NORTH CAROLINA
STATE BOARD OF COMMUNITY COLLEGES
LIBRARIES
SAMPSON COMMUNITY COLLEGE

P9-EMB-706

LEARNING RESOURCES CENTER
SAMPSON COMMUNITY COLLEGE
CLINTON, N.C. 28328

ASSESSMENT
FOR
EXCELLENCE

The Philosophy and Practice of
Assessment and Evaluation in
Higher Education

ASSESSMENT FOR EXCELLENCE

The Philosophy and Practice of
Assessment and Evaluation in
Higher Education

Alexander W. Astin

AMERICAN COUNCIL ON EDUCATION
MACMILLAN PUBLISHING COMPANY
New York

COLLIER MACMILLAN CANADA
Toronto

MAXWELL MACMILLAN INTERNATIONAL
New York   Oxford   Singapore   Sydney

LEARNING RESOURCES CENTER
SAMPSON COMMUNITY COLLEGE
CLINTON, N.C. 28328

Copyright © 1991 by American Council on Education and Macmillan Publishing Company,
A Division of Macmillan, Inc.

All rights reserved. No part of this book may be reproduced or
transmitted in any form or by any means, electronic or mechanical,
including photocopying, recording, or by any information storage
and retrieval system, without permission in writing from the
Publisher.

Macmillan Publishing Company
866 Third Avenue, New York, N.Y. 10022

Collier Macmillan Canada, Inc.
1200 Eglinton Avenue East, Suite 200
Don Mills Ontario M3C 3N1

Library of Congress Catalog Card Number: 90-38753
Printed in the United States of America

printing number
1 2 3 4 5 6 7 8 9 10

Library of Congress Cataloging-in-Publication Data

Astin, Alexander W.
    Assessment for excellence : the philosophy and practice of
assessment and evaluation in higher education / Alexander W. Astin.
        p.   cm. – (The American Council on Education/Macmillan series
on higher education)
    Includes bibliographical references and index.
    ISBN 0-02-897022-5
    1.   Universities and colleges–United States–Examinations.
2. Education, Higher–United States–Evaluation.   3. Education,
Higher–United States–Aims and objectives.   I. American Council on
Education.   II. Title.   III. Series: American Council on
Education/Macmillan series on higher education.
LB2366.2.A89   1990
378.1′664–dc20   90-38753
                                                                    CIP

To my parents
Allen V. Astin
and
Margaret Mackenzie Astin

CONTENTS

Preface   ix

1   The Philosophy and Logic of Assessment   1

2   A Conceptual Model for Assessment   16

3   Assessing Outcomes   38

4   Assessing Student Inputs   64

5   Assessing the Environment   81

6   Analyzing Assessment Data   94

7   Use of Assessment Results   128

8   Building a Data Base   151

9   Assessment as Direct Feedback to the Learner   178

10 Assessment and Equity   194

11 Assessment and Public Policy   216

12 The Future of Assessment   231

Appendix: Statistical Analysis of Longitudinal Data   255

References   315

Index   325

PREFACE

For the past twenty-five years I have been more or less continuously engaged in assessment activities in the field of higher education. This work has involved collecting data from literally millions of students, several hundred thousand college faculty and administrators, and more than a thousand different colleges and universities of every conceivable type. While much of this assessment has involved standardized tests and self-administered questionnaires, it has also included personal interviews, focus groups, case studies, and other qualitative approaches. I have also made personal visits to many campuses to assist them in developing their own assessment programs. Finally, for the past sixteen years I have been a faculty member in a major research university where I have been writing books and articles based on my assessment work and teaching graduate courses in educational assessment and evaluation. All these experiences have convinced me of one thing: although a great deal of assessment activity goes on in America's colleges and universities, much of it is of very little benefit to either students, faculty, administrators, or institutions. On the contrary, some of our assessment activities seem to conflict with our most basic educational mission. It was this realization that has prompted me to write this book.

Why does all this assessment activity produce so little of value? What can be done to improve assessment in higher education? How can we get more use from our existing assessment activities? What new assessment practices might we undertake in order to utilize this powerful educational tool more effectively? These are the broad questions to which this book is addressed.

The book is designed for use by anyone who is involved in or interested in the practical uses of assessment: faculty, administrators, researchers, policy analysts, and governmental officials. Not all chapters, however, will necessarily be of equal interest to different readers. Teaching faculty, for example, would be particularly interested in chapters 1 and 9. Administrators should probably be most interested in chapters 1, 7, and 8. Policymakers, legislators, and other public officials should find chapters 1, 10, and 11 of most relevance to their concerns. Students of higher education should be interested in most chapters, and higher education scholars and researchers should be interested in the appendix as well. Indeed, social scientists in general might find chapters 2 and 6 and the appendix to be of special interest.

The idea for the book originally grew out of two graduate seminars on assessment and evaluation that I have been teaching at the University of California at Los Angeles (UCLA) for the past fifteen years. Much of the material covered in these courses was nowhere to be found in the published literature, and students frequently complained about having to rely entirely on their lecture notes in the absence of any written exposition of many of the ideas and concepts covered.

For years the book idea remained just one of those numerous latent projects that I would undertake "someday" but never really found the time to start. Then along came the assessment movement. I do not pretend to any special expertise in historical analysis, but I find it hard to avoid the conclusion that a major catalyst in the development of this movement was the performance funding system developed for public higher education institutions in the state of Tennessee (Bogue and Brown, 1982). The idea that institutions would be awarded or denied state funding according to how their students performed on standardized tests was not only a radical concept but also an idea that was extremely unsettling and even threatening to the higher education community in general. In retrospect I still cannot understand why the higher education leadership in Tennessee at that time either could not or would not kill this idea before it got off the ground. While the jury is still out on the matter of how the public education system in Tennessee will ultimately be affected by performance funding, there is little question in my mind that the Tennessee program had at least two major impacts: it alerted legislators and public officials in other states to the possibility of using student assessment as a tool for achieving a greater degree of "accountability" in public higher education, and it motivated some higher education leaders to take a more critical look at their own assessment practices.

As more states got on the assessment bandwagon, and as governmental agencies and higher education associations began to look at the assessment issue, two interesting things happened. First, those few institutions that had quietly pioneered the use of sophisticated student assessment programs—I think particularly here of Northeast Missouri State University and Alverno College—emerged suddenly into the limelight and became objects of intense scrutiny. Second, there appeared on the scene a number of assessment "experts" who found themselves in tremendous demand by states and institutions that wanted to improve and strengthen their assessment procedures. As grants from public and private agencies were awarded to institutions and educational associations to support new assessment activities and programs, as assessment conferences and workshops proliferated across the country, and as articles and monographs on assessment began to appear, a kind of conventional wisdom about assessment began to emerge.

While there is much in this conventional wisdom that is valid and useful, it began to occur to me that something was missing. When you piece together the various tidbits of wisdom and advice to be found in the current literature on assessment, the resulting mosaic that emerges is deficient on at least two counts. First, the disparate items of wisdom and knowledge simply do not fit together into a coherent whole. And second, certain critical issues and items of information are missing altogether. As a consequence, the collective wisdom that one encounters in the assessment field today does not really address the practical needs of those college faculty, administrators, researchers, institutions, or state governments that might wish to use assessment to improve the educational process.

What do I mean by practical needs? A hypothetical example might help to clarify the point. Suppose officials of an institution or a state agency decide that they want to evaluate their current assessment procedures, to try out new approaches to assessment, or even to develop a comprehensive new assessment program. Below are four issues that such officials need to consider:

- Any new assessment program should be predicated on a clear and explicitly stated understanding of what the institution's mission is and should be designed to further that mission. In other words, it should be possible to rationalize the assessment program—in all of its essential details—in terms of how it can facilitate the institution's basic mission.
- Existing assessment practices should be scrutinized in terms of that same institutional mission, and those that do not appear to be enhancing that mission should be revised or abandoned.
- Faculty, administrators, and others who conduct assessment activities need to understand *why* they assess and *how* the results can be used to enhance educational policy and practice. To achieve such a level of understanding will normally require time as well as exposure to some of the issues and topics covered in the book.

- Persons who will be responsible for designing and operating an assessment program should ideally possess a unique combination of skills and competencies not usually found in graduates of traditional doctoral programs in education, psychology, or the social sciences. (To a certain extent, this book represents a kind of "curriculum" that focuses on many of these skills and competencies.)

This is not just a book about assessment. It is also a book about how to do applied research in education and the social sciences. The reasoning behind my decision to include major sections on research methodology (especially chapter 6 and the appendix) is as follows: Good assessment is really good research, and the ultimate aim of such research should be to help us to make better choices and better decisions in running our educational programs and institutions. Since assessment and evaluation should thus be designed to improve decision making, and since decision making inevitably involves causal reasoning ("Alternative A is chosen over Alternatives B or C because we believe that it will lead to a better outcome"), *assessment results are of most value when they shed light on the causal connections between educational practice and educational outcomes.* There are basically two issues here: What can our assessment results tell us about how different educational policies and practices are likely to affect various educational outcomes? How much confidence can we have in the results? The recommended research methodology (the input-environment-outcome [I-E-O] model) is thus designed to yield assessment results that will simultaneously (a) yield maximum information on the possible causal connections between various educational practices and educational outcomes and (b) minimize the chances that our causal inferences will be wrong.

Some of my colleagues who are experts in the methodology of social science or educational research may cringe at my frequent references to "causal" relationships or to the "effects" of educational programs. Most of them, like me, were brainwashed during their graduate training about the superiority of "true experiments" over "correlational studies." We were all repeatedly reminded that "you can't make causal inferences from correlational data." It has taken me several decades to realize that all of this well-intentioned advice is simply wrong: true experiments are no panacea, in part because they are very difficult if not impossible to conduct with live human beings in real educational settings, and in part because they create at least as many inferential problems as they solve (see chapter 2). And while it is true that you can't prove causation with correlational data, you most certainly *can* make causal inferences from such data; people do it all the time. In fact, it would be impossible for most teachers and administrators to make it through an average work day without making literally dozens of causal inferences based either on correlational data or, as is more often the case, on no data at all. The real challenge for us researchers and practitioners is to use assessment in such a way as to minimize the chances that our causal inferences will be wrong. This is basically the aim of the methodological procedures described in chapters 2 and 6 and the appendix. I make no claim that the recommended assessment methodology is the only or even the best approach to estimating causal relationships between educational practices and educational outcomes, but I do believe that these procedures represent a substantial improvement over what most institutions are currently doing or what most contemporary assessment experts are currently recommending.

In this book I have consciously mixed personal observations and experiences with more technical "how to do it" material. The selection of technical content, such as how to measure different kinds of variables (chapters 3, 4, and 5), how to set up a data base (chapter 8), and how to analyze assessment data (chapter 6 and the appendix) is admittedly selective and makes no pretense at comprehensiveness. My selection decisions have been guided primarily by my understanding of what people most need to know and what is generally unavailable from other publications. Wherever possible, I have used references to try to steer the reader to omitted material that is available elsewhere.

As far as the more personal aspects of the book are concerned, the reader will no doubt note the effects of my early educational roots. My undergraduate training in music is reflected in my predilection for a "performing arts" theory of how best to utilize assessment results (chapter 7) and in my use of the piano lesson as a metaphor for understanding the principles of good assessment in the classroom (chapter 9). My graduate training in quantitative psychology is reflected in my heavy emphasis on how to analyze assessment data (chapter 6 and the appendix), and my early employment as a clinical and counseling psychologist is reflected both in the developmental (longitudinal) view of assessment that I have taken throughout the book and in my preference for a talent development approach to institutional quality or excellence.

A number of people have contributed in important ways to the production of this book. First are the students—the thousands of undergraduates who over the years have cooperated in our freshman and follow-up surveys to provide us with assessment data—and the many UCLA graduate students who have helped me sharpen my thinking about assessment. In particular, I want to acknowledge the help of my research assistants—Eric Dey and Sylvia Hurtado, who regularly offered critical commentary on various parts of the book, and Jesus Trevino and Yinte Wang, who helped me considerably with my review of the assessment literature.

I also want to acknowledge the key role played by the Value-Added Consortium project, a three-year field experiment carried out during the late 1980s under a grant from the Fund for the Improvement of Postsecondary Education (FIPSE) (see chapter 8). Peter Armacost (Eckerd

College) and Willard Enteman (Rhode Island College) originally conceptualized this project, and its implementation was greatly facilitated by the involvement of Lena Astin (UCLA), Tim Lehmann (Empire State College), Don Stewart (Spelman College), Barbara Hetrick and Martha Church (Hood College), and Chuck Kiesler, Jay Devine, and Tony Penna (Carnegie-Mellon University). I especially appreciate the help of our three consultants—Trudy Banta, Peter Ewell, and Charles McClain—all of whom have themselves made substantial contributions to our understanding of assessment. Maryann Jacobi and Frank Ayala were my staff colleagues on this project, and their involvement made the whole thing worthwhile. FIPSE, of course, helped to make this consortium project run smoothly, not only through its financial support but also by adopting its usual supportive and noninterfering role. Most other government agencies that fund outside projects could get a lot more "bang for the taxpayer's buck" if they imitated FIPSE's approach.

Peter Ewell of The National Center for Higher Education Management Systems (NCHEMS) kindly provided a very insightful and helpful anonymous review of chapters 1-11 after I had sent them to the publisher. I was so impressed by the perceptiveness of the review that I asked Lloyd Chilton, my executive editor at Macmillan, if I could learn the identity of the reviewer so that I could acknowledge (him) (her) personally in this Preface. Lloyd and Peter both agreed, so here it is: Many thanks, Peter!

I also want to thank my old friend and colleague, David E. Drew, for providing a number of helpful suggestions concerning chapter 2 and the appendix. Finally, I want to express my appreciation to the several people who helped with the manuscript preparation: Laura Birely, Judy Liggett, and especially Robin Bailey, who, in spite of my crazy work habits, somehow managed to keep track of all the references and many chapter drafts.

ALEXANDER W. ASTIN

ASSESSMENT FOR EXCELLENCE

The Philosophy and Practice of
Assessment and Evaluation in
Higher Education

1

THE PHILOSOPHY AND LOGIC OF ASSESSMENT

One of the distinguishing features of American colleges and universities is their fondness for assessment. Practically everybody in the academic community gets assessed these days, and practically everybody assesses somebody else. Students, of course, come in for a heavy dose of assessment, first from admissions offices and later from the professors who teach their classes. Recently students have also gotten in on the other end of the assessment business, with the end-of-course evaluations of teaching that are now so widely used by colleges and universities. Professors, of course, subject each other to the most detailed and rigorous assessments when new professors are hired or when a colleague comes up for tenure or promotion. Administrators also get in on the act of assessing faculty and in many institutions have the final say in faculty personnel decisions. Administrators, of course, regularly assess each other, and sometimes the faculty and the trustees also take part in assessing the administrators. Finally, the whole institution is regularly assessed in a highly detailed fashion by external accrediting teams made up of faculty and administrators from other institutions.

Why do we do all this assessment and what does it accomplish? Perhaps my principal motive for writing this book is the strong impression that assessment in American higher education is in a generally wretched state. Our assessment efforts are handicapped in part because we are not really very clear about what we are trying to accomplish, and in part because we perpetuate questionable practices out of sheer habit, for convenience, or to fulfill purposes that are unrelated or at best tangential to the basic mission of our colleges and universities. The book thus presents a detailed critique of assessment practices in higher education and outlines specific ways in which assessment can be strengthened and improved. Much of the book is devoted to procedures for assessing *students*, not only because the current assessment movement is primarily focused on student assessment but also because the usefulness of our faculty, administrator, and institutional assessments depends in part on how effectively we assess our students.

The inadequacies of current student assessment practices have been responsible to some degree for the emergence of two trends in American higher education. First, several of the recent national reports on higher education (e.g., Study Group, 1984; Association of American Colleges, 1985) have been highly critical of contemporary assessment practices, and increasing numbers of individual institutions are undertaking major revisions in their student assessment activities (Paskow, 1988). Second, there is a rapidly growing interest among federal and state policy makers in improved *outcomes assessment* and *accountability* in postsecondary education (Ewell and Boyer, 1988). Some states—notably Florida, Georgia, New Jersey, and Tennessee—have already introduced extensive new outcomes assessments for students in public institutions. However, in many important respects these programs do little to overcome the limitations of traditional assessment procedures, and in some cases they threaten to make things even worse (see chapter 11). Considering that a majority of the remaining states have either begun or are considering similar statewide assessment activities, this would seem to be an opportune time to take a critical look at assessment in higher education and to consider how this potentially powerful tool might be utilized for the benefit of students, faculty, and institutions alike.

ASSESSMENT, MEASUREMENT, AND EVALUATION

In this book I shall consider *assessment* to include the gathering of information concerning the functioning of students, staff, and institutions of higher education. The information may or may not be in numerical form, but the basic motive for gathering it is to improve the functioning of the institution and its people. I use *functioning* to refer to the broad social purposes of a college or university: to facilitate student learning and development, to advance the frontiers of knowledge, and to contribute to the community and the society.

As commonly used today, the term *assessment* can refer to two very different activities: (a) the mere gathering of information (measurement) and (b) the utilization of that information for institutional and individual improvement (evaluation). I believe that there is a fundamental distinction here between the information we gather and the uses to which it is put, and that we often forget this distinction when we talk about assessment in higher education. Evaluation, of course, has to do with motivation and the rendering of value judgments. For example, when we give an examination in a college course (measurement), there are many ways in which the results can be used or evaluated. Many of us who teach in academia sometimes give course examinations primarily for record-keeping purposes: since our institution requires us to give grades, we make students take exams so we have some basis for awarding a grade.

Under these conditions, we professors are merely measuring and not evaluating, since the evaluating is done by others: by the college registrar who determines whether the student should be put on probation or awarded honors, by the students who are trying to judge their own academic progress, and by the employers or graduate and professional schools who use college transcripts to help them make employment or admission decisions.

In other situations we professors might indeed be interested in evaluating the information generated by our examinations. We might want to gauge the effectiveness of our pedagogical efforts or to decide what kind of written or oral feedback to give to our students in order to facilitate their learning of the course material. Students might be interested in evaluating their own test results for the same reasons: to know their strong and weak points in order to become more effective learners.

Similar distinctions between measurement and evaluation could be made for almost any other higher education assessment activity: admissions testing, placement testing, testing of graduates, assessment of faculty and staff, and institutional accreditation. Since assessment and evaluation are inextricably linked, I will argue that assessment policies and practices in higher education should always give full consideration to the evaluative uses to which our measurements will be put.

THE GOALS AND VALUES OF HIGHER EDUCATION

A basic premise of this book is that *an institution's assessment practices are a reflection of its values*. In other words, the values of an institution are revealed in the information about itself that it gathers and pays attention to. A second, and perhaps more fundamental, premise is that *assessment practices should further the basic aims and purposes of our higher education institutions*. We might consider these two premises, respectively, as the "is" and the "ought" of assessment in higher education.

What, then, are the goals or aims of higher education? Despite the enormous diversity of American higher education institutions, most of us subscribe to the notion that the system has three basic goals: education, research, and public or community service. I like to call these the *social purposes* of higher education, in the sense that it is primarily for these purposes that these 3,000 institutions were created in the first place, and that the society and the public continue to support them. It is true that individual institutions now espouse many other goals and purposes—to grow, to achieve "excellence," or merely to survive—but education, research, and public service continue to be their fundamental reasons for existence.

While different types of institutions assign different priorities to these three purposes—the major universities put more emphasis on research; the community colleges put more emphasis on serving the community—all types of institutions share a common commitment to the educational function. Indeed, the very fact that we call our colleges and universities *educational* institutions signifies this shared responsibility to educate our students. It is also worth noting that much of the current debate about assessment and reform in higher education focuses on the educational process. Research universities have been criticized for emphasizing research to the neglect of undergraduate education, and community colleges have been criticized for emphasizing such things as funding and enrollment growth over high quality teaching and learning. Similarly, public pressures to use more competency testing or outcomes assessment reflects a concern about how much students are actually learning in our colleges and universities.

While the three basic functions of higher education institutions are frequently seen as competing with each other, there are many ways in which they can be complementary and even mutually reinforcing. Thus, effective education and effective research are clearly important forms of public service. And to conduct research on teaching, learning, and the educational process is certainly one way to enhance teaching. At the same time, effective teaching can obviously contribute to the development of more skilled researchers.

Since most of the current interest in assessment in higher education is concerned with the assessment of students, a good portion of this book is concerned with assessment as it relates to the teaching-learning process. More specifically, I argue that *the basic purpose of assessing students is to enhance their educational development.* Another way of saying this is that assessment of students, more than anything else, should advance the educational mission of our colleges and universities.

In the same spirit, I argue that *assessment of college and university faculty should enhance their performance as teachers and mentors of students and as contributors to the advancement of knowledge.* Again, this is another way of saying that assessment of faculty should enhance the teaching and research functions of the institution.

These propositions about the proper function of assessment in higher education might appear, on the surface at least, to be straightforward and reasonable, perhaps even self-evident. The problem seems to be that most assessment practices today are not well-suited to higher education's basic purposes, and some practices would appear even to undermine those purposes. How did we reach such a state? And what can be done about it?

ASSESSMENT AND EDUCATIONAL EXCELLENCE

Most of us who serve as higher education faculty or administrators would agree that we are committed to promoting the "excellence" of our institutions. If pressed a bit on the matter, most of us would also say that by excellence, we mean excellence in teaching and excellence in research (the third basic function of higher education, service to the community, is usually not mentioned, especially in the four-year institutions, but for the rest of this discussion we can assume that the community is being well served if the institution is able to deliver excellent teaching and excellent research). So far, so good. We are committed to excellence and by that we mean excellent teaching and excellent research.

Up to now I have been dealing with the excellence concept on a purely verbal level, and at that level it seems that we are indeed promoting the purposes for which our institutions were established. However, we all know that actions speak louder than words, and it is in the things we actually do to promote excellence that difficulties begin to arise. Assessment, of course, is one of the means by which we try to operationalize our notions about excellence.

Traditional Views of Excellence

What specific policies and practices in higher education do we justify on the grounds that they promote excellence? What really matters to us? Where do we direct our attention, and to what ends do we direct our energies? What do we pay attention to? What, in other words, are the values that govern our efforts to achieve excellence? Although there are many possible answers to such questions, during the past few decades I have come to realize that there are two conceptions of excellence that govern much of what we do. For simplicity I have labeled these, respectively, as the *resources* and *reputational* conceptions of excellence. What is especially important about these two views is that they are seldom stated explicitly, but rather are implicit in our policies and practices. The problem here is that the pursuit of excellence in terms of resources and reputation is only tangentially related to our more fundamental societal purposes, and especially to our educational function.

The *resources* conception is based on the idea that excellence depends primarily on having lots of resources: the more resources we have, the more excellent our institution. The resources that are supposed to make us excellent are of three different types: money, high-quality faculty, and high-quality students. Money can be measured in terms of our endowment, income from public and private sources, the amount we actually spend, and the things money can buy: libraries, laboratories, physical plant, faculty, and students. Faculty can be of high-quality according to several different definitions, such as the highest academic degree they hold or the reputation (see below) of the institution where they received it, but the "highest-quality" faculty (i.e., the ones who are most sought after and who command the highest salaries) are almost always the ones who are widely known for their research and writing. "High-quality" students are those who earned high marks in high school and who receive high scores on college admissions examinations.

The reputational view of excellence is based on the idea that the most excellent institutions are the ones that enjoy the best academic reputations. In American higher education, there is a folklore that has evolved over the years that implicitly arranges our institutions into a kind of pyramid-shaped hierarchy, or pecking order. A few prestigious institutions such as Harvard, Yale, Berkeley, and Stanford occupy the top positions in the hierarchy while the bottom layers include most of the two-year colleges and a large number of small four-year colleges that are largely unknown outside of their local communities. I refer to the pecking order as folklore largely because it is part of our belief system rather than something that has been established independently through systematic study and analysis. It is possible, I might add, to determine the positions of institutions in the pecking order by means of reputational polls in which people are asked to rate the "excellence" or "quality" of colleges and universities (Astin and Solmon, 1981; Solmon and Astin, 1981). Under the reputational view, then, the excellence of an institution is determined by its position in this reputational hierarchy or pecking order.

An important feature of these two traditional views of excellence is that they both produce very similar rankings of institutions. That is, the institutions that occupy the top positions in the reputational hierarchy tend to be the same ones that have the most resources of money, prestigious faculty, and high-performing students (Astin, 1985a). On reflection, this close correspondence is really not so surprising: having a great deal of resources can help to enhance your reputation, and having an outstanding reputation can help to attract money, prestigious faculty, and bright students. Reputation and resources, in short, tend to be mutually reinforcing.

The Talent Development View

In recent years I have been very critical of these traditional conceptions of excellence (Astin, 1985a), primarily because they do not directly address the institution's basic purposes: the education of students and the cultivation of knowledge. To focus our institutional energies more directly on these fundamental missions, I have proposed the adoption of an alternative approach called the *talent development* conception of excellence. Under the talent development view, excellence is determined by our ability to develop the talents of our students and faculty to the fullest extent possible. The fundamental premise underlying the talent development concept is that true excellence lies in the institution's ability to affect its students and faculty favorably, to enhance their intellectual and scholarly development, to make a positive difference in their lives. As far as *educational* excellence is concerned, the most excellent institutions are, in this view, those that have the greatest impact—"add the most value," as economists would say—to the students' knowledge and personal development.

Excellence and Assessment

These different conceptions of excellence have obvious implications for assessment activities. For example, if we operate according to the resources and reputational views of excellence, we would tend to focus our student assessment activities on the entering student, since excellence in these terms depends on enrolling a student body with the highest possible grades and test scores. On the other hand, if we believe that our excellence is a function of how well we educate our students, that is, if we embrace a talent development approach, we would be more inclined to assess changes or improvements or growth in our students over time. Under the talent development view, then, excellence is determined by the quality and quantity of student and faculty *learning* and *development*.

If we consider for a moment the assessments that attract the greatest attention from college faculty and administrators, most, if not all, seem to reflect adherence to the reputational and resource views of excellence: the average test scores and grade-point averages (GPAs) of the entering freshmen, rankings in reputational polls, faculty salaries, the size of the endowment, the dollar amount of annual giving, the annual income from state appropriations, and the size of the enrollment (which, for most institutions, translates directly into income). This relative lack of institutional interest in assessments that relate to the educational or talent development mission is probably responsible, in part, for the growing interest of public officials in outcomes assessment and in making institutions more accountable. Unfortunately, most of the assessment remedies that have been proposed or tried at the state level are ill-conceived and may actually do more harm than good. (The pros and cons of such state-mandated assessment activities are discussed in detail in chapter 11.)

This brief critique of our traditional views about excellence in higher education is not intended to suggest that resources and reputations are not important. Institutions need resources to function and they need reputations to attract both students and resources. At issue here is whether abundant resources and excellent reputation are viewed primarily as ends in themselves rather than as means to achieving excellent educational ends (talent development). In this connection research has shown that the quality and quantity of student talent development that an institution is able to achieve bears only a weak relationship, if any, to its level of resources or to its reputation (Astin, 1968b, 1977;

Bowen, 1980, 1981). This finding would suggest that those institutions with the most resources do not necessarily use their additional resources to enhance the talent development process.

To recapitulate: my major purpose in reviewing these different notions about excellence has been to show that the values underlying our traditional notions about institutional excellence or quality in higher education are not necessarily consistent with our fundamental societal missions of education and research. While there are numbers of other problems connected with these traditional views of excellence (see chapter 10 and Astin, 1985a), our immediate concern is how adherence to these views has affected our assessment activities. Let us now consider what some of these effects have been.

WHY WE ASSESS

Why do we test and grade students? What ends are served when we evaluate faculty performance? For many forms of assessment, there are really two levels at which such a question can be answered: the immediate purpose of the assessment activity, and the underlying value. For example, one could argue that we require prospective students to take admissions examinations in order (a) to help us select our students (the immediate purpose), or (b) to enhance the excellence of the institution (the underlying value). Any given assessment activity can also serve multiple purposes and multiple values. However, in this discussion my focus is primarily on the values—and in particular the different views about excellence—that undergird our principal assessment activities in higher education.

There are at least four different institutional activities that involve assessments of students: admissions, guidance and placement, classroom learning, and credentialing or certification. What types of assessments do we utilize in connection with each activity and what values and what conceptions of excellence do they support? Let's start with admissions.

Admissions

Many of us who work in colleges and universities tend to forget that we are responsible for much of the assessment activity that goes on in the secondary schools. These activities include the grading system that produces class ranks and grade-point averages (GPAs), as well as a number of large-scale testing programs that examine more than two million secondary school students each year. The largest of these, of course, are the Preliminary Scholastic Aptitude Test (PSAT) given to eleventh graders and the Scholastic Aptitude Test (SAT) and American College Test (ACT) given to twelfth graders.

Such tests and the student's GPA and class rank are used by individual colleges and universities to help decide whether or not a student applicant should be admitted: the higher the scores, the better the student's chances of being admitted. Although other factors are also given consideration in the admissions decisions of many colleges, the immediate goal in using GPAs and test scores is to enroll students with the best possible GPAs and the highest possible test scores.

One immediate consequence of reliance on these assessments in admissions is that it encourages a great deal of competition among institutions. The competition among colleges for high-scoring students is so great that many colleges these days employ generous scholarships, personalized direct mail, and a variety of other sophisticated and expensive marketing techniques to try to attract such students. The National Merit Scholarship Program, which annually utilizes the PSAT to screen about one million candidates, encourages colleges and universities to sponsor a number of Merit Scholars each year. In return for agreeing to attend one of the sponsoring colleges, high-scoring students can greatly increase, and sometimes guarantee, their chances of being named Merit Scholars.

What motivates colleges and universities to use admissions assessments in this fashion? Why is the high-scoring student so heavily favored over other students? While there are many ways to answer such questions (see below), anyone who has worked in academe for very long will tell you that *selective admissions signifies academic excellence.* The more selective the institution, the more excellent it is presumed to be. Indeed, many college faculty and administrators routinely use the average high school GPAs or average admission test scores of the entering freshmen as a sort of barometer of institutional quality or excellence. If scores go up, quality is assumed to be on the increase; if scores go down, quality is assumed to be on the decline.

Why is such an index so closely watched and so highly valued? There are at least two respects in which high scores are valued. First is the belief that "having bright students makes us a better institution." This is, of course, the *resource* notion of quality, namely, that we attain quality merely by having a lot of resources (in this case, bright students). The more we have, the higher the quality.

The second sense in which having a select student body signifies quality has to do more with its market implications: "if so many bright students want to come here, we must be pretty good." This is, of course, the *reputational* conception, in which we view our excellence or quality in terms of what others (in this case, bright prospective students) think of us.

While there are many colleges and universities that are not in a position to practice selective admissions (especially community colleges and other "open admissions" public institutions), nearly all institutions value the highly able student and virtually no institution deliberately seeks out or favors the less well prepared student.

Assessment for admission to graduate and professional schools follows very much the same pattern as assessment for undergraduate admissions. Indeed, just as the undergraduate colleges determine much of the assessment that goes on in the secondary schools, so do the graduate and professional schools determine much of the assessment that involves undergraduates. Undergraduate colleges and universities give course grades and compute undergraduate GPAs in part because the graduate and professional schools need them for admission purposes.

At the same time, the graduate and professional schools utilize a variety of nationally standardized tests in making their admission decisions: the various Graduate Record (GRE) examinations, the Medical College Admission Test (MCAT), the Law School Aptitude Test (LSAT), and the Graduate Management Aptitude Test (GMAT), to name just a few. These test scores together with undergraduate GPAs are used in much the same way as are the undergraduate admissions devices, and for pretty much the same reasons.

In short, this discussion of the admissions process suggests that the student assessments that we require as a part of the admissions process are utilized primarily to promote the resources and reputational conceptions of excellence.

Before leaving the subject of admissions, I should note that it is possible to rationalize the practice of selective admission in terms of how it can also promote talent development. While such arguments seldom constitute the real reasons for selective admission, they will be considered in some depth in chapter 10 ("Assessment and Equity").

Guidance and Placement

A second major student assessment activity concerns student guidance and placement. Here, more than with any other assessment activity, the basic motive seems to be to enhance the teaching-learning process (i.e., to promote talent development). Institutions use a variety of tests—national as well as local—to place students in appropriate courses and to help them make decisions about courses, majors, and career plans. Since this type of assessment is designed to enhance the talent development process, it will be discussed in more detail in chapter 6.

Classroom Assessment

The third major area of student assessment activity occurs in connection with college courses. Three major forms of assessment are involved here: course examinations, assessment of course projects (homework, term papers, etc.), and course grades.

Some educators believe that the mere use of these classroom assessments can facilitate the talent development process by serving as incentives for the student to learn. Since the possible incentive value of assessment will be considered later in chapter 9, we are concerned here with the use of the information generated by these different classroom assessment procedures. A major reason for assessing class projects and for giving classroom examinations is to grade students. Thus, all forms of classroom assessment can be and often are used to generate course grades. These grades, in turn, contribute to the overall grade-point average (GPA) for each student. The principal justification for GPAs, of course, is that they are needed to help employers and admissions departments of graduate and professional schools make decisions about applicants. Since most of the graduate and professional schools, like the undergraduate colleges, rely on GPAs to identify the "best" students, classroom grading is frequently used to support the resources and reputational views of excellence. Just as a high GPA can be used to award various types of academic honors, so can a low GPA be used to expel students or to put them on probation. But high GPAs can also be used to assign students to special honors courses and a low GPA can be used as an indicator that the student needs special assistance. It would seem that these last two uses of the GPA are perhaps its only truly educational functions. Practically all other uses of the GPA are either adminsitrative (to determine eligibility for probation, suspension, graduation, or honors) of for purposes of screening and selection (by employers and graduate and professional schools).

An interesting aspect of the GPA is that it tells us very little about what a student actually knows or what that student's competencies or talents really are. The GPA is thus primarily a relativistic or normative measure. That is, the primary information contained in a course grade pertains to the student's performance in relation to other students. Thus, the "best" students get As while the "worst" students get Cs or lower grades. This relativistic quality of grading is reinforced by the practice of grading "on the curve." Such a procedure attempts to allocate certain numbers of As, Bs, and Cs, and so forth, regardless of how well the class as a whole is performing.

Besides their relativistic quality, course grades also reflect little of what the student has actually learned in the course. Harris (1970) studied the relationship between course grades and actual learning as measured by tests given before and after a course. He found that test score gains of students who had received failing or near-failing grades were comparable to the gains of the students who had received high grades. In other words, course grades did not really reflect the amount of learning that was occurring among students. In short, course grades appear to be a relatively poor indicator of how much students are actually learning in a course. Rather, what they tell us is how well the students are performing in relation to one another at a particular point in time.

Many teachers evaluate course examinations and class projects primarily for purposes of grading: they read the test results or examine the class project and simply assign a grade. Such practices would not appear to contribute much to the talent development process. Grading of course examinations and class projects can, of course, be used to enhance talent development. In such cases the nature of the feedback provided by the professor normally goes considerably beyond merely assigning a grade (see chapter 9). The assessment of the exam performance or the class project involves specific feedback concerning particular aspects of the student's work. In this connection it is unfortunate that most such assessment occurs only after the course has been completed, at a time when students are probably not very motivated to benefit from the feedback and are instead looking forward either to vacations or to the next academic term. Clearly, these assessment techniques can be of most benefit when they come in the form of midterm projects or examinations. Feedback provided to the student at such times is more likely to benefit the learning process because the student is still in the process of attempting to master the course material.

Credentialing and Certification

We have already described what is probably the most widely used credentialing technique: the class grade and the GPA. Students are awarded degrees if their GPAs are above a certain minimal level. But there are other ways in which student assessment in higher education is used to support credentialing and certification. For example, new students entering an undergraduate institution for the first time can frequently "test out" of certain introductory courses if they are able to achieve relatively high scores on various types of standardized tests. The most widely used technique of this type is the Advanced Placement (AP) examinations administered by the College Entrance Examination Board. Nearly 40 percent of all full-time freshmen entering college for the first time have taken at least one advanced placement examination, and better than 20 percent of the students have taken two or more such examinations (Astin et al., 1989). Provided that students are able to achieve certain minimal scores on these examinations, most colleges will award course credits simply on the basis of the examination score.

Certification by examination exists in many other forms. One entire unit of the State University of New York, the Regents' External Degree Program, relies on a battery of standardized tests to award credits toward completion of the baccalaureate degree. Still another common use of assessment for certification purposes is the professional credentialing that occurs in fields such as medicine, law, accounting, nursing, and school teaching. Since these tests are generally administered by professional associations or by state agencies rather than by higher education institutions, they will not be considered further here. There are, however, other widespread uses of testing for certification within academe. The nineteen campuses of the California State University require each student to pass a certification test in English composition as a condition for receiving the bachelor's degree. Similarly, entire states (Florida and Georgia, in particular) are now requiring students to pass a battery of standardized tests before they are permitted to advance from sophomore to junior year status in the state's public institutions. Such tests are more or less forced on the private institutions as well, since passing them becomes a prerequisite for students to receive state financial aid.

Assessing Faculty Performance

Much of the assessment of college faculty is carried out for purposes similar to the assessments of students: to support the resources and reputational views of excellence and to support certain administrative practices. Thus, candidates for faculty positions are frequently assessed in terms of how much their presence will enhance the institution's reputation and of the quantity of resources that the candidate is likely to attract in the form of research grants or top students. In many research universities, the prospective faculty member's capacity to contribute to talent development (teaching competence and commitment to students) gets little, if any, consideration in the review process.

Much the same can be said of how we assess incumbent faculty. While the faculty member's ability to develop student talent (as reflected, for example, in student course evaluations) gets some consideration when faculty members come up for review, research productivity and national visibility (or the promise of such productivity and visibility) usually receive much greater weight in hiring decisions and in decisions concerning tenure and promotion. Except for the pre-tenure review that some universities now utilize several years in advance of the final tenure review, practically all assessments of faculty or prospective faculty are designed for purposes other than to develop the faculty member's talents.

SUMMARY

This brief overview of traditional uses of student assessment suggests that much of the assessment that goes on in academe (particularly the use of classroom grades and standardized tests for admission to undergraduate and graduate school) is intended primarily to support the resources and reputational conceptions of institutional excellence. High-achieving students are not only viewed as prized "resources" by the undergraduate, graduate, and professional schools, but their presence in the institution is also regarded as a means of enhancing the institution's reputation. Much of the rest of the student assessment that goes on in academe is employed either for administrative or certification purposes.

About the only form of student assessment that is clearly designed to support the talent development view of excellence is the testing done in connection with guidance and course placement. Of course, feedback from classroom examinations and assignments or course projects *can* be used to enhance talent development if the feedback is informative and well timed, but such examinations and projects are often used primarily, if not exclusively, to generate course grades.

Much the same can be said about our assessments of college faculty and administrators: they are done primarily to serve the reputational and resources views rather than to enhance talent development. Assessments of faculty for hiring, tenuring, and promotional purposes tend to put disproportionate weight on qualities that are likely to enhance the institution's resources and reputation. Similarly, administrators (especially chief executive officers) are heavily rewarded if they are successful in expanding the institution's resource base and in enhancing its reputation or image. Since faculty and especially administrators are seldom judged in terms of their contribution to the talent development process, assessments of faculty and administrator performance seldom yield any information bearing directly on this process.

HOW CAN ASSESSMENT PROMOTE TALENT DEVELOPMENT?

The major purpose of this book is to show how assessment can be used to enhance the educational and research functions of colleges and universities by promoting talent development among both students and faculty members.

There are essentially two different ways in which assessment activities can contribute to talent development among students: through direct effects on the learner and indirectly by enlightening the educator. Assessment can directly affect the learner, for example, when students are motivated to learn because they know they will be examined, or when they improve their knowledge or competence as a result of the feedback they receive from a test. Similar direct effects occur when professors strive to be more effective teachers because they know they will be evaluated by their students, or when they improve their teaching as a result of the feedback they receive from such evaluations or from their assessments of students. The use of assessment as direct feedback is discussed in detail in chapter 9.

Assessment promotes talent development more indirectly when it enlightens or informs the educator about the effectiveness of various educational policies and practices. It is interesting that most of the discussion and debate about assessment these days concerns this indirect use of assessment rather than assessment designed to influence the learner directly. For this reason, most of this book (with the exception of chapter 9) is devoted to a consideration of how assessment can be utilized to inform educators about those educational policies and practices that are most likely to be effective in enhancing talent development. (Direct feedback of assessment results to students and faculty, incidentally, happens to be one of these educational practices.)

The principal means by which assessment results can help to enlighten professors and administrators is their use as an aid to *decision making*. Educators are continually confronted with decisions that can affect the talent development process: what to teach, how to teach it, whom to admit and on what basis, how to orient and advise students, what courses to require, how to structure the students' residential and social life, and how to test and evaluate students' performance. These decisions involve choices among alternative courses of action: this requirement rather than that requirement, this teaching method rather than these other methods.

Assessment results can be of considerable value in making such decisions because they can provide information about the likely impact of alternative courses of action. Chapter 2 presents an evaluation model— the input-environment-outcome model—which shows how assessment information can be most effectively used for this purpose. Chapters 3, 4, and 5 elaborate different aspects of the model (outcomes, inputs, and environments, respectively). Chapter 6 discusses various ways of analyzing assessment data. (Readers who desire more detail about statistical methods for data analysis should also read the appendix.) Chapter 7 discusses how assessment results can be used to enlighten and inform the practitioner.

Chapter 8, "Building a Data Base," discusses the practical, technical, and political problems associated with building an adequate data base consisting of student input, environment, and output data.

Chapter 9, "Assessment as Direct Feedback to the Learner," discusses how assessment can be used to affect the learning process directly among both students and faculty. Chapter 10, "Assessment and Equity," reviews various ways in which assessment has been used to limit educational opportunity and suggests how it might be used instead to enhance and expand opportunity.

Chapter 11, "Assessment and Public Policy," discusses the assessment "movement" in various states, suggesting ways in which institutions can minimize the negative impacts of such externally mandated assessments and employ them instead to strengthen the talent development process.

The final chapter (12), "The Future of Assessment," summarizes the major points of the book and considers various future directions that assessment in American higher education might take.

2

A CONCEPTUAL MODEL FOR ASSESSMENT

How can assessment be used to enlighten and inform college faculty and administrators? If an educator is interested in using assessment to learn how effective particular educational practices or programs are in developing student talent, it is not enough simply to go out and collect some "outcomes assessments." Unfortunately, a good deal of educational "evaluation" is done in this fashion, and as a consequence it ends up shedding very little light on the educational questions being investigated.

For the past couple of decades, I have been using what I call the input-environment outcome (I-E-O) model as a conceptual guide for assessment activities in higher education. The I-E-O model is very simple, yet it provides a powerful framework for the design of assessment activities and for dealing with even the most complex and sophisticated issues in assessment and evaluation. Since this model is something that evolved during my early years as a higher education researcher, I will introduce it by providing a brief autobiographical account of how it originated.

My doctoral training in psychology and my early employment as a clinical and counseling psychologist in a variety of medical settings conditioned me to look at human behavior in a developmental framework: people come to you for help in a certain condition, and you strive to work with them in such a way as to improve their condition. The success of the treatment that you provide is thus judged in terms of how much the patient or client is able to improve. Since some clients are in much worse shape than others when you first see them, you cannot judge the efficacy of your treatment simply in terms of the outcome, the condition of the patient at the termination of treatment; on the contrary, the effectiveness of treatment has to be judged in terms of how much *improvement* takes place.

My initial exposure to educational research occurred when I accepted a position as a research associate at the National Merit Scholarship Corporation (NMSC). Moving from clinical to educational psychology represented a major shift in orientation, but the problems in education seemed at least as interesting as—and probably more tractable than—those in the mental health field. The move also gave me an opportunity to work with a former mentor—psychologist John L. Holland—whom I greatly liked and admired.

My first research project at NMSC was concerned with something called *Ph.D. productivity.* The study was supported by the National Science Foundation which, at the time, was concerned with finding ways to encourage more undergraduates to pursue graduate work, especially in the sciences. Researchers at Wesleyan University and the University of Chicago (Knapp and Goodrich, 1952; Knapp and Greenbaum, 1953) had found that certain colleges were much more likely than others to produce graduates who eventually went on to win graduate fellowships and to earn the Ph.D. degree. Since the highly productive colleges also tended to have larger libraries, smaller student-faculty ratios, and more faculty who themselves had Ph.D.s than did the less productive colleges, the researchers concluded that these superior facilities and resources were somehow responsible for the colleges' higher productivity.

Holland and I noticed that the highly productive colleges tended to be the same ones that the Merit Scholars preferred to attend. This fact prompted us to ask a rather simple question: Could a college's output of Ph.D.s be explained simply in terms of its initial input of talented freshmen? To test this possibility, we conducted a series of studies which showed that, as far as Ph.D. output is concerned, the student input is by far the most important determining factor (Astin, 1962, 1963). It turned out that, when you took student inputs into account, some of the so-called highly productive institutions were actually *underproducing* Ph.D.s, whereas some of those with more modest outputs were actually producing more than one would expect from their student inputs.

These early studies were critical in teaching us three fundamental lessons about assessment in higher education:

1. The output of an institution or program—whether we measure this in terms of how many graduates earn advanced degrees, how much money the alumni earn, or whatever—does not really tell us much about its educational *impact* or educational *effectiveness* in developing talent. Rather, outputs must always be evaluated in terms of inputs. This is a particularly important principle for American higher education, given the fact that the three thousand institutions in our system differ so greatly in the kinds of students they enroll.
2. An output measure such as Ph.D. productivity is not determined solely by a single input measure such as student ability. On the contrary, even in our earliest studies of this phenomenon we found that input variables such as the student's sex and major

field of study are at least as important as ability in determining Ph.D. outputs.

3. Even if we have good longitudinal input and student output data, our understanding of the educational process will still be limited if we lack information on the college *environment*. Thus, it is one thing to know that your college overproduces or under-produces Ph.D.s, but quite another to understand why. What is it about the environment of a college that causes it to over- or underproduce? This last lesson suggests that input and output data, by themselves, are of limited usefulness. What we need in addition is information about the students' educational environment and experience: the courses, programs, facilities, faculty, and peer groups to which the student is exposed.

These early studies convinced us that any educational assessment project is incomplete unless it includes data on student inputs, student outcomes, and the educational environment to which the student is exposed (Figure 2.1). *Outcomes*, of course, refers to the "talents" we are trying to develop in our educational program; *inputs* refers to those personal qualities the student brings initially to the educational pro-gram (including the student's initial level of developed talent at the time of entry); and the *environment* refers to the student's actual ex-periences during the educational program. Environmental information is especially critical here, since the environment includes those things that the educator directly controls in order to develop the student's tal-ents. A fundamental purpose of assessment and evaluation, it should be emphasized, is to learn as much as possible about how to structure educational environments so as to maximize talent development.

To put the I-E-O in a more familiar terminological context, we could also refer to the outcome variables as dependent variables, criterion vari-ables, posttests, outputs, consequents, ends, or endogenous variables. Environmental and input variables are both types of independent vari-ables, antecedent variables, or exogenous variables. Inputs could also be called control variables or pretests. Environmental variables might also be referred to as treatments, means, or educational experiences, practices, programs, or interventions.

The three arrows in Figure 2.1 (A, B, and C) depict the relation-ships among the three classes of variables. Assessment and evaluation

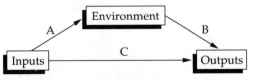

FIGURE 2.1 The I-E-O Model.

in education are basically concerned with relationship B—the effects of environmental variables on outcome variables. However, as the history of research on Ph.D. productivity shows, the relationship between environments and student outcomes cannot be understood without also taking into account student inputs. Student inputs, of course, can be related to both outputs (arrow C) and environments (arrow A). Another way of saying this is, first, that differences among students tend to show some consistency (i.e., correlation) over time (arrow C), and second, that different types of students often choose different types of educational environments (arrow B). The fact that inputs are thus related to both outputs *and* environments means that inputs can, in turn, affect the observed relationship between environments and outputs.

This problem can be illustrated with a simple example. Suppose we are concerned that many of our students do not seem to have very well-developed skills in English composition by the time they graduate, and that we decide to try to learn whether there are particular course-taking patterns that facilitate or inhibit the development of writing talent among our students. Accordingly, we administer a test of skill in English composition to all graduating seniors (outcome measure) and compare the average test performance of students who took different patterns of courses (different environments). We might well find, for example, that students who majored in engineering do relatively poorly on the test, whereas those who major in journalism do substantially better. Would such a finding justify the causal conclusion that majoring in engineering is detrimental to the development of talent in writing, and that majoring in journalism facilitates the development of writing talent? Probably not. Is it not reasonable to suppose that students who as freshmen choose to major in journalism *already* have better-developed writing skills when they first enter college (input) than do students who choose engineering? If so, we would expect journalism majors to score better than engineering majors on the senior test of writing skill, *even if the different course-taking patterns had identical effects on the development of writing talent!*

The basic purpose of the I-E-O design is to allow us to correct or adjust for such input differences in order to get a less biased estimate of the comparative effects of different environments on outputs. (Details of how to make such adjustments and interpret the results are given in chapter 6 and the appendix.)

Perhaps the need for these three kinds of data can be better understood with an analogy from the field of horticulture. Suppose we go to a county fair and examine the different entries in a rose contest. While it might be interesting to observe that some people's roses are bigger, more beautiful, or more fragrant than the roses of others, such output information, by itself, is not very useful in telling us how to grow roses successfully. We might improve our understanding somewhat if we also had input information on the types of seeds or cuttings that each grower had used. But would we be justified in concluding that output differences in rose quality were simply a matter of input differences in the seeds or cuttings from which they grew? Clearly we would not. What is missing here, of course, is environmental data concerning the conditions under which the different roses were grown: type of soil, method of planting, light, fertilizers, watering schedule, and fungicides and pesticides used. These environmental factors are important considerations in how effectively the grower can develop the rose's "talent."[1]

In other words, simply having input and outcome data of a group of students over a period of time is of limited value if you do not know what forces were acting on these students during the same period of time.

Perhaps an even better analogy can be found in the field of health care. The basic evaluation problem in medical research is to learn which treatments (environments) are most effective. If we were trying to enhance our understanding of how best to treat patients in a hospital, imagine how difficult it would be if all we did was to collect output information on how long patients stayed, whether they lived or died, and what their condition was as they left the hospital. We would improve the situation considerably if we also got input (diagnostic) information on the patients' condition at the time of admission. But we would still be greatly handicapped without environmental data. That is, how could we expect to learn much about how best to care for our patients if we did not know which patients got which therapies, which operations, or which medications? This is the equivalent of studying student development with no environmental data on what courses they took, where they lived, how much they studied, and so on.

There is nothing magical or even necessarily real in the I-E-O model. For me personally it represents nothing more than a convenient way of looking at phenomena that interest me—a tool for trying to understand why things are the way they are and for learning what might be done to make things different if we feel the need to change them. The model seems applicable to almost any social or behavioral science field—history, anthropology, economics, sociology, psychology, or political science—as long as the interest is in studying the development (input to output) of human beings or groups of human beings and in understanding more about factors (environments) that have influenced

---

1. This agricultural example is not entirely accidental. The earliest sophisticated forms of statistical inference—the analysis of variance and covariance—were developed as a means of determining the effect of various environmental variables (water, fertilizer, etc.) on the output of crops (growth rate, size, etc.).

(or might influence) that development. I have chosen education (especially higher education) as the focal point for most of my discussion of the model, but I see no reason why it could not be used just as readily in any of these other fields.

Although most of the illustrations and applications of the model used in this book are *quantitative* (that is, they involve quantifiable measures of inputs, environments, and outcomes and statistical analyses of the data), the logic underlying the model would seem to apply equally to *qualitative* problems. Qualitative research, like quantitative research, ordinarily seeks to identify causal connections between certain antecedent events or conditions (environments) and certain subsequent events (outcomes). Even if no quantitative data are involved, the qualitative investigator who is striving to understand why a certain event (outcome) occurred would be well advised to consider the possible contribution of inputs as well as environment.

Let's take as an example one of the most primitive forms of qualitative assessment: the testimonial. A testimonial is a verbal statement by an individual that is basically causal in nature. In effect, a testimonial attributes a particular outcome to the effects of a particular environment: "that teacher [environment] really helped me to understand calculus [outcome]." Note that the testimonial always implies an environmental *variable*, in the sense that it implicitly argues that some other environment (e.g., no teacher or a different teacher) would have produced a different outcome (less knowledge of calculus).

Often the testimonial also implies an input "pretest" condition (e.g., the student's lesser knowledge of calculus prior to encountering the teacher), but it usually ignores other inputs that might have had an important bearing on the outcome (e.g., the student's degree of determination to learn calculus).

What are we really trying to accomplish by applying such a model? First, it is important to keep in mind what higher education is attempting to accomplish: to enhance the educational and personal development of its students and faculty. (To simplify this particular discussion, I shall focus on student development, but remember that practically everything said applies equally to faculty development.) Taken together, student input and student outcome data are meant to represent student development—*changes* in the student's abilities, competence, knowledge, values, aspiration, and self-concept that occur over time. Because the notion of change is so basic to the purposes of higher education, we need to have at least two (and probably more) snapshots of the student taken at different times in order to determine what changes have actually occurred. At the same time, knowing what particular environmental experiences each student has had helps us to understand why some students develop differently from others.

Input and outcome refer simply to the state of the person at two different time points, and environment refers to the intervening experiences. We are particularly interested in learning about environmental experiences that can be controlled or changed, since it is these experiences that offer the possibility of improving outcomes in the future. Some environmental experiences, of course, can't be controlled. It is one thing to know that a death in the family (environmental event) contributed to a decline in a student's performance, but quite another to know what could have been done to prevent it or what can be done to prevent such events from occurring in the future. By contrast, if we know that a particular teaching method or particular curriculum is better than others, we are in a much better position to utilize such findings in designing educational environments that will produce more favorable outcomes in the future.

Nothing in human experience is intrinsically an input, an output, or an environment. How we should assign these labels depends entirely on what aspects of experience we choose to study and how we formulate the questions we wish to answer. To see why this is so, we can look at a single variable: the student's score on the SAT taken in the senior year in high school. We might want to know why students score as they do on this test and to find the most effective ways to help future generation students achieve better scores. In such a case the SAT score would probably constitute an *outcome* measure. For possible environmental measures we have an almost infinite range of possibilities: the type of secondary school students attended, the kinds of courses they took, the quality of teaching they received, whether they took preparation courses for the SAT (and which ones they took), how they prepared for the test, what kind of peer group stimulation they had, what kind of home environment they had. For input measures we would, obviously, need some sort of pretest, maybe the PSAT or a special earlier administration of the SAT. Our choice here would be determined in part by the period of time covered by our environmental variables (e.g., the last year of high school, the last two years, or whatever). We would also need to assess a variety of other input variables (sex, ethnicity, socioeconomic status, and so on) that might affect SAT performance, especially if these variables could also affect the set of environmental variables to which the students were exposed.

But we might have a very different interest in the SAT. Perhaps we wish to evaluate its usefulness in college admissions. From this particular perspective we would probably consider it an *input* variable and select such variables as college GPA, retention, or GRE performance as our outcome measures. Even in this situation, we would no doubt want to include environmental variables such as college major and place of residence in our analysis, since the effects of SAT on certain outcomes may be mediated by such variables. For example, it has been well established that student retention (completion of the baccalaureate) is facilitated by living in a campus residence hall during their freshman year (Astin, 1975, 1977, 1982; Chickering, 1974; Pascarella, 1985). Since the students with high SAT scores are more likely to live on campus than students with low scores (Chickering, 1974; Karabel and Astin, 1975), it may well be that the "effect" of SAT on retention is an indirect one which is, in fact, mediated by campus residence and possibly other environmental variables.

Still another perspective on SAT scores is to use them to construct an *environmental* variable. It has long been recognized (Feldman and Newcomb, 1969) that one of the most important sources of environmental influence on students is the peer group. We could define each student's peer group as all the students who were majoring in the same field. If we were to compute the average SAT scores of the students separately by major, we would then have an estimate of the average ability of the peer group within each major field. A variation on this idea would be to use the SAT score of each student's roommate (or the average score if there is more than one roommate) as an environmental measure (see chapter 5.)

COMPARATIVE EVALUATION AND THE CONTROL GROUP CONCEPT

Educational policy-making and educational decision making in general inevitably involve choices among alternatives. The student can decide to go to college instead of going to work, joining the military service, becoming a homemaker, traveling, or just loafing. The student can choose college A over college B or C, or decide to live on campus rather than at home. The student can also pick a particular college major over dozens of others, or decide to put off the decision for a few years. Finally, the student can decide how to go about studying and how much effort to devote to it. For their part, college officials make choices when they decide to offer particular programs, to hire particular faculty or staff, or to set particular standards of performance. Similarly, the faculty make choices when they decide what to teach, how to teach it, how to counsel and guide students, what to study, and how to treat their colleagues.

The point is a simple one, but one which is frequently overlooked in treatises on assessment and evaluation: all educational evaluation is "comparative," in the sense that whatever is being evaluated is being compared with something else. Often these comparisons are implicit rather than explicit, and often neither the evaluator nor the decision maker is aware of what the (implicit) comparison really is.

To take the most primitive kind of educational assessment and evaluation as an example, a common educational assessment practice is to administer some kind of standardized competency test to students as they reach an important educational transition point. Such testing has become especially popular in the elementary and secondary schools and may be gaining popularity in higher education. The state of Florida, for example, requires such an exam (the College Level Academic Skills Test, or CLAST) of all students before they are allowed to move from the sophomore to the junior year. While the original intent of such testing was that of quality control—to establish and maintain minimal performance standards for persons before they are allowed to go beyond certain educational levels—the temptation to aggregate such scores for certain groups of students (by institution, for example) may eventually prove too great for many educators to resist. Suppose we were trying to evaluate a particular course and that we used this approach by administering some kind of test to the students just as they completed the course. As with any other evaluation problem, our ultimate interest is in decision making: to continue the course as is, to make certain modifications, to revise completely and even abandon it, to recommend or not recommend it to others, and so on. By looking at how well or how poorly the students do on the end-of-course test, we then make a judgment about the effectiveness of such things as the syllabus, homework assignments, the teacher, the teaching method, and the course in general.

To simplify this discussion, suppose we are the teachers and we do this evaluation to determine whether changes in the course are needed. The wary reader may by now have already detected a flaw in our approach: we have an output measure but no input measure. How can we know how much our students have learned during the course if we don't know how well they were doing at the start of the course? But suppose we are sophisticated enough to have also administered a pretest (input measure) at the beginning of the course. Now we can determine how much *improvement* took place between the beginning and end (input to output).

Let us assume further that we are not satisfied with the amount of improvement that took place in a certain aspect of the students' performance, and on the basis of that evaluative judgment, we decide to change something about the way we teach the course. In effect, what we are doing here is comparing the actual improvement that occurred under our current teaching approach (environment A) with what we expect to happen under the new approach (environment B). That (implicit) comparative evaluation has led us to conclude that the outcome would be better under the new approach. Note that we must assume not only that the particular outcome performance that concerns us under the old approach will improve under the new approach, but that all other aspects of the student's outcome performance will be at least as good under the new approach (i.e., that there will not be any undesirable side effects caused by the new environment).

Exactly the same kind of comparative judgment would be involved if our evaluation led us to conclude that nothing needed to be changed. In effect, such a decision is based on the assumption that our current method of teaching the course (environment A) produced an overall outcome performance that is just as good or better than what could be produced under all other approaches that we might consider (environments B, C, D, and so on).

All educational choices, regardless of whether they result in a decision to change something or a decision merely to keep things as they are, involve comparative judgments such as the one just discussed. A decision to change something implies that the new environment is expected to produce a better outcome than the current environment. When the decision is not to change anything, the current environment is judged to be equal to or better than all possible alternative environments.

Control Groups and the True Experiment

Comparisons of the type discussed here are very similar in principle to what experimental scientists call the *control group* approach. In experimental science, we try to understand the effects of a particular environment by simultaneously studying the effects of at least one other environmental situation and comparing the results. Typically these two situations are called the experimental condition and the control condition, respectively. One group of subjects or cases is exposed to the experimental condition and a second, equivalent group is exposed to the control condition. The idea is to try to make the environments of the two conditions identical in every respect, with the exception of the one variable of interest, which is deliberately made to be different in the experimental group (in experimental jargon, this is *manipulating* or *controlling* the independent variable, which is also sometimes called the *treatment*). Through the processes of random selection or matching, the people exposed to the two situations (the experimental group and the control group) are presumed to be equivalent at the start (input). If the outcome performance of the experimental group turns out to be different from the outcome performance of the control group, the experimenter is justified in concluding that the difference was caused by the environmental variable of interest, since the two groups were comparable in every other respect.

We can illustrate the control group approach with an example. Let's say that we wish to introduce a radically different approach to teaching English composition in our undergraduate curriculum, but that there is some controversy within the faculty about whether the new approach will really work. We agree to conduct an experiment. We will select 10 percent of next year's new freshmen as an experimental group who will be given the new course, and the remaining 90 percent of the students will constitute the control group. While in reality we would probably want to use several different measures to compare the outcomes of our two groups, let us temporarily assume that we use only a single outcome measure consisting of a test of competence in English composition. If we picked our 10 percent of the freshman class by lot (i.e., randomly), and if the rest of the curriculum and freshman year experience was comparable to that of the other freshmen (the control group), then we would be justified in saying that we had a true experiment. In fact, if the experimental group was really selected by lot, we would not even need a pretest input measure, since we could assume that the two groups' average levels of skill in English composition were comparable at the beginning when they first started the course.[2] Then, if the two groups' average performance on the test of composition ability (outcome measure) turned out differently, we would be justified in concluding that the two approaches to teaching English composition produce (or cause) different results.

The approach taken in this hypothetical example is, unfortunately, used all too infrequently in academe. Typically, proposed changes in the curriculum are either implemented across the board for all students or, more typically, not implemented at all because of resistance and controversy within the faculty. But note here that such decisions involve precisely the same kind of logic that one finds in a control group experiment. When the faculty decides to change the curriculum, it has (implicitly) reasoned that if it *had* done a controlled experiment, the results would have favored the new curriculum. A negative faculty decision on the new curriculum also involves similar reasoning, but with a different result: they assume that the experiment would *not* have favored the new curriculum.

Most students who do graduate work in education and the social sciences are told that true experiments are the ideal, and that we use other, less elegant research methods only because experimentation is usually unfeasible. While it is true that a classical control-group experiment generates results about which one can make causal inferences with a high degree of confidence, control-group experiments in education (or in any other social science field, for that matter) create a number of other problems which, in my experience, greatly limit their usefulness.

First, when we conduct a true experiment by assigning students at random to experimental and control groups, we create a highly artificial situation that can distort our findings. Since it is very difficult (and possibly unethical) to keep the students from knowing what is being done

---

2. Having pretest measures would, however, increase the odds of detecting a significant difference in the effects of the two courses.

to them, they usually know that they are participants in an experiment, and they usually know the group to which they have been assigned. This knowledge will almost certainly affect the results of the experiment, and unfortunately, such effects are frequently unpredictable.[3]

We can see how this might work in the curriculum experiment just described. Students who have been assigned to the new course in English composition might resent the fact that they are being used as "guinea pigs," a reaction which in turn could have a detrimental effect on their motivation to perform well in the course. On the other hand, they might feel that they are sort of an elite group that has been singled out for special treatment, a response that might stimulate them to work especially hard. Students in the control group might feel grateful that they have been spared the fate of being used as guinea pigs, or they might resent having been deprived of this innovative and exciting new course. Since nobody can be sure just how students in each group are really being affected by the knowledge that they are part of an experiment, it is not possible to know how this knowledge will ultimately affect their performance on the outcome measure.

From a practical point of view, the real problem here is not so much that the experimental results can be affected by the students' knowledge of the experiment, but rather that *the environmental conditions created by the experiment cannot be reproduced in the future.* Suppose the outcome of the experiment clearly favors the new English composition course and that this result prompts the faculty to replace the old course with the new one. Now all students must take the same new course, and the students no longer think they are part of an experiment; the course is now simply another part of the required core curriculum that everybody has to take. How can we be sure that the course will continue to have the same beneficial effect? How do we know that the superiority of the new course in the experiment was not just a temporary consequence of student enthusiasm generated by the knowledge that they had been singled out for special treatment? How do we know that the inferior performance of the control group was not just a consequence of their indifference or resentment?

Similar problems arise when we consider the effects of the experiment on the faculty. The real dilemma here is how to assign faculty responsibility for the experiment. The rules of classical control group experimentation require that we do one of two things: either assign the faculty to teach the two composition courses by lot, or have each faculty member who teaches the traditional course also teach one section of the experimental course. Neither of these requirements is entirely

---

3. The situation described here is very much like the "Hawthorne effect" in social science research or the "Heisenberg principle" in physics: the very *act* of studying something changes the nature of what is being studied.

satisfactory, but the second is probably preferable to the first, since it simulates more closely the results that would occur if a decision were made to drop the old course and have all students take the new one.

The point of this discussion is to stress that control-group experiments in education are no panacea. We can learn much from true experiments, but they are not necessarily preferable to *natural* experiments, which we will now consider.

Natural Experiments

The I-E-O model was developed primarily for use in what I like to call *natural* experiments. In such experiments we try to study naturally occurring variations in environmental conditions and to approximate the methodological benefits of true experiments by means of complex multivariate statistical analyses. In a sense, with natural experiments we try to study the real world rather than the artificial ones that are created by experimentation. Natural experiments have two principal advantages over true experiments. First, they avoid the artificial conditions of true experiments that are created by the establishment of experimental and control groups and the random assignment of students to these groups. Second, natural experiments make it possible to study the effects of many different environmental variables at the same time. Since natural experiments permit us to compare and contrast the great variety of educational approaches and practices (i.e., the different environments) that characterize higher education in America, they can help us to understand which educational environments and practices are most effective and under what conditions.

The principal limitation of natural experiments—and it is a very serious one—is that the students are not assigned at random to the various educational environments. Another way of saying this is that the input characteristics of students who are exposed to one environment are usually different from the input characteristics of students who are exposed to another (comparison) environment. Students to some extent pick their environments and environments sometimes pick their students. This inequality of inputs means that the outcome performance of students exposed to different environments will almost certainly differ, even if the actual *effect* of the different environments is the same. The main purpose of the I-E-O model is to control for initial input differences among the students by means of multivariate analyses (see chapter 6 and the appendix for details of these procedures). In effect, such statistical equating of initial input differences attempts to accomplish by statistical means what random assignment accomplishes in pure control group experiments. The real question about any natural experiment is this: have all of the potentially biasing input variables been adequately controlled? Chapters 4 and 6 and the appendix suggest a number of specific techniques for addressing this question.

To return to our hypothetical example involving the new method of teaching English composition, if a few members of the English department became interested in such an approach, they might well want to try it out in some of their classes and to evaluate the results using a natural experimental design rather than the classical control group experiment described earlier. They might persuade some of their colleagues who would be teaching with the traditional approach to let their classes serve as natural (i.e., nonrandomized) control groups, or possibly they themselves could teach different sections using the two methods. No matter who does the teaching, it would be important to obtain input as well as outcome data from students in all classes. The input data should obviously include a pretest measure of competence in English composition as well as measures of any other characteristics (sex, prior grades in English courses, etc.) that might affect students' outcome performance.

Before leaving this discussion, I would like to add a word about a topic that has been much debated among social science methodologists: correlation and causation. Graduate students in education and the social sciences are routinely told that only true control group experiments permit the investigator to make causal inferences about environmental effects on outcomes, and that "you can't make causal inferences from correlational data" (this, of course, is the equivalent of saying you can't make causal inferences from natural experiments). The fact is that you *can* make causal inferences from correlational data; people make such inferences all the time. Indeed, it would be hard to get through an average day without making such inferences. Each of us implicitly makes a causal inference when we make choices between alternatives, such as what to eat for breakfast, how to spend our day at work, and so on. Each such decision implicitly involves causal reasoning—the selected alternative is assumed to lead to a better outcome than the rejected alternative—even though we almost never have data from a pure control group experiment to help us choose.

The real issue in making causal inferences from correlational data is not that such inferences are methodologically unsound or immoral, but rather to *minimize the chances that our inferences are wrong*. In natural experiments, the best insurance against making invalid inferences is to control as many of the potentially biasing input variables as possible. While we can never be sure that we have controlled all such variables, the more we control, the greater confidence we can have in our causal inferences.

INCOMPLETE DESIGNS

Perhaps the best way to understand the importance of the three components in the I-E-O design is to consider what happens when one or two of the three components is missing. Since typical assessment activities in higher education more often than not leave out components from the I-E-O model, I would like to discuss these incomplete designs using examples taken from real-life experiences that I have encountered on various college campuses. Four different incomplete designs will be considered: outcome-only assessments, environment-outcome assessments, input-outcome assessments, and environment-only assessments.

Outcome-Only Assessments

With the accountability and outcomes assessment movements gaining so much popularity during the past few years, outcome-only assessment is probably the fastest growing approach of all. This approach involves the utilization of some kind of end-of-program assessment designed to determine whether the learning objectives of the particular program are being achieved. The most common application of this model is the course final examination. However, the model has been increasingly used in much broader contexts. Many institutions now require all students to demonstrate some minimal levels of competency in basic skills such as mathematics and written composition before they are permitted to reach certain levels (the junior year, for example) or to receive a degree. Similarly, some public systems now require undergraduates to demonstrate minimal competency in one or more areas. A good example is the upper-division writing requirement now mandated in all nineteen campuses of the California State University system. On an even broader level, Florida's CLAST program tests student competence in several different areas as a condition for achieving junior year status. Finally, the outcome-only model is being used even at the national level. The national assessment of educational progress (NAEP) periodically examines national samples of students at various levels of educational development to determine their skill levels in a variety of areas. Similarly, the national college admissions tests (the SAT and the ACT) have been used as a kind of annual barometer to gauge the effectiveness of our elementary and secondary school systems across the country. The sharp declines in these scores that occurred between the 1960s and the early 1980s provided the principal empirical foundation for the widely discussed critical report on our educational system, *A Nation at Risk* (National Commission on Excellence in Education, 1983).

The main advantage of assessments that use this model is that they focus attention on the fundamental problems of defining and measuring those outcomes that are relevant to the goals of the educational program in question. Even the process of trying to define and measure the goals of educational programs can be a very useful learning experience for faculty members and policy makers. The major drawback to this approach, however, is that it produces data that are extremely difficult, if not impossible, to interpret. In other words, the *meaning* of the data generated by this approach is very unclear.

Ambiguities and interpretive difficulties occur at all levels at which the outcome-only model is applied. Let's start with classroom final examinations. Without additional information, the professor who attempts to evaluate his or her teaching using the course final examination is implicitly forced to assume that *what is being tested is what has been learned*. In most academic fields, such an assumption is very difficult to justify. There are very few courses, for example, in which students do not begin with at least some knowledge of the course subject matter. And students usually differ in this respect: some know much more than others about the subject matter before the course ever starts. Furthermore, most course final examinations test a lot more than knowledge of course content, since exam performance is affected by factors such as writing skill and reasoning ability. All of us who have taught college students over the years know well that if a student is sufficiently bright and talented at the start of the course, it is possible for that student to do quite well on a final examination without really learning much of anything in the course. On the other hand, it is possible that a student whose performance on the final examination is mediocre may, in fact, have learned a great deal in the course, especially if the student began the course with no knowledge of the subject matter and with minimal examinatinon performance skills. Perhaps the only time a professor has a reasonable basis for assuming that what is being tested is what has been learned is when the course has such highly specialized content that it would be unreasonable to assume that the students had any knowledge of the content prior to enrolling in the course. Outside of a few courses in highly technical fields or in certain natural science fields, it seems safe to assume that such situations are quite rare.

Problems associated with the application of the outcome-only method are compounded whenever the method is applied on a broader scale beyond the classroom. Take the much-heralded *A Nation at Risk*. The steadily declining college admissions test scores were cited in this report as one of the principal bases for concluding that the nation was "at risk." While such a conclusion may have indeed been warranted by the data, the real problem is to understand *why* the decline occurred and what can be *done* about it. Is the problem with the high schools? In order to answer this, one would have to know how much improvement in performance the most recent classes of students exhibited during their three or four years in high school, and to compare the results with a similar longitudinal assessment done during the late 1960s. If such a study were to show that the problem was not in the high schools, we would be confronted with other questions. Was the problem at the primary or intermediate levels? Or was it at the preschool level? To answer such questions, of course, it would be necessary to have input data at the beginning of each school level as well as outcome information.

But even if the decline could be isolated in terms of school levels, we would still be confronted with the even more difficult problem of understanding why the decline has occurred and what can be done about it. If we did indeed locate the problem in our secondary schools, what are we doing in the secondary schools that has created the decline? A definitive answer to this question would require us not only to have input and outcome assessments at the beginning and end of secondary school but also to have such assessments on different types of secondary schools and school programs. Since we lack such data, a great deal of effort has been invested over the past decade in speculating about the reasons for the decline. Dozens of theories have been proposed ranging from changes in the curriculum to radioactive fallout from atmospheric testing conducted during the 1950s (Turnbull, 1985; Wirtz, 1977). The commission that produced *A Nation at Risk* concluded that the decline was caused in part by changes in the school curriculum and thereby recommended substantial increases in the number of basic academic subjects that students should be required to take in secondary school. While such curricular changes may indeed have a beneficial effect on test scores, available test data were really of very little help in assisting the commission to come to such a conclusion and, in the long run, the commission was forced to resort to hunches and guesswork in making its recommendations. For all we know, the test score declines were not caused by curriculum changes. Perhaps there are many more cost-effective ways in which these declines can be turned around.

In short, the outcome-only approach to assessment is flawed on two accounts. First, there is no way of knowing how much has actually been learned as a result of an educational program because there is no input information with which to compare the outcome assessment. Second, in the absence of information on how students performed under different environmental circumstances, there is no way to tell from the assessment data which educational programs and practices are likely to be most effective.

Environment-Outcome Assessments

The environment-outcome approach to assessment represents an improvement over the outcome-only approach in that it incorporates information on environmental differences that can aid in the interpretation of student performance on the outcome assessments. However, this improvement can well turn out to be counterproductive as it encourages causal interpretations of environmental effects when these may indeed be unwarranted. The principal limitation of this approach is that no information on student input performance is included.

There are many examples of the use of the environment-outcome approach. Some institutions, for example, compare retention rates of students across different majors or between different colleges within the university. At the multi-institutional level, different institutions can be compared with each other in terms of their retention rates, alumni achievements, and so on. The "Ph.D. productivity" studies discussed at the beginning of the chapter represent another example of the use of this approach.

As we have already shown, the main difficulty with the environment-outcome approach is that it exercises no control over differential inputs. The only situation in which we would be justified in concluding that output differences across different environments were, in fact, caused by the environmental differences is one in which the students have been assigned at random to the different environments (that is, when we have the conditions of a true experiment). A possible exception to this caveat is the situation in which, although the subjects are not assigned at random, we have good reason to believe that there are no important differences in input characteristics of students entering different environments. However, without actual input data, such assumptions are usually very difficult to defend.

Perhaps the most egregious application of this model occurs in the achievement testing done annually in the public school systems of our states. Typically, the students at different schools within a system are examined on some achievement test and the average results are computed on a school-by-school basis. Each school is thus regarded as a different "environment." Schools in which the students get the highest average scores are thus presumed to be the best schools whereas those whose students get the lowest scores are considered to be the weakest schools. If we had reason to believe that the students entering the different schools were comparable at the point of entry, such causal conclusions would perhaps be justified. However, as we all know, different schools recruit students from vastly different socioeconomic backgrounds; their input levels of performance are almost certainly different. Under these circumstances, we would clearly expect to find outcome differences in achievement from school to school, even if the schools had identical true effects on the students' educational development. It may well be that many of the schools whose students do well on such achievement test comparisons are doing a mediocre educational job with their students, and that some of the schools whose students do relatively poorly are, in fact, doing an outstanding job. Without input information on the students' initial levels of achievement and family background, there is simply no way to know how effective the different educational programs of the different schools really are.

Such problems are compounded in American higher education, what with the enormous diversity of student bodies entering a variety of institutions. Even within many institutions, there can be substantial input differences between students who pick different majors, between commuters and residents, between part-time and full-time students, and between financial aid recipients and students who receive no aid. There is no way that we can reliably assess the impact of environmental experiences such as major or place of residence without input information on the characteristics of students at the point of entry.

Input-Outcome Assessments

Perhaps the prototypical study of college impact involves the testing and retesting of students at a single institution (Feldman and Newcomb, 1969). Characteristically, students complete some kind of questionnaire or inventory when they first enter college and take it again one year later, four years later, or in a few cases, many years after graduation. Measures of change or growth are obtained by comparing the students' input scores from the initial administration with outcome scores from the follow-up administration. In subsequently interpreting these change scores, we typically assume that any observed changes are due to the students' experiences in the educational program. In other words, such studies equate *change* with *impact*.

When such assessment studies involve the use of achievement tests or other cognitive measures, they are sometimes referred to as *value-added* assessments. I personally prefer the term *talent development*, for at least two reasons. First, the value-added concept is basically economic rather than educational in its derivation. Second, talent development seems to come much closer to describing the fundamental educational mission of most colleges and universities. Nevertheless, it should be recognized that the terms *value-added*, *talent development*, *pretest-posttest*, and *longitudinal* basically relate to the same phenomenon: repeated assessment of the same qualities on the same students done at different points in time.

This type of design has the advantage of focusing attention on the longitudinal nature of the talent development process, as it views the student's outcome performance not in isolation but rather in relation to entering input performance. Its basic weakness is that it really produces no information that bears directly on the question of environmental impact. Would the same changes have occurred if the student had been exposed to a different kind of program or to no program at all?

These inferential problems are probably not as severe at the level of the individual course or class, given that course examinations are usually more specialized and focused on a relatively short time interval. It is probably reasonable for a professor to assume that changes or improvements in student performance that occur during a quarter or semester are largely attributable to the course experience. Clearly, the availability of input information can be of significant value to those of us who teach in higher education for at least two reasons. First, it tells us about the students' strengths and weaknesses early enough to give us an opportunity to adjust our teaching during the course. Second, it provides us with a baseline for assessing how much students actually learn and how much their performance improves between the beginning and the end of the course. Even so, if the results of such pretest-posttest assessments lead us to conclude that the students are not learning as well as we would like them to learn, there is really no way for us to know for sure what needs to be changed in order to bring about the desired degree of improvement. For this reason it would be useful for all of us who teach in higher education to begin to experiment with different approaches to teaching (i.e., with different environments) in order to learn more about how best to facilitate learning. The experimentation can take several forms. We might give different students different types of assignments. Or, we might teach one section of a course using one approach and another section using a different approach. In effect, such experiments introduce *environmental variation* into our input-outcome model.

Because of the cost and time associated with collecting longitudinal pretest and posttest data, many investigators have tried to shortcut the process by simultaneously assessing freshmen and upper classmen on some measure. In addition to the problems already mentioned, this shortcut method is so full of pitfalls that one wonders if there is the slightest justification for supposing that the observed changes are related in any way to the college experience. For example, such an approach forces us to assume that upperclassmen are a representative sample of the total cohort of freshmen from which they were drawn. We also need to assume that this original cohort was drawn from the same population as the current freshmen who are being compared to the upperclassmen. In other words, this shortcut approach assumes that the successive entering freshmen classes have not changed with respect to the outcome measure, and that the dropouts, persisters, and transfer students are all comparable on the outcome measure. Except under very unusual circumstances, neither of these assumptions can be justified.

In short, the input-outcome model produces inferential difficulties that result from the need to assume that *change* is equivalent to *environmental impact*. This problem suggests that it would be useful to regard changes in students that occur during the course of an educational program as comprising two components: change resulting from the impact of the educational environment and change resulting from other influences (maturation, effects of other unmeasured environmental variables, and so on). Note that the program being assessed may (1) bring about changes that otherwise would not occur, (2) exaggerate or accelerate changes resulting from other sources, or (3) impede or counteract changes resulting from other sources. In other words, it is even conceivable that the true effect of the environment being assessed is the *opposite* of the observed change that occurs between pretest and posttest, and that the change would actually have been greater if the student had been exposed to a different environment.

Environment-Only Assessment

When some people speak of evaluation, what they have in mind is environment-only assessments. In this type of assessment we focus our attention on the educational program itself: teaching techniques, curriculum content, course materials, course assignments, physical facilities, the qualifications of professors. When faculty members evaluate each others' courses by examining course syllabi, they are practicing environment-only assessment. Perhaps the best-known application of this method is the regional accreditation process in higher education. Traditionally, accreditation has involved an examination of the institution's libraries, physical plant, faculty-student ratios, teaching loads, required and elective courses, and the academic qualifications of the faculty such as the percentage with doctoral degrees. In recent years regional accrediting associations have begun to request information on "outcomes," but typically this information is collected in isolation from other data about the institution. In effect, this merely adds an outcome-only component to the usual environment-only component of regional accrediting. A notable exception is the Southern Association of Colleges and Schools, which recently requested all of its institutions to produce what amounts to talent development or value-added data on student learning.

Another well-known example of environment-only assessment is the periodic ratings of the "quality" of graduate programs (Cartter, 1966; Roose and Anderson, 1970; Jones, Lindzey, and Coggeshall, 1982). While these are, in effect, reputational surveys, they appear to be primarily a reflection of the scholarly productivity and reputation of the faculty in the particular graduate department being rated (Drew and Karpf, 1981).

The problem with environment-only assessment is that it runs afoul of the same difficulties noted in our earlier critique (see chapter 1) of the reputational and resources approaches to excellence: no information bearing directly on learning or the talent-development process is gathered. In other words, no matter how detailed the descriptive information made available through this method, no data concerning the actual impact or effectiveness of the educational program is provided. In the absence of such information, we are forced to *infer* it in order to make any evaluative judgments about the program. For example, if a particular course syllabus is regarded as deficient in some respect, it is necessary to assume that the alleged deficiency produces some unwanted result in terms of the desired educational outcomes of the course (student learning). It is also necessary to assume that the recommended remedy in the syllabus will produce a better outcome. Similarly, if a visiting accrediting team decides that the institution's library is deficient in some respect and recommends that it be changed, the team is implicitly assuming that the alleged deficiency causes some decrement in student (or faculty) talent development which would, once again, be remedied by implementing the recommended change.

Since the environment-only method is particularly popular in evaluating curricula, one should recognize that such evaluations necessarily assume that "what is taught is what is learned." There is, however, one situation in which this method can be applied with a reasonable degree of confidence. Assume, for example, that prior longitudinal research has shown that a particular kind of educational intervention, curriculum, or program produces better results (in terms of improvements from input to outcome) than other approaches. Armed with such information, the assessor can then examine the content and method of the program being evaluated to determine whether it possesses the most desirable components (as determined by the earlier research). Recommendations for change under these conditions would not be based on speculation but on previously established empirical findings. Once well-designed longitudinal research has established the causal connections between environmental characteristics and particular educational outcomes, such information can provide the basis for environment-only assessments that can be carried out much more rapidly and at much lower cost than elaborate longitudinal studies.

SUMMARY

This chapter has presented a conceptual model to be used as a general guide in designing and implementing assessment activities on any campus. The input-environment-outcome (I-E-O) model is predicated on the assumption that the principal means by which assessment can be used to improve educational practice is by enlightening the educator about the comparative effectiveness of different educational policies and practices. The I-E-O model is specifically designed to produce information on how outcomes are affected by different educational policies and practices. Use of this model should allow those responsible for assessment activities to enhance their understanding of how student or faculty development is affected by various educational policies and practices.

The three informational components of the model—inputs, environments, and outcomes—are discussed in more detail in the next three chapters.

3

ASSESSING OUTCOMES

Of the three classes of assessment variables discussed in the preceding chapter, outcomes are, generally, the most critical and important to educators and researchers. In the jargon of scientific research, outcomes are the *dependent variables* while inputs and environments are the *independent variables*. Outcomes are sometimes also called *criterion variables*, *output variables*, *aims*, *goals*, or *objectives*. In essence, student outcomes refer to those aspects of the student's development that the institution either does influence or attempts to influence through its educational programs and practices.

OUTCOMES AND VALUES

Because they reflect the desired aims and objectives of the educational program, outcome measures are inevitably value based. The very act of choosing to assess certain outcomes rather than others clearly requires us to make value judgments. In this connection, it is important to distinguish between the value statement—a verbal description of some future condition or state of affairs that is considered desirable or important (e.g., competence in critical thinking)—and the actual *measure* selected to represent that outcome. The former might be referred to as the *conceptual outcome*; the latter as the *outcome measure*. The task in developing an appropriate outcome measure is thus to operationalize the conceptual outcome in some way (e.g., to develop a test of competence in critical thinking).

Controversy about outcome assessment often results from a failure of the respective parties to understand this fundamental distinction between conceptual outcomes and outcome measures. Sometimes disputes about the use of particular outcome measures may mask fundamental values differences over the conceptual outcomes implied in the measures, whereas in other situations a disagreement about conceptual outcomes may really represent a difference of opinion over the particular measures selected to represent these outcomes.

One of the basic ideas underlying modern testing and assessment is the concept of validity. A test or assessment instrument is valid to the

extent that it measures what it purports to measure. Given that conceptual outcomes are basically value statements, there is no way that they
can be validated empirically. The same goes for outcome *measures*: their
validity must ultimately be judged in terms of how well they reflect
the values underlying the conceptual outcome. In other words, there is
no way one can validate an outcome measure except through a logical
analysis of its relevance to the conceptual outcome (Astin, 1964). One
can, of course, validate an outcome measure by determining whether
it correlates with some more ultimate outcome measure, and then validate that second measure by correlating it with still another (even more
ultimate) measure. But at some point one reaches the end of the chain,
and at that point one must resort to logical analysis and argument to
validate the final measure.

A key consideration that is often overlooked is what I like to call *perspective*: from whose perspective are we attempting to assess outcomes?
It is my impression that our final choices of conceptual outcomes and
outcome measures are heavily influenced by perspective. Let me give a
few examples to show how much our ultimate measures can vary as a
function of perspective.

Perhaps most common is the *departmental* perspective. From this
perspective, the development of outcome measures is generally guided
by existing course content required of undergraduate majors. Basically,
we faculty are trying to capture or summarize whatever materials we
happen to be teaching at that point in time. Departmental comprehensive exams (Banta and Schneider, 1988) are a good example of an
outcome assessment developed from this perspective.

A variant on the departmental perspective is the *disciplinary* perspective. Here we are trying to utilize outcome assessments that reflect
a kind of national consensus as to what our field or discipline should
include. The most obvious example of the disciplinary perspective is the
GRE. Northeast Missouri State University, for example, has utilized the
GRE in many of its departments as an outcome assessment for graduating seniors in different major fields (Krueger and Heisserer, 1987;
McClain and Krueger, 1985).

Note how these first two perspectives affect the interplay between
curriculum and outcome assessment: under the departmental perspective we tend to "test what we teach," whereas under the disciplinary
perspective we are more inclined to "teach to the test." (Chapter 7 includes a detailed discussion of this latter practice.)

Closely related to the disciplinary perspective is the *professional* perspective. Here we attempt to assess those outcomes that are relevant to
entry to a profession or professional school. Some colleges, for example, use the National Teachers Exam (NTE) as the outcome assessment
for teacher training graduates. At the graduate or professional school
level, a similar perspective would lead us to use the state bar exam as

an outcome assessment for law school graduates or the National Board exam for medical school graduates.

Still another variant is what we might call the *employer* perspective. Here we try to gear our definition of relevant outcomes to the skills and personal qualities that are most valued by the employers of our graduates. Among traditional baccalaureate institutions, this perspective is perhaps best illustrated by the assessment program at Alverno College, (Mentkowski, 1988; Mentkowski and Doherty, 1984). Many of the trade and proprietary schools also assess from this perspective.

A perspective that leads to the assessment of basic skills—reading, writing, computation, and so on—is the *state* perspective (see chapter 11). An interesting aspect of the state perspective is that it tends to focus at the low end of the performance continuum on minimal competencies. There are many contemporary examples of this perspective: the "rising junior" exams in Florida (Ciereszko, 1987) or the upper-division writing competency exam that is now required on all nineteen campuses in the California State University.

Before leaving the issue of perspective, I would like to say a word about an approach that has received very little consideration so far in selecting outcome assessments: the *student* perspective. Students come to college with a wide variety of personal goals and aspirations. Shouldn't any system of outcome assessment be at least partially responsive to this perspective? Beyond the usual student aims of a good job or a good graduate or professional school, some students want to develop their social and interpersonal skills; others want to hone their performing arts skills; still others are concerned with increased self-understanding or with making a contribution to society. My personal bias here is that no system of outcome assessment is adequate if it fails to incorporate some of this student perspective. But if we are going to take a student perspective, this almost forces us to tailor-make part of our assessment to the particular needs and aspirations of the individual student. This may seem like an onerous task, but I think it can be done.

Why do these different perspectives lead to such different types of outcome assessments? Again, I think the key to understanding this issue is one of *values*. What is most important and most dear to us? Faculty in the departments place a very high premium on what they teach: they have developed a high level of expertise in a particular content area and are thus inclined toward cognitive tests that assess students' mastery of that same content. Proprietary and trade schools put a very high value on their ability to place their graduates and to have these students perform well on the job; hence their identification with the employer's perspective is strong.

States are concerned with protecting taxpayers' investments by making institutions accountable, which helps to explain the strong value they place on basic skills and minimal competency levels. The state, in other words, wants to ensure that its graduates are certified as being capable of performing certain tasks competently.

SINGLE OR MULTIPLE MEASURES?

The entire assessment process in higher education would be simplified greatly if there were a single outcome measure that could be used in assessment and evaluation programs. Our discussion of perspective, however, shows that there are many possible outcomes of a higher education experience, and no one of these will really suffice as an adequate assessment of the impact of our educational programs. Since higher education is in the business of developing multiple talents, it is not possible for any single measure adequately to reflect the institution's educational mission. Indeed, there is good reason to believe that the different constituencies served by higher education—students, parents, faculty, legislators, policy makers, and taxpayers—would each attach somewhat different priorities to different educational outcomes. Even within a given constituent group, such as students, there is likely to be considerable diversity in the motives for attending college. Some students may be interested primarily in developing their intellectual talents, others might be interested in developing their interpersonal or leadership skills, others might be interested in getting a better job or in making more money, while still others might simply be looking for a spouse. And even if we limited our outcome assessments to just those students who are attending college to develop their intellectual talents, we have an extremely broad range of talents to assess: mathematical, scientific, artistic, literary, analytical, and so on.

What is interesting about our current assessment practices in higher education is that an observer from another planet might conclude that there is only one or at best a handful of student outcomes that are important. Many institutions rely heavily or even exclusively on a single measure of student progress—the grade-point average (GPA). A few institutions employ senior comprehensive examinations, but even here the measurement may be limited to a single score or grade. Increasing numbers of institutions are also using their retention rate as an outcome measure, but again we are looking at a single measure. Clearly, traditional assessment practices in American higher education do not adequately reflect the multidimensionality of student outcomes.

OUTCOMES OR IMPACT?

The distinction between outcome measures and measures of educational impact is one that is often poorly understood by educators and policy makers alike. While such a semantic issue may seem pedantic or even trivial, it has profound implications for how we use outcome assessment in higher education.

Many educators are inclined to use the term *outcome* as synonymous with *impact*. This confusion is perhaps understandable, given that outcome can be viewed as having a kind of causal connotation: to say that something is an outcome is to imply that it is an outcome *of* something (in this case, the educational program of the institution). The implication is that the institution can somehow take credit (or blame!) for its graduating students' level of competence. However, as was noted in chapter 2, the performance of students at the end of an educational program is substantially affected by their performance at the point of initial entry (input). In other words, one cannot simply assume that the students' outcome performance after completion of a program of study has been caused by that program of study. At the same time, one cannot assume that differences in outcome performance between students exposed to different kinds of programs can be attributed to the differential effects of those programs unless we first take into account their differing input performances at the beginning of the program.

In short, the term *outcome* as used in this chapter and throughout the book refers simply to the students' performance on an outcome measure at a particular point in time, and does not, in itself, imply any antecedent causal factors that may account for that performance.

OUTCOME TAXONOMIES

Given the multidimensional nature of student outcomes, it is necessary to confront the question of *which* outcomes should be assessed and *how*. A number of investigators have suggested taxonomic schemes for classifying various types of student outcome measures. In his major review of the literature on higher education outcomes, Bowen (1977) suggests that student outcome assessments should cover the following categories of traits: verbal skills, quantitative skills, substantive knowledge, rationality, intellectual tolerance, aesthetic sensitivity, creativeness, intellectual integrity, and wisdom. A similar listing has been suggested by a recent report of the Association of American Colleges (1985): The Project on Redefining the Meaning and Purpose of Baccalaureate Degrees.

Lenning, Lee, Micek, and Service (1977) suggest a highly detailed taxonomy of outcomes organized under five major headings: economics; human characteristics; knowledge, technology, and art form functions; resource and service provision; and aesthetic and cultural activities. Still another approach to outcome classification has been utilized by Mentkowski and Doherty (1983). Their system, developed collaboratively with faculty and administrators at Alverno College, includes eight categories: communications, analysis, problem solving, valuing, social interaction, taking responsibility for the environment, involvement in the contemporary world, and aesthetic response. Unlike the other outcome taxonomies mentioned in this section, the Alverno model is designed to reflect the faculty's views about the goals of the undergraduate liberal arts program in a particular institution. For a more detailed description and critique of these taxonomies, see Jacobi, Astin, and Ayala (1987).

Given that any college or university's outcomes will be to some extent idiosyncratic, it would probably not be appropriate for an institution simply to adopt lists of outcomes that were developed elsewhere. Rather, I would like to suggest a conceptual scheme for developing outcome measures that would probably fit almost any institution's specific needs and requirements. This taxonomic scheme, which has been proposed in some of my earlier writings (Astin, 1970a, 1977), involves three dimensions: type of outcome, type of data, and time.

Type of Outcome

Measurement specialists have traditionally classified student outcomes into two broad domains: cognitive (sometimes called *intellective*) and affective (sometimes called *noncognitive*). Cognitive outcomes have to do with knowledge and the use of higher order mental processes such as reasoning and logic. Of all the possible outcome measures that one might devise for assessing student progress, those involving cognitive learning and the development of cognitive skills are most likely to be judged as relevant to the educational objectives of students, faculty, administrators, trustees, parents, and the general public.

Affective outcomes have to do with the student's feelings, attitudes, values, beliefs, self-concept, aspirations, and social and interpersonal relationships. Although the number of possible affective or noncognitive outcomes is very large, techniques for measuring such outcomes are probably not as far advanced as are those for measuring cognitive outcomes. Nevertheless, crude measures of affective outcomes are relatively easy to obtain through self-administered questionnaires and inventories whereas measurements of cognitive outcomes normally require the more controlled conditions of proctored test administration and larger amounts of the student's time.

Educators are inclined to shy away from assessing affective outcomes because they think they are too value-laden. They feel much more comfortable limiting their assessments to cognitive outcomes. College, they argue, is supposed to develop the student's intellect, so how can we go wrong if we focus on cognitive variables? However, if you read through a few college catalogues, you begin to realize that this argument is really inconsistent with the stated aims and goals of most undergraduate institutions. Most colleges claim to be concerned about such affective qualities as good judgment, citizenship, social responsibility, and character. Indeed, most descriptions of the liberally educated person sound at least as affective as they do cognitive (Grandy, 1988). Under these conditions, no program of student outcomes assessment would seem complete without due consideration for assessment of relevant affective outcomes.

Type of Data

Whereas the first dimension of this taxonomy—Type of Outcome— reflects *what* is being assessed, the second dimension—Type of Data— reflects the *how* of assessment. This second dimension of the taxonomy relates to the types of information that are gathered in order to assess the cognitive or affective outcomes under consideration. Again, two broad classes can be identified: *psychological* data reflecting the internal states or traits of the student, and *behavioral* data relating to the student's observable activities. The measurement of psychological traits is usually indirect, in the sense that we are trying to infer some underlying state within the individual from responses to a set of test questions. The responses to the questions themselves are not of intrinsic interest but are considered important because of what they reflect about some internal state. Standardized tests such as the SAT or GRE are common examples of such psychological assessment data.

Behavioral measures, on the other hand, are usually of intrinsic interest because they directly reflect transactions between the person and the environment. Behavior such as dropping out of college or changing one's choice of a major would be considered examples of behavioral measurements. Since behavioral (as opposed to psychological) measures typically involve interactions between the person and the environment, such measures might also be termed *sociological*.

By combining the first two dimensions in the taxonomy—type of outcome and type of data—we can generate the four combinations shown in table 3.1. The cell in the upper left, for example, includes cognitive outcomes that are typically measured through course grades or performance on tests of ability and achievement. Outcomes such as knowledge of subject matter, basic skills, and academic aptitude are often assessed by means of test batteries like the SAT and GRE. The upper-right cell includes psychological measures of affective states such as the student's motivation and self-concept as well as subjective feelings of satisfaction and well-being. Most of the published research on college impact has emphasized the use of such measures, in part because of the logistical ease with which such outcomes can be assessed via self-administered questionnaires (Feldman and Newcomb, 1969; Astin, 1977).

The lower-left cell of table 3.1 gives examples of behavioral or sociological measures of cognitive outcomes. This category covers outcomes that reflect the behavior of the student (or former student) in society

TABLE 3.1 A Taxonomy of Student Outcomes: Type of Outcome by Type of Data

	TYPE OF OUTCOME	
TYPE OF DATA	*Cognitive*	*Affective*
Psychological	Subject-matter knowledge Academic ability Critical thinking ability Basic learning skills Special aptitudes Academic achievement	Values Interests Self-concept Attitudes Beliefs Satisfaction with college
Behavioral	Degree attainment Vocational achievement Awards or special recognition	Leadership Citizenship Interpersonal relations Hobbies and avocations

and are assumed to require the use of cognitive skills. Presumably, these real-life achievements represent the behavioral manifestations of the cognitive traits listed in the cell above. The fourth cell, located in the lower-right quadrant, includes behavioral manifestations of the student's development that are presumed to reflect affective states. These might include hobbies and avocations or the amount of time spent in various recreational pursuits. Citizenship might be measured by voting behavior or by the amount and quality of participation in community activities, the earning of special awards for service to the community, or, on the negative side, welfare or arrest records.

It should be emphasized that the two dimensions making up table 3.1 are really more continua than true dichotomies. For example, a person's earned income and job status (which would presumably be covered under vocational achievements in the cognitive domain) may also involve noncognitive or personality traits. Whether particular outcomes are correctly classified into these four cells is really of little consequence; the point of the taxonomy is to provide a conceptual scheme within which any institution can identify the widest possible variety of outcome measures for use in assessment and program evaluation.

The Time Dimension

Given that college can have both short- and long-term effects on student development, the four cells in table 3.1 can be extended into a third dimension representing different time periods following initial entry into college.

Table 3.2 provides one example of each type of outcome from table 3.1 for both short- and long-term assessment. Most assessments used in higher education so far have tended to focus on relatively short-

TABLE 3.2 The Time Dimension: Examples of Short- and Long-term Outcomes

Type of Outcome	Type of Data	Short-Term (During College)	Long-Term (After College)
Cognitive	Behavioral	Completion of college (versus dropping out)	Award for outstanding job achievement
Cognitive	Psychological	MCAT score	Score on medical licensing exam
Affective	Behavioral	Participation in student government	Involvement in local or national politics
Affective	Psychological	Satisfaction with college	Job satisfaction

term outcomes that can be measured while the student is still in college. However, most educational institutions (and most of the people who support such institutions) are focused on longer term changes. The goals stated in many college catalogues, for example, imply that the institution is concerned primarily with making an impact that will last at least into early adulthood and ideally throughout the student's lifetime. For many prospective college students, however, such long-term effects are too remote and too difficult to comprehend. These students are primarily interested in much more immediate goals—their actual experiences during the undergraduate college years—rather than in how these experiences will affect their later development. Educators frequently overlook the fact that the two, four, or eight years of college represent a sizable proportion of the student's total life span. To students, then, outcomes during college are important in themselves, not merely for what they will mean later on. (See also chapter 10 for a discussion of "existential" outcomes.)

COGNITIVE OUTCOMES

Cognitive outcomes in the behavioral realm are relatively few in number, but they include some of the most important outcomes for higher education institutions. Short-term behavioral outcomes comprise such things as retention (completing a degree program versus dropping out), the grade-point average, and receipt of various academic honors. Longer-term behavioral outcomes include entry to and successful completion of school, receipt of graduate fellowships, subsequent job performance, and earnings. We might also include here such special achievements as inventions, patents, and artistic or musical productions. However, the line between cognitive and affective accomplishments begins to disappear when we get into the area of one's vocation and work.

The cognitive-psychological realm is where most of us focus our attention when we discuss issues related to outcome assessment. This bias is perhaps understandable, given that most professors and other educators are inclined to view the transmission of knowledge as the core goal of education. As knowledge is ordinarily considered to be something internal to the individual psyche, it stands to reason that we would employ psychological tests to assess that knowledge. Since classroom tests devised by individual professors will be discussed separately in chapter 9, I shall focus this discussion on the many commercially developed instruments for assessing cognitive outcomes.

What are the various types of psychological tests for assessing cognitive outcomes and what are some of the issues concerning their use? I have found it convenient to differentiate among four different classes of cognitive outcomes for which tests have been devised: specific skills, general education outcomes, subject-matter competency, and vocational and professional competencies (except for the last category, this taxonomy is similar to one recently suggested by Millman, 1988). In considering each of these four types of cognitive measures, I shall occasionally make reference to specific assessment instruments. Readers interested in a much more complete and critical discussion of specific instruments for assessing cognitive-psychological outcomes should consult Jacobi, Astin, and Ayala (1987, pp. 37–59) or the *Mental Measurements Yearbook* (Mitchell 1985).

Specific Skills

Tests of specific skills fall into two general categories. First we have the so-called basic skills, which include mathematics and communication skills (reading, writing, speaking, listening). Such skills are typically among those tested for course placement and advisement purposes when the student initially enters the institution. For interesting accounts of attempts to assess basic skills in mathematics and language, see Appelbaum (1988a) and Dunbar (1988).

The other category includes more complex skills such as verbal reasoning and critical thinking. Of all of the skills that are considered basic to the purposes of a liberal education, critical thinking is probably at the top of the list. Even so, there appears to be little agreement as to how this particular skill should be measured. By far the most commonly used instrument is the Watson-Glaser Critical Thinking Appraisal (Helmstadter, 1985).

General Education

General education outcomes are closely connected to specific skills outcomes, in the sense that most accounts of the goals of general education speak of such skills as communication and critical thinking. The basic difference between tests of general education outcomes and tests designed to assess specific skills is that the general education tests more often attempt to assess how effectively students can use their basic skills in approaching different kinds of tasks. General education tests also emphasize the synthesis of basic skills with subject-matter knowledge.

Of all of the areas of cognitive-psychological assessment, general education is the least well developed and probably the one that causes the most difficulty (Curry and Hager, 1987). Nevertheless, many educators believe that it is the most important cognitive assessment task facing us in higher education today. For this reason, it may be useful to review briefly some of the latest approaches that have not yet been reviewed in the *Mental Measurements Yearbook* (Mitchell, 1985).

Attempts to assess the outcomes of general education programs have led recently to the development of some rather innovative approaches. One of these is the College Outcomes Measurement Program (COMP) test of the American College Testing Program (ACT), which is designed to assess the student's ability to "apply specific facts and concepts in work, family, and community roles" (Forrest and Steele, 1982, p. 1). The ACT-COMP comes in two forms: a six-hour composite and a shorter objective form requiring three hours for administration. Students are required to respond to a variety of stimuli, including text, audio tapes, and films. In the longer composite form, the student's mode of response includes multiple choice, short answers, essays, and tape-recorded speeches. The shorter form of the ACT-COMP is probably the most widely used test of general education outcomes today; the six-hour form, despite its appealing response format, engenders a number of logistical problems in administration (Astin and Ayala, 1987).

Another innovative approach to assessing general education outcomes is the Behavioral Event Interview (BEI) of the Student Potential Program sponsored by the Council for Adult and Experiential Learning (CAEL). The BEI consists of an intensive one-hour interview that is designed to elicit information about critical incidents in the student's life. Interviewers, who require an intensive one-week course in addition to periodic calibration exercises, spend another hour coding the interview responses of the subject in terms of specific capabilities such as initiative, persistence, influence, and leadership. Preliminary research with the BEI (Astin, Inouye, and Korn, 1986) suggests that the BEI scales do indeed have some validity, although the BEI is not as accurate in predicting traditional college outcomes, such as GPA and retention, as are the traditional measures of high school grades and admissions test scores. Perhaps the major limitation of the BEI at this point is the labor-intensive nature of its administration, which requires two hours of a trained professional's time. Nevertheless, the information elicited from the BEI appears on its face to be of considerable importance and the interview experience itself appears to be of substantial value to the student. Much more use of and research on the BEI is needed, however, before any definitive conclusions about its value in assessing general education outcomes can be drawn.

Because of the growing interest in general education issues and the increasing state and national interest in outcome assessment, several of the major testing organizations have recently developed test batteries specifically designed to assess general education outcomes. One such instrument that is rapidly gaining popularity is the Academic Profile II of the Educational Testing Service. This instrument is designed to combine subject-matter competency with basic skills. Four skills (college level-reading, college-level writing, critical thinking, and using mathematical data) are tested within each of three broad academic areas (humanities, social sciences, and natural sciences). While it is available in the traditional norm-referenced format, Academic Profile II has recently appeared in a criterion-referenced format. Criterion-referenced scores have a number of advantages over norm-referenced scores (see the section below entitled "The Multiple Choice Test").

Another relatively new instrument of this type is College Base, a criterion-referenced achievement test that is designed somewhat along the lines of Academic Profile II. College Base assesses student proficiency in English, mathematics, science, and social studies together with three cross-disciplinary cognitive competencies: interpretive reasoning, strategic reasoning, and adaptive reasoning. Each of the four academic subjects is organized into levels of increasing specificity ranging from subjects, on the one hand, through clusters and skills to "enabling sub-skills," on the other. The basic purpose of College Base is "to assess content, knowledge, and skill development at a level commensurate with students completing the general education component of their college experience" (Osterlind, 1989).

Another major class of instruments for assessing general education outcomes comprises the various admissions tests used for undergraduate, graduate, and professional schools. Some of these instruments might as well be classified as specific skills measures, but they are included here because they are used to estimate the students' readiness to do undergraduate or graduate work. The most common instruments are the SAT and ACT used for undergraduate admissions and the GRE, LSAT, MCAT, and GMAT tests used for admission to graduate and professional schools. (For a detailed analysis and critique of these and other general education assessment devices, see Centra, 1988; and Jacobi, Astin, and Ayala, 1987.)

Given the obvious difficulties in assessing general education outcomes in the cognitive domain, the best solution may be for faculties to develop their own instruments and procedures. While this can be an extremely complex and time-consuming task, the very process of developing such assessments can have a number of beneficial results:

faculty engage in productive and informative discussions of curricular objectives, course requirements, and—perhaps most important—the teaching-learning process (Baird, 1988; Ewell, 1984). In fact, experience at Alverno College (Alverno College Faculty, 1985) and Kean College (1988) shows that the process of trying to develop measures of general education outcomes can actually result in major curricular revisions.

Subject-Matter Competency

Most test manufacturers have made available a wide range of instruments for assessing student competency in specific subject-matter areas. For almost all of the major academic fields, there are instruments (and usually several) available to test student competence at the undergraduate as well as the graduate levels. The most widely used batteries at the undergraduate level are the Achievement Tests of the College Board, the College Level Examination Program (CLEP) Subject Examinations of the Educational Testing Service, and the ACT Proficiency Examination Program. Another test with extensive use at the undergraduate level is the Advanced Placement Examination of the College Entrance Examination Board which includes examinations in twenty-four introductory college courses covering thirteen different fields. The Advanced Placement Examination is administered to high school students who can receive credit for college-level courses if they achieve certain minimal scores specified by the college. At the graduate level, the most used instruments are the GRE subject tests.

The most widely used tests of subject-matter competency, of course, are the examinations given in individual undergraduate and graduate classes. Beyond this, an approach that was popular several decades ago and seems to be gaining some popularity currently is the senior comprehensive examination given in the student's major field of study or concentration. For a much more complete discussion of the use of and construction of subject-matter tests, see Appelbaum (1988b), Adelman (1988a), and Jacobi, Astin, and Ayala (1987).

Vocational and Professional Competency

This final category of devices for assessing cognitive outcomes covers a wide range of tests, most of which have been devised by the professions. At the undergraduate level, professional competency tests are used to screen people for admission into such diverse professions as school teaching, nursing, and accounting. At the advanced professional level, national competency examinations are available in fields such as medicine, dentistry, and pharmacy. The competency exams for the legal profession (the bar exams) are not national in scope but are administered by each of the fifty states independently.

Pretesting and Posttesting

Given the widespread use of all these cognitive assessment instruments at virtually all levels of undergraduate and graduate education, institutions could learn a great deal about the effectiveness of their academic programs if they were to "posttest" all of the instruments given at the entry level (college admissions and placement tests for undergraduates; admissions tests for graduate and professional schools) and if they were to "pretest" the instruments used at the end of the undergraduate years (graduate and professional schools admissions tests, subject-matter competency tests, some professional competency tests) or at the end of graduate or professional study (professional competency tests). By having such longitudinal data available, institutions would be in a position to measure actual growth or change in the competencies and skills being measured by these instruments. Eckerd College in Florida, for example, tests all of its entering freshman with the Graduate Record Examination. Northeast Missouri State University, on the other hand, repeats its ACT admissions test after the first two undergraduate years.

THE MULTIPLE-CHOICE TEST

When academics hear the words *assessment* or *evaluation*, they often assume that we are speaking of standardized multiple-choice tests like the SAT or GRE. This is perhaps an understandable assumption, given our heavy reliance on this particular assessment method. Furthermore, most of the commercially available devices for assessing cognitive outcomes involve norm-referenced, multiple-choice tests (Pace, 1985). There is nothing inherent in the assessment process, however, that dictates that multiple-choice testing should be the only or even the most appropriate approach to the assessment of student outcomes. There are several other assessment techniques—largely untried in academe—that one can consider as alternatives to the multiple-choice test: oral examinations, essays, short-answer tests, fill-ins, matching, products or work samples, and performance tests. Readers interested in learning more about these various assessment methods are advised to consult some of the standard texts on psychological testing such as Anastasi (1988) or Cronbach (1984).

Standardized multiple-choice tests have been criticized on a variety of technical grounds and also because they are seen as testing narrow or superficial knowledge (Hefferman, Hutchings, and Marchese, 1988). Such tests are also said to be biased against women and certain minority groups (see chapter 10 for a discussion of such biases). While this is not the place to launch into a full-blown technical critique of standardized multiple-choice tests, the fact that academia has come to be so dependent on such tests suggests that some discussion of their merits and disadvantages is in order. In discussing them I hope to make it clear that *values* also play a crucial part in our choices of assessment methods. In other words, values determine not only *what* outcomes we decide to assess, but also *how* we choose to assess them.

Multiple-choice tests are popular for at least two reasons: they can be administered and scored very cheaply in large groups, and they naturally yield quantitative scores that make it easy to differentiate among students. My concerns about our heavy reliance on this assessment technology, which are in part practical and in part value based, will be discussed under three general headings: methods of scoring, the nature of the task itself, and the impact on student-faculty relations.

Methods of Scoring

My first concern is with the way multiple-choice tests are scored. Typically, the number of right answers (or a weighted combination of rights minus wrongs) is converted into some type of normed score, either a percentile or a standard score (see the appendix). What do we really do when we make such a conversion? We discard the basic data about how many questions (and which ones) the student answered right or wrong, and replace this information with a score indicating only how well the student performs in relation to other students. Here we have the so-called norm-referenced test. By using tests that are scored normatively, we are putting students in competition with each other. The implied value underlying this type of test seems to be that the cognitive performance of any given student should be judged competitively: How much better or worse did the student do when compared to other students? This competitive scoring procedure is identical in spirit to traditional classroom grading, especially if the grading is done on the curve. I might add that these relativisitic and competitively scored tests are difficult to use in assessing talent development because they make it virtually impossible to determine *how much* a student has actually changed or improved over time. All we can say is that the student's performance has increased or decreased in relation to other students.

There is another, perhaps even more subtle problem with normative assessment, whether it be through letter grades or standardized tests: when we choose to assess performance using a normed instrument, we create what the economists would call a "scarce good." Only so many students can be at the top of their class and only so many students can score above the 90th percentile. No matter how hard students work and no matter how much they actually learn, there will always be only so many "excellent" test scores or grades or students! Normative assessment, in other words, automatically constrains how much "excellence" you can have. The important thing to realize is that this shortage is a completely *artificial* one rather than something inherent in the outcome being assessed. The shortage, in other words, is something created by the assessment method itself.

As with any scarce good, the scarcity itself tends to exaggerate the importance of being at the top, so that below-average or even average performance is often viewed as failure. *Normative scoring, in other words, guarantees that a substantial number of students, if not the majority, will view themselves as failures.*

The principal alternative to norm-referenced tests is a technique that has come to be known as criterion-referenced testing (Popham, 1978). The idea behind criterion-referenced testing is that we can establish certain absolute standards of performance (criteria) against which any given student's performance can be assessed. For example, we might devise a senior comprehensive examination consisting of a set of questions in some subject field and decide that students should answer at least 70 percent of the questions correctly in order to qualify for a bachelor's degree in that field. We might also decide that answering 90 percent or more of the questions correctly qualifies the student to graduate with honors. Under these conditions, no predetermined proportions of students will graduate or receive honors. Theoretically, all students (or none, for that matter) could reach either performance standard. What is also important about this approach is that students are not being assessed against each other, so that one student's success does not mean failure for others. Each student has a set of defined standards to aim for and attaining these standards is not contingent on what others do.

Criterion-referenced testing has a number of additional advantages for the educator. Since such tests use absolute rather than relative standards, they provide a concrete standard for assessing the effectiveness of our teaching. If we decide that 70 percent correct answers should be our minimal standard for successful teaching, we have a ready-made basis for judging our effectiveness. In theory, we can succeed (or fail) with all of our students when criterion-referenced assessments are used.

As suggested in chapter 1, norm-referenced tests like the GRE and SAT are well suited to the competitive value framework underlying the resources and reputational conceptions of excellence, since they can be used in selection and screening and lend themselves readily to competitive comparisons. But they are ill suited to the talent development approach, as they make it difficult to measure growth or change over time. Criterion-referenced tests, on the other hand, not only make it possible to establish absolute standards of performance but also allow us to assess *how much* students actually change with time. In short, reliance on norm-referenced tests promotes the values of selection and competition, whereas reliance on criterion-referenced tests promotes the value of teaching and learning.

Those of us who rely on norm-referenced tests often fail to realize that since virtually all of these tests *could* be used as criterion-referenced tests with some minor changes in scoring and reporting procedures, there is something that we can do to overcome the negative consequences of most such tests. Very simply, we can insist that the testing companies give us back the raw score results and, ideally, the results from individual test questions. Raw scores provide a way to measure how much each individual student is actually learning or improving over time, without requiring any competitive comparisons with other students. Furthermore, results from individual test questions can be useful to individual students in understanding their particular strengths and weaknesses. Results from individual questions aggregated across a group of students can also be very useful in curriculum planning and course evaluation since they tell us which questions the students are having trouble with and which incorrect answers they are choosing. I feel strongly that all of us who utilize standardized tests should begin insisting that the test makers give us this kind of feedback.

Nature of the Task

Another concern about multiple-choice tests is the artificiality of the task itself. After students finish their formal education, the ability to find a correct answer from a predetermined set of alternatives has a very limited usefulness. How often in real life is any of us presented with a prepackaged set of possible answers to a question, only one of which is correct? And how often are we required to read a question and find the answer under intense time pressure? How often do life's problems take such a bizarre form? And what about the myriad real-life problems that call for creative solutions? My point here is that the ability to perform well on such tasks is so highly specialized and so foreign to real-life problems that I really wonder whether we educators have been wise to make such liberal and uncritical use of the multiple-choice test. The test makers might respond that such tests have "predictive validity," and indeed they do. But in such validity studies the outcome being predicted is almost always school or college grades or simply another test constructed in the same manner! (See also chapter 10 for a critique of the predictive validity argument.)

This problem is perhaps best illustrated by the observation that the multiple-choice test is not well suited to many important kinds of educational outcomes, but especially not to those that require the exercise of creative talents. Creativity can be expressed basically in two ways: through *products*, and through some sort of creative *performance*. Creative products include such things as essays, research papers, inventions, scripts, films, videos, works of art, and musical compositions. Creative performances include equally diverse activities such as public speaking, dance, musical recitals, and theater productions. Depending upon how broadly one chooses to define creativity, performance outcomes such as leadership behavior, public service, and athletics might also be included. Clearly, the multiple-choice test is an inappropriate technology for assessing many types of creative outcomes that are highly valued not only in the academic community but also in later life. Thus, when we insist upon putting our principal assessment emphasis on student outcomes that can be measured through multiple-choice tests, we are implicitly assigning a low value to student creativity.

Student-Faculty Relations

My final concern about multiple-choice tests is the distance they put between the student and the professor. The administration and scoring is done impersonally and the numerical feedback is dry and impersonal as well. Reliance on such tests makes it possible for professors to assess student outcomes without ever having to interact with students or even learning the students' names. Clearly, this approach to assessment is inimical to the close student-faculty contact that much of the research in higher education shows to be so important (Astin, 1977; Study Group, 1984).

ALTERNATE METHODS

By this time the reader may wonder, "If Astin is so dubious about course grades and standardized multiple-choice tests of cognitive outcomes, what would he put in their place?" There is no question but that the student needs feedback of some kind, and the institution needs some way to document the student's progress. In the preceding discussion of creative performance, it was suggested that the individual creative products and performances of students probably have to be assessed in some kind of holistic fashion. Many educators already have a good deal of experience in making such judgments, as, for example, in grading essays or research papers or in judging science contests or musical or artistic competitions. Holistic judging does not necessarily mean that only a single or unidimensional judgment is made since any creative product can be evaluated along a number of dimensions.

The more I think about the problem of assessing cognitive outcomes, the more convinced I become that holistic feedback, whether written or spoken, is far and away the most powerful assessment tool we have for directly enhancing talent development in particular and the educational process in general (see also chapter 9). Specifically, I am referring to the kinds of written feedback that students receive at schools such as Hampshire College, Alverno College, Empire State College, and the University of California at Santa Cruz. It has been my experience that most academics who have merely seen a few real examples of such feedback have been impressed by its potential educational value. Not only is the feedback itself extremely informative and useful to the student, but since the process itself requires the professor to get to know the individual student's work personally, narrative feedback strengthens and enhances the relationship between student and faculty member.

One problem with holistic written evaluations of student performance, of course, is that they do not readily yield quantitative estimates of student performance that can be utilized in an I-E-O evaluation design. There is, however, nothing inherent in the narrative or in any other qualitative assessment method that precludes quantification, although it should be recognized that not all institutions that use narrative feedback try to quantify their evaluations. One very simple approach is to have the evaluator also complete a brief set of rating scales, with each scale representing a different skill, area of knowledge, or personal quality. Such an approach is not unlike the quantification involved in scoring essays or in judging musical and artistic competitions.

Another, perhaps more serious objection to holistic narrative evaluations is that they are highly labor-intensive. In this connection it should be realized that much of the work required for narrative evaluation may already have been done in order to award course grades. The grade, or course, attempts to reduce all of the relevant information about the student to a single normative measure. If professors are going to be asked to undertake the more personalized evaluations of their students required for normative evaluations, what kinds of trade-offs are we going to make in terms of the professors' other job responsibilities? I believe that the best way to approach this question is first to recognize that we are once again dealing with a question of values. If we believe that students can benefit significantly from the experience of having a professor get to know their work well enough to write a detailed narrative evaluation of it, then what other, presumably less useful, activities can be traded off against the time required for the professor to carry out the evaluation and discuss it with the student? Each institution, of course, will have to answer this for itself, but it seems to me that one reasonable trade-off would be for professors to do a bit less lecturing or even to teach one less class. Not only would the students benefit from the personalized feedback, but the professors would probably welcome the variety introduced into their pedagogical activities. Certainly it behooves us to begin to study the potential efficacy of such trade-offs.

AFFECTIVE OUTCOMES

It has already been suggested that the importance of affective outcomes is implied in the mission statements appearing in many college catalogues as well as in the notion of the liberally educated person. What are some of these outcomes and how can they be assessed? In the area of affective *skills* we have a variety of potentially important qualities such as interpersonal competence, leadership ability, and empathy. The ability to empathize with others is, incidentally, probably dependent to some extent on one of the most neglected communications skills: listening ability.

There are other affective outcomes that seem to be relevant to the goals of a liberal education, although we do not ordinarily consider them to be skills. A very interesting but little-studied affective outcome is student motivation (Graham, 1988). Other potentially important affective outcomes would include self-understanding, honesty, maturity, motivation for further learning, understanding of other peoples and societies, self-esteem, social responsibility, and even good mental and physical health (see Grandy, 1988).

One affective area that needs more attention in our assessment activities is the student's own values. I have been involved in monitoring the values of incoming freshmen through the Cooperative Institutional Research Program (CIRP) surveys for some twenty-three years now, and what I see happening is unsettling. During the past two decades, students have become markedly more materialistic and more concerned with having power and status. They are increasingly coming to see an undergraduate education primarily as a means to make more money and less as a way to get a general education. At the same time, students have become less concerned about the well-being of others, the environment, and the community, and less interested in developing a meaningful philosophy of life. These value changes have been accompanied by similar changes in the students' career plans, with careers in business reaching all-time highs in popularity, and careers in the human service occupations reaching all-time lows (Astin, Green, and Korn, 1987).

Lately the higher education community has begun to react to some of these trends by creating programs to encourage student participation in public and community service activities. The Campus Compact project, for example, is a consortium of some 180 institutions that are working together to establish community service programs for undergraduates under the sponsorship of the Education Commission of the States. The California state legislature has passed a law requiring the University of California and the California State University to establish some kind of volunteer or public service program for undergraduates. And at the national level, several members of Congress have introduced legislation promoting a period of national service for all young people.

In his 1987 report to the Board of Overseers, Harvard president Derek Bok said that "universities should be among the first to reaffirm the importance of basic values such as honesty, promise keeping, free expression, and nonviolence . . . [and] there is nothing odd or inappro-priate . . . to make these values the foundation for a serious program to help students develop a strong set of moral standards." Bok also notes that "students must get help from their universities in developing moral standards or they are unlikely to get much assistance at all."

These trends suggest that the notion that liberal education ought to be "value-free" is no longer tenable; indeed, our political and ed-ucational leaders seem to be suggesting that social responsibility and concern for others is one of the qualities that higher education insti-tutions should try to foster in their students. Under these conditions, it would seem appropriate for any attempt at outcome assessment to include measures of qualities such as empathy, concern for others, tol-erance, and social responsibility.

This discussion suggests that there are many affective outcomes that might be judged relevant to the goals of a liberal education. How, then, do we go deciding which outcomes to measure and how to measure them? In deciding which ones to assess, my personal preference is to assess as wide a range of affective outcomes as possible and to be more inclusive than exclusive. However, if one chooses to be highly inclusive, there are certain constraints on how these outcomes can be assessed. The greater the number and range of affective outcomes to be assessed, the simpler our methodological approach must be. Conversely, if we prefer to use highly sophisticated psychometric approaches to assessing affective outcomes, we are necessarily limited in the number of such outcomes that we can assess.

Much of the early research on college impact utilized sophisticated psychometric instruments such as the Allport, Vernon, Lindzey (1960) *Study of Values* and the Omnibus Personality Inventory (Buros, 1978). Since these instruments were devised for use in counseling individual students, it was important to make sure that each affective trait being assessed could be measured with a reasonable degree of precision or reliability. Thus, each scale in these instruments is based upon a large number of individual questions or items. The main limitation of such an approach in assessing affective outcomes is that a substantial amount of the student's time is required to produce information on a relatively small number of affective outcomes. In the terminology of information theory, we might say that these instruments have relatively high "fi-delity" with a relatively narrow "band width."

Investigators who rely on such instruments for assessing the affec-tive outcomes of college are inclined to forget that the psychometric requirements for reliability in the case of individual students are very different from what is required in the case of groups of students. Thus, it is possible to use a single item from an attitudinal questionnaire to measure some affective outcome for a group of students with a considerable degree of reliability, provided the sample of students is large enough. Since we are normally interested in assessing student outcomes using groups of students who have been exposed to particular educational programs, we have the luxury of being able to study a wide range of outcomes using individual items with the results aggregated across groups of students. It is, of course, possible to combine individual items into scales when studying groups as well as individuals (see, for example, Astin, 1977). However, when applied to groups of students it would appear that scales with as few as three items are just about as reliable as scales based on thirty items (Astin, 1971).

The economics involved in using items rather than scales have enormous practical implications for the study of affective outcomes. Assume that we have about thirty minutes of each student's time available to assess affective outcomes. It might be reasonable to expect that we could ask the student to respond to perhaps fifty affective questions within thirty minutes. Following the traditional psychometric approach, we could measure only five or fewer outcomes, since few psychometric instruments designed for use with individuals have scales of fewer than ten items (indeed, it is not uncommon for many psychometric devices to have scales based on forty or fifty items). By contrast, if we considered each item as measuring a potentially different affective outcome, we could assess as many as fifty different affective outcomes using the individual item approach.

The individual item approach has been taken in the Freshman Survey of the Cooperative Institutional Research Program (CIRP), which as of 1989 had been administered to more than seven million students during the twenty-three years since it was initially begun in 1966. Although the freshman surveys "pretest" a number of affective outcomes, it is the Follow-Up Surveys (FUS) that are primarily focused on assessing affective outcomes. The FUS has been administered to more than 500,000 students over intervals ranging from three months to nine years after college entry. Currently the FUS is administered annually to samples of freshman after two and four years. While individual institutions may find it more useful to design their own instruments for assessing affective outcomes, I believe that our experience with the FUS provides a number of useful guidelines for the development of local instruments. These guidelines are summarized below separately for both behavioral and psychological outcomes in the affective realm.

Behavioral Measures

There are many affective-behavioral outcomes that might be considered relevant to the goals of an undergraduate education. How one chooses to assess these outcomes depends in part upon how frequently they are likely to occur. For example, there are behavioral outcomes that normally occur only once and can be assessed through a simple checklist: the student either did or did not experience the outcome. These would include joining a social fraternity or sorority, being elected to a student office, participating in an honors program, working on a professor's research project, dropping out of college, getting married, and winning an award. On the other hand, there are other behavioral outcomes that can occur with varying frequency and which should probably be assessed in a slightly more quantitative fashion. These would include outcomes such as personal contacts with faculty or with fellow students, being late to class or missing class, participating in campus protests or demonstrations, discussing various topics with others, doing independent study, drinking, smoking, or participating in athletic or cultural activities. After experimenting with various ways of quantifying the frequency of such activities, I have found that the most useful approach is to ask students to indicate whether they participate in each such activity frequently, occasionally, or not at all.

Still another approach to assessing behavioral outcomes is the time diary. There are student activities and behaviors that can be assessed by getting students' best estimates of the number of hours per week they devote to each activity. Behavioral outcomes that might be assessed with a time diary would include studying, doing volunteer work, watching television, reading for pleasure, pursuing hobbies, and participating in religious or cultural activities. It is also possible to use time diaries to assess longer-term postcollege behaviors such as time spent with spouse, children, job, and civic activities.

A final set of behavioral outcomes concerns the student's educational and career decisions. These would include the student's choices of undergraduate and graduate majors; decisions about dropping out, stopping out, or transferring; decisions about graduate or professional school attendance; occupational choices and choices of employers; income and earnings; job performance; and special achievements or awards. We might also include here the preliminary or tentative career choices that students express at the time of college entry and at later points prior to actual career entry, although these outcomes might just as well be considered "psychological" since they have no behavioral manifestation until the student actually enters employment.

Another way to assess student behavior is through the use of independent observers rather than self-reports. While there are several advantages to the use of observers such as faculty and student affairs personnel, these advantages may well be outweighed by costs, inconvenience, and other considerations (Pace, 1985). On the other hand, the very successful assessment program at Alverno College (Mentkowski and Loacker, 1985) has made effective use of behavioral observations by outside evaluators.

Psychological Measures

While a few psychological outcomes might be assessed using the response formats for behavioral outcomes described above, I have found in general that a different kind of item and response format is needed to assess most psychological-affective outcomes.

One area of considerable interest to educators is the student's self-concept. While there are many ways that self-concept can be assessed, a particularly useful and simple approach is to generate a list of self-descriptive traits (academic ability, intellectual self-confidence, leadership ability, emotional health, popularity, etc.) and to ask the student to rate himself separately on each trait. Students can be asked either to make absolute judgments as to the applicability of each trait (very descriptive, somewhat descriptive, not descriptive) or to make a normative judgment in terms of how they compare to the average person of their own age (top 10 percent, above average, average, below average, and so on).

A second psychological area is the student's personal values. In the CIRP and FUS questionnaires we have regularly included a variety of value or life-goal items such as raising a family, being very well-off financially, helping others who are in difficulty, helping to promote racial understanding, and developing a meaningful philosophy of life. For each value statement, the student is asked to indicate the degree of importance to him personally (essential, very important, somewhat important, or not important).

Still another affective-psychological area is student *attitudes*. There is an almost infinite range of issues that can be examined (abortion, capital punishment, students' rights, women's rights, the value of education, federal policy, and so on). Although there are many possible response modalities that can be employed, I personally prefer the time-tested Likert-type response mode: strongly agree, agree, disagree, strongly disagree.

A particularly interesting area of affective outcome assessment is the student's political orientation (party preference; preference for liberal, conservative, or radical political identifications) or religious preference and religious behavior. It is also possible to get rough measures of mental health by asking students how frequently they feel anxious or depressed or whether they have sought any kind of psychological counseling or treatment.

But perhaps the single most important affective-psychological area for outcomes assessment is student *satisfaction*. Banta's (1985) experience at the University of Tennessee–Knoxville is that satisfaction data obtained from student surveys can lead to substantial changes in institutional policy. This category of affective outcomes encompasses the student's subjective experience during the college years and perceptions of the value of the educational experience itself. Given the considerable investment of time and energy that most students make in attending college, their perception of the value of that experience should be given considerable weight. Indeed, it is difficult to argue that any other outcome category—cognitive or affective, behavioral or psychological—should be given greater priority than student satisfaction.

The simplest way to approach the issue of assessing satisfaction is to consider ways of assessing overall satisfaction as well as satisfaction with specific aspects of the college experience. Concerning overall satisfaction, I prefer at least two different approaches that are probably more complementary than duplicative. The first approach simply asks the student to express a degree of satisfaction or dissatisfaction with the overall college experience on a simple scale (very satisfied, satisfied, on the fence, dissatisfied, very dissatisfied). The other approach is to pose the question in terms of a hypothetical decision: "If you could make your college choice over again, would you still choose to enroll at the same institution?" (definitely yes, probably, don't know, probably not, definitely not). These two approaches generate similar but not identical responses.

Regarding satisfaction with specific aspects of the college experience, it is possible to conceive of literally dozens of specific services or experiences that could be rated: general education requirements, courses in the majors, relevance of course work to everyday life, overall quality of instruction, laboratory facilities, libraries, computer facilities, social life, contact with faculty, relationship with students, cultural events on campus, housing, financial aid, health services, advising, counseling, and job placement. The student's degree of satisfaction with each of these services or experiences can be rated on a four- or five-point scale, but it is also important to allow the student to indicate that no rating is possible because the service was not actually received or experienced.

SUMMARY

Defining and measuring the outcomes of higher education programs necessarily require the use of value judgments. Given the many different goals of educational programs, it is unrealistic and unwise to think that a single outcome measure can possibly be adequate to the task of assessing outcomes.

In speaking of outcome assessment it is important to distinguish between a simple outcome measure obtained at the end of an educational program and a measure of program impact. The latter can be accomplished only by comparing an outcome measure either with a pretest measure or with some sort of expected outcome based on the student's entering characteristics (see chapter 6 and the appendix).

There are several taxonomies that can be used to classify student outcome measures. One that has proved useful in the Cooperative Institutional Research Program classifies measures according to type of outcome (cognitive or affective), type of measure (behavioral or psychological), and time (short term or long term). Most discussions of outcome assessment implicitly focus on a single cognitive-psychological type of outcome measure: the norm-referenced, standardized, multiple-choice test. Despite its popularity, this method of outcome assessment has a number of serious flaws that limit its usefulness.

Current assessment efforts seem to underutilize affective outcome measures, especially those that assess the student's reaction to and satisfaction with the undergraduate experience.

4

ASSESSING STUDENT INPUTS

It is very difficult, if not impossible, to learn how our educational policies and practices affect student outcomes in the absence of input data on the entering student. Any application of the I-E-O model to assessment data requires the inclusion of input data for two basic reasons: (1) inputs are always related to outputs; and (2) inputs are almost always related as well to environments (educational programs and practices). Because inputs are related to both outputs and environments, any observed relationship between environments and outcomes might well reflect the effects of inputs rather than the actual effects of environments on outcomes. The Cooperative Institutional Research Program (CIRP), which has been in progress for nearly a quarter of a century and which now includes input data on nearly 8,000,000 students and 1,300 institutions, was initiated in 1966 specifically to collect input data that would make it possible to apply the I-E-O model to a national study of student outcomes in American higher education. Because it is an omnibus instrument that includes demographic and other background data as well as pretests and self-predictions (see below) on a wide variety of college outcomes, the CIRP is used extensively throughout this chapter to illustrate certain issues related to the collection and use of student input data. Other potentially important sources of input data would include admissions and registration data, results of placement tests, and any other special assessments that may be carried out during orientation and registration.

Experience with the CIRP suggests that input data have a number of other uses beyond their utilization in longitudinal applications of the I-E-O model. A profile of information on new entering freshmen, for example, can be put to a variety of uses in student recruitment, curriculum review, program planning and evaluation, and public information. In this chapter we shall first consider the principal ways in which student input data can be used, after which we shall review different types of input data that can be collected.

THE FUNCTION OF STUDENT INPUT MEASURES
IN THE I-E-O MODEL

In applying the I-E-O model the most obvious use of student input data is as a pretest of student outcome measures. With very few exceptions, pretests are more highly correlated with outcome posttests than any other input or environmental variable (see below). For many cognitive and affective outcome measures, exactly the same measure can be used as an input pretest at the time of entry into college. For other outcomes such as college grades, for which an identical pretest is not feasible, a parallel measure of performance at the high school level (high school grades) is available. Similarly, college outcome measures that reflect interaction with faculty or with other college students can be pretested at the high school level using comparable measures of interaction with school teachers and classmates.

For many other outcome measures, however, there is really no parallel pretest at the input stage. A good example is the outcome, student retention (completing a degree versus dropping out). How can you "pretest" retention, given that anybody who drops out at the high school level will, by definition, be eliminated from the college sample? In this situation it is important to understand what other input characteristics are most likely to be strongly related to the outcome measure in question. In the case of college retention, high school grades and standardized test scores are generally found to be the best input predictors (Astin, 1971).

Another class of outcome measures that cannot really be pretested are satisfaction measures. One might argue that a parallel pretest at the high school level would be satisfaction with the high school. However, the two types of institutions are sufficiently different and the nature of the student's experience in each is different enough to raise some questions as to the sufficiency of such a pretest measure.

One way around the problem of outcome measures that have no obvious pretests at the input stage is to obtain students' *predictions* or *expectations* with respect to the output measure in question. One can, for example, ask entering students to estimate their chances of dropping out or the chances that they will end their college experience being satisfied. A long history of research on college impact suggests that students' expectations or self-predictions do indeed carry substantial predictive weight over time (Astin, 1977). In other words, most students can make a reasonably accurate guess about what is likely to happen to them in college. What is particularly interesting about these self-estimates is that they often add to the predictive capacity even of pretests. Table 4.1 shows an actual example of how self-predictions can contribute to the prediction of an outcome measure over and above the contribution of the pretest. The figure in the lower right-hand corner

TABLE 4.1 **Percentage of Students Earning at Least a B+ Average in College, as a Function of High School Grades and Freshman Self-Predictions**

Average High School Grade	SELF-PREDICTED CHANCES OF OBTAINING AT LEAST AN A− AVERAGE IN COLLEGE				
	None	Little	Some	Very Good	Total
A or A+	34	52	65	64	61
A− or B+	20	26	31	41	29
B	9	10	11	*	10
B− or C+	4	5	7	6	5
C	2	3	5	*	3
Total	6	11	22	39	14

Source: Astin (1977).

* Too few cases to compute a reliable percentage.

of table 4.1 shows that 14 percent of the students earned at least a B+ average in college. By looking at the last column and bottom row of table 4.1, one can see that both high school grades (last column) and freshman self-predictions (bottom row) are substantially related to the student's chances of getting a B+ average in college. However, school grades seem to be the stronger predictor, since the percentages vary from 3 percent (C average in high school) to 61 percent (A or A+ average in high school), compared to only 6 percent (self-prediction of "none") to 39 percent (self-prediction of "very good chance"). What is particularly important about the data in Table 4.1, however, is that the self-prediction is related to college grades *within* each category of high school grades. Thus, among students who earned A or A+ averages in high school, those who were most optimistic about their chances of getting at least an A minus average in college ("very good") were much more likely to obtain a B+ average (64 percent) than were those who said that their chances were "none" (34 percent). The same goes for self-predictions within the category of students whose average high school grades were A minus or B+: those saying that their chances were "very good" were twice as likely (41 percent) to obtain at least a B+ average as were those whose estimated chances were "none" (20 percent). Since the percentages for different self-predictions do not vary much in the lower grade categories, it appears that the effect of self-predictions is confined primarily to those students with high school grade averages above B.

Self-predictions have been found to correlate with practically every type of outcome measure. For example, students who say when they enter college that their chances of marrying while in college are "very good" are more than three times as likely to be married four years later (66 percent) as are students who say that there is "no chance" of marrying while in college (21 percent). Similarly, students who say when they enter college that they are planning to obtain a law or medical degree are better than three times as likely to be enrolled in graduate school five years later (50 percent) as are students who say they plan to obtain only a bachelor's degree when they enter college (15 percent) (Astin, 1977).

This discussion of self-predictions as input measures underscores two important points:

- Self-predictions are useful predictors of student outcomes, especially when there is no appropriate pretest available for the outcome in question.
- Even when pretests are available, self-predictions can still add substantially to the prediction of some outcomes.

We may be missing a potentially important source of input variance when we fail to incorporate self-predictions in our battery of input measures.

It should be emphasized that there are many student characteristics other than self-predictions that can affect outcome measures over and above the effects of input pretest measures. Longitudinal multivariate studies (Astin, 1975, 1977, 1982) suggest that an average of fifteen to twenty freshman input characteristics other than the pretest contribute to the prediction of most student outcome measures. Thus, it would seem that the best way to ensure that the bias resulting from student input characteristics has been adequately controlled is to incorporate as many input characteristics as possible into the analysis, with special attention to those that are likely to relate to the outcome measure under study.

A final use of student input information within the I-E-O model is in the study of possible *interactions* between student input and environmental characteristics. As will be pointed out in chapter 6, a knowledge of interaction effects can be of particular value in selection and placement of students, since it can enhance our understanding of how to effect an optimal fit between the student and the educational programs available. Among the student input characteristics that might be examined for potential interaction effects with environmental variables are the student's gender, ethnicity, age, ability, and socio-economic level.

OTHER USES OF INPUT DATA

Controlling for the effects of student input characteristics in the I-E-O design is not the only purpose of collecting student input measures.

Many student input characteristics are of intrinsic interest because of what they tell us about our institution and because of their potential use for a variety of administrative purposes. There are at least three areas of institutional functioning that can make effective use of student input information: admissions and recruitment, curriculum and program evaluation, and public information.

Admissions and Recruitment

Given the heavy commitment of institutions to the resources and reputational conceptions of excellence, high school grades and especially admission test scores of the entering freshmen are closely monitored by many colleges and universities on a regular basis. While I have raised serious questions about this use of assessment in several places throughout this book, it is important to realize that there are many other attributes of the entering student that are of intrinsic interest because of what they suggest about the institution's recruitment and admissions effort. One such characteristic that has generated renewed interest in the academic community is student ethnicity. Institutions are especially interested in increasing their enrollments of African-Americans, Hispanics, and American Indians, given the long-standing underrepresentation of these groups in the student bodies of most institutions (see especially chapter 10 for a more detailed discussion of educational equity). Recently, interest in still another ethnic minority group—Asian— has emerged as a result of two factors: the growing Asian population in the United States and the belief in some quarters that institutions are actually attempting to limit Asian enrollments. It is not clear just how this controversy is going to be resolved, but in the meantime institutions are monitoring their Asian enrollments closely, paying particular attention to the academic qualifications of Asian students in comparison to non-Asians.

Another important use of input data is to identify factors that may be affecting prospective students' decisions about college choice. In the CIRP Freshman Survey, we regularly ask students to assess the importance of various factors in their decision to attend that particular college (academic reputation; social reputation; low tuition; location; special educational programs; advice of relatives; teachers; counselors and college representative). We also ask students to indicate the number of other colleges to which they applied, the number of acceptances they received, and whether the college of entry is their first or second choice. All of this information can be extremely useful in gaining a better understanding of factors that might influence students' decisions to attend our own institution and in identifying potential new students that might be tapped in the college recruitment process.

Curriculum and Program Evaluation

One peculiarity of American higher education is that many institutions develop their curricula and other educational programs in a vacuum without considering the characteristics of the student clientele with which they are dealing. One major purpose of the CIRP Freshman Survey is to provide institutions with a profile of student characteristics that can be used in curriculum planning and program review. Among the many items of information that can be used for this purpose are the courses taken by students in secondary school, degree aspirations, probable major field of study, life goals, reasons for attending college, and perceived need for remediation in various fields.

One particularly useful application of input data is to chart trends in the characteristics of entering students. While most institutions monitor changes in such areas as standardized test scores, gender, and ethnicity, they could collect additional useful information charting changes in students' plans, aspirations, values, and attitudes. As pointed out in the previous chapter, during its twenty-four years of operation the CIRP Freshman Survey has revealed some rather dramatic changes in students' interests and values. Compared to students of the early 1970s, today's students show a strong inclination toward careers in business and relatively little interest in the human service occupations. They are much more interested than earlier students in achieving wealth, power, and status, and much less interested in altruistic goals and in "developing a meaningful philosophy of life" (Astin, Green, and Korn, 1987). It may well be that such changes have been in part responsible for the decision by many colleges and universities to establish programs of public and community service for their undergraduates and, in some cases, to require some form of community or public service as part of the undergraduate general education curriculum.

Public Information

A comprehensive profile of the new students entering a college or university can provide excellent material for use in public addresses by institutional officials, feature articles in the campus press, articles for alumni bulletins and magazines, and press releases to local, regional, and national news media. Such informational uses of input data are greatly enhanced when there are norms against which an institution's freshman profile can be compared. One of the principal appeals of the CIRP Freshman Survey is that it yields national norms not only for institutions in general but also for subcategories of institutions broken down by type (public versus private, two year versus four year versus university, religious affiliation, and predominant race of the student body) as well as by level of selectivity. The ability to compare one's students with students at comparable institutions greatly enhances the usefulness of student input data for public information purposes.

TYPES OF STUDENT INPUT MEASURES

Given the many uses of student input measures in the I-E-O model and the many other administrative uses that can be made of such information, the number and variety of student input measures that might be obtained from the new students is very large. Although there does not seem to be any natural taxonomy of student input measures similar to the one developed for outcome measures (see chapter 3), input measures can be placed in two broad classes: fixed or invariant characteristics of the students, and characteristics that can change over time. The latter category can be further broken down into at least six subcategories: cognitive functioning, aspirations and expectations, self-ratings, values and attitudes, behavioral patterns, and educational background characteristics. Each of these types of student input data is considered separately.

Fixed Student Attributes

Another label for the category of fixed student attributes might be demographic characteristics. Included here would be measures of the student's gender, race or ethnicity, family size (including the number of siblings currently in college), birth order, citizenship, place of residence, language spoken in the home, racial composition of the home neighborhood, and the marital status, income, education, religion, and occupation of the student's parents. Some of these characteristics are not permanently "fixed" in the literal sense (e.g., parents can change their occupation, income, or education, or have more children), but for most purposes it is reasonable to assume that these demographic characteristics will remain quite stable during the student's time in college. One demographic characteristic—age–changes regularly, of course, but each student's age in relation to every other student's age remains invariant.

A number of other student characteristics, discussed below, might also be considered as invariant—for example, the type of high school attended and the year of graduation. However, these will be discussed subsequently in the section on educational background characteristics.

Cognitive Functioning

The admissions procedures of many colleges and universities produce several types of input measures that can be used as pretests for I-E-O studies of cognitive functioning. Most prominent among these are the high school GPA and the various standardized admissions tests

(ACT, SAT, and achievement tests in various subject-matter fields). There are the Advanced Placement (AP) tests and College Level Examination Program (CLEP) tests that many colleges now use to award college credit as well as placement tests in fields such as English and math. In theory, any or all such input measures could be used in longitudinal studies in which the same instrument is subsequently posttested to yield measures of change or growth. Placement tests, in particular, are well suited to such longitudinal analyses since the results would presumably allow the institutions to answer two critical questions: Does differential course placement based on test results really pay off in terms of enhanced student progress? Do remedial courses really succeed in developing those basic skills on which the course content is focused?

Aspirations and Expectations

The aspirations and expectations category of student input characteristics includes students' self-predictions, degree aspirations, probable career choice, probable major field of study, and life goals. Each of the twenty-four annual freshman surveys has included a number of self-predictions covering a variety of possible outcomes such as academic performance, retention, getting married, changing major or career choice, getting a job to help pay for college expenses, needing extra time to complete degree requirements, getting vocational or personal counseling, participating in student protests, transferring before graduation, and participating in various extracurricular activities (social fraternity or sorority, clubs, athletics, and election to a student office). On occasion, the CIRP questionnaire has included students' felt need for remediation in various subject matter fields.

The CIRP survey also asks students about the highest degree they plan to obtain, their probable career choice, and their probable major field of study. Although most American college freshmen are not required to elect a major field of study until after they have been in college for a while, more than 90 percent of the freshmen are willing to name a probable major field of study.

It is also useful to know why students are attending college. The CIRP survey has regularly asked students to indicate the importance of each of a number of possible reasons for going to college: to get a better job, to gain a general education, to improve reading and study skills, to become more cultured, to make more money, to learn more, to prepare for graduate school; other reasons are pressure from parents, desire to get away from home, inability to find a job, and "nothing better to do."

A final type of information that can be obtained in this category has to do with the students' larger goals in life. In the CIRP survey students are asked to indicate the relative importance of goals that are occupationally or vocationally oriented (science, performing arts, business, creative writing, and fine arts), as well as a number of more general life goals (being very well-off financially, becoming an authority, obtaining recognition, influencing social values, raising a family, helping others, helping to promote racial understanding, and participating in community action programs). Many of these, of course, are pretests for the same items when they will be used as outcome measures in subsequent follow-up surveys.

Self-Ratings

During the past decade the concept of self-esteem has taken on increasing interest among educators and even some public policy makers. The California Legislature recently passed a bill authorizing the creation of a State Commission on Self-Esteem. The Commission has been charged with responsibility for reviewing the evidence concerning the effects of self-esteem on students' school achievement, crime and delinquency, and economic productivity (California Task Force, 1990).

The early CIRP Freshman surveys included student's self-ratings every third or fourth survey, but in recent years the self-ratings have become a regular part of each new annual survey. Students are asked to compare themselves with other persons of the same age in a variety of personal characteristics: academic ability, artistic ability, drive to achieve, emotional health, leadership, mathematical ability, physical health, popularity, public speaking ability, intellectual self-confidence, social self-confidence, and writing ability. These self-ratings have proved to be related to a variety of student outcomes (Astin, 1977).

Values and Attitudes

As pointed out in chapter 3, the history of research on student development in American higher education is replete with studies of how the undergraduate experience influences students' values, attitudes, and beliefs. The freshman survey has routinely included a long list of questions for assessing students' attitudes on a wide variety of social issues (abortion, homosexuality, women's rights, capital punishment, sex, drugs, disarmament, and federal policy) together with a group of questions concerned more with educational issues (school busing, the costs of college, students' rights, and the purposes of higher education). While the primary reason for including such items is to have pretests on these same questions when they are used as outcome assessments, educators have shown an increasing interest in recent years in how freshman responses to these questions change from one survey to the next.

Another item of considerable interest in this category is the student's political self-labeling: far left, liberal, middle-of-the-road, conservative, far right. This question has been included primarily as a pretest for subsequent longitudinal posttesting, but the item itself has shown interesting changes across successive generations of entering college students (Astin, Green, and Korn, 1987).

Behavioral Patterns

Getting students to report on their own behavioral patterns is a relatively easy matter, although our experience with this kind of question suggests that at least two different response formats are necessary. In the previous chapter it was suggested that specific behaviors that can be reported but which do not lend themselves to precise quantification can be assessed using a response format that permits only crude quantification: the behavior is reported as occurring frequently, occasionally, or not at all. A list of these behaviors usually includes items such as attending religious services, participating in demonstrations, winning a varsity letter for sports, failing to complete a homework assignment on time, tutoring other students, smoking cigarettes, feeling overwhelmed, feeling depressed, and being a guest in a teacher's home.

Other behavioral patterns can be reported in terms of the number of hours per week, on the average, that the student spends in different activities. In recent years we have included in the freshman questionnaire a "time diary," in which students indicate the number of hours per week they spend in activities such as studying or doing homework, socializing, talking with teachers, exercising, partying, working, participating in student clubs or organizations, and watching television. While these time diary questions serve primarily as pretests for similar questions to be asked after exposure to college, some of the items are of intrinsic interest (hours spent studying versus watching television, for example), especially when it becomes possible to assess trends over several years' time.

Educational Background Characteristics

It is possible to incorporate a wide variety of questions about the student's educational background in a comprehensive assessment of student input characteristics. These characteristics have typically shown consistent relationships with a variety of student outcome measures, especially those concerned with academic activities or academic achievement.

The CIRP Freshman Survey has regularly incorporated a number of different educational background characteristics: type of secondary school (public, private, sectarian), year of high school graduation, high school grades and rank in class, racial composition of the high school attended, number of years of study in basic subject-matter fields (English, mathematics, foreign language, physical science, biological science, history/ government, computer science, art/ music), special courses taken (honors or Advanced Placement), and any prior college courses taken. Other areas of possible interest that have been incorporated in CIRP surveys from time to time include the students' study habits in high school and whether they have taken remedial work or had special tutoring in particular subject-matter fields.

Other Input Measures

Several other types of student input characteristics that do not fall neatly into any of the above categories may nevertheless be relevant to a comprehensive input assessment. Included here would be the number of colleges applied to, the number of acceptances, students' reasons for selecting a particular college (see above), concern about college finances, religious preference, and disability status.

A final category of especially interesting student input characteristics might be labeled as bridge measures. This term is meant to suggest that the variable in question could be construed as both a student input characteristic and as a college environmental characteristic (see the next chapter). That is, although these variables are being measured at the time the student enters college (input), they also signify environmental experiences that can continue to affect the student's development during the college years. Included among these would be the student's initial choice of a major field of study, financial aid (loans, grants, work-study), jobs currently held, where the student lives while attending, how far the college is from the student's home, and whether the student is attending on a part-time or full-time basis. Whether such variables are used as input or environmental characteristics depends in part upon the particular problem being studied and how the investigator chooses to conceptualize that problem (see chapter 2 and the appendix).

CORRELATIONS OF INPUT MEASURES WITH ENVIRONMENTAL AND OUTPUT MEASURES

As mentioned earlier in this chapter and in chapter 2, the principal reason that input measures need to be controlled in studies of environmental effects is because inputs tend to be related to both outcome measures and environmental measures. How pervasive are these correlations and how concerned should investigators be about controlling inputs? Perhaps the best way to answer this question is to examine a sample of student input characteristics and see how they are correlated with both output and environmental characteristics.

Input-Output Correlations

With only very rare exceptions, an outcome posttest measure has a higher correlation with its corresponding input pretest measure than with any other independent variable. Nevertheless, these pretest-posttest correlations can range from very high to very low, depending upon the reliability of the measure in question and the length of time separating pretest from posttest. The longer the period of time, the lower the correlation.

Some of the highest correlations can be obtained with standardized tests, interest inventories, and objective personality tests in which each scale is based on a relatively large number of items (20 or more per scale). For example, in chapter 6 it will be shown that the SAT (which really turns out to be a kind of pretest for the GRE) has a correlation of roughly .85 with the GRE administrated four or more years later.

What about the pretest-posttest correlations involving questionnaire items such as those used in the CIRP Freshman Survey? Table 4.2 shows the pretest-posttest (input-outcome) correlations involving a selected sample of items from the CIRP Freshman Survey administered in 1983 and the CIRP follow-up administered to the same students in 1987.

TABLE 4.2 **Correlations between Selected Input (Pretest) and Output (Posttest) Measures (3,897 Freshmen in 1983 Followed up in 1987)**

Measure	Correlation between 1983 and 1987
Grade-point average (high school with college)	.54
Level of highest degree aspired to	.32
Political liberalism	.33
Self-ratings:	
Mathematical ability	.68
Academic ability	.53
Writing ability	.50
Leadership ability	.50
Intellectual self-confidence	.40
Values and attitudes:	
The activities of married women are best confined to home and family	.25
The chief benefit of a college education is that it increases earning power	.24
Choice of major:	
Engineering	.65
Fine arts	.48
Education	.48
Agriculture	.44
History or politcal science	.40
Mathematics	.33
English	.26

The correlation of .54 between high school grades and college grades may seem modest, but it is really quite substantial considering the four-year gap and the great variation in grading standards across high schools and across colleges. The next two items in table 4.2, level of highest degree aspired to and political liberalism, show substantially lower pretest-posttest correlations of .32 and .33, respectively. Although these low correlations might suggest that the two items are unreliable, the explanation is that students' aspirations and political beliefs undergo substantial changes during the undergraduate years. The observation that pretest-posttest correlations tend to decline with time suggests that the longer the time interval between pretest and posttest, the greater the opportunity for students to change their position on a particular measure. The best way to differentiate between unreliability and change over time is to compare pretest-posttest correlations over very brief periods of time (a few hours or days) with comparable correlations over much longer periods of time. The larger the drop from one correlation to the other, the greater is the amount of differential change shown by the students.

Note my use of the adjective *differential*. When a pretest correlates significantly with a posttest, all we have demonstrated is that the relative positions of and distances separating the individuals being assessed show some consistency over time. (See chapter 6 and the appendix for a more detailed discussion of correlation.) In other words, if all the individuals change over time but all change by roughly the same amount, their relative positions and the distances separating them will remain relatively stable, thereby producing a very high pretest-posttest correlation. So, when we speak of pretest-posttest correlations being attenuated by change, what we are really speaking of is differential change from one person to the other: some people increasing their scores, others decreasing their scores, and others showing no change. The more inconsistent the change from person to person, the lower the pretest-posttest correlation.

Table 4.2 shows that, *within* a given category of questionnaire item, consistency over time can vary substantially from item to item. For example, among the student self-ratings, the correlations vary from a high of .68 (mathematical ability) to a low of .40 (intellectual self-confidence).

Even greater variation occurs among pretest-posttest correlations involving choice of a major. Engineering shows the highest pretest-posttest correlation (.65) whereas English shows the lowest correlation (.26). The high correlation involving engineering occurs primarily because virtually all people who choose engineering on the posttest also chose it on the pretest. Thus, even though many people switch from engineering to other fields during the undergraduate years, very few people switch *into* engineering during the same period of time. The situation is very different with a major such as English. Here we not only have many students switching from English to some other major, but an even greater number switching into English from other freshman majors. The changes from pretest to posttest, in other words, are much more chaotic with the choice of an English major than with the choice of an engineering major.

It is possible to obtain somewhat higher pretest-posttest correlations by combining several related questionnaire items into larger scales measuring more general student characteristics. Multi-item scales generally have less measurement error (greater reliability) than do single items, provided that the items being combined are measuring similar qualities.

Input-Environment Correlations

It probably comes as no surprise that pretest input measures tend to correlate with posttest outcome measures. This is just another way of saying that people's relative positions on a measure tend to show some stability over time. The real problem for analysis of environmental effects is caused not by the correlation between input and outcome but by the correlation between input and environment. As pointed out in chapter 2, people are seldom distributed across different environments at random; they generally pick their environments and environments to a certain extent select their people. Thus, in any real-life situation we tend to find different types of people (in terms of input characteristics) being exposed to the different environments. A simpler way to say this is that input characteristics tend to be correlated with environmental characteristics.

Which input characteristics are related to environmental characteristics, and how large are the correlations? To explore this question, correlations were computed between selected input and environmental variables. Table 4.3 shows the correlations of four input demographic characteristics with various environmental measures. Each of these characteristics actually had more statistically significant correlations with environmental characteristics than those reported in table 4.3; only the largest correlations are shown. The data indicate that students from well-to-do families are much more likely than are students from poorer families to attend selective institutions and, in particular, private universities. Students from poor families, on the other hand, are substantially more likely to attend predominantly black colleges and to work while attending college.

A similar pattern occurred for father's education: students with highly educated fathers tend to attend selective institutions, private universities, and institutions that spend a lot of money on their educational programs. Students whose fathers are relatively uneducated, on the other hand, are more likely to attend predominantly black col-

TABLE 4.3 Correlations of Selected Student Demographic Input
Measures with Environmental Measures

INPUT MEASURE	ENVIRONMENTAL MEASURE	CORRELATION
Parental income	Selectivity	.33
	Black college	−.25
	Private university	.15
	Hours spent working in college	−.15
	Institutional size	.14
Father's education	Selectivity	.34
	Private university	.17
	Expenditures per student	.17
	Black college	−.16
	Hours spent commuting	−.15
	Two-year college	−.14
Race: black	Black college	.79
	College region: Southeast	.49
	Selectivity	−.45
	Protestant college	.27
	College region: Mideast	−.19
Attended private high school	Catholic college	.20
	Selectivity	.17
	Private nonsectarian college	.13
	Public college	.13
	Private university	.11
	Black college	−.09

leges or two year-colleges and to spend above-average amounts of time commuting to college.

Black students, not surprisingly, are much more likely than non-black students to attend black colleges, colleges located in the Southeast, or Protestant colleges. Nonblacks, on the other hand, are more likely than blacks to attend highly selective colleges or colleges located in the mideast region of the country.

Finally, students who attend private high schools are more likely than students from public high schools to attend Roman Catholic colleges and highly selective colleges. Students from public high schools, by contrast, are more likely than private school students to attend public colleges.

Table 4.4 shows how environmental measures are correlated with three personal characteristics of entering students: their average high

TABLE 4.4 Correlations of Selected Student Personal Characteristics
(Input Measures) with Environmental Measures

INPUT MEASURE	ENVIRONMENTAL MEASURE	CORRELATION
High school grades	Selectivity	.43
	Enrolled in honors program	.25
	Black college	−.22
	Live in dormitory	.21
	Per-student expenditures	.20
	College region: Southeast	−.19
	Two-year college	−.17
	Private university	.16
Years of foreign language in high school	Selectivity	.40
	Per-student expenditures	.19
	College region: Plains	−.18
	College region: Mideast	.17
	Two-year college	−.17
	Private university	.17
	Institutional size	.17
	Black college	−.16
Political liberalism (versus conservatism)	College major: English	.07
	College major: engineering	−.07
	Participated in college sports	−.06
	College major: humanities	.06

school grades, the number of years they studied foreign language in high school, and their degree of political liberalism (versus conservatism). As expected, students with good grades in high school are much more likely to enroll in selective institutions than are students with mediocre or poor grades. Students with good grades are also more likely than other students to enroll in private institutions and in institutions with substantial per-student expenditures, to live in a dormitory rather than commute, and to enroll in honors programs in college. Students with relatively poor grades, on the other hand, tend to enroll in two-year colleges, predominantly black colleges, and colleges located in the southeastern United States.

Students who have taken foreign languages in high school are most likely to enroll in highly selective institutions, large institutions, private universities, and institutions with high levels of per-student expenditures. (Possibly this has something to do with the admissions policies of such colleges.) Students with little or no foreign language study in high school are most likely to enroll in two-year colleges, black colleges, and colleges located in the plains states. The last input characteristic shown in Table 4.4, political liberalism, was measured along a five-point scale: far right (1), conservative (2), middle-of-the-road (3), liberal (4), far left (5). Political liberalism is significantly related to several environmental measures although the correlations are considerably smaller than those involving the other input characteristics. Politically liberal students are most likely to major in English or other fields of the humanities whereas politically conservative students are most likely to major in engineering and to participate in college sports.

In short, these selected findings demonstrate that student input characteristics are significantly related to a wide variety of environmental measures. Of all the environmental variables examined in this analysis, college selectivity clearly bears the most consistent relationships to student input characteristics. Obviously, it makes no sense to try to assess the impact of college selectivity and other environmental characteristics on student outcome measures without first controlling for several student input characteristics. Even *within* individual institutions there are significant correlations between input characteristics and such environmental experiences as living in a dormitory, enrolling in an honors program, participating in extracurricular activities, time spent working, time spent commuting, and the student's major field of study. Again, assessing the impact of such environmental experiences on student outcomes may lead to erroneous causal inferences unless one first controls for relevant student input characteristics.

SUMMARY

In this chapter we reviewed the different types of student input characteristics and showed how measures of such characteristics can be used in the I-E-O model. The most crucial inputs to include are pretests on the various student outcomes. When pretesting is not feasible for a particular outcome, a good substitute is to assess the students' expectations for that outcome. Input measures can also be used for a variety of other purposes such as curriculum review, admissions and recruitment, and public information.

Controlling student inputs is important, as inputs were shown to be related to both outcome and environmental measures. Moreover, because inputs other than the pretest are almost always predictive of a given outcome, it is important to control as many input measures as possible in order to minimize bias in assessing the impact of college environments on student outcomes.

5

ASSESSING THE ENVIRONMENT

Environmental assessment presents by far the most difficult and complex challenge in the field of assessment. It is also the most neglected topic. In its broadest sense, the environment encompasses everything that happens to a student during the course of an educational program that might conceivably influence the outcomes under consideration. The environment thus includes not only the programs, personnel, curricula, teaching practices, and facilities that we consider to be part of any educational program but also the social and institutional climate in which the program operates. Thus, for a student attending college, the environment might include the courses taken, the personalities and pedagogical techniques of the professors who teach these courses, the physical surroundings in the classroom and on other parts of the campus, the behavior of roommates and friends, the organizations and other co-curricular activities in which the student participates, as well as any special programs to which the student is exposed (e.g., orientation, registration, counseling, remediation, and honors). The task of assessing the college environment, then, involves the identification and quantification of these external circumstances and events.

Before considering specific approaches to assessing higher education environments, we first need to discuss several conceptual and methodological issues: the unit of observation, self-produced environments, and the source of environmental data.

WHICH UNIT OF OBSERVATION?

One of the first considerations in trying to assess any student's environmental experiences is to define the person or thing on which we focus our attention. In assessment jargon the entity to which any measurement applies is called the *unit of observation*. In the case of collecting input and output information such as SAT or GRE scores, the student is typically the "unit" being described by our measures (or, in the case of studies of faculty, the individual faculty member is the unit). That is, we gather the actual data—such as test scores and demographic characteristics—about each individual student. However, in trying to capture the essence of any student's environmental experiences, there are several other units that we might wish to measure or characterize. We could, for example, try to describe the student's entire institution in terms of its size (enrollment), selectivity, location, type of control (public, private, sectarian), level of degree offered (associate, bachelor's, doctorate), money spent per student, characteristics of the faculty (percentage with doctorates, sex composition, and so on), characteristics of the overall student body (ethnic composition, average age, average admissions test scores, and so on), the student-faculty ratio, the size of the library, and so forth. For all such environmental measures, the *total institution* is the unit of observation being described.

If we wanted to personalize these measures a bit more, we might obtain them instead on some smaller unit of observation such as the student's major department within the institution. Or, we might measure characteristics of the student's individual classes, such as class size, instructor characteristics, course content, and instructional method. On a still more personal level, we might measure the characteristics of the student's roommates, faculty adviser, counselor, or closest friends. We might also collect information about the particular organizations of which the student is a member.

What I am describing here, of course, is a kind of continuum of environmental measures beginning with the most distal units of observation such as the entire institution to the most proximate units that reflect particular teachers, associates, or classroom experiences to which the student is exposed. The more proximate the measure is to the student, the greater the significance that measure is likely to have for most student outcomes. However, it is usually much easier and less costly to obtain distal measures of the student's environment in which the entire institution is the unit of analysis than to obtain the most proximate measures that reflect the particular people or events that impinge directly on each student's experience. The practical difficulties in gathering proximate data about each student's environment is one of the major reasons that environmental assessment is still in such a primitive state.

The issue of the proximity of environmental measures is probably much greater in the larger and more complex institutions than in the smaller and more homogeneous ones. That is, a measure of the overall environment of an institution is more likely to provide an accurate picture of the individual student's environment in a small residential college than in a large urban community college.

SELF-PRODUCED ENVIRONMENTS

Still another problem in trying to assess the student's environment is that any student's environment is, to a certain extent, self-produced. Students, in other words, can choose and form their own environmental experiences. For example, if we consider three college freshmen who are taking exactly the same courses and living on the same floor of the same residence hall, the actual environmental experiences of the three might still be quite different if one of them chooses to spend her evenings studying in her dormitory room, another spends her evenings studying in the library, and the third spends her evenings socializing in the student union. Similar differences in experience would occur for students who studied in groups as contrasted with those who study alone or for those who study primarily during the weekends rather than during the week. The number of specific situations in which self-produced environmental experience might be highly significant is almost limitless.

Because many environmental experiences are in part self-produced, sometimes they can also be regarded as input or even outcome variables. Take the student's major field as an example. If a new freshman elects engineering as a major, that choice could be regarded as an environmental variable since the student may well be exposed to a different set of courses, professors, and student peers than will a freshman who begins college with some other preliminary choice of a major. On the other hand, because the freshman engineering student entered college with a decision about a major already made, the choice could also be regarded as an input variable. (See also page 74 on bridge variables.)

And what of the student's final selection of a major, the one in which he or she eventually earns a bachelor's degree? Since the final choice, just like the freshman choice, has important implications for the kinds of peers, faculty, and courses to which the student is exposed, it could readily be viewed as an environmental variable. At the same time, since the student's environmental experiences during the first two undergraduate years may well influence that final choice of a major, it could also be utilized as an outcome variable. In short, there is nothing inherent in the nature of self-produced environmental variables that dictate their status as environmental variables; whether we choose to utilize variables such as the student's choice of a major as environmental variables depends to a large extent on how we conceptualize the problem under investigation.

Self-produced environmental experiences present a number of other technical and conceptual challenges. To begin with, it is obviously unrealistic to expect that we could even enumerate, much less measure, all or even most of the important self-produced environmental experiences that a typical college or university student might encounter. Second, because self-produced environmental experiences can also be regarded as outcomes, they pose formidable chicken-egg problems for our input-environment-output model. While there are certain approaches to analyzing such environmental experiences that alleviate some of these conceptual difficulties (basically, they involve considering such experiences as *intermediate* outcomes falling between input and outcome; see the appendix), no technique for analyzing such environmental experiences is entirely satisfactory and the results are therefore inherently ambiguous. The best we can hope to do is to measure some of these experiences and explore their possible effects while maintaining a full awareness and recognition of the inherent ambiguities.

THE SOURCE OF ENVIRONMENTAL DATA

Where do we get the information with which to develop measures of each student's environmental experiences? Obviously, the source of the data is closely related to the unit of observation, but it also has implications for the problem of self-produced environmental variables. Data about the entire institution (its size, control, selectivity, and facilities) are usually obtained from the institution itself. But environmental data pertaining to an entire institution can also be obtained through surveys of faculty and staff. In this approach a sample of people at the institution is given a standard set of questions, and the *mean* answer given by the respondents becomes the measure of the environment. (Such measures will be described in more detail in the next section.) It is also possible to use faculty and staff as the source of information about themselves. Thus, one might characterize the environment of a college or university in terms of the percentage of faculty who hold doctoral degrees, the average number of contacts they have with students outside of class, or the average number of articles they have published.

Environmental measures describing the entire institution are useful when several institutions are being studied simultaneously; they are of less value in studying a single institution since each student would have the same environment. Under such conditions, the environmental measure would be a constant (all students would get the same score) rather than a variable (whereby different students could get different scores). To overcome this problem, we might gather similar information from definable *sub*environments within the institution, such as the student's program or major field of study. Different departments within an institution, for example, can be characterized in terms of the mean characteristics of the faculty or the size of the department. Or, we might wish to characterize individual classes taken by the students in terms of their size, time of day, professor, or method of instruction.

An extremely important source of potential environmental information is institutional records on individual students. Practically all institutions maintain extensive records about each student's academic experiences (courses taken, grades, credits) and financial aid, and many also keep records of students' places of residence, participation in special services and programs, and extracurricular participation.

But perhaps the richest source of data on the students' environmental experiences is the students themselves. In this instance we are basically using the student as an observer or informant to tell us what kinds of environmental experiences he or she has had. Usually, the gathering of such information is done by questionnaires which the student completes after being exposed to the environment. In this manner students can be used to generate information about a wide range of environmental experiences that might not be available in institutional records.

Data from student records or from individual students can be aggregated to produce environmental measures that essentially describe the characteristics of groups of students. Thus, in multi-institutional studies in which several different institutions are being compared and contrasted, institutional records or questionnaire responses from the entire student body (or a representative sample of the student body at each institution) can be aggregated by institution to produce mean scores describing the entire student body. Or, in the case of a single-institution study, data can be aggregated on smaller subgroupings based on the student's major field, residence hall, or organization. The environment for any individual student thus becomes the mean score of all fellow students who are majoring in the same field, living in the same residence hall, or participatiing in the same organization. At an even more atomistic level, a student's environment might be characterized in terms of the mean characteristics of roommates or best friends. The possibilities are virtually limitless.

TWO TYPES OF MEASURES

I have found it convenient to differentiate between two broad classes of environmental measures: (1) the characteristics of the total institution (its size, selectivity, etc.) which can, in theory at least, affect all students at the institution, and (2) particular educational experiences within the institution (living in a particular dormitory, being a member of a particular student organization, participating in a remedial program, etc.) to which only some of the students at a given institution are exposed. The latter category comprises *within*-institution environmental variables, whereas the former comprises *between*-institution environmental variables. Since this book is directed primarily at people working in a single institution rather than at investigators who are studying several institutions simultaneously, most readers will have a greater interest in within-institution variables. Nevertheless, since many of the measures designed for between-institution comparisons can also be used within a single institution, we shall first examine some of these measures.

Between-Institution Measures

Most of the published research that contrasts the effects of different types of institutions has utilized what sociologists might refer to as structural characteristics of institutions: size, selectivity, type of control (public, private, denominational), highest level of degree offered (associate, bachelor's, graduate or professional), gender (colleges for men, colleges for women, coeducational institutions), expenditures (usually computed on a per- student basis), size of the library, level of training of the faculty (e.g., percentage with doctoral degrees), student-faculty ratio, tuition charges, percentage of applicants accepted, and geographic region. With a few exceptions, information on these characteristics can be obtained from annual surveys conducted by the U.S. Department of Education, from commercial college guides, or from college catalogues. Such measures obviously have little use within a single institution since they would yield the same score from student to student.

There is, however, another class of between-institution environmental variables developed by researchers in the field of higher education that can be of use in single-institution studies. The principal purpose of such measures is to obtain information that describes the institution's environment or climate in a more personal and sophisticated manner than the structural characteristics listed in the preceding paragraph. For example, many educators believe that the size of an institution (as measured by the number of students who are enrolled) can have significant effects on the development of the individual student. Few would argue, however, that size per se is the important variable. Rather, they might argue that having a large or small student body tends to create a particular type of climate which in turn can affect the development of the student. Thus, it might be argued that the climate of a small institution is more likely to be characterized by a strong sense of community than is the climate of a very large institution. Rather than simply using a measure of size as a proxy for community, the investigator would attempt to measure directly the perceived degree of community at the institution.

This is in fact what one UCLA colleague, C. Robert Pace, has attempted to do in his College and University Environmental Scales (CUES) (Pace, 1960, 1963). In Pace's CUES the degree of community in a particular college environment is determined by surveying groups of faculty, administrators, or students to learn the extent to which they view the environment as characterized by cohesiveness and by a friendly, congenial atmosphere in which common values are shared by faculty, staff, and students. The Community scale in Pace's instrument contains thirty true-false questions, as do each of his four other environmental scales: Scholarship, Awareness, Propriety, and Practicality. The CUES was derived from a larger environmental assessment instrument, the College Characteristics Index (CCI), which comprises 300 true-false questions that are used to form thirty different scales measuring the environmental press of the college (Pace and Stern, 1958). Most recently, Pace has developed the College Student Experiences (CSE) questionnaire, an instrument designed to measure the "quality of effort" that students "put into using the facilities and opportunities provided for learning and development in college." Like his other environmental assessment instruments, Pace's College Student Experiences questionnaire is administered to groups of people at the institution (in this case, students) to generate scores on a series of scales measuring the quality of effort that students devote to such things as course learning, student acquaintances, clubs and organizations, library experiences, and experiences with faculty. The CSE includes fourteen quality of effort scales, with an average of ten items per scale. A given institution's score on each scale is determined by the aggregated responses of the students to each item on the scale. Currently, the College Student Experiences questionnaire is the most widely used instrument of this type.

The several instruments developed by Pace have utilized quite different types of items. In the CCI and the CUES, respondents report primarily their perceptions of the institutional climate (e.g., "There is a lot of group spirit on campus"). The more recent College Student Experiences questionnaire, on the other hand, relies primarily upon behaviorally oriented questions eliciting more factual information from students about their own activities ("Took detailed notes in class").

An earlier environmental assessment instrument that utilized behaviorally oriented items is the Inventory of College Activities (ICA)(Astin, 1968). The ICA is based on the assumption that any student's environment consists of a large and diverse set of stimuli. A stimulus is defined as any behavior, event, or other observable characteristic of the institution that is "capable of changing the student's sensory input, and whose existence or occurrence can be confirmed by independent observation" (Astin, 1968, p. 18). The ICA involves twenty-seven such stimulus measures covering four general areas: the peer environment, the classroom environment, the administrative environment, and the physical environment. Also included in the ICA are eight image measures based on perceptual items similar to those used in CUES. Even though the ICA image scales have an average of only three items per scale, they appear to capture much of the same information as the thirty-item CUES scales (Astin, 1971).

Still another approach to assessing between-institution environmental variables is the environmental assessment technique (EAT) (Astin and Holland, 1961). The EAT is based on what might be termed the student characteristics approach to assessing the environment in that it attempts to characterize the individual student's environment in terms of the average or mean characteristics of the other students in that environment. The EAT utilizes eight scales reflecting the interests and abilities of the students enrolled at the institution.

A major longitudinal study of student development at 246 four-year institutions (Astin and Panos, 1969) afforded an opportunity to compare and contrast these different approaches to assessing college environments. In general, the results supported the assumption that the stimulus approach based on observable student behaviors generates environmental scales that account for more of the differential impact of colleges than do the perceptual, structural characteristics, or student characteristics approaches. Even so, each of these other assessment techniques appeared to capture some important information not fully reflected in the stimulus approach.

Despite its popularity, a major difficulty presented by the perceptual approach to measuring environmental characteristics is that the student's perception of the college environment can be affected both by what the environment is really like and by how the student has been influenced by that environment. That is, the student's subjective view of his college environment may well reflect college *outcomes*. In the jargon of research methodology, we would say that we have partially "confounded" outcomes with environments. Thus, if a particular environmental scale based on student perceptions is found to be related to change in some student outcome, we cannot be sure that the scale really explains the change simply because the direction of causation might well be reversed; that is, the student's perceptions may actually have been influenced by the outcome itself.

This problem can be illustrated with a simple example. Suppose the perceived degree of community in the college environment is shown to be positively related to persistence toward the degree (outcome measure), after student inputs are controlled. While it might seem reasonable to conclude that a college's retention rate can be positively affected by the degree of community in the college climate, another interpretation is possible: The perceived degree of community may well have been influenced by the retention rate. Is it not likely that students will perceive the environment as being strong in community if nearly all students stay to complete their degrees? Will not a college where large numbers of students drop out tend to be seen as lacking in community? Perceptual measures of the college environment, in other words, can themselves be influenced by college outcomes. This confounding of environmental variables with outcome variables is less likely to occur with the structural, student characteristics, and stimulus approaches to environmental assessment since they do not rely on the student's perceptions and impressions. (For further discussion of this issue, see Astin, 1970c, pp. 440–441).

Two other widely used instruments for assessing the environmental characteristics of colleges and universities are the Institutional Functioning Inventory (IFI) (Peterson et al., 1970) and the Institutional Goals Inventory (IGI) (Peterson and Uhl, 1972). The IFI grew out of a systematic attempt by a number of prominent educators to develop a measure of institutional vitality (Hefferlin, 1969.) It includes 132 multiple-choice "perceptual" items (e.g., "Power here tends to be widely dispersed rather than tightly held") which are combined to yield scores on eleven dimensions or scales such as Concern for Improvement of Society, Concern for Undergraduate Learning, and Institutional Esprit. The IGI is designed to assist a college in identifying its basic goals and in determining priorities among these goals. Ninety goal statements (e.g., "to help students achieve deeper levels of self-understanding") are organized into twenty goal areas such as Academic Development, Vocational Preparation, Research, and Social Egalitarianism. Respondents rate the goal statements in terms of how important each goal is perceived to be, as well as how important it should be at the institution. Institutions using the IGI are encouraged to administer it to different constituent groups (students, faculty, administrators, trustees) in order to permit comparisons among the priorities given to different goals by each group. Even though it is designed to measure goals of the entire institution, the IGI, unlike the other environmental assessment instruments described in this section, is not intended to be used for normative comparisons between institutions. Rather, it is recommended for use by individual institutions to determine local priorities among the various goals. The IGI is the only such instrument that does not provide norms that allow the individual institution to compare itself with other institutions. Both the IGI and IFI were used extensively during the 1970s, but their popularity has declined markedly in recent years.

Even though most of the instruments discussed in this section are designed for between-institution comparisons, they are generally used much like the IGI: for assessing a single institution. Typically, the institutional research office will administer one of these instruments to a sample of students, faculty, or administrators and use their aggregated responses as a kind of description of the environment. Profiles of scale scores can be plotted and compared visually against norms in order to see how the institution's environment compares with the environments of other colleges and universities. Areas in which the institution deviates substantially from the norm can be viewed as the distinctive features of that college's environment.

At the same time, aggregated responses to individual survey questions (e.g., the percentage agreeing with the item) can be examined to determine the specific areas in which there is a consensus among the respondents and those in which there is significant disagreement as to what the environment is like. The closer the percentages are to 100 or 0, the greater the consensus and the more likely the statement is to be true or false with respect to that institution's environment; the closer to 50, the greater the disagreement and the less the certainty there is about whether the item accurately describes the environment.

Such descriptive information about an institution's environment can be used productively to generate discussion and debate within the academic community about the institution's policies and practices. If the ultimate aim of using environmental information in this manner is to enhance educational outcomes through improvements in the educational environment, then we have what amounts to an environment-only model of assessment and evaluation (see chapter 2). As already noted in chapter 2, this assessment model forces the practitioner to assume that particular environmental circumstances produce particular outcomes, even when there is no independent empirical basis for such assumptions.

To see how this works with an example, suppose we administer the CUES to a sample of students and find that the degree of community in our environment is substantially below the norm for similar institutions. Let us assume further that subsequent discussion of these results among faculty and administrators leads to the conclusion that the community score is too low and that measures should be taken to strengthen the sense of community on the campus. Such a conclusion is either explicitly or implicitly based on the following kind of reasoning: since the degree of community on the campus is causally related to one or more desired outcomes (student satisfaction, student retention, faculty morale, etc.), by increasing the degree of community we can also facilitate the attainment of these desired outcomes. Such reasoning is most likely to be believed when one or more of the outcomes (e.g., the student retention rate) is also judged to be unacceptably low. This environment-only approach forces us to make such causal assumptions even when there is no independent evidence showing that the environmental variable in question (community) is even correlated with, much less causally related to, the desired outcome variable (retention).

Educators who advocate the use of purely descriptive information about the college environment or climate might respond to this last discussion by arguing that environmental information can be useful without requiring one to make unsubstantiated causal assumptions about outcomes. I would be the first to agree that descriptive environmental information can be of significant value as a basis for generating critical discussion about the institution among faculty, administrators, trustees, and students. But ultimately such discussions must lead to significant changes in policy, practice, attitude, or belief. Otherwise, the environmental data are of little value or significance beyond being interesting.

Assessment data that are merely interesting are likely to generate the "So what?" response (see chapter 7).

Another problem that comes with using environmental assessment instruments in isolation from other data is a lack of information about the *genesis* of institutional climate variables. What are the antecedent conditions that cause environments to be the way they are? Why do some college environments have more or less community than others? Without such knowledge on the genesis or origin of college environments, we are flying blind when it comes to any attempt to change or improve the environment. This is a problem not only for measures based on perceptions such as the CUES or the IFI, but also for instruments based on students' behavior such as the ICA or the Quality of Effort scales of the CSE. The most important unanswered question about such measures is the extent to which they are under the control of the institution. Both the characteristics of the peer environment (ICA) and the quality of effort shown by students (CSE) will to some extent (and probably to a great extent) depend on the characteristics of the students who enroll at the institution. Given the particular student body that enrolls in any institution, how much control does that institution actually have over such environmental circumstances? And assuming that the quality of student effort and the behavior of the student peer group is not entirely a function of the types of students entering the institution, what, specifically, can institutions do to enhance these environmental variables? These are among the most neglected questions in the field of higher education research today.

Within-Institution Measures

A major limitation of between-college measures is that they are generally designed to assess the environment of a total institution rather than the environment actually encountered by individual students within that institution. Since there are unquestionably many distinct *sub*environments within any college or university, especially within the larger institutions, measures of the total institutional environment may not be especially useful because they will confound these subenvironmental differences.

It has already been suggested that the most obvious subdivisions for environmental assessment within a single institution are academic departments and, in the more complex universities, schools and colleges within the university. Nevertheless, the mere existence of organizational units such as schools or departments does not necessarily mean that the different units are, from the student's perspective, functionally independent. In certain universities, for example, students attending the technical college may have little or no contact with students or professors in any of the other colleges of the university. In other universities such students may live in dormitories and attend classes with students from a variety of other colleges.

Most within-institution environmental variables cut across the formal organizational subunits within the institution. That is, not all students within a given department or school will encounter such experiences, and the experiences will usually apply to at least some students in every organizational subunit. There are, of course, a great many within-college environmental experiences that cut across organizational subunits such as schools or departments. The methodological challenge for the researcher is to identify such experiences and to devise an appropriate means for measuring them and for determining whether each student encountered each experience while enrolled. While the list shown below is not exhaustive, it is provided as a preliminary framework for determining which within-institution environmental experiences an institution may wish to assess and evaluate.

- Characteristics of individual classes in which the students enroll (content, size, teaching method, etc.)
- Characteristics of the student's peer group, roommates, or closest friends
- Characteristics of significant others among employees of the institution (professors, advisers, counselors, administrators)
- Utilization of campus services and facilities (health service, study skills center, library, etc.)
- Courses taken (individual as well as aggregated by various forms of "transcript analysis"; see Boyer and Ahlgren, 1987; Ratcliff, 1988; and Zemsky, 1989).
- The amount of time devoted to various activities (studying, outside reading, recreation, sleeping, etc.)
- The type and amount of counseling and advisement received
- Participation in special educational programs (honors program, independent study, year abroad, developmental or remedial, Washington semester, etc.)
- Living arrangements (dormitory, fraternity or sorority house, private room, commuting from home)
- Use of alcohol or drugs (tranquilizers, sleeping pills, tobacco, psychedelics, etc.)
- Type and amount of financial aid received
- Employment status (type and place of work performed, hours employed, pay received, etc.)
- Availability of a private automobile
- Marital status and number of children
- Participation in student organizations and other extracurricular activities

Information about some of these within-environment experiences can be obtained from institutional records, although much of it may have to be gathered directly from the students by means of questionnaires.

CONCLUSIONS

In this chapter we have considered some of the conceptual and practical issues in assessing the student's environmental experiences. Several instruments for assessing environmental characteristics have been developed, and while they are intended primarily for assessing the environment of a total institution, they might also be useful in assessing subenvironments such as schools or departments.

By far the most important type of environmental information comes from within institution experiences to which some, but not all, students are exposed. While institutions do not ordinarily record such information in any systematic fashion, it offers the greatest opportunity for learning how particular educational experiences affect student development. Even though a good deal of this within-institution information can be supplied by the students themselves via follow-up questionnaires, institutions need to find better ways of recording such information so that it will be available for all students. (Issues related to inclusion of environmental data in a comprehensive student data base are discussed in chapter 8.)

6

ANALYZING ASSESSMENT DATA

For at least two reasons, I consider this chapter and the next one to be among the most important in the book. First, even the most comprehensive and sophisticated assessment program will be of little benefit to an institution that does not analyze the data properly or utilize the results appropriately. Second, without some concrete notion about how assessment data are to be analyzed and utilized, we are likely to assess the wrong things or use the wrong assessment devices. If I were limited to only one criticism of contemporary practices in assessment, I would say that in the typical institution, major decisions about assessment practices are made with little or no thought given to matters of analysis and utilization.

At the outset it is important to clarify the distinction between the analysis of raw assessment data (chapter 6) and utilization of assessment results (chapter 7). Analysis refers primarily to the statistical or analytical procedures that are applied to the raw assessment data and to the manner in which the results of these analyses are displayed visually; utilization has to do with how the results of assessment analyses are actually used by educators and policy makers to improve the talent development process. The statistical analysis must be designed with the user in mind; however, there are certain minimal statistical requirements that must ordinarily be satisfied, regardless of the potential audience of users. My own experience has been that the results of even the most complex and esoteric statistical analyses can be presented in such a way as to be understood by academics who are not versed in statistical methods.

STATISTICAL PROCEDURES

Assuming that many readers of this book will not be familiar with methods of statistical analysis, I realize that I run the risk of discouraging or confusing some readers by introducing statistical concepts. But I made the decision to include this chapter (as well as the appendix) for two very important reasons. First, my nearly three decades of experience in working with institutions on assessment issues convinces me that most academics cannot expect to make better use of assessment results without acquainting themselves with at least some of the basic statistical tools that are available today. An understanding of statistical concepts is important not only in helping us understand what assessment results *mean*, but also in suggesting what *actions*, if any, we might take on the basis of the results.

My second reason for deciding to incorporate statistical concepts in this book is the belief, based on many years of experience in teaching educators who know little of statistics and care even less about learning, that any reasonably intelligent academic can master some basic statistical ideas with a little effort and a modest investment of time.

METHODS OF ANALYSIS

Over the years I have found it convenient to distinguish between two quite different ways of analyzing information. Let's assume we have two individuals about whom we have collected a great deal of assessment information concerning their abilities, interests, background characteristics, talents, and behavior. The simplest approach to analyzing this information would be to compare and contrast the two persons in terms of the various measures: Person A is more intelligent and ambitious and comes from a more advantaged family; person B is more politically liberal and has a better sense of humor. Such an analysis of assessment data is basically *descriptive*, in that it is simply describing how the two individuals are alike and how they differ. On the other hand, we might wish to understand *why* the two people are the same or different in certain ways. We could, for example, investigate the two individuals' family backgrounds, early childhood experiences, and kinds of educational institutions they have attended with the aim of understanding how they came to be similar or different in certain attributes. The latter kind of analysis is *causal* in that it helps us understand *why* the people are the way they are. Descriptive analyses ordinarily focus on the question "What?" while causal analyses are concerned with the questions "Why?" and "How?" The two methods are closely related: descriptive analyses often raise causal questions, and causal analyses presuppose a descriptive knowledge of the phenomena under investigation. Since descriptive and causal analyses of assessment data typically utilize somewhat different types of statistics, let us now consider how to perform each type separately.

DESCRIPTIVE ANALYSES

Descriptive analyses ordinarily involve somewhat simpler statistics than causal analyses. The simplest level of description involves a single measure. As a concrete example, one outcome measure that has received a great deal of attention in higher education in recent years is an institution's retention rate. In a baccalaureate-granting institution, a student's retention score would normally consist of a simple dichotomy: the student completed a baccalaureate degree within some specified period of time (score 1) or the student did not complete the degree (score 0). Our raw assessment data thus consists of 0's and 1's, with each student obtaining a score of 0 or 1, depending on whether he or she completed the degree or dropped out. If we were to add up these retention scores for all of the students in a given entering class and divide it by the number of students, we would obtain a retention rate (that is, the proportion of students who completed their degrees). What I have just described is the application of a statistical procedure (the computation of a mean or average) to a single outcome measure (retention). The retention mean is obviously a very simple piece of information, but it is much more interesting and significant than a crude listing of the 0's and 1's for each individual student. In other words, the basic assessment data (the individual retention scores for each student) have been converted into a more useful form by the application of a simple statistical procedure (computation of the mean). Other than multiplying the mean by 100 to obtain a percentage, there is little besides computing a mean that can be done with a "dummy" variable—one that has only two possible values—such as retention.

Another example of a single measure that generates some interest through the application of descriptive analyses is the admission scores (SAT or ACT) of entering freshmen. As pointed out in chapter 1, such scores attract much attention from faculty and administrators alike, largely because they are seen as an index of the institution's quality or prestige. Many institutions closely monitor changes from year to year in the mean admissions test scores of their entering freshmen. Like retention scores, the raw SAT scores of the entering freshmen are difficult to comprehend or use if they are simply presented as a long list of individual scores. These scores take on much greater significance once we apply the same simple statistical procedure, the computation of the mean score. However, since individual SAT and ACT scores can assume many different values, there are other kinds of descriptive analyses besides the mean that we can apply to the raw scores. We can compute the *median* (middle-ranking) score ot the *mode* (the most common score). We can also determine how much *variation* there is in the scores by calculating the range (from highest to lowest) or the *standard deviation* (see the appendix). Furthermore, we can examine the variation in scores visually by generating a *frequency distribution* (see the appendix) which shows us how many students have each different score. Finally, we can use more esoteric statistics to tell us whether the distribution of SAT scores is symmetrical or asymmetrical in shape (skewness) and whether the shape of the distribution is very peaked or flat (kurtosis). These latters statistics are seldom used, but I mention them here to point out that it is possible to analyze scores on a single measure like the SAT in a number of different ways.

Single-variable descriptive analyses can be performed on almost any input, outcome, or environmental variable. Other outcome measures besides retention might include performance on comprehensive examinations, scores on admissions tests for graduate or professional school (GRE, LSAT, GMAT, MCAT), or enrollment in graduate or professional school. Individual input measures that can be of intrinsic interest include ethnic minority enrollments, class ranks or GPAs from secondary school, or scores on advanced placement examinations. Among the many individual environmental measures that might be considered important in their own right would be class size, faculty salaries, teaching loads, and student/faculty ratios. I can personally recall a number of situations in which a descriptive analysis (computation of the mean or percentage) using one of these variables has attracted a good deal of institutional attention and has even led to modifications in institutional policy or practice.

It is especially interesting that the results of even the simplest descriptive analysis can often raise questions that call for an additional causal analysis. If when we compute our retention rate we decide that it is too low, we might naturally ask two additional causal questions: Why is it so low? What might be done to increase the retention rate? Similarly, if we compute a mean score on the SAT for our most recent crop of freshmen and decide that that score is too low, we might ask the same two causal questions: Why is it so low? What can be done to raise it? Note that while descriptive information can give rise to causal questions, descriptive information based on a single measure cannot, by itself, supply any causal answers.

Descriptive analysis of assessment data becomes more complicated and far more interesting when we analyze two or more variables simultaneously. We might want to compute our retention rates separately for men and women undergraduates. Here the two variables are gender (male versus female) and retention (degree attainment versus dropping out). Or, we might wish to compute mean SAT scores separately for science majors, humanities majors, and so on. Similarly, we may wish to compute the average class size for science and nonscience students. Descriptive analyses involving more than one variable are of special interest because they permit us to assess the degree of *relationship* or *association* between the variables.

What statistical analyses can be performed to describe the relationship between two variables? By far the most common and popular methods are *cross-tabulation* and *correlation*. Each of these is considered in turn.

Cross-Tabulation

Cross-tabulation is a statistical procedure for determining whether the categories on one measure are associated with the categories on another measure. Take two simple categorical variables such as gender (male or female) and retention (completed degree or dropped out). By cross-tabulating one against the other, we can determine whether a student's gender bears any relationship to retention. The cross-tabulation analysis might show, for example, that women are more likely than men to complete their degrees. In other words, it would show that there is a higher proportion of degree completers among the women, and a higher proportion of dropouts among the men. The same cross-tabulation would also show that the proportion of women is greater among degree completers than among dropouts, and that the proportion of men is greater among dropouts than among degree completers. In other words, the results of a cross-tabulation involving two variables can be described in two different ways.

To put this discussion in more concrete terms, let us examine some actual assessment data from a large public university, located in a western state, which we shall call Western University. From the full-time freshmen who completed the CIRP Freshman Survey when they entered college in fall 1982, we have selected 472 students who also completed the CIRP follow-up Survey (FUS) four years later in the summer of 1986. In addition to the freshman and follow-up survey data we also obtained from the university SAT scores, cumulative undergraduate grade-point averages (GPA), final major field, and retention information. The different variables and data sources are summarized in table 6.1 according to the I-E-O model. Since there are literally hundreds of two-way cross-tabulations that we can do with such data, I shall select a few to illustrate this type of analytic approach.

We can take a simple outcome measure (retention) and cross-tabulate it against a simple environmental measure (the student's major). Partial results are shown in table 6.2. To simplify the presentation of results I have selected only two major fields (English and engineering) that showed dramatically different retention rates. The table actually shows three different retention rates for each major, the most stringent requiring that the student obtain the bachelor's degree in four years. The next most stringent retention measure also classifies as retained those who have no degree after four years but who have completed four years of undergraduate work. The most liberal definition counts those who are still enrolled as being retained, even if they did not complete four years. English majors show higher retention rates regardless of the measure used, although the differences are greatest with the most stringent measure (earning a bachelor's degree in four years). Engineering majors, on the other hand, show lower than average retention

TABLE 6.1 Variables Used for Analyses of Assessment Data on Western
University Undergraduates

Input (freshman) data (1982):
1. CIRP survey data (race, sex, parental income and education, high
   school grades, future plans, values, attitudes)
2. SAT scores[a]

Outcome data (1986):
1. Posttests on selected CIRP attitudes and values (FUS)
2. College GPA
3. Retention[a]

Environmental data:
1. Major [a]
2. Place of residence (FUS)
3. Financial aid (FUS)
4. Participation in special programs (FUS)
5. College activities (FUS)

Note: CIRP refers to the annual freshman survey of the Cooperative Institutional
Research Program (Astin et al., 1989); FUS refers to the annual follow-up survey
conducted two and four years after college entry (Hurtado et al., 1989).

[a] Provided by the institution from its student records.

rates on the most stringent measure, but average rates on the two more
liberal measures. The explanation for this discrepancy is probably that
engineering students simply take longer to complete their degrees than
do students with other majors. But why should English majors have
much higher retention rates than students in general? Is it because they
are better prepared or more highly motivated when they enter as freshmen? Can we explain the higher rates in terms of input characteristics?
Is there something about the program offered by the English department that facilitates retention? Obviously, it is difficult to answer such
causal questions without additional data.

Table 6.2 uses a *within*-institution environmental measure, the student's final major field of study. What if we were to take the same
three retention outcome measures and cross tabulate them by a *between*-
institution environmental measure? Table 6.3 compares Western University's overall retention rates with the rates for two groups of institutions:
four-year colleges and universities, and highly selective public universities (of which Western is one).

Using the most stringent measure, we find that Western University
has a slightly higher rate than four-year institutions in general (42 percent versus 39 percent), but a slightly lower rate than its peer group, all
selective public universities (42 precent versus 47 percent). However,
on the most liberal retention rate, Western University is virtually iden-

TABLE 6.2 Retention Rates by Major at Western University: 1982
Freshmen Followed up in 1986

	RATE (%) AMONG		
RETENTION MEASURE[a]	All Students	Freshman English Majors	Freshman Engineering Majors
Earned bachelor's degree	42.4	68.8	35.6
Earned degree or completed 4 years	64.2	85.1	64.0
Earned degree or completed 4 years, or still enrolled	74.8	88.8	75.5

[a] Data provided by the institution.

tical to selective universities in general and substantially higher than all
four-year institutions. Once again we are confronted with an interesting
causal question: Why do Western University students earn bachelor's
degrees at a slightly lower rate than students at selective public universities and why are Western's rates on the two more liberal retention
measures so much higher than all four-year institutions? Once again, it
is difficult to answer such questions with any certainty without adding
input data to our analysis.

Cross-tabulation is ideally suited to variables that occur naturally in
discrete categories such as gender, race, ethnicity, retention or program
completion, participation in special programs (honors, remedial), and

TABLE 6.3 Three Measures of Retention: 1982 Freshmen Followed up in
1986

	PERCENTAGE RETAINED		
		National Norms	
RETENTION MEASURE[a]	Western University	Selective Public Universities	All Four-Year Institutions
Earned bachelor's degree	42	47	39
Earned degree or completed 4 years	64	67	52
Earned degree or completed 4 years, or still enrolled	75	74	61

[a] Retention norms are based on data provided by a national sample of institutions (see
Dey and Astin, 1989).

the choice of a major field of study or a career. If a variable does not occur naturally in such discrete categories (SAT scores, for example), we can still use the cross-tabulation technique if we are willing to group the scores on such variables into broader discrete categories (composite SAT scores might be grouped into intervals such as 400–499, 500–599, and so on).

Correlation

The correlation coefficient is another procedure for describing the relationship between two measures. Correlation basically describes the *strength* and *direction* of the association between two variables in terms of a coefficient that can range from −1.0 (a perfect negative relationship) to + 1.0 (a perfect positive relationship). A correlation of .00 means that there is no association between the two variables. There are many types of correlation coefficients, but the one that is used far more frequently than any others is the Pearson product-moment correlation coefficient, which is ordinarily designated by the lower-case r. Unless specified otherwise, the generic terms *correlation* and *correlation coefficient* are used by researchers to refer to the Pearson r. Any variable (SAT scores, GRE scores, etc.) can be correlated with any other variable.

What, exactly, does a correlation mean? Perhaps the best way to understand this statistic is with a concrete example. Suppose we have a group of 20 people and that we have measured two variables on each person: height and weight. If we line up the 20 people according to their height, the tallest person who is at the head of the line will be ranked number 1, the shortest person at the end of the line will be number 20, and the other 18 people will be ranked in between from 2 to 19. If we then line up the same 20 people according to their weight, their rankings will change somewhat. However, because tall people generally weigh more than short people, the tallest people will tend to have higher ranks in the weight line and the shortest people will tend to have low ranks in that line. At the same time, the heavier people will tend to have higher ranks in the height line than will the lighter people. If we were to compute the correlation between height and weight, it would be positive rather than zero (because height and weight are *positively correlated*) but less than 1.0 (because some tall people are skinny and some short people are fat). The coefficient tells us how similar the height and weight rankings are. In other words, *a correlation coefficient tells us how similar the rankings of a group of people are on the two measures being correlated*.[1] A zero correlation tells us that there is no correspon-

---

1. The actual *distance* between people who occupy adjacent ranks can also affect the correlation, but the comparative rankings are the most important determinant of the size of the correlation coefficient.

dence between the rankings of the people on the two variables, while a negative correlation tells us that there is an inverse correspondence; that is, people who have high ranks on one measure tend to have low ranks on the other, and vice versa. If we compared 20 people's rankings on income with rankings on family size, we would probably find a negative correlation because people with high incomes tend to have fewer children than do people with low incomes. (For a much more detailed discussion of the meaning and computation of a correlation coefficient, see the appendix).

The correlation coefficient is a very powerful statistic, not only because it tells us how two measures are related (positively, negatively, or not at all) but also the strength of the relationship. The correlation coefficient is thus the basic statistic used in most of the more complex statistical analyses like multiple regression and factor analysis (see below). One limitation of the correlation coefficient is that the mathematical model on which it is based assumes that the two measures satisfy some rather stringent assumptions (for example, that the shapes of their frequency distributions are normal). However, a number of technical studies have shown that the correlation coefficient is extremely robust, meaning that it is still a highly useful statistic even when the measures do not satisfy the classical assumptions.[2]

Cross-tabulations, correlations, and other statistics that describe the relationship between two variables might be characterized as *bridge* statistics between descriptive and causal analyses since they can be used both descriptively and causally. We might find, for example, that there is a positive correlation between the students' scores on the GRE Quantitative test and the number of science courses they have taken in college. A conservative investigator might simply report this correlation as a descriptive statistic without suggesting any causal relationship between the two variables. Other investigators, however, might interpret such a correlation as evidence that taking courses in science can enhance one's performance on the GRE Quantitative test. As pointed out in chapter 2, such causal interpretations of correlations between environmental and outcome measures are hazardous, especially when no

---

2. About the only assumption that absolutely must be satisfied is that the variables involved in computing the correlation coefficient are ordinal in nature. By ordinal, we mean that each successively higher score on the variable indicates that the person possesses more of the particular trait being measured. Consequently, purely qualitative variables such as the student's race or choice of major field, where the actual values assigned to each category are arbitrary, should never be used in computing correlation coefficients. Instead, one should create a separate "dummy" variable for each of the different qualitative categories. Thus, to be able to correlate the student's race with anything else we would first have to convert each racial category (black, white, Asian, and so on) into a separate dummy variable. Note that a dummy variable is, by definition, ordinal because one category represents all of the quality being measured while the other category represents none of that quality. Thus, the dummy variable for Asian would be scored either 1 (Asian) or 0 (not Asian).

effort has been made to control student input variables. Nevertheless, educators can and do interpret many such simple correlations in causal terms. Indeed, the very reporting of a simple correlation between an environmental measure and an outcome measure tends to encourage such causal thinking.

CAUSAL ANALYSES

During the many years that I have worked with a variety of institutions on assessment matters, I have come to realize that assessment data that are analyzed primarily for descriptive purposes are of very little use because they are easily subject to misinterpretation and because they may serve to discourage institutions from further attempts at systematic assessment. At best, purely descriptive analyses will be construed as "interesting"; at worst, such data generate the "So what?" reaction (see the next chapter). Causal analyses, on the other hand, are less likely to generate such reactions because they ordinarily deal more directly with the "why" and "how" of educational outcomes. Causal analyses, in other words, are concerned with understanding how student development (from input to outcome) is affected by educational practice (the environment). Clearly, causal analyses have much more direct implications for the formulation of educational policy and the improvement of educational practice than do descriptive analyses.

As shown earlier in chapter 2, the I-E-O model provides a convenient framework for conducting causal analyses using assessment data. Now let us employ some real assessment data to illustrate how cross-tabulation and regression can be used to implement the I-E-O model.

Cross-Tabulations

The examples of cross-tabulation analyses provided in the preceding section involve only two variables. If we wish to apply the I-E-O model using cross-tabulations, we need at least three variables: one each for input, environment, and output. Let's consider how we can use cross-tabulation to do a simple causal analysis of the effect of an environmental variable on an outcome measure. For this illustration the student's response to the value of "promoting racial understanding" in the 1986 follow-up survey has been selected as the dependent or outcome measure. The relevant input variable is the student's response to this same value question four years earlier in 1982 (i.e., the pretest). The environmental measure is a simple dichotomy formed by selecting the two majors whose students showed the greatest differential change between 1982 and 1986 (see table 6.4). When they started college in the fall of 1982, the engineering students were twice as likely as the fine arts students (44 percent versus 20 precent) to say that promoting

TABLE 6.4 **Importance of Promoting Racial Understanding Effects of Two Different Majors**

| | | PERCENTAGE RESPONDING | | | |
| | | Essential or Very Important in | | Not Important in | |
MAJOR IN 1982	N	1982	1986	1982	1986
Fine arts	42	20	65	10	5
Engineering	68	44	23	9	23

Note: Responses of "Somewhat important" are not shown.

racial understanding was either essential or very important. By 1986 the relative positions of these two groups of students had actually reversed so that the fine arts students were much more likely to endorse this value than were the engineering students (65 percent versus 23 percent). A complementary pattern emerged for the response of *not important*. Whereas in 1982 roughly equal percentages of fine arts and engineering majors (10 percent and 9 percent, respectively) indicated that promoting racial understanding was not important, by 1986 the proportion of fine arts students giving this answer was down to only 5 percent while the percentage of engineering majors giving this response had more than doubled to 23 percent.

It should be emphasized that the use of the term *effects* in table 6.4 may be presumptuous, since there are many other input characteristics of the fine arts and engineering students that might have contributed to the differential changes. The fine arts group, for example, is likely to contain a substantially higher proportion of women than is the engineering group. Possibly, women are more likely than men to become more interested in promoting racial understanding during the undergraduate years. Indeed, there are probably many other ways in which fine arts and engineering majors differ from each other at the time of college entry; any one of these differential characteristics could, in theory, affect how their values developed during college. Nevertheless, the differential changes are so great as to raise the possibility that the environmental experiences of fine arts and engineering students during the undergraduate years encourage quite different attitudes toward the importance of promoting racial understanding.

The three-way cross-tabulation shown in table 6.4 could be elaborated to include a fourth variable such as gender. It is possible to control any number of input variables using cross-tabulation, provided the sample size is sufficiently large. Sooner or later, however, it becomes practically impossible to use cross-tabulation to control a large number of variables, not only because the number of cases in any cell is likely to become too small for reliable results, but also because multidimensional cross-tabulations become extremely difficult to interpret.

Correlation and Regression Analysis

A much more powerful and efficient technique for controlling large numbers of variables at the same time is multiple regression analysis. Multiple regression is a procedure whereby the investigator can use two or more independent (input) measures to predict a dependent (outcome) measure. The example of multiple regression analysis used here will be a simple one designed to illustrate how the technique can be employed in conducting an I-E-O analysis. Readers who want more information or more complex examples of the application of this technique are advised to consult the appendix.

Suppose we are interested in finding better ways to prepare our undergraduate students for admission to graduate or professional school. As many graduate schools use the Graduate Record Examination (GRE) general test as one of the criteria for deciding which applicants to admit, being able to help students get better GRE scores has a lot of practical value for students who are headed for graduate school. Moreover, if we assume that the GRE is measuring important skills and talents that we are trying to develop during the undergraduate years, scores on this test can be regarded as a kind of outcome measure for assessing the effectiveness of our undergraduate programs.

How, then, do we go about identifying environmental factors that affect the student's performance on the Graduate Record Examination? For this illustration we shall pick two outcome measures (the GRE Verbal [GRE-V] and the GRE Quantitative [GRE-Q] tests), one environmental measure (the student's undergraduate major classified as being in science or engineering versus nonscience), and three input variables: SAT Verbal (SAT-V) and Math (SAT-M) scores (the pretests for the GRE) and the student's sex (female $=1$, male $=0$). Normally we would use more than three input variables to control as much input bias as possible, but to simplify this illustration we shall use only these three.

The basic ingredients used in multiple regression and other multivariate statistical procedures are the *correlations* among the independent variables. Table 6.5 shows all the correlations among the two outcome and three input variables. Not surprisingly, the largest correlations are between each of the outcome measures and their corresponding input (pretest) measures. Thus, the SAT-Verbal score correlates .85 with the GRE Verbal score, and the SAT Math score correlates .84 with the GRE Quantitative score. Considering that the interval of time involved here is four years, these are very high correlations, suggesting that the SAT and the GRE are measuring very much the same qualities. Being female has substantial negative correlations with the SAT-M ($-.50$) and

TABLE 6.5 Correlations between Input and Outcome Measures ($N = 97$)

MEASURE	SAT-V	SAT-M	GRE-V	GRE-Q
SAT Verbal				
SAT Math	.23			
GRE Math	.85	.30		
GRE Quantitative	.21	.84	.27	
Female	.00	−.50	.07	−.43

Source: Data on UCLA undergraduates who applied to graduate school in 1985.

the GRE-Q (−.43). Women, in short, get substantially lower scores on the Mathematical and Quantitative tests than the men do. Being female is uncorrelated (.00) with the SAT-V, and has a very weak positive correlation (.07) with the GRE-V, meaning that women earn slightly higher scores than men do on the latter measure and that women and men get virtually identical mean scores on the former.

The next step is to conduct two separate regression analyses using the two GRE scores as the dependent variables. It is a characteristic of multiple regression that only one dependent (outcome) variable can be utilized in any given analysis, although the number of independent (input or environmental) variables is limited only by the capacity of the computer software and hardware. The idea is that in any given regression analysis, we are trying to get the best possible prediction or estimate of a particular dependent variable. In the present example we thus conducted two regression analyses, one for each GRE score. In each analysis, the two SAT scores and gender were used as the three independent (input) variables.

The main product of any regression analysis is a mathematical formula which, when used in conjunction with the independent variables, produces the best possible estimate or prediction of the dependent variable. Table 6.6 shows the two formulas provided by the two regression analyses. Note that the formula for predicting the GRE Verbal score uses all three input variables. This means that all three of the input variables contributed independently to the prediction or estimation of the GRE Verbal score. To use this formula for estimating the GRE Verbal score, one would simply (a) multiply the SAT-V by .85, the SAT-M by .23, and gender (being female) by 41.7, (b) sum the three products, and (c) subtract the constant a (−127.6). The formula for estimating the GRE Quantitative score is much simpler since only the SAT-M score proved to have any predictive power. Thus, to estimate a person's GRE Quantitative score, one needs only to multiply the SAT-M by .997 and add the result to 35.4.

TABLE 6.6 Regression Formulas for Predicting GRE Scores

GRE SCORE (DEPENDENT VARIABLE)		CONSTANT (a)		COEFFICIENT (b) TO BE MULTIPLIED BY		
				SAT-V	SAT-M	*Female*
Verbal	=	−121.0	+	+.85	.23	41.7
Quantitative	=	35.4	+		.997	

How can these formulas be used to estimate the effect of the student's major on GRE performance? The logic behind the use of regression formulas for this purpose is as follows. The formulas shown in Table 6.6 enable us to estimate what a student's GRE score *should* be, given his or her SAT scores and gender four years earlier at the time of admission to college. In other words, they permit us to answer the question, "What GRE score would we *expect* this student to obtain, given his or her SAT scores and gender at the time of college entry four years earlier?" For example, a female freshman with a SAT-V of 650 and a SAT-M of 600 would be expected to get a GRE-V score of 611.2. A student of either sex with a SAT-M score of 400 would be expected to get a GRE-Q score of 434.2. (Readers are invited to check these computations for themselves to see how the formulas actually work.)

If we were to perform these calculations on each student in our sample, we would have an estimated GRE-V and estimated GRE-Q score for each student based upon his or her entering freshman characteristics. An important characteristic of these estimated scores is that if we were to average them across all students in the sample, the average estimated score would be equal to the average actual score. (See the appendix for more details.) However, the average expected score does not have to equal the average actual score for any *subgroup* of students. What if we were to examine the average GRE scores for just science and engineering majors? Would the average estimated score for this subgroup also equal their average actual score? If majoring in science or engineering has no effect on GRE performance, we would expect the average *actual* GRE scores of science and engineering students to be the same as their average *estimated* scores based on SAT and gender. But if majoring in science and engineneering has a positive effect on the GRE-Q score, then we should expect to find that the actual GRE-Q score for science and engineering majors is higher than the expected score based on their entering freshman characteristics.

Table 6.7 shows the results of such an analysis of the effects of majoring in science or engineering on the student's GRE-V and GRE-Q scores. Note that science and engineering students' expected mean score

TABLE 6.7 Effects of Majoring in Science or Engineering on
GRE Performance (N = 56 Science or Engineering
Majors)

GRE SCORE	ACTUAL MEAN SCORE	EXPECTED[a] MEAN SCORE	DIFFERENCE (EFFECT)
Verbal	491.8	536.6	−44.8
Quantitative	700.1	642.0	+58.1

[a] Based on formulas from Table 6.6.

on the GRE Verbal is 536.6, but that their actual mean score of 491.8 is
44.8 points lower. This result shows that students who major in science
or mathematics do not do as well on the GRE-V as one would expect
from their entering SAT scores and gender. The reverse pattern occurs
with the GRE Quantitative score: the actual score (700.1) exceeds the
expected mean score (642.0) by fully 58.1 points. Thus, although these
students had a very high expected score on the GRE Quantitative test,
their actual score was nearly 60 points higher.

This pattern of effects is exactly what one would predict: students
who major in science or mathematics during their undergraduate years
will enhance their quantitative skills relative to their skill level at the
time they entered college as freshmen, and their verbal skills will not
develop as far as expected from freshman characteristics. As one would
expect, precisely the opposite pattern of effects is associated with majoring in a nonscience field: these students do better than expected on
the Verbal GRE and worse than expected on the Quantitative GRE.

Multiple regression analysis is an excellent statistical procedure with
which to implement the I-E-O assessment model because it permits the
investigator to control a very large number of potentially biasing student
input characteristics. Note that the regression formula allows the investigator to express the entering characteristics of the student in terms of
an expected output score. By comparing the expected and actual output scores of students who experienced different types of environments
(such as majors, place of residence, financial aid, and special programs),
we can evaluate the effects of almost any environmental variable on the
outcomes of interest. How much confidence educators can place in these
effects depends primarily on the adequacy with which potentially biasing student input characteristics have been controlled. In the example
shown in the last few tables, we could not place much confidence in
any effects derived from an analysis that was not able to include some
kind of cognitive pretest such as the SAT. And while the pretest on

the outcome measure is by far the most important input characteristic to control, the pretest is almost never the only biasing input characteristic. Note that in the simple illustrative example given here, the student's gender added substantially to the prediction of GRE Verbal scores. If we had included more student input characteristics in the analysis, some of them would surely have been found to add to the prediction of both GRE scores. A general rule of thumb for evaluating causal analysis is that the more inputs one controls, the greater confidence one can have that the observed environmental effects are indeed true effects. (See the appendix for a much more thorough discussion of this issue.)

The foregoing example using GRE scores as the dependent variable was designed to test the effect of a *within*-college environmental variable, science versus nonscience major. Another way to approach the analysis of assessment data is to compare your own institution's results with data from other institutions. We might, for example, want to know how our institution's retention rate compares with the rates of other institutions in the state or nationally. To illustrate using regression to test such *between*-college effects, we can use the same three measures of retention shown earlier in tables 6.2 and 6.3. Retention data on random samples of 1984 freshmen were provided by institutions in the fall of 1988. Stepwise regression analysis was conducted using SAT scores provided by the institutions and items from the 1984 freshman questionnaires as independent (input) variables. The two input variables showing the strongest predictive power were the students' high school grades and SAT scores. Table 6.8 shows how retention rates vary as a function of high school grades and SAT scores. More than 80 percent of those students who have both the highest grades and the highest test scores complete degrees in four years, contrasted to less than 10 percent with the lowest grades and test scores. Note that since the percentages increase consistently across the rows as well as up the columns, grades and test scores both contribute independently to the student's chances of completing a degree. (As results for the other two retention measures show similar patterns, we shall confine the rest of this discussion to the most severe retention measure; completing a bachelor's degree in four years.)

The actual regression analysis ultimately used thirty-three variables to predict retention. In other words, each of thirty-three different student input characteristics was shown to carry some independent predictive weight in the stepwise regression. Not surprisingly, variables related to the student's academic preparation carried by far the largest predictive weights in the analysis. Figure 6.1 shows these variables in graphic form to illustrate their relative predictive power. The figure shows nine entering freshman characteristics, identified in the left-hand column. Corresponding to each characteristic is a dark horizontal bar.

TABLE 6.8 **Percentage Receiving Bachelor's Degrees, by High School Grades and Test Scores in Four-Year Colleges and Universities: 1984 Freshman Followed up in 1988**

Average Grade in High School	SAT Verbal + Math Score[a]					
	Less than 700	700–849	850–999	1,000–1,149	1,150–1,299	1,300 or more
A, A+	—	—	40	58	68	82
A−	—	45	39	55	64	65
B+	—	25	38	50	55	63
B	12	26	29	41	46	—
B−	10	15	27	34	—	—
C+	7	17	—	—	—	—
C	—	7	—	—	—	—

Source: Cooperative Institutional Research Program, Higher Education Research Institute

[a] Act scores have been converted to SAT equivalents following Astin, Henson, and Christian (1978).

The length of the bar indicates the relative importance of that variable as far as its effects on retention are concerned. (For the statistically inclined reader, the width of each black bar is proportional to its standardized regression coefficient or beta weight.) The vertical gray line in the middle of the chart corresponds to the mean or average score on each of the variables as well as to the average expected retention rate of 39 percent. If a person got an average score on each entering characteristic, that person's estimated retention chances would be 39 percent. We can illustrate how to interpret this chart with the first variable, the SAT composite score. If a person scored extremely low, somewhere in the 400s, that person's expected retention rate would be cut by one-fourth, from 39 percent to 29 percent. On the other hand, if a person were able to achieve a very high score of 1500, this would add about the same amount, yielding an expected retention probability of 49 percent. If we take the next variable, average high school grades, having an A average in high school adds nearly 11 percent to the chances of completing a bachelor's degree in four years, whereas having only a C average reduces the chances by 20 percent.

As the horizontal bars for SAT and high school grades are much longer than the bars for the other variables, these two entering freshman characteristics are clearly much more important than the others. Most of the other predictors relate to the number of high school courses the student has taken in various subject-matter areas: with the exception

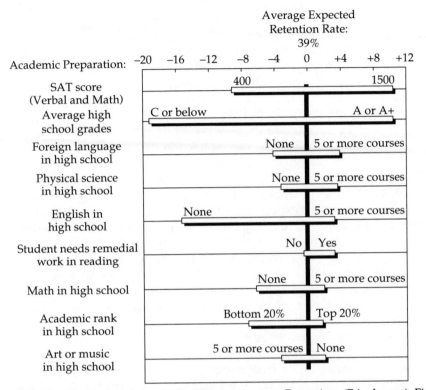

FIGURE 6.1 Effect of Academic Preparation on Retention (BA degree) Final Regression Equation (Effect Sizes in Percentages, 1988 Follow-up of 1984 Freshmen)

of courses in art and music, the more courses taken in any area, the better. Judging from the length of the bars, secondary school courses in English are more important factors in retention than are courses in other fields.

Readers may wonder why the vertical gray line representing the average expected retention rate does not bisect each horizontal black line in the middle. The reason is that the horizontal black bars have been located according to the position of their mean scores. To illustrate, with the second variable, high school grades, more of the black line is to the left of the vertical gray line than to the right because the *mean* high school grade is closer to the A end of the grade continuum than it is to the C end.

It would be theoretically possible to develop a chart showing all thirty-three freshman characteristics that predicted retention rather than just the nine academic characteristics shown in figure 6.1. However, to conserve space we will not present these here; readers should remember that these other input characteristics involve such things as the student's expectations for college, socioeconomic background, and values and attitudes. With few exceptions, the horizontal black bars for these twenty-four other variables would be relatively short, indicating that their individual contribution to the prediction of retention is very modest.

Keep in mind that this thirty-three-variable equation was developed using data from students at several hundred institutions across the country. The same formula can be used to calculate an expected retention rate at any college in the country; the only constraint is that the institution must have available the relevant information on the thirty-three student input characteristics for each of its entering freshmen. If we were to calculate expected retention rates for each of the several hundred institutions that participate in our annual freshman survey, we would find that they differ markedly from one institution to another. Some institutions would have expected retention rates of less than 20 percent, whereas others would have expected retention rates above 70 percent. This is not surprising, considering that American higher education institutions differ so greatly in the characteristics of the students they admit.

Our regression equation permits an institution not only to calculate its expected retention rate but also to understand why that expected retention rate may deviate from the population average of 39 percent. This can be illustrated with examples taken from an institution that had a very high expected rate—61 percent—rather than the average rate of 39 percent. What is it about the freshmen at this institution that leads us to expect a much higher retention rate than at the typical institution? By looking at the mean scores for that institution's entering freshmen on the relevant variables, we can discover precisely why the students at that institution were expected to have a much higher than average retention rate. Figure 6.2 illustrates how to approach this question. In this particular institution—which we shall call Western Mythical University—the major factor accounting for the higher retention rate is the students' high SAT scores. Other factors include the high educational level of their parents, the large percentage of students who have taken several years of foreign language, and their above-average high school grades.

After the expected retention rate is computed based on entering student characteristics, an institution is now in a position to evaluate its own retention rate. Is the actual retention rate higher than expected, lower than expected, or about as expected? It is not surprising that institutions' actual retention rates tend to correspond reasonably well with their expected retention rates. Nevertheless, there are several in-

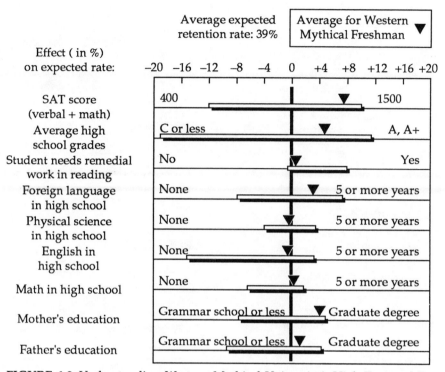

FIGURE 6.2 Understanding Western Mythical University's High Expected Retention Rate: 61 Percent versus 39 Percent

stitutions for which two rates differ by a substantial amount, indicating that these institutions are doing something different that makes their actual retention rate deviate from the expected rate. What is it in the environment of these institutions that explains the deviation? To answer this question let's examine another institution which we shall call Acme College, to understand why its actual retention rate (22 percent) is so much lower than its expected rate (39 percent) based on entering freshman characteristics. Recall that the regression analysis for predicting retention identified thirty-three entering freshman characteristics that predicted retention. Once having controlled for these entering freshman characteristics by calculating an expected rate and subtracting it from the actual rate, it is then possible to determine whether any measurable environmental characteristics of institutions add anything to the prediction of retention. As it turns out, there are several such environmental characteristics that we identified in our analysis of these same data. By examining how Acme College's environment differs from the typical college environment, we come a little closer to being able to explain its lower than expected retention rate.

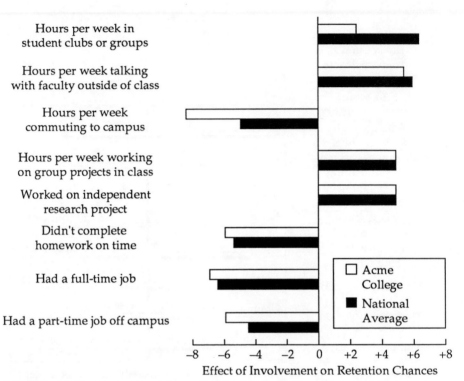

Hours per week in
student clubs or groups

Hours per week talking
with faculty outside of class

Hours per week
commuting to campus

Hours per week working
on group projects in class

Worked on independent
research project

Didn't complete
homework on time

Had a full-time job

Had a part-time job off campus

☐ Acme
College

■ National
Average

-8   -6   -4   -2   0   +2   +4   +6   +8

Effect of Involvement on Retention Chances

FIGURE 6.3 Understanding Acme College's Lower than Expected Retention Rate: 22 Percent versus 33 Percent

Figure 6.3 shows a chart that can be used to understand, at least in part, why Acme College's retention rate is lower than expected. The horizontal bars in figure 6.3 come in pairs: the gray bar shows the data for Acme College and the black bar shows data on the same environmental variable for institutions nationally. For illustrative purposes we have selected those environmental variables that indicate the level of involvement shown by undergraduates. (Involvement has been found to be a major factor affecting student retention; see Astin, 1975, 1977, 1982.)

It would appear that Acme College's low retention rate can be at least partially explained in terms of three environmental variables: a relatively low degree of involvement by students in clubs or groups, a greater than average amount of time devoted to commuting, and a higher than average number of students holding part-time jobs off campus. Is there anything that Acme might do about these involvement variables to improve its retention rate? As far as commuting time is concerned, there might be little the college can do since it is not in a very good position to control commuting time. As a long-range strategy, of course, it might consider building more residential facilities, but in the short term there may not be much that can be done. One remote possibility is to try to take advantage of the commuting time as a possible learning experience. Students might be encouraged to tape record some of their classroom lectures, or faculty might be encouraged to supply students with tape-recorded materials that they can play on their car cassettes while commuting to and from school. Still another possibility might be to provide special orientation or counseling for students who have to commute over substantial distances to help them make better use of their time while on campus, to help them understand the problems posed by commuting, and to help them devise compensatory strategies.

The other areas of deviation offer much more hopeful prospects for significant change. On the matter of involvement with student clubs or groups, there are several possibilities. One obvious approach would be to expand the number and quality of student organizations, with special attention to the unique interests and needs of the student clientele at Acme College. Students could also be given special encouragement during student orientation and registration to participate in such organizations.

For the third factor, holding a part-time job off campus, the implications are very clear: if Acme College can find a way to develop more part-time employment opportunities on the campus, it might reap a double benefit in terms of retention. First, this action would obviate the need for students to hold part-time jobs off campus (which has a negative effect on retention), and it would involve more students in on-campus employment, a condition that has been shown in previous research to have a positive effect on retention (Astin, 1975, 1977).

The example of predicted and actual retention rates shown here has been taken from regression analyses that involved all types of institutions across the country. It may well be that some institutions would rather compare their retention rates with what they consider to be comparable peer institutions (for example, state colleges or Catholic liberal arts colleges). Regression formulas like the one used in these illustrations are available for different subgroups of institutions from the Higher Education Research Institute, along with similar formulas for institutions nationwide (Dey and Astin, 1989). Formulas are also available separately for men and women and for different ethnic minority subgroups, allowing institutions that wish to focus on a particular subpopulation to employ the specific formula and norms developed for that population.

The reader should note that the analysis just described of between-institution characteristics can also be done by an individual institution on a local basis without any national data. That is, if an institution were to collect data on its students similar to what we collect for our national freshman and follow-up surveys, it can develop institution-wide formulas and apply them to different environmental subunits within the institution. *Subunits* refers to schools, departments, resident and commuter populations, full-time and part-time students, Educational Opportunity Program (EOP) or developmental students, and other units. By applying the overall institutional formulas to these various subpopulations, institutions can develop expected retention rates for each subpopulation to compare with their actual retention rates. Once again, such within-institution analyses are possible only if an institution has a data base containing input, environment, and output data (see chapter 8).

I-E-O SHORTCUTS

One drawback of the I-E-O model is that it normally requires the collection of longitudinal (input and outcome) data over a period of time before any tangible results can be produced. The resulting time lag between the decision to apply the I-E-O design and the availability of results can often serve to discourage institutions from undertaking the data collection needed to implement the model. While I believe that the best long-term solution to this dilemma is to start *now* to develop a comprehensive longitudinal student data base (see chapter 8), there are one or two short-term solutions that can help to stimulate and sustain faculty interest in assessment while the longitudinal assessment plan is being implemented. These two strategies are "satisfaction" studies and "quick-and-dirty" value-added analyses of talent development.

Satisfaction Studies

One of the most important areas of student outcome assessment is the student's satisfaction with various aspects of the undergraduate experience. It is possible to assess the student's degree of satisfaction with a wide range of undergraduate experiences (such as instruction, student support services, and facilities) by means of a simple list of items to which students respond on a satisfaction scale (e.g., very satisfied, satisfied, neutral, dissatisfied) (see chapter 3). In the most recent follow-up survey conducted in connection with the Cooperative Institutional Research Program (Hurtado et al., 1989), we assessed the student's satisfaction with twenty-seven different aspects of the undergraduate experience.

Of all the types of student outcomes that have been studied so far in college impact studies, student satisfaction shows the weakest relation to student input characteristics. The multiple correlations between most satisfaction measures and student input characteristics tend to be very low (generally much less than .20), and weaker than the correlation of satisfaction with environmental experiences (Astin, 1977). Virtually every other type of outcome measure is more strongly correlated with student input characteristics than with environmental characteristics. In other words, student satisfaction seems to be the only type of college outcome that is not heavily dependent on student input characteristics.

The practical significance of the weak association between student input characteristics and student satisfaction with college is that causal inferences based on correlations between environmental characteristics and student satisfaction entail fewer risks of error than do causal inferences involving most other kinds of outcome measures. This is not to say that the risk of making erroneous causal inferences is completely eliminated when we study the outcome of student satisfaction (student input does, after all, have weak but significant correlations with most satisfaction outcomes; see Astin, 1977); what it does mean is that the risks are smaller, especially when there are strong associations between satisfaction and environmental experiences.

We can look at a concrete example that once again uses the student's major as the environmental variable. The first two columns of table 6.9 show overall satisfaction rates across thirteen different majors. Students in communications and sociology report the highest overall satisfaction rates whereas students in the biological sciences, history, and engineering report the lowest rates. Somewhat surprisingly, the percentage of students who report being either neutral or dissatisfied does not follow very closely the percentage who are very satisfied. Indeed, the large majority of students report being either satisfied or very satisfied, so that the primary differences among majors are in whether they say they are very satisfied or merely satisfied. Note that it would be possible to show similar comparative percentages for commuters versus residents, freshman versus seniors, regularly admitted students versus those in developmental or remedial programs, athletes versus nonathletes, fraternity or sorority members versus nonmembers, or any other environmental variables. It may also be of interest to tabulate satisfaction rates by input characteristics such as sex, ethnicity, or socioeconomic level.

The last two columns in table 6.9 show satisfaction with courses in the major. Here we find more consistency in extreme responses, with the percentages reporting neutral or dissatisfied being highest among those fields in where the lowest percentages report being very satisfied. Although the ranking of majors in table 6.9 is similar to the ranking in table 6.8, some noticeable differences emerge. History, which was next to last in terms of overall satisfaction (table 6.8), shows the second highest degree of satisfaction with courses in the major (table 6.9). Interestingly, table 6.9 suggests that courses with considerable quantitative content (science, engineering, and economics) tend to get low ratings.

TABLE 6.9 Student's Satisfaction with the Overall College Experience and with Courses in the Major, by Major; 1982 Freshmen Followed up in 1986

	OVERALL		COURSES IN MAJOR	
FINAL 1986 MAJOR	"Very satisfied" (%)	"Neutral" or "Dissatisfied" (%)	"Very satisfied" (%)	"Neutral" or "Dissatisfied" (%)
Communications	52	17	64	9
Sociology	50	5	60	5
Political science	44	6	44	6
Economics	43	11	38	14
English	41	5	55	5
Psychology	38	9	54	16
Other majors	37	24	44	16
(All majors)	(37)	(14)	(46)	(14)
Mathematics	36	18	36	14
Fine arts	35	25	42	16
Electrical engineering	33	17	33	22
Other engineering	32	18	32	26
History	31	6	63	6
Biological sciences	21	14	40	17

Source: Higher Education Research Institute.

Note: "Satisfied" category has been omitted.

One way to present satisfaction results so as to pique the interest of individual departments is to provide summaries across a number of satisfaction questions. To illustrate this procedure we have taken the results from just six satisfaction items (overall, courses in major, opportunities to talk to professors, contact with faculty, academic advising, and computer facilities) and displayed them in table 6.10 for three different departments. Students majoring in mathematics tend to be dissatisfied with courses in the major, library facilities, and computer facilities, but very well satisfied with their academic advising. As a matter of fact, mathematics students reported the highest degree of satisfaction with academic advising, a result that might prompt some further investigation of their advising procedures to determine whether other departments might be able to learn from the way that the mathematics department does its academic advising. This would be especially true of the fine arts departments, given that their generally favorable pattern of student satisfaction is marred by a low rating on academic advising. Another interesting feature of table 6.10 is the high rating given to computer facilities by the electrical engineering students, in contrast to the low rating given by mathematics students. Perhaps this discrepant pattern has something to do with who controls the computer

TABLE 6.10 Satisfaction Patterns for Students in Three Different Majors

FINAL 1986 MAJOR	HIGH RATINGS	LOW RATINGS
Mathematics	Academic advising	Courses in the major Library facilities Computer facilities
Fine arts	Contacts with faculty Opportunity to talk with professors Overall quality of instruction Library facilities	Academic advising
Electrical engineering	Computer facilities	Courses in the major Contact with faculty

facilities, the types of facilities available, or the relative accessibility of these facilities to students in the two departments. Whatever the reason, these contrasting patterns would suggest that it might be useful for the mathematics and engineering departments to discuss the possible reasons for the discrepant ratings. Note that the possibility for such follow-up investigation and self-study would be even greater if we were to present the results for all twenty-seven satisfaction items and every individual major.

"Quick-and-Dirty" Assessment of Talent Development

The time lag between the collection of input and outcome data is one of the prime deterrents to the implementation of the I-E-O model. Educators and policy makers tend to avoid data-collection exercises that do not produce usable results more or less immediately. One simple way around this problem is to ask the students themselves to make an estimate of how much change has occurred between input and outcome. For a number of years we have been doing this with our national follow-up survey by means of an item which reads: "Compared with when you entered college as a freshman, how would you now describe your—." This statement is followed by a list of nineteen skills, talents, or other qualities such as general knowledge, analytical and problem-solving skills, ability to think critically, foreign language skills, and job-related skills. Students indicate whether they believe that their current skill level, compared to the freshman (input) level, is much stronger, stronger, no change, weaker, or much weaker.

Such "quick-and-dirty" assessments of value-added or talent development are clearly no substitute for actual before-and-after assessments of input and outcome skill levels, but they can produce some interesting information for institutional debate and discussion. One recent study (Astin, 1989) indicated that while there is a considerable amount of error in such retrospective reports, they do tend to have some validity. Students who report that a particular talent is much stronger tend to show larger true pretest-posttest gains than do students who report "no change" or "weaker." Even so, such retrospective self-reports should not be accepted uncritically as a completely adequate substitute for real before-and-after assessments, simply because there is a substantial amount of error in the reports and the degree of accuracy varies substantially according to the particular quality being assessed (Astin, 1989).

Such self-reported gains can produce interesting material for self-evaluation and discussion. Table 6.11 shows results at Western University for one self-reported growth measure: improvement in writing skills. It is not surprising that English majors reported by far the highest rate of improvement in writing skills, with twice as many students (73 percent) reporting much stronger skills than the next-highest field, political science (37 percent). Bringing up the rear are the biological sciences and engineering, two majors in which students are unlikely to get much practice in developing their writing skills. More than half the students majoring in electrical engineering reported that their writing skills showed either no change or were weaker at the time of the follow-up than when they entered college as freshmen.

It is also possible to apply quick-and-dirty value-added assessments to affective outcomes. Table 6.12 shows the results at Western University for one such outcome: ability to work independently. Here we find the highest rates of growth among students in political science, fine arts, and communications; the lowest rates are found among students in engineering and economics. More students in these latter fields reported "no change" or "weaker" than reported "much stronger." Certainly these findings ought to be regarded as a possible cause for concern among faculty in these departments.

INTERACTION EFFECTS

Interaction effects are among the most important results that can emerge from any analysis of assessment data. At the same time, the interaction effect is one of the most difficult statistical concepts to grasp. There are two conceptual difficulties here that must be overcome: the *meaning* of an interaction effect, and its *practical significance*.

What are Interaction Effects?

What, precisely, do we mean by an interaction effect? First, we must be precise about terminology. In common usage we might speak of

TABLE 6.11 Self-Reported Growth in Writing Skills, by
Major: 1982 Freshman Followed up in 1986

FINAL 1986 MAJOR	MUCH STRONGER (%)	NO CHANGE OR WEAKER (%)
English	73	0
Political science	37	3
Sociology	35	10
Communications	35	13
Fine arts	30	20
Other majors	30	14
Economics	27	22
(All majors)	(26)	(18)
History	25	6
Mathematics	18	23
Other engineering	18	39
Psychology	12	14
Biological sciences	12	24
Electrical engineering	6	56

"interactions" among students, among faculty, or between faculty and students, usually meaning a kind of reciprocal give-and-take: the respective parties may carry on a dialogue, spend time together, or engage in other similar activities. This is *not* what we mean when we speak of interaction effects in analyzing assessment data. In data analysis an interaction effect occurs when the effect of one variable on another depends upon the value of a third variable. If the effect of an environmental variable on some student outcome variable is not the same for men and women, we would say that the particular environmental variable interacts with an input variable (in this case, the variable of gender). Suppose the environmental variable was place of residence (on campus versus off campus), and the outcome variable was retention (persisted versus dropped out). If on-campus living has a strong positive effect on retention among women but a different effect among men, we would say that, when it comes to their effects on retention, there is an interaction effect between place of residence and sex. The different effect on retention among the men could mean a stronger positive effect, a weaker positive effect, no effect, or even a negative effect. As long as the effect of place of residence is not the same for men as it is for women, we have an interaction effect.

Note that an interaction effect always involves at least three variables: the outcome (dependent variable), and the two independent (interacting) variables. Since these independent variables can be any com-

TABLE 6.12 Self-Reported Growth in Ability to
Work Independently, by Major:
1982 Freshman Followed up in 1986

FINAL 1986 MAJOR	MUCH STRONGER (%)	NO CHANGE OR WEAKER (%)
Political science	55	8
Fine arts	55	15
Communications	48	9
Sociology	40	15
History	38	13
(All majors)	(33)	(22)
English	32	41
Biological sciences	31	21
Psychology	29	24
Other majors	29	27
Mathematics	23	18
Electrical engineering	22	28
Economics	22	30
Other engineering	21	29

bination of input and environmental variables, there are three types of simple interaction effects (see table 6.13).[3]

Any simple interaction effect can be described in two ways. In the first example (table 6.13), we might say that the effect of place of residence is different for men than it is for women, but we could also say that the effect of sex on retention is not the same for commuters as it is for residents. Or, in the last example, we could say that the effect of place of residence on retention is different among honors program participants than it is among nonparticipants.

So far we have been discussing interaction effects involving categorical or "dummy" variables, that is, variables such as gender that have only two possible values (male or female). Interactions involving continuous variables such as SAT or GRE scores involve exactly the same principle, but interpreting and describing such effects is a bit more difficult. For example, if we found an interaction between place of residence and SAT scores, we might say that the effect of place of residence (dormitory living versus commuting) on retention among high-scoring students is different from its effect on retention among low-scoring stu-

---

3. When two independent variables interact, we say there is a *simple* interaction effect. *Higher order* interactions involving more than two independent variables will not be considered here.

TABLE 6.13 Simple Interaction Effects

Type of Interaction	Example
Input-environment	Effects of place of residence (on campus versus commuting) on retention is different for men that it is for women.
Input-input	Effect of sex on retention is different for blacks than it is for whites.
Environment-environment	Effect of participation in honors programs on retention is different for commuters than it is for residents.

dents. Suppose retention is once again our outcome measure and we find an interaction between place of residence (dormitory living versus commuting) and SAT scores. Just where on the continuum of SAT scores does the interaction occur? Does place of residence affect retention differently for high-scoring, middle-scoring, or low-scoring students? We might find, for example, that living in a dormitory positively affects retention among low-scoring and middle-scoring students but has no effect among high-scoring students. We could say that the effect of SAT scores on retention is different among commuters than among residents, but describing the exact nature of such an effect accurately might prove difficult. In this connect we should note that interactions between environmental variables and input variables are usually described in the former sense, that is, how the environment affects the ouput separately by student type. (The detection of interaction effects requires the use of special procedures in the analysis of assessment data; see the appendix.)

The Practical Significance of Interaction Effects

In certain situations, a knowledge of interaction effects can be of considerably more value for educational policy and practice than a knowledge of simple ("main")[4] effects of environmental variables. For example, while it is useful to know that living in a residence hall on campus (compared to commuting) can be of significant benefit to students, it may not be practicable to build enough residential units to house all students. Under such conditions, it might be especially useful to know which types of students are most likely to benefit from the residential experience. Such knowledge can be of significant value in deciding which students should be selected to live in campus residence halls.

---

4. In statistical parlance the overall effect of any independent variable (ignoring all other independent variables) is called a *main effect*

Knowledge of interaction effects can be of significant value in a variety of other practical decision-making situations, but such knowledge is of special importance in two general types of situations: selection and placement. Let us consider each of these separately.

Selection decisions abound in American colleges and universities. We make such decisions when we decide which applicants to admit to our institution, whether to admit the applicant to various academic units within the institution (engineering, nursing, etc.), and whom to select for special treatment (remediation, probation, honors, etc.). As pointed out in chapter 1, any selection decision (and especially admissions decisions) can be made on the basis of two very different models: to maximize *outcome* performance, and to maximize learning or *talent development*. Since the former type of decision is concerned only with selecting those individuals who are most likely to perform well on an outcome measure and ignores the issue of talent development, it does not require any consideration of input-environment interaction effects. We will therefore focus this discussion on the question of how information on interaction effects can facilitate decisions that are intended to maximize talent development.

Consider the problem of how to select students for special programs. If we establish an honors program and decide that only students with GPAs above a certain level are eligible to participate in the program, we are implicitly assuming that such students will benefit more from the honors program than will students with lower GPAs. This kind of reasoning assumes an interaction between the environmental variable (honors participation versus nonparticipation) and an input variable (GPA). The outcome measure could be amount learned, retention, or some combination of such measures. It is important to realize that these assumptions are seldom made explicit when we establish special programs that necessitate selection decisions; indeed, most of us who participate in the implementation of such programs are probably not aware of the implicit assumptions that underlie our selection decisions. How do we know that arbitrary selection criteria such as minimum GPAs are really valid? How do we know that students who fail to meet these criterai will not benefit as much as, or even more than, those students who satisfy the criteria?

The notion that the particular group of selected students will benefit more than the other (rejected) students is really a very tricky concept. It does not mean just that the high GPA students will do better in the honors program than they would in the regular program[5] (this is not necessarily an interaction effect, since the same might be true of lower

5. In statistical parlance this would be called the *main effect*, meaning simply that the honors program benefits the students who participate, regardless of their GPAs.

GPA students). And it does not mean simply that if all students were allowed to participate in the honors program, the high GPA students would perform better than lower GPA students[6]. In other words, an interaction effect occurs only when the *effect* of one variable (e.g., honors participation versus nonparticipation) is different for people with different scores on another variable (e.g., GPA).

Consider what such interaction effects mean in practical terms. Remember that we are interested in getting the maximum educational mileage (measured in terms of talent development) from existing programs. If certain students benefit more than other students from certain programs, the overall talent development for all students considered as a group will be greatest if we are able to select the right students for the right program. If all students benefit equally from a given program (i.e., if there is no interaction between environment and input), then it really makes no difference how students are selected; the overall benefits to the entire student group will be the same regardless of who participates.

In short, selective admissions to an educational program contributes to the overall talent development process only when there are interaction effects between the program and the input variables used to admit students to the program.

Placement decisions are very much like selection decisions. In chapter 1 it was pointed out that selective admission to a particular institution is really a form of placement when viewed in a larger context, since the rejected students eventually end up somewhere. This is especially true in a three-tier public higher education system like California's, where some of the students who fail to qualify for admission to the university are eligible to be admitted to the state university, and where all the remaining students are eligible for admission to the community colleges. To rationalize such a system in educational (i.e., talent development) terms, it is necessary to assume an interaction effect between the environmental variable (university versus state university versus community college) and the input variable (high school grades). If the educational benefits of attending the University of California (UC) were no greater for the UC-eligible students (those who graduate in the top one-eighth of their high school classes) than for other students, there would really be no educational justification for limiting university access just to these students.

Most legislators and other public officials who determine admission policy for public institutions are not aware that these policies are inevitably based on assumptions about interaction effects. Thus, if one

---

6. Again, this would be just another main effect, meaning that high GPA students do better than low GPA students, regardless of whether they participate in honors programs.

wishes to justify the California Master Plan for Higher Education in educational terms, it is necessary to assume the following:

1. that students graduating in the top one-eighth of their high school classes will be more favorably influenced by attending the university than will students in the other seven-eighths of the class;
2. that students graduating in the top one-third of their classes will be more favorably influenced by attending the state university than will the other two-thirds of the graduates; and
3. that students graduating in the lower two-thirds of their class will be more favorably influenced by attending a community college than will students graduating in the top one-third.

The California Master Plan is also based on implicit assumptions about freedom of student choice. Since university-eligible students are not precluded from attending the state university or the community colleges, it is implicitly assumed that such students will benefit more than will other students from having a free choice among the three segments.

The three interaction assumptions listed above can also be rephrased in terms of the environmental variable, for example, "Students graduating in the lower two-thirds of their high school classes will be benefited more by attending a community college than by attending either of the university segments." Such assumptions, of course, have seldom, if ever, been tested empirically in any of our state systems.

But what about placement activities that occur on an individual campus? Most colleges regularly make a variety of student placement decisions: course placement, assignment of students to advisers, assignment of students to residence halls, assignment of roommates. Why are such activities implicitly based on the assumption of interaction effects? The reasoning process here is very much like what we just described for selection. For example, if we give each new freshman a battery of tests to guide our course placement decisions, we are implicitly assuming that only students who score above certain levels will do better in certain courses. Again, by "do better" we mean that they will learn best or learn fastest (i.e., develop their talents more fully) in the courses in which we place them. Thus, if we give all new freshmen a test of their competence in English composition, we might place the poorest performers in remedial English classes, the best performers in an advanced creative writing course, and the rest of the students in the regular English composition course. Such a placement system involves a complex set of assumptions about interaction effects:

1. the remedial course will benefit the lowest-scoring students more than will either of the other two courses.

2. the advanced course will benefit the highest-scoring students more than the remedial course or the regular course.
3. the regular course will benefit the remaining (middle-scoring) students more than either the remedial or the advanced course.

Such assumptions are seldom tested empirically, even though they are basic to any placement activity in which students are selectively assigned to particular educational environments on the basis of their input characteristics.

CONCLUSION

There are basically two types of data analyses that can be applied to assessment data: *descriptive* and *causal*. Descriptive analyses are concerned simply with describing the current state of affairs while causal analyses are designed to estimate the comparative effects of different environments on student outcomes.

The two most commonly used statistical techniques for analyzing assessment data are cross-tabulation and correlational analyses. Correlational and regression analyses are especially well suited to causal studies because they permit the investigator to control simultaneously a large number of potentially biasing input variables.

7

USE OF ASSESSMENT RESULTS

Proper utilization of assessment data has one primary objective: to stimulate actions that will ultimately enhance the talent development process. These actions can include changes in curriculum, pedagogical technique, advising procedures, assessment tools, faculty reward system, or sometimes merely a decision to review some aspect of institutional policy or practice.

Among the many issues surrounding optimal utilization of assessment results are identifying the proper audience for the assessment results, selecting methods of communicating the results, developing of assessment expertise within the faculty and staff, and dealing with resistance. Before addressing these specific issues, however, let us first consider the theoretical perspective from which we can approach the question of utilization.

A THEORY OF UTILIZATION

While some readers might be inclined to view a theory of utilization as a very abstract or even esoteric issue, the reality is that anyone who attempts to collect and utilize assessment data on a campus is operating on the basis of some kind of theory. All too frequently these theories are implicit rather than explicit. Most persons who are involved in assessment activities probably give relatively little attention to the implicit theory underlying their assessment activities. The theory of utilization summarized below is one that has evolved over the past two decades as a consequence of my heavy involvement in assessment activities at both the national and campus levels. This theory is only one of many possible ones. It is presented not as any final word on the utilization question but rather to emphasize that we all operate on the basis of some theory and that it is important for each of us involved in assessment activities to try to make our implicit theories as explicit as possible so they can be scrutinized. Readers who find this particular theory unsuitable are strongly encouraged to develop one of their own.

As might be assumed from the arguments presented in chapters 1 and 2, my own theory of utilization is predicated primarily on the feedback principle. I am assuming here that the recipient of the feedback is a faculty or staff person who is in a position to use the assessment results to improve the talent development process. (A similar discussion of feedback theory in which the student is the recipient is discussed in chapter 9.)

I have found it convenient to view college faculty, administrators, counselors, and other academic practitioners much like performing artists. Teaching, counseling, advising, and other forms of staff-student interaction are very much like artistic activities in the sense that one learns them by doing them and the learning process is not something that can be easily programmed in a "how to do it" manual. An essential ingredient in developing the technique and skills necessary for effective performance in an artistic endeavor is the opportunity to review the results of one's own work. People learn how to paint or draw by observing what comes out on the canvas and by subsequently adjusting their behavior. Similarly, instrumentalists or singers learn by listening to the results of their playing and singing and making appropriate adjustments. Feedback is at the heart of the process of developing technique or skill in any artistic endeavor.

While feedback is no doubt equally important in learning how to be an effective teacher, counselor, or administrator, these academic performing artists almost never have feedback as good or as immediate as that available to painters, dancers, or musicians. In the arts, useful sensory information is automatically generated by the very act of performing the art. In academe, however, teaching or counseling or administering a program does not usually generate the needed feedback. A professor may give what he or she believes to be a stimulating and provocative lecture and yet never really know how much of it was understood by students, how much of it will be retained, or what other effects it might have had on students. Similarly, a counselor or adviser may spend twenty minutes talking to a student without ever knowing whether the student benefited from the encounter. Or, administrators may establish certain policies and procedures concerning student conduct and never learn whether the policies or procedures had the desired impact on the students. In a sense, learning to become an effective teacher, counselor, or administrator is a little like learning to paint blindfolded or learning to play the piano with your ears plugged up.

It is true that faculty and staff periodically receive informal verbal feedback from students during class discussions, office visits, and informal encounters, but all too often these students are the "squeaky wheels" and not at all representative of the typical student. One could also argue that faculty members receive feedback on final examinations, but acting on the basis of such feedback is a little like closing the barn door after the horse has escaped.

The role of assessment is to enhance the feedback available to faculty and staff in order to assist them in becoming more effective practitioners. Assessment, in other words, is a technology that educational practitioners can use to enhance the feedback concerning the impact of their educational practices and policies. Even though performing artists can generate their own direct sensory feedback without technological aids, it is also true that they are willing to rely on technology to enhance feedback: for example, dancers use mirrors, musicians use recorders.

As noted above, the immediate purpose of assessment feedback is to generate action that will lead to improvements in the educational program. The actors in this context are, of course, the professors, counselors, administrators, and other members of the academic community whose actions impinge either directly or indirectly on the students. Their individual and collective actions help to create the educational environment to which students are exposed. However, since most practitioners have no means to connect their specific actions to student progress and development, it is difficult for them to know whether the environments they create are having their intended effects on student outcomes. A basic function of assessment, then, is to provide feedback that will enhance practitioners' understanding of the connections between their actions (the environment) and the talent development process (student outcomes). In short, the function of assessment is to provide educational practitioners with feedback concerning the causal connections between their policies and practices and various student outcomes.

THE "SO WHAT?" REACTION

Of all the faculty or administrator reactions that an assessment specialist can generate when presenting assessment results, the "So what?" reaction is not only one of the most frustrating and demoralizing but also one of the most destructive to the development of a comprehensive and useful assessment program. There are two circumstances in which we are likely to elicit this reaction. The first is a situation in which the negative reaction is a kind of ploy or game played by a faculty member or administrator who is hostile to the purposes of assessment. (This kind of defensiveness is discussed below under "Involving Faculty and Staff.") The second and more common situation occurs when the assessment results being presented have no obvious meaning or significance for policy or practice. Findings are presented, sometimes with a good deal of detail, but without a clear statement of the implications the results might have for educational policy or practice. The "So what?" reaction does not necessarily involve these particular words, but the message and its impact are the same. Sometimes the reaction is expressed merely as nonresponse or pure silence. At other times, the findings may be regarded merely as "interesting." To refer to findings as interesting with no further explanation and no suggestion for action is a virtual kiss of death.

I have personally witnessed the "So what?" reaction on more occasions than I would care to remember. We encountered this response on several campuses in connection with our value-added consortium project (see chapter 8). Results from a one-time administration of an unfamiliar standardized test were presented to various faculty groups in the absence of any environmental data. About the only thing these groups could do was to compare their students' performance with national "norms," and in most cases the results of the comparison were difficult if not impossible to explain. The net result was that the faculty groups generally rejected the whole assessment concept.

Despite its devastating consequences, the "So what?" reaction is likely to appear under conditions that are fairly easy to define. Further, the means for avoiding this response are readily available. The reaction is likely to occur when outcome data are reported in the absence of environmental data, or when environmental data are reported in the absence of outcome data. With the increasing enthusiasm of institutional researchers for trying out new assessment techniques, the indifferent reaction of faculty is becoming more common. Ironically, the purveyors of environmental and outcome assessment instruments have contributed to the problem by encouraging institutions to use their instruments on a one-shot basis without incorporating other data about the students.

"TEACHING TO THE TEST"

A more active form of resistance to assessment activities is the argument that the use of particular assessment instruments will encourage faculty to "teach to the test." This kind of reaction can, of course, reflect legitimate concerns. There may be fears that professors will circumscribe their course subject matter, homework assignments, and teaching methods so as to produce maximum student performance on a test. The test may also discourage experimentation.

One obvious strategy for getting around the problem of teaching to the test is to use multiple measures of student outcomes (see chapter 3) and to avoid total reliance on commercially developed instruments (which are difficult to change or modify). Nevertheless, there are certain circumstances under which teaching to the test may be appropriate, as when we are trying to evaluate student performance in a highly specialized area of knowledge or expertise. Classical test theory provides an interesting way of looking at this issue. Most of the major testing organizations have developed what they refer to as achievement tests that measure student competency in specific subject matter fields such as chemistry, mathematics, and American history. In theory, the test questions represent a random sample from a domain of all possible questions that might be asked about that subject matter. Assuming that the domain is appropriate to the aims of the course or program being evaluated, teaching to the test would seem to be an appropriate goal, as long as the test questions are a representative sample of questions from the relevant domain.

Many of us who teach college students, however, are inclined to forget that most of our students are already "studying for the test." In most cases this happens to be the test that we concoct for their final exam, one which is likely to be much more arbitrary and idiosyncratic and less well constructed than a nationally standardized test covering the same subject matter. In other words, our particular course examination is much less likely to include a representative sample of questions from the domain than is a nationally standardized test. The critical issue is whether the domain represented by the national examination is appropriate to the course in question.

Academics are also inclined to forget that we actively encourage teachers in the secondary schools to teach to the test. This is true not only for the college admissions tests (ACT, SAT, and various achievement tests), but especially for the Advanced Placement (AP) examinations. The success of teachers who teach AP classes in the secondary schools is ordinarily judged by the proportion of students who pass AP examinations (that is, who achieve high enough scores to receive course credit from higher education institutions). Jaime Escalante, the nationally recognized calculus teacher at Garfield High School in Los Angeles, achieved notice almost entirely because he succeeded in enabling a large proportion of the minority students in his calculus classes to pass the calculus AP examination. The popular movie, *Stand and Deliver*, was based on Escalante's life and teaching.

Teaching to the test is most likely to be acceptable to the faculty when they have personally developed the outcome assessment instruments. Two excellent examples of faculties that have successfully developed their own instruments are those of Alverno College (Mentkowski and Doherty, 1983) and Kean College (Kean College of New Jersey, 1986).

INVOLVING FACULTY AND STAFF

It is possible to collect and analyze a great deal of good assessment data without having support from the top administration or even without involving faculty members. However, when it comes to utilization of the results, there is simply no way that one can hope to make a difference with assessment data without the involvement of the faculty and the support of the administration. Strong administrative backing serves at least two critical functions: it provides the assessment specialists with an incentive to move ahead with the implementation of a systematic assessment program, and it maximizes the chances that any resulting recommendations will be put into action.

Faculty involvement is necessary for obvious reasons. Any change in the curriculum or in instructional methodology obviously must involve the faculty. Moreover, since faculty, especially those in the larger research institutions, are oriented primarily toward their disciplines and their departments, any recommendations for significant changes in these basic academic functions must gain departmental support if there is to be any hope of action based on the assessment findings. If significant changes in academic policy or procedures are recommended and key faculty members are not a party to their formulation, the changes are unlikely to be implemented.

Involving faculty in the development and implementation of assessment programs does not guarantee that proposed changes will be accepted by their faculty colleagues, since faculty are by nature inclined to resist change. One strategy for avoiding total dependence on faculty support is to concentrate significant parts of the assessment activities on nonacademic areas of institutional functioning, such as admissions, recruitment, orientation, advisement and counseling, job placement, co-curricular participation, and residential life. Changes in institutional policies and practices in these areas normally do not require the same degree of faculty support needed for changes in course requirements, teaching techniques, grading, advising, or other academic functions.

Another point to keep in mind is that most faculty are neither hostile to nor highly enthusiastic about assessment; they are, rather, indifferent or uninvolved. Indeed, if indifference were the only problem, the task of dissemination and utilization would be much easier. The difficulty is that the assessment specialist can usually expect to encounter one or more faculty members who are actively opposed to assessment and that these activists can often sway their otherwise uninvolved colleagues.

Academic Games

One of the most frustrating experiences encountered by those who attempt to implement significant change in academic institutions is the variety of defensive tactics that faculty can invoke to avoid coming to grips with significant proposals for reform. Some twenty years ago I was involved in a major attempt to use longitudinal assessment data on undergraduate students at nineteen different institutions to bring about change in institutional policy and practice (Astin, 1976). Task forces were appointed on each campus to examine the assessment results and based on these, to devise proposals for change. Our analyses of the behavior of these task forces revealed a wide variety of defensive strategies used by faculty to avoid any significant action. In a paraphrase of Eric Berne's (1964) best-selling book *Games People Play*, I labeled these various defenses "games academics play" or simply "academic games."

Identifying and describing these academic games may seem to some readers merely a tongue-in-cheek exercise, but this exercise should not be regarded simply in terms of its entertainment value. Faculty members have become so expert at these games and so accustomed to playing them that the games pose a serious obstacle to any attempt to use assessment data to improve institutional policy and practice. By identifying these games, readers should be in a better position to deal with academic gamesmanship when it occurs on their campuses.

While academic games bear some resemblance to the interpersonal games described by Berne, they are unique in certain ways. Academic games are less interactive than they are declarative: the typical academic game consists mainly of making a verbal statement. The statement may or may not be in direct response to a statement by another academic, and it may or may not require a response. Thus, many academic games may be played by one person because they are, in effect, ends in themselves. However, since the game also requires an audience of some sort, the player (faculty member) becomes a performer.

Because academics place such a high value on intellectual competence, one immediate object of many academic games is to make the player look brilliant or creative. A more subtle consequence, however, is to relieve the player or the audience of any responsibility to act on the basis of assessment results. Psychologically, the function served here is tension reduction. The immediate source of these tensions might be the suggestion of the assessment results that certain pedagogical objectives or student developmental needs are not being met, or guilt about past failure to deal effectively with student issues. Using academic games to reduce tensions serves to preserve the status quo. By fending off action on new proposals, insights, or ideas, the player of academic games, perhaps unwittingly, becomes a party to a kind of institutional conservatism. Failure to act, in other words, is tantamount to endorsing current policies and procedures.

The following catalogue of academic games by no means covers all techniques used by academics to avoid coming to grips with problems requiring action, but it does describe some of the more common ones that academics are inclined to play.

Rationalization is one of the most commonly played games in academia. A familiar defense mechanism, rationalization is especially suited to the style of academics because it is highly verbal and depends heavily on abstract reasoning. The gamesmanship project cited earlier (Astin, 1976) indicated that academics tend to rationalize away the results of assessment data under two conditions: when data are perceived as unflattering or negative, and when the data are not accompanied by any concrete recommendations for change or reform. Typical games of rationalization use statements such as "the proposed changes are unrealistic" or "we just don't have the resources to deal with this problem." The basic function of rationalization is to avoid having to take action based on the results of assessment data by invoking real or imagined obstacles or by suggesting somehow that the proposed reforms have already been implemented or are in the process of being implemented.

One especially bizarre form of rationalization is a game that, in Orwellian jargon, might be labeled *bad is good*. Here the academic manages to cope with a clearly negative finding by concluding that the finding is, in fact, positive. Many academics, for example, can rationalize a high dropout rate for an institution by suggesting that it reflects rigorous academic standards. Similar kinds of rationalizations can be invoked to account for poor ratings of classroom teaching: "Their complaints are the best evidence that they are really being challenged by my course."

Another frequent academic game is called *passing the buck*. Academics frequently attempt to sidetrack an issue by forming a committee or a task force to study it. Passing the buck is an especially maddening academic game because it avoids the need to formulate policy or to take action while at the same time it creates the impression that something is being done about the problem. In academe, we frequently find ourselves taking a report from a task force or a committee and appointing another task force or committee to study the implications of the report. Assessment data are especially vulnerable to this game because any assessment is by nature imperfect and thus lends itself easily to "further study."

Perhaps the most frustrating academic game is *obfuscation*. Since academics are masters at obfuscation, this game is often difficult to detect until its damage has been done. Let me quote here from the comments of one of the consultants on the gamesmanship project, the late Joseph Katz: "The academic reflex is often to talk when faced with the need for action which requires some change of established habits. Academics often do not recognize this particular form of lassitude, because for academics words, after all, are action, perhaps the most favorite action." One common form of obfuscation is to invoke platitudes or highsounding generalizations that lead nowhere but create the impression of genuine concern and interest.

One interesting form of obfuscation might be called the *rhetorical question game*. Here the academic poses what appears to be a serious and thoughtful question, but which in fact calls for no particular answer and either deflects the issue or shuts off further discussion and debate.

Still another academic game might be labeled *co-optation*, to borrow a term from the student New Left of the 1960s. Co-optation is an especially effective defense against action because it incorporates an unqualified acceptance of the assessment results. In effect, co-optation involves the open acceptance of the existence of a problem as suggested by assessment results, together with the suggestion that steps have already been taken to remedy the problem, or in its extreme form, that the problem has already been solved. The obvious danger of this game is that it preempts any further action on the problem: "The student survey underscores one of our major campus problems, and it is fortunate that we have a task force in place that is working on the problem." Assessment data are especially susceptible to this game since there is always some lag between the collection of the data and the presentation of findings. The purpose of co-optation is to suggest that the problem has been solved in the interim. The use of co-optation does not necessarily justify the conclusion that the problem is not in the process of being solved. (It is entirely possible that the "solution" is in fact alleviating the problem.) However, playing this game often closes off inquiry into the matter and precludes further discussion of solutions, even though direct evidence that the problem has been solved is lacking.

A game which has the effect of mesmerizing its audience is *recitation*. Committees or task forces that are assigned responsibility for reviewing assessment data sometimes manage to avoid any serious attempts to relate the results to institutional policy by plodding methodically from one result to the next and simply converting the numbers into prose statements: "Six percent of the respondents said this, forty percent said that," and so on. I often find a good deal of recitation in early drafts of doctoral dissertations or even in articles published in academic journals. When there is much assessment data to interpret, recitation tends to mesmerize the reader while at the same time creating the impression of serious concern and involvement. Besides encouraging the "So what?" reaction, recitation of dry empirical findings can also serve to confound the audience by suggesting that there is really no way to make coherent sense out of the results.

The final two games are *displacement* and *projection*. These games cover a wide range of strategies that all have the effect of shifting attention away from the possible substantive implications of the assessment data and focusing it instead on some external issue. The basic function of displacement and projection is to obviate the need for serious consideration of the findings by undermining confidence in the assessment instruments or in those responsible for designing the instruments or collecting and analyzing the data. This is an especially effective academic game because all assessment data have technical deficiencies, no matter how sophisticated nor how well analyzed and presented. This is not to suggest that technical limitations should not always be kept in mind when utilizing assessment data. The critical distinction between legitimate criticism of the data and the use of displacement or projection is whether the criticisms are presented constructively (that is, to make appropriate qualifications in the interpretations or to clarify certain points about the data) or whether they are used to undermine the entire assessment project.

A version of displacement or projection that is frequently played by persons with some knowledge of psychological testing or test theory is the *reliability-validity* game. This game is designed to undermine confidence in the assessment instrument through the use of such questions as "What is the reliability of this measure?" or "Have any validity studies been done with this instrument?" In truth, the issue of the reliability of measures (i.e., the amount of measurement error they contain) becomes paramount only in the face of generally negative findings, that is, when no environmental variable is found to make much of a difference in outcome performance. Also, as pointed out in chapter 5, traditional notions of reliability, which are entirely appropriate when applied to assessment instruments that are to be used to evaluate and advise *individuals*, are not applicable when the main concern is aggregated data derived from *groups* of individuals. Measures that are relatively unreliable on an individual basis can yield highly reliable results when the scores are aggregated across a number of individuals. Similarly, as was pointed out in chapter 3, traditional psychometric notions about validity simply do not apply to outcome assessments. Since most academicians are not aware of these finer points of measurement and psychometrics, confidence in assessment results can easily be undermined by persons who like to play the reliability-validity game.

Another variant on displacement might be called *caution*. This game involves a litany of technical limitations in the data, followed by a statement indicating that it would be hazardous to attempt to formulate meaningful interpretations or generalizations concerning policy because of these imperfections. Ewell (1988) calls this the "perfect data fallacy." Still another variation on the displacement game might be called *red herring*. In this version the game player identifies a deficiency that is real but which could not possibly invalidate the results. Attention is diverted from the interpretive task at hand and, by implication, confidence in the assessment results is undermined. A close relative of red herring might be called *innuendo*. Here the academic gamesman attempts to discredit the assessment results by suggesting that some minor deficiency might indicate more far-reaching but unspecified defects. The purpose of innuendo is to discourage others from taking the assessment results seriously or making recommendations for action by implying that the data cannot be trusted. Innuendo can also be expressed in the form of sarcasm. In effect, sarcasm shifts attention away from the substance and, by implication, discredits the data.

Countermeasures

The most important consideration in coping with academic games is to detect them in time to take appropriate countermeasures. Dealing with academic games involves two major challenges: identifying gamesmanship when it occurs, and taking appropriate remedial action. If one is familiar with the major varieties of games that can be played and monitors early reactions to the assessment data closely, detection should not be a major problem. A more difficult challenge is how to cope with academic games in a constructive manner.

If a group of faculty members is reviewing some assessment results, a frontal attack on gamesmanship is probably inadvisable, except in the unusual circumstance in which the participants are a close-knit group who know each other reasonably well and have established a mutual trust. By frontal attack, I mean that the person countering the game simply points out the game when it appears and asks the player to adopt a more constructive approach. With persons who do not know and respect each other, the frontal attack is likely to provoke defensiveness, hostility, and other nonproductive responses.

A more effective approach to the gamesman is diversion. This technique is applicable to verbal exchanges when a particular participant disrupts group functioning by playing displacement and projection games that focus attention on, say, methodological deficiencies. A potentially effective countermeasure is to divert such a discussion by suggesting that it is time to move to another topic, that other participants cannot follow technical discussions, or that there will not be enough time remaining to consider what the assessment results might mean. A variation on this approach is to isolate the gamesperson. People who play displacement and projection games might be asked to prepare a written analysis of technical problems to be discussed at some future time. The request for the analysis in effect shuts off the discussion and provides a pivotal moment for shifting to more substantive issues. Isolation of games in a written report can be accomplished by removing undesired portions (highly technical criticism, for example) from the main body of a report and locating them instead in an appendix.

Most academic games can be countered by suggesting that the player (and the other participants) should consider also the implications of the findings (this is a particularly important countermeasure to the game of recitation). For certain games, however, the player should probably be challenged more directly by a suggestion that alternative explanations might be possible (this is particularly important for games such as rationalization and co-optation). Still another approach is to ask the gamesperson to explain or clarify a particular statement (this approach is essential in a game such as obfuscation).

Particularly difficult strategic challenges are posed by games such as passing the buck. Since academics are so used to playing these games, the other participants may be tempted to go along with the gamesman as a way to avoid the hard work of trying to interpret and understand the assessment results and to formulate appropriate recommendations for action. Passing the buck also avoids the risk taking that is usually associated with making recommendations for institutional change. A faculty member playing passing the buck should probably be confronted more or less directly, and be reminded that this behavior represents an abdication of responsibility.

These suggested strategies represent only some of the many countermeasures that might be employed to cope with academic games. While their use by no means guarantees that the negative consequences of academic games will be eliminated entirely, simply being attuned to gamesmanship when it occurs puts us in a much better position to reduce its negative impact.

THE PROBLEM OF EXPERTISE

One of the most neglected topics in the contemporary literature on assessment is the problem of finding people who have the expertise needed to run an effective assessment program. There seem to be two different models that permeate this literature: the *independent assessor* model and the *collegial* model.

The Independent Assessor

Many treatises on assessment and evaluation implicitly assume that the collection, analysis, and dissemination of assessment results is to be done by one person or a small group of people (i.e., the assessor, evaluator, or researcher) and that the utilization of findings is to be done by an independent set of people (practitioners and policy makers) (De Loria and Brookins, 1984). Under this model the main work of designing and conducting assessment activities is done by "experts" such as directors of institutional research offices or outside consultants. A report summarizing the findings is prepared and disseminated to the faculty and staff.

In my view, this *independent assessor* concept is the worst possible model for effective utilization of assessment results. It not only puts the assessors and practitioners in a potentially adversarial relationship, but it also tempts assessment experts to view their dissemination work in a manipulative way, much like the proverbial salesperson who is trying to sell refrigerators to Eskimos. Practitioners are seen as naive and uninformed, at best, and as hostile and defensive, at worst. From the perspective of administrators or faculty members, assessors are often perceived as number-crunching interlopers who really do not understand the complexities and subtleties of academe; assessment results are viewed accordingly as an unwarranted intrusion into their academic work and as a threat to their autonomy. The independent assessor model is, in short, a formula well designed for failure.

The Collegial Model

A far more effective approach to effective utilization of assessment results is the *collegial* model, in which faculty and staff colleagues play a significant part in all phases of the assessment process. Aside from the obvious political advantages that come with greater personal involvement, reliance on this model also increases the odds that the assessment data will address real institutional issues and problems and that the findings and recommendations will be intelligible and meaningful to practitioners and policy makers. Reliance on a collegial model by no means precludes the involvement of institutional researchers or outside assessment experts; indeed, it increases the chances that the expertise of such assessment professionals will be effectively utilized. The basic difference between the two models is in the degree of faculty and administrative involvement in and control over the entire assessment process.

What Expertise Do We Need?

Mere involvement of faculty and administrators, however, by no means guarantees the success of any assessment program (Ewell, 1985b). My long involvement in assessment work and my many visits to college and university campuses persuades me that *lack of expertise is a major impediment to the effective use of assessment in American higher education*. This is not to say that most colleges and universities in the United States do not have faculty and staff who are expert in many of the relevant fields: testing, measurement, statistics, research design, computer technology, learning theory, group processes, instructional methods, curriculum, administration and governance, and long-range planning. The problem is, first, that one seldom finds these talents combined in a single person or even in a committee of two or three people and, second, that the challenge of effective assessment in academia really requires a unique kind of expertise that is simply not being produced currently by our existing doctoral training programs in education or the social sciences.

What, then, should the ideal assessment expert have in the way of expertise? I have listed below some of the most critical qualifications.

> *Vision*: A broad understanding of institutional purposes and ideals and a clear conception of how assessment activities can be used to further these purposes and ideals
>
> *Understanding of Academia*: A clear conceptual grasp of how academic institutions function and of the unique strengths and

limitations of faculty and administrators as they perform their individual and corporate roles within the institution

Functional Knowledge of Measurement and Research Design: A thorough knowledge of measurement theory, statistical methods (especially multivariate statistics), and research design. By using the word "functional" I mean to emphasize that this knowledge would serve to facilitate action, that is, the implementation of useful assessments and procedures of data analysis, rather than to immobilize the person by emphasizing all the imperfections and limitations that are inherent in real-world data

Technical Know-how: Familiarity with modern techniques of data collection (e.g., optical scanning or mark sensing), data organization (e.g., file structure), methods of storage and retrieval, and data analysis (e.g., statistical packages such as SPSS-X [1988] and SAS [1985]).

Understanding of Relevant Educational and Social Science Concepts: Familiarity with learning theory, instructional methods and theory, curriculum, support services, student development theory, group dynamics

Good Communication Skills: Ability to listen, speak, and write clearly; persuasiveness; ability to express complex ideas and findings in clear, concise terms

Academic Qualifications: Training, experience, and accomplishments at a level commensurate with appointment as a tenure-track faculty member

One could also add to this listing such personal qualities as patience, nondefensiveness, empathy, creativity, and initiative. Ideally, in each institution at which there was the desire to implement a substantial assessment program to enhance the talent development process, there would be one or more persons possessing most of these qualifications who could assume responsibility for the design and implementation of a comprehensive assessment program.

THE AUDIENCE

Assessment results will be most effectively utilized when they are designed specifically for particular audiences (Ewell, 1987). There are at least four major audiences toward which assessment results can be directed: the faculty, student affairs personnel, academic administrators, and students. (Another audience might be the public; see chapter 11.) For each of these groups we shall examine three issues that need to be considered in designing effective feedback: environmental variables, outcome variables, and student sampling.

Faculty

The environmental variables of most direct concern to faculty are the courses they teach, the pedagogical techniques they use, and the climate of the department or discipline in which they teach. Since faculty members are strongly identified with their departments and disciplines, every effort should be made to aggregate assessment results at the level of the individual department. Institutionwide results may generate some interest among faculty, but the same assessment results can generate much more interest when they are available at the departmental level (Kinnick, 1985). Departmentally based results are of even more interest to a given department, however, if they can be compared with norms based on other departments.

Assessment results aggregated at the level of the individual course will also generate a great deal of interest among faculty, although course-level assessment results are generally difficult to interpret unless they are available from different sections of the same course. The reason is that courses vary so much in content and purpose that it is difficult to compare results, especially from cognitive assessments, across different courses. Course-level assessments can also be potentially threatening to faculty members, especially if these findings are made public.

Pedagogical technique is a complex and difficult environmental variable to incorporate into an assessment program. Again, unless such information is obtained across different sections of the same course, it tends to be confounded with course subject matter. Nevertheless, there are some interesting possibilities for studying pedagogical technique. For example, faculty can conduct mini-experiments in which they deliberately try out different instructional techniques at different times. Also, if it is possible to obtain assessment data on a large number of different courses, it might be possible to study the impact of different instructional techniques and approaches using the course as the unit of analysis. Such studies also make it possible to study the effects of variables such as class size, time of class meeting, age of the instructor, and similar factors.

As far as outcome measures are concerned, faculty are obviously interested in cognitive outcomes, especially those that are relevant to the subject matter of their own courses. In this connection it should be noted that assessments in the area of general education outcomes are especially difficult to utilize effectively since most faculty do not see themselves as primarily engaged in teaching general education courses. At the same time, most cognitive outcomes in the area of general education cut across courses in such a way that it is difficult to assign responsibility to any particular course or department for particular general education outcomes. Some of the most effective approaches to utilization of assessment data in the area of general education are illustrated by the assessment activities at Alverno College (Mentkowski and Doherty, 1983) and Kean College (Kean College of New Jersey, 1986). In both of these institutions the faculty responsible for developing general education curricula and for teaching general education courses were persuaded to work collaboratively to develop tailor-made outcome assessments.

There are many outcome assessments in the affective area that can generate interest among faculty. Perhaps the most obvious of these are satisfaction measures in areas such as academic advising, quality of instruction, courses in the major, general education requirements, and student-faculty contact. Faculty are also interested in affective outcomes such as aspirations for graduate study, the value of liberal learning, and choice of a major or career.

As far as student sampling is concerned, faculty members are most interested in students whose majors are in their own departments, who attend their classes, and who are their academic advisees. If it is possible to aggregate assessment results separately for these groups, the data will generate a great deal of interest among individual faculty members.

Student Affairs Personnel

The environments of greatest interest to student affairs personnel would include the particular services for which they are usually responsible: personal and career counseling, tutorial help or other academic assistance, housing, financial aid, career placement, and health services. The simplest and most straightforward approach to assessing these different environmental experiences is to use student satisfaction as the appropriate outcome measure (Banta and Fisher, 1987). Student affairs personnel will also have a great deal of interest in students' satisfaction with more general nonacademic outcomes such as campus social life, opportunities to participate in extracurricular activities, opportunities to attend cultural events, and regulations governing campus life. Another outcome of special significance for student affairs personnel is student retention. Finally, while the student subsample of greatest interest would probably be student leaders, student affairs personnel are also very interested in students in general.

Academic Administrators

Among the environmental variables of particular interest to academic administrators are facilities such as laboratories and equipment, libraries, and computers. Because most academic administrators are or have been members of the faculty, their interests tend to be similar to those of faculty members except that they are ordinarily focused at a higher level of aggregation. This group would thus tend to be more interested in data aggregated at the level of the entire institution or by division, school, or college. They might also be interested in results at the departmental level, but primarily for interdepartmental comparisons rather than as a means of looking at any particular department.

Academic administrators have a particular interest in inter-institutional comparisons. It is thus no accident that practically all the representatives for the more than 1300 colleges and universities that have participated in the Cooperative Institutional Research Program are administrators rather than faculty members.

As far as cognitive outcome measures are concerned, academic administrators tend to be more interested in the area of general education than in particular departments or courses. An outcome of particular interest to academic administrators these days is student retention. Retention is of significance not only because of its academic implications (students are "voting with their feet"), but also because it has significant fiscal implications. Because of the substantial cost of recruiting students these days, administrators have a strong incentive to find ways to encourage students to complete their programs rather than drop out.

Academic administrators also have a considerable investment in outcomes related to student satisfaction for many of the same reasons: satisfaction implies that the academic program has been successful; it also has implications for recruiting future generations of students.

Students

The environmental variables of greatest interest to students are those that concern the decisions they have to make throughout their undergraduate years: housing, individual courses and professors, departments or majors, social fraternities and sororities, student organizations, and special programs (year abroad, honors, remedial). Students are also interested in aggregation of assessment data by class year (freshman, sophomore, etc.), by gender, and by ethnic subgroup.

As far as outcome measures are concerned, students have a considerable degree of interest in satisfaction, retention, entry to graduate and professional school, success in graduate or professional school, job placement, and career development. Other outcomes would include student satisfaction with various aspects of the undergraduate experience: quality of instruction, campus social life, relevance of course work to everyday life, academic advising, financial aid, and other student services. Students may also have an interest in knowing results separately for particular student subgroups, especially those to which they belong: for example, commuters, adult students, part-time students, and ethnic minorities.

COMMUNICATION OF ASSESSMENT FINDINGS

Once we have identified the appropriate audiences and generated the kinds of assessment results of greatest interest to those audiences, we are then confronted with the task of how best to communicate these findings so as to capture the interest of each audience. A good deal of conventional wisdom has been developed about how to accomplish this task; my personal experience with this problem, however, persuades me that none of us in the assessment business really has any final answers to this issue and that the conventional wisdom is wrong just about as often as it is right.

One item from today's bible of conventional wisdom is that we must eliminate technical detail from reports or presentations of assessment results. This recommendation seems to run directly counter to another item of conventional wisdom: that the faculty (or other users of the assessment results) must come to "own" the assessment findings (Ewell, 1984). Given the considerable critical and analytical skills of most college faculty members, it is difficult to imagine how they can ever develop a proprietary interest in assessment findings without being provided a good deal of technical detail. If such details are withheld, faculty may feel that they are being patronized or simply reject the findings as trivial.

One approach to the problem of too much detail is to report results at several different levels of detail and complexity. The first level might consist of an executive summary that presents only the highlights of the results in one or two pages at most. The next level might be presented like a brief journal article in which a good deal more detail is presented with selected tables of data and some extended discussion of interpretations and implications. The final and most elaborate level might consist of an appendix containing much more quantitative detail and possibly technical discussions of more complex statistical and methodological matters. A report of findings containing all three levels of detail could be used in several different ways. Practitioners who want simply to familiarize themselves with the basic findings can do so by investing just a few minutes of time and effort. Practitioners wanting more detail can consult the other two sections of the report in any degree of specificity they desire.

The matter of how much detail to provide takes on a somewhat different flavor when the communication is oral rather than written. My own experience in making literally hundreds of presentations of assessment results to different audiences in different kinds of institutions leads me to suggest three principles that should be considered in making oral presentations of such results:

1. Always insist on having enough time to communicate the essential methodology, findings, and implications. For assessment results of even modest complexity, a minimum of thirty to forty-five minutes is usually needed to satisfy this requirement.
2. Use visual aids (charts, slides, film clips) whenever possible.
3. Try merely to whet the audience's appetite rather than communicate every detail of the results. By whetting the appetite, the

presentation will tend to generate more comments and questions in search of further detail.

4. Always allow some time for questions and discussion.
5. Design the presentation so that there are next steps to be carried out, ideally involving members of the audience. This requirement tends to give the audience a sense of future involvement and to show specific ways in which they can act on the basis of the findings or become more involved in interpreting or generating new findings.

Another issue concerning the admonition about technical detail relates to language. A chronic problem in the social sciences is the inability or unwillingness of professional researchers and scholars to communicate their ideas in terms that are intelligible to the nonspecialist. I happen to believe that much of this difficulty is self-inflicted and that even the most complicated and technical concepts can be communicated meaningfully to a lay audience without substantially distorting the facts. Even when we are trying to communicate a purely technical message, we have considerable latitude in the language we choose. For example, in discussing multiple regression analysis used to control differential student inputs, there is a continuum of jargon we can use to communicate what is basically the same concept. On the extreme technical end of this continuum, we can say that we "partialled out" the effects of student input characteristics using blocked, multiple stepwise regression analysis. Such a statement is likely to be obscure to nonspecialists. A less technical version of this statement would be that we "controlled for" the effects of student input characteristics. A much more intelligible way of saying the same thing would be to state that we "took into account" the effects of entering student characteristics. If further explanation is needed, we can say that we used sophisticated statistical procedures to match students in terms of their entering characteristics.

Researchers usually find it difficult to translate technical and disciplinary jargon into understandable English because of the type of graduate training they have received and because of the reward system they encounter once they enter the academic labor force. Social scientists are trained and evaluated by peers. Under these circumstances, we are expected to use precise technical terminology and disciplinary jargon, not only in our professional writing but also in our presentations at conferences, meetings, and symposia. Those of us who might have the temerity to report our research procedures and findings in lay terms run a considerable risk of rejection and ridicule by colleagues. No wonder, then, that social scientists and educational researchers have developed such poor communication habits when interfacing with practitioners.

In spite of this heavy and long-term conditioning, I believe that most of us are capable of greatly improving our use of language when we communicate with nonspecialists. Let me give just a few examples using the I-E-O model. Instead of talking about "dependent variables," we can talk about "student outcomes" or "student outcome measures." Instead of talking about "independent variables" or "treatments," we can talk about "programs," "educational practices," or "factors in the college environment." Instead of talking about "independent variables," "control variables," or "input variables," we can speak instead of "characteristics of the entering freshman." These more familiar alternatives in no way distort the meaning of what is being communicated.

SOME MORE PRACTICAL SUGGESTIONS

Following are a number of practical suggestions that might facilitate the utilization of assessment results on a campus.

Emphasize Feedback, Not Evaluation

Faculty and staff are much more likely to be receptive to assessment results if the assessments are carried out as a form of feedback rather than as part of an attempt to evaluate the persons involved. Even the terminology used is important: terms such as *feedback* and *assessment results* are much less loaded and less threatening than terms such as *testing* and *evaluation*.

But the problem is not merely semantic. The *spirit* in which assessment activities are carried out is by far the most important consideration in creating the proper climate for effective utilization. As suggested in chapter 1, a program of outcome assessments is most likely to be effective if it is based on a talent development approach—geared toward the improvement and facilitation of faculty teaching and of student learning and development—rather than on the resource and reputational approaches, which are inherently competitive, comparative, and adversarial. Students, faculty, and staff are much more likely to resist any form of assessment if they believe the results will be used to allocate rewards and punishments than if they believe that the assessments are being done to facilitate their own development.

In short, the feedback concept that is basic to the talent development approach to assessment creates a climate much more conducive to effective utilization of assessment results than the evaluation approach with its emphasis on reward, punishment, and competition. This is not to say that well-conceived assessment programs do not in fact *evaluate* according to the formal definition of this term in chapter 1; rather, it is to emphasize that faculty and staff will be less receptive to assessment results if they believe that they are being evaluated in the common sense in which this term is used.

Fit the Instrument to the Task

In searching for instruments to assess cognitive outcomes, many assessment specialists are tempted to grab some off-the-shelf instrument that has been developed by a professional testing agency and which has been standardized on a national or regional basis. Unless the subject matter being assessed is highly specialized or the instrument itself has some national credibility (e.g., the SAT or GRE), it may be very difficult to convince faculty to take the results seriously. This is especially true in the case of so-called general education outcomes, despite the recent proliferation of commercially available instruments to assess this important area of cognitive functioning (see chapter 3). Among the many lessons to be learned from the model assessment programs of Alverno and Kean College is that locally developed instruments for assessing general education outcomes have much more credibility with faculty. This is not to suggest that the nationally developed instruments should be avoided entirely, but simply that locally developed instruments are much more likely to produce results that will actually be utilized for program improvement.

A related issue is the temptation to use multiple-choice tests to assess practically everything. Even with locally developed instruments, the multiple-choice methodology is a tempting alternative because it easily generates quantitative results and because the scoring is objective and inexpensive. Multiple-choice tests are not suitable, however, for many of the important outcomes of higher education. Moreover, their apparently low cost is in part illusory. While multiple-choice tests are indeed inexpensive to score, they are extremely expensive to construct: item writing is a highly refined and time-consuming art, especially if one expects to develop good items that are relatively unambiguous. Also, many commercially available multiple-choice tests are quite expensive to administer and score (costs per student tested can range well above twenty dollars).

Expect Faculty Resistance

One of the best lessons learned from our three-year project involving the value-added consortium (Astin and Ayala, 1987; see chapter 8) was that faculty resistance to any new assessment activity is an integral and probably necessary part of any successful assessment program. Faculty who are unaccustomed to utilizing systematic assessment results will naturally be skeptical and critical of assessment findings when initially presented. This is not only a reflection of the faculty's strongly conservative stance with respect to institutional change and their highly developed habit of criticism (Astin, 1985a) but also a manifestation of some degree of involvement in the utilization process. The absence of faculty resistance or criticism might well reflect an impotent assessment program that either has little of substance to say or is being ignored by the practitioners. The real challenge is to capitalize on this early critical involvement and to channel the faculty's energy into positive and constructive involvement.

Try to Achieve Faculty Ownership

The suggestion that the researcher attempt to achieve faculty ownership has become almost a cliche' in contemporary assessment circles (Banta, 1988; Ewell, 1984; Halpern, 1987). I personally do not believe that it is absolutely essential in order for assessment results to be effectively utilized, but it certainly helps. If the faculty can learn to trust and respect the people carrying out the assessment program, faculty ownership may not be an absolute necessity in order for the results to be used.

Among the more obvious ways to attain ownership is through use of locally developed assessment instruments, involvement of faculty in the early stages of instrument selection or assessment design, and responsiveness to legitimate faculty concerns and criticisms from those doing the assessment. If faculty believe that they can shape the future direction of an assessment program by becoming involved to the extent that they are willing to offer constructive criticism of assessment procedures, they are much more likely to attain some minimal level of ownership over the assessment program.

Maintain Flexibility

An admonition merely to be flexible sounds almost like a truism, but in the case of assessment programs it is an extremely important ingredient in successful utilization of results. Flexibility is especially important in the case of instrument selection. Many assessment specialists reduce their effectiveness by becoming locked into a particular commercial instrument. With the exception of those few instruments that are regularly revised and allow the user to add some locally developed questions, most commercially available assessment instruments are more or less set in stone. As a result, it is difficult for the assessment specialist to be responsive to faculty concerns and criticisms that will inevitably be expressed when initial results are analyzed and presented.

Capitalize on Serendipity

Any effective assessment program is going to produce unexpected results or generate novel and unanticipated ideas. Indeed, an assessment program that merely validates the obvious is of little or no use in program improvement. My own view of this issue is perhaps a bit eccentric, but I believe it has paid off handsomely in terms of substantive results. Generally, my approach is to try to assess the variables that are of obvious importance and relevance, and then to add some other variables on a more or less intuitive basis without any clear idea as to just how the results might be used. While some critics might characterize this as a "shotgun" approach to assessment, I feel strongly that our state of knowledge about the dynamics of student learning and development is so meager that we are unrealistic in assuming we can learn all there is of importance through a purely rational approach to the selection of instruments and methods of analysis.

One of the most interesting ways to maximize serendipity in data analysis and in interpretation of results is to "play" with the data using various analytical techniques and selecting different subgroups of variables and students to analyze. It is also possible to attain greater degrees of faculty ownership by encouraging faculty colleagues to experiment with the data in the same manner. This open-ended approach to analysis offers the greatest potential for productive payoff if the data set itself includes the widest possible array of input, environmental, and outcome variables.

SUMMARY

Any utilization strategy should be predicated on some kind of theory that indicates how users of the assessment data are supposed to translate results into action. A performing arts theory is suggested whereby faculty and staff use the results as feedback to enhance their understanding of educational practices that are most likely to enhance talent development.

For maximum mileage to be realized from assessment results, they should be tailored to a specific audience (faculty, student affairs, etc.). Consideration should also be given to strategies for avoiding the "So what?" reaction and for dealing with the many academic games that faculty are inclined to play when they are confronted with data suggesting the need for change.

There are several strategies for involving faculty and staff in active use of assessment results and for identifying personnel who are most likely to be effective directors of assessment programs.

8

BUILDING A DATA BASE

In the preceding chapters we have considered in some detail a number of issues concerned with the measurement of student outcomes, student inputs, and college environments and have discussed various ways of analyzing such data and using the results to improve educational practice. All such assessment activities, however, assume the existence of some kind of data base which simultaneously incorporates input, environment, and outcome data and which is accessible for the kinds of analyses and applications discussed in chapters 6 and 7.

Some readers may be tempted to skip this chapter on the assumption that the creation of such a data base is primarily a technical matter that can be left to the computer specialists. My experience with several attempts to implement comprehensive assessment programs in institutions suggests quite the opposite. Not only is the creation of an adequate data base an extremely complex and difficult task that requires the involvement and support of the top leadership, but the lack of an adequate data base is one of the most serious obstacles confronting any institution that wishes to implement a comprehensive assessment program. One of the experiences that led me to this conclusion was a three-year project initiated in the summer of 1984 under a grant from the Fund for the Improvement of Postsecondary Education (FIPSE). This discussion of data base issues begins with a brief review of the relevant findings from this project.

WHY THE DATA BASE IS SO IMPORTANT: EXPERIENCE FROM THE FIPSE VALUE-ADDED PROJECT

The FIPSE project was in many respects a grass roots undertaking. Early in 1984 I was approached by two friends—Willard Enteman, provost of Rhode Island College, and Peter Armacost, president of Eckerd College in Florida—with the suggestion that a small consortium be formed to experiment with value-added student assessment programs. Both Enteman and Armacost knew of some of my research and writing on the subject of assessment and were interested in starting longitudinal student assessment programs on their own campuses. After several discussions, the three of us agreed to organize a consortium of perhaps six or seven diverse institutions and to seek federal funding to support a consortium project. We eventually added five more institutions: Carnegie-Mellon University, UCLA, Spelman College, Empire State College, and Hood College. These participants were selected not only because of their diversity but also because the presidents or chief academic officers were known personally by one or more of us and supported the aims of the project. With involvement and support from top administration, we felt that the project had a very good chance of success. Our proposal was submitted to the Fund for the Improvement of Postsecondary Education and was funded in the late summer of 1984.

The philosophical underpinnings of the project in many respects resemble the arguments set forth in chapter 1. Our proposal argued that an institution's assessment procedures inevitably reflect its conception of its own excellence. Rather than merely promoting the resource and reputational views, we felt that an *educationally* oriented assessment program would instead focus on *change* or *growth* in students during the undergraduate years. Such repeated assessment would make it possible to gauge how much students actually learn and develop while attending the institution. Thus, the formal title of the original proposal submitted to FIPSE was "Value-Added: A New Approach to Institutional Excellence." (I have subsequently come to prefer the phrase "talent development" over "value added," primarily because it seems to capture more of what institutions are really trying to accomplish in their educational programs.)

The project called for pretesting students at each institution in 1984 and for follow up posttesting one year later in 1985. Developmental changes in both cognitive and affective outcomes would be assessed. Changes in affective outcomes would be assessed using the CIRP freshman and follow-up questionnaires. Cognitive outcomes would be assessed using the ACT-COMP, an instrument specifically designed to assess the outcomes of general education programs (see chapter 3). Results from input pretests would be used to enhance early advisement, placement, and curriculum planning. The longitudinal value-added or talent development data resulting from the pretest-posttest assessments would be used to evaluate and strengthen the academic and student service programs on each campus through faculty retreats, student-faculty workshops, and related approaches.

While the project produced a number of interesting results (see Astin and Ayala, 1987), one of the most important insights (and certainly the most unexpected) concerned the issue of institutional data bases. We learned about the importance of the institutional data base the hard way during a two-day workshop we conducted at UCLA in 1986 for project teams from each of the seven institutions. One major component of the workshop was devoted to a rather technical presentation concerning how to analyze longitudinal student data. These presentations assumed that participants would be able to link their longitudinal assessment data to other data about their students. This assumption soon proved to be naive, however. The participants were largely unable to apply what they had learned in the workshop because their institutions really had no comprehensive longitudinal student data base to which they could tie the new assessments they had carried out in connection with the consortium project. In my many visits to college campuses during the past few years I have come to realize that there are very few institutions around the country that have anything remotely resembling an ideal longitudinal student data base that links together critical information from admissions, the registrar, financial aid, student affairs, institutional research, career placement, and alumni offices. Without such a data base, the benefits of new assessment data hardly justify the costs. It is my impression that many sincere attempts at improved assessment have yielded very little of value because the institutions lacked such a data base. Subsequent attempts to assist the consortium institutions to establish such a data base through campus visits from our staff proved that it is no easy task.

In the rest of this chapter we shall consider the various issues and problems connected with establishing a comprehensive student data base and present a number of specific recommendations for institutions in which there is an interest in creating such a resource for better utilization of assessment results.

THE PRACTICAL AND SYMBOLIC SIGNIFICANCE OF THE STUDENT DATA BASE

At this point the reader might be tempted to conclude that institutions need to collect input, environment, and output data on their students merely to fulfill certain methodological requirements for doing environmental impact (I-E-O) studies. However, over the years I have become increasingly convinced that the need for input, environment, and output data on any college campus is much more basic than satisfying the requirements of I-E-O studies of environmental impact. I can demonstrate this need through a series of questions.

Input Data. Is it reasonable to suppose that an institution should want to know something about its new students? What are their plans and aspirations? What do they want out of college? Why did they pick this college? What are their academic strengths and weaknesses? What is their socioeconomic background? What were their activities and achievements in high school?

Environmental Data. Is it reasonable to expect that we should know what educational experiences our students are having in college? Beyond the courses they are taking (which almost all colleges *do* know), should we not also be interested in what kinds of extracurricular activities different students participate in, how they are supporting themselves, how many of them work and what kinds of jobs they hold, what their study habits are, what goes on in their residence halls, whether they are participating in special educational programs, and how extensively and how effectively they are using the laboratories and libraries?

Outcome Data. Is it reasonable to expect that we should know something about the educational progress of each student? How long is it taking them to complete their programs of study? How many students (and which ones) are dropping out or stopping out? What are students actually learning in their classes? How do they perceive their educational experiences? How do they rate the quality of instruction they get in different fields? How do they view the different student services they receive? Are they getting what they want out of college? What happens to students when they leave? What kinds of jobs do they hold? Do they feel we have prepared them adequately for work, for marriage, or for parenthood?

The point of raising such questions is to underscore that student input, environment, and output data are fundamental to the operation of any educational institution, even if we never bother to do any environmental impact studies. Indeed, *not* to collect and use student input, environmental, and outcome data on a regular basis would seem to be educationally irresponsible.

Who Are the Data Collectors?

Although most institutions do gather some input, environment, and outcome data, the manner in which they collect, store, and use such data is highly compartmentalized and fragmented. Admissions offices collect primarily input data: applications, transcripts, admissions test scores. Orientation directors may also collect a variety of input data such as placement test scores and various questionnaire data from orientation sessions. Financial aid offices collect some input data (parents' confidential financial statements, financial aid applications), but they also collect and update environmental data (type and amount of aid actually received, college employment information). Registrars collect environmental data (majors, courses taken) as well as outcome data on the student's academic standing, grades, credits, honors, and degrees earned. Offices of student affairs or student activities sometimes collect a wide range of environmental data on student housing, extracurricular participation, and student health, although such information is often not recorded in any systematic fashion. Alumni offices sometimes collect outcome data on former students' jobs and earnings. Beyond this, institutional researchers and individual administrators or faculty members might collect a wide range of both environmental and outcome data in connection with accreditation self-studies or other special evaluation or research projects.

How Are the Data Used?

Each of these data collection activities serves an important purpose (e.g., to make admissions and financial aid decisions, to keep track of students' academic performance); however, each data set is usually maintained independently of every other data set. Consequently, it is very difficult to get a comprehensive longitudinal picture of the progress and talent development of any individual student or any given class of students. We might be able to look up a student's grade-point average in the registrar's files, but we would normally have to look somewhere else to find out about that same student's housing, financial aid, placement test scores, marital status, socioeconomic background, and extracurricular activities. Much of this other information might not be available anywhere. Since the optimal use of assessment data depends on our ability to *link* any student's outcome performance with relevant input and environmental data about him or her, such a fragmented and disconnected data system creates enormous problems for anyone trying to do input-environment-outcome studies.

Parenthetically, the lack of an integrated student data base makes it very difficult to advise and counsel students. To take another analogy from medicine, advising students in most colleges today is a little like trying to prescribe treatment for a patient without a medical chart. In most medical treatment facilities each patient normally has a single comprehensive file (the chart) which includes admissions or input data (history, presenting symptoms, results of initial physical exam, x-ray and lab pretests), environmental data (drugs, surgery, or other therapies administered), and outcome data (changes in symptoms, posttests on lab tests and x-rays). Any medical professional who is trying either to advise a patient or to make a decision about further treatment can consult the chart to get a comprehensive picture of the patient's past and current situation. It would be irresponsible for a hospital or clinic not to have all such data on a given patient combined in a single file, and it would be irresponsible for a physician to prescribe treatment without first consulting that file. In most academic institutions, however, counselors and advisers seldom have access to a comparably complete source of information about the individual students they advise.

But an integrated longitudinal student data base has considerable significance beyond its usefulness for I-E-O assessment studies and for student counseling and guidance. That an institution creates and maintains such a comprehensive data base represents an important symbolic statement about that institution's commitment to and interest in the educational and personal development of its students. It signifies the institution's interest in answering the most fundamental educational questions it can ask about its programs: Who are the students who come to us? What happens to them while they are here? How are they being affected by their experiences?

In another sense, the existence of an integrated student data base containing input, environmental, and outcome data symbolizes the wholeness of both the student and the student's educational experiences. Having such a data base implies that we are interested not only in knowing how our students change from entry to exit, but also in knowing *why* some students change differently from others and how the different programs and experiences to which they are exposed contribute to these changes. To create, maintain, and use an integrated data base thus constitutes concrete evidence of the institution's commitment to critical self-study and to enhancing its impact on student development.

STRUCTURE OF THE DATA BASE

Before discussing the practical question of how best to begin developing a student data base, we should first consider what an ideal data base would look like. The integrated student data base should consist of a series of cohort files. In this context a cohort is defined as any group of newly admitted students. Depending upon the type of institution involved, it may be desirable to create separate cohort files for any student groups that have unique educational objectives. In most baccalaureate granting institutions, each new crop of first-time freshmen would constitute a separate cohort, and separate cohort files would probably be desirable for each new group of transfer students and each new group of first-time graduate students. In a community college, on the other hand, it might be desirable to create separate cohort files for transfer, vocational, or nondegree credit students. The best way to determine whether separate cohort files are appropriate is to ask the following question: Is the same measure of program completion appropriate for all students in the cohort? In a traditional undergraduate liberal arts college, for example, completion of the bachelor's degree would probably be an appropriate measure of program completion for all first-time, full-time entering freshmen. However, in most community colleges, completion of the associate degree (or successful transfer to a four-year institution) would almost certainly not be an appropriate program completion measure to apply to terminal occupational or vocational students. Thus, rather than maintaining a single cohort file for all students who enter the college in a given year, it would be more appropriate to create several independent subfiles from that cohort.

Any individual cohort file consists of a series of records, one for each entering student. Each student's record is laid out in exactly the same way as every other student's record, although it will probably not be possible to gather all data on all students. Given that it is possible to collect an enormous amount of input, environmental, and outcome data on individual students, the cohort file should be designed and maintained so that new data can be added to each student's record with relative ease.[1]

What does each student's record contain? The most grandiose answer to this question is "anything that might be worth knowing about the condition of the student at the point of entry (input), the student's educational programs and experiences while in college (environment), and how the student develops after entering and subsequent to graduation (outcome)." Some of the data—admissions, financial aid, academic performance, enrollment status, degree completion—is already collected by various offices on the campus. Additional input, environmental, and outcome data would have to be collected through special questionnaires, inventories, and tests. While most of the information will probably be in numerical form, there is no reason that prose or other nonquantitative information cannot be incorporated into the file. It must be acknowledged, however, that such non-numeric information can take a great deal of file space and that analyzing it may be extremely difficult.

The integrated student data base is not meant to be a substitute or replacement for other existing data files needed by the admissions office, the registrar, the alumni office, the institutional research office, or other administrative offices. As each of these units has its own operational needs and responsibilities, it must operate and maintain its own data files in a manner best suited to its particular purposes and functions. These offices must understand, however, that they must periodically make their files available so that selected information can be copied and incorporated into the various cohort files making up the integrated student data base. The integrated data base, in other words,

1. A technical note: Ease of analysis is facilitated when all student records in a given record file are stored in the same physical record (disk, tape, etc.). However, since the physical record can become extremely long, some institutions may find it necessary to store different parts of the students' records in different physical files. If this becomes necessary, it is extremely important to design software for accessing the files so that selected data from the physically separate files can be easily merged into a single record for purposes of analysis.

is not meant to replace or compete with the data bases needed by other operational units on the campus. It is my strong belief, however, that once an integrated data base is put into operation, many of the offices on the campus will come to rely on it for a veriety of evaluation and self-study purposes. An interesting account of the development of a cohort data base at the University of Colorado—Boulder has been written by Endo and Bittner (1985).

Why a cohort file? Why not some other form of file design? Perhaps the best way to answer this question is to recall once more the philosophical underpinnings of this book as discussed in chapter 1: the need for institutions to define their excellence in terms of the talent development concept. If we are committed to maximizing talent development among our students, it is necessary to know how students change after they matriculate. Matriculation, in other words, defines the point of initial contact with our programs (input). Once students are admitted, we retain the capability of influencing talent development until they leave. Each cohort, then, represents a separate I-E-O study. It is possible to combine students across several different cohorts (entering classes), but the talent development concept requires us to begin our study of student development at the point of initial student entry to the institution.

One should note that cohort files do not lend themselves to certain kinds of statistical studies that are often carried out by planning offices or offices of institutional research. For example, the statistical reporting required by the federal government and by many states often requires information on all enrolled students. An agency may wish to know the ethnic composition of the entire student body. Similarly, the planning office may periodically need such information as how many students are currently enrolled in remedial courses. Note that such queries are static rather than developmental in that they are concerned with the state of the student body at a particular time rather than with changes in individual students over time.[2]

Another point to keep in mind about cohort files is that once a student becomes a member of a cohort, that student remains in that cohort indefinitely. Students are not removed from a cohort simply because they transfer, drop out, or graduate. (Techniques of cohort tracking have been recently described by Ewell and Jones, 1985.) Regardless of how long a student remains in the institution and regardless of how often

2. Most such administrative requests for information would probably produce much more useful feedback, however, if the request were reformulated so that it could be answered with cohort files. For example, rather than knowing merely what percentages of currently enrolled students were members of different ethnic subgroups, wouldn't it be more useful to know these percentages separately for the four or five most recently admitted classes (cohorts) and also to know what percentages from each class had dropped out or completed their programs?

the student drops out or stops out of college, the possibility of institutional environmental influence on that student remains. By following each cohort over time, by observing how they change and develop, and by relating these developmental changes to their particular environmental experiences, we can learn a great deal about how different programs and educational practices affect student development.

Since details about the possible types of data that might be incorporated in the integrated student data file are provided in chapters 3 (outcomes), 4 (inputs), and 5 (environments), specific suggestions about items of data to be included in the comprehensive file will not be presented here. However, as it will probably not be feasible or even desirable to include every conceivable item of data currently collected by different administrative units on campus, discrimination will have to be exercised in deciding what to include. It is strongly recommended that student outcome data be the first consideration, since the particular outcomes selected will largely determine the minimal requirements for input data.

GETTING STARTED

The ideal data base described in the preceding section obviously cannot be achieved overnight. Several years of intense effort may be required before an institution can successfully integrate data from all the relevant data collection agencies on campus. Therefore, it is important to initiate the development of an integrated student data base with both short-term and long-term objectives in mind.

The principal short-term objective should be to initiate some assessment activity that can produce meaningful and useful results in a relatively brief period of time. The surest way to undermine campus support for the idea of a comprehensive student data base is to embark upon a costly and time-consuming developmental effort that yields no useful results for several years. The short-term effort described here will not only produce useful results in a relatively brief period of time but will also provide the beginnings of the more comprehensive data base described above. The short-term plan has two major components: a retention file and preliminary student surveys.

The Retention File

In most institutions the retention file can be constructed from data that already exist on the campus. The basic idea in building the retention file is to select a single cohort of entering students and to develop a longitudinal file based on data already available in the institution. Institutions that have the capability to do so can, of course, construct several retention files using more than one cohort; the idea is to begin with at least one cohort.

The cohort should be chosen from some recent entering class of students who would normally have completed their degree program by the time the initial file development effort begins. In a baccalaureate granting institution this might be an entering class from five or six years earlier; in a community college it might be those who entered as new students three or four years before. The minimal data needed for a usable retention file would include the following:

- outcome information (completed degree, dropped out, still enrolled)
- input information (demographics, high school grades or class rank, admissions test scores, and any other available information such as freshman survey results or placement tests)
- Environmental data (at a minimum, major or program taken; preferably also information on place of residence, financial aid, and individual courses taken)

The basic retention file will enable a variety of studies focusing on a wide range of questions relating to the retention issue: What kinds of students (in terms of input characteristics) complete their programs and which students drop out? Which majors or which types of programs seem to facilitate program completion? Do particular types of students (in terms of input characteristics) seem to do better in particular types of programs?

If it is possible to include other outcome data in the retention file (academic performance, for example) without a great deal of trouble and without significantly slowing down the development of the file, they should be added. Their inclusion would expand the number of possible studies that can be done. It should also be noted that the retention measures used in the example presented here may have to be modified for particular types of institutions and particular types of programs. Thus, in a cohort file for community college transfer students, the associate degree may not be the most appropriate measure of program completion. It might be more useful to use a measure such as years of study completed, number of credits completed, or (if available) whether the student transferred to a four-year institution.

Preliminary Student Surveys

The single most important survey to be incorporated into a newly developing student data base is a follow-up of students who have just completed (or are about to complete) their programs. The survey should include at least three basic types of information:

- student satisfaction (overall as well as with quality of instruction, advising, student services, contact with faculty; see chapter 3)

- self-reported talent development (retrospective reports of how much students have gained or improved in various areas since entering college: general knowledge, knowledge of specific subject matter, critical thinking; see chapter 3)
- environmental experiences (major, place of residence, extracurricular participation, time diary, work history, financial aid, participation in special programs; see chapter 5)

Ideally, the follow-up survey would be conducted with the same cohort on which the retention file is based so that the follow-up questionnaire data could be merged with the retention file data. However, if this is not feasible, the follow-up survey can still provide a great deal of useful information for analysis (see chapters 3 and 6 for more details).

The CIRP follow-up survey contains all three data elements described above plus a variety of other information that can be useful for preliminary analyses. The special advantages of the CIRP are (a) the opportunity for institutions to add additional, locally developed items to cover follow-up information not included in the standard questionnaire; and (b) the availability of national norms (Hurtado and Astin, 1989) with which any institution can compare its own follow-up data. Nevertheless, there is no reason why an institution cannot develop its own follow-up questionnaire if it decides the CIRP instrument is inappropriate for any reason.

For institutions not currently collecting survey data on entering freshmen it is strongly recommended that some kind of entering freshman survey be initiated simultaneously with the follow-up survey. Ordinarily one would want to know, at a minimum, the following things in an entering student survey:

- basic demographic and biographical information (sex, ethnicity, family background)
- plans and aspirations (probable major, probable career choice, highest degree sought)
- high school achievements and activities
- pretests on any outcomes likely to be posttested in subsequent follow-ups (e.g., values, attitudes, aspirations, self-concept; see chapter 4)

As with the follow-up questionnaire, institutions can develop their own entering student surveys or use one of several national surveys currently available. The College Entrance Examination Board and the American College Testing Program both offer student surveys in connection with their admissions testing program for college seniors. The CIRP Freshman Survey, of course, contains all the suggested data elements listed above as well as a number of other potentially useful items. CIRP also provides national norms as well as the opportunity to add additional local questions. Whatever survey is used, the major point is to begin supplementing the data normally available from admissions so that when the time comes to conduct longitudinal follow-ups of the students, sufficient input and pretest data will be available for longitudinal studies. Although some interesting results can be obtained by doing cross-sectional analyses of the freshman survey data (see chapter 4), the primary reason for including such a survey in this start-up phase is to begin building the capability for a comprehensive longitudinal data base that can be used for assessment studies in the future. For every year the freshman survey is delayed, the possibility of conducting comprehensive longitudinal assessment studies is delayed another year.

As pointed out in chapter 5, the biggest practical problem in developing a comprehensive longitudinal student data base is the difficulty of retrieving information on environmental experiences. With the exception of information on course-taking patterns maintained by the registrar, there is ordinarily very little environmental information that can be readily obtained from other units across the campus. Ideally, different units within the areas of student affairs should regularly be able to provide information about which students are living in residence halls and which ones are participating in various student organizations and activities. While it may eventually be possible to work out arrangements to obtain such information from the offices of student housing, student health, student activities, financial aid, and other units, the best interim solution is to rely heavily on a student follow-up questionnaire for these data.

SECURITY AND CONFIDENTIALITY

The development of a comprehensive student data file of the sort described in this chapter will almost surely raise questions of student anonymity and privacy in the minds of some faculty, students, or administrators. It is important, if not essential, to develop the data file in such a way that the privacy of each student is protected and that unauthorized persons cannot have access to data on individuals. Before discussing the specifics of how the confidentiality of student data can be protected, we should understand that there is a fundamental distinction between the integrated I-E-O student data base discussed in this chapter and the kinds of student data bases usually maintained by different administrative offices within a college or university.

The type of data base one is likely to find in the admissions office or the registrar's office is what might be called an administrative data base. The basic purpose of an administrative data base is to provide a way to retrieve data on *individuals* for purposes of taking specific actions related to those individuals. Admissions offices must make decisions about whether to admit particular applicants. Similarly, the registrar's office needs to report grades and to provide transcripts on individual students.

The integrated student data base, on the other hand, is not designed to supply data on individual students to anyone, including the investigators who utilize the data in assessment studies. Rather, the integrated student data base is to be used for analyses of data on *groups* of students. Thus, in contrast to the administrative data files maintained by various campus administrative offices, the integrated student data base might be called a research file.

Because it is necessary to update and add information in the records of individual students in the integrated student data base, there has to be some indirect way to identify individuals, even though the direct linking of the student's identity with the data is never really necessary. How, then, can we add new data to the integrated student data base and simultaneously protect the anonymity of the individual student?

My recommended approach to accomplishing both of these objectives is to develop and maintain two independent data files. The first of these might be called the *identifying file*. It contains all the identifying information on the student: name, address, birth date and social security number. The second file, which might be called the *assessment data file*, includes all the input, environmental, and output data with no identifying information except a number. It would be most convenient for purposes of updating if the number used were the social security number. However, since it might be possible to decode somebody's social security number and thereby reveal their identity, a better solution is to include a completely arbitrary (but unique) identification number in each student's record in the assessment data file. This same arbitrary number could also be included in the identifying file in order to make it possible to add information or update the assessment data file. For example, if a follow-up survey is done, the outgoing questionnaires can be addressed to each student by using information from the identifying file. When the results come in, all identifying information can be stripped away from the follow-up data and the arbitrary identification number added. The inclusion of the arbitrary identification number with the follow-up data makes it possible to merge the follow-up data with the data already resident in the assessment data file.

As long as the identifying file (containing the arbitrary identification number as well as all the identifying information) is kept secure, the possibility of violating someone's anonymity is virtually eliminated. Under these conditions, it would be possible to make the assessment data file generally available to the campus community for use in a variety of assessment studies.

Under the scheme just described, the only way that student anonymity could be violated would be for someone to obtain both the identifying file and the assessment data file. However, there is another still more elaborate system that can be used to prevent even this unlikely possibility from happening. This is a system I developed in the late 1960s at a time when we were conducting a major national study of campus unrest (Astin et al., 1976). At that time, several different courts and committees of Congress were threatening to subpoena student data in connection with various investigations or trials. As we were at the time collecting longitudinal data on a national scale from individual participants in student protests, we were especially vulnerable to the charge that we might release our data in order to avoid being jailed for contempt of court or Congress. I was discussing this problem with a former FBI agent at a cocktail party when he suggested, "Why don't you do what the Mafia does to protect its financial records?" He said that in order to prevent having their records subpoenaed, the leaders of organized crime in the United States keep their records in a foreign country where subpoenas have no validity.

While the idea of having our student data stored in a foreign country was not particularly appealing, the FBI agent's suggestion did bring to mind another possibility: why not have the *capability* of linking students' identities with their data stored in a foreign country? This would allow us to maintain student assessment data for research purposes and to maintain identifying files for collecting follow-up information but would prevent anyone (including us) from directly linking identifying information with student assessment data.

We managed to accomplish this seemingly impossible objective by creating *three* data files, as follows:

- a student identifying file containing names, addresses, social security numbers plus an arbitrary identification number (1) for each student
- a research file containing all the assessment data together with a different arbitrary identification number (2) for each student
- a "link" file containing only the pairs of arbitrary identification numbers (1 and 2 from the identifying and assessment data files above)

The link file was subsequently stored in a foreign country (Canada) where it would be invulnerable to subpoena by a U.S. court or legislative body. When we collected follow-up data on any given cohort of students, we would use the identifying file to address the mailed questionnaire. When the questionnaire data were returned to us, we would convert the students' responses to tape and include no identifying information other than the arbitrary identification number 1. We would then send the tape to the Canadian agency that maintained the link file with a request that they copy our follow-up data file, replacing identification number 1 with the identification number 2. The new copy, in other words, would contain all the same follow-up data as the original; the only change would be in the identification numbers. They would then return the new copy of the follow-up tape to us so that we could merge the follow-up data with the other data we already had on the students. The merging became possible when our Canadian colleagues replaced each student's identification from the identifying file with his or her corresponding identification number from the data file. The security of the link procedure was such that even we could not retrieve data on individual students. (For further details on the link procedure, see Astin and Boruch, 1970.)

While the use of a foreign country is certainly unwieldy and probably not recommended for most institutions, the principle underlying the use of the link file can be used, with some modification, by any institution. One strategy would be to have the link file maintained by an external data processing facility or a neighboring institution. Or, the link file could simply be kept under extremely tight security and unlocked only when it was necessary to merge follow-up data with existing student data.

Even with the security procedures described here, there is still another way that student anonymity can be violated. This is the well-known "twenty questions game," in which certain students can be identified by narrowing down the possibilities based on known characteristics of those students. The twenty questions game will not work for all students, but it can be used to identify students with unique characteristics (such as people majoring in unusual or unpopular fields, or members of very small ethnic minority groups or very small student organizations). By setting certain requirements based on known characteristics of the student (age, sex, race, major field), some students can probably be identified by playing this game. While there is probably no absolutely sure way to prevent persons from playing twenty questions, there are certain rules of thumb that can be followed to make sure that individual identities are not inadvertently revealed. Perhaps the most important requirement is to report no tabulations of data based on a single individual or on a very small group of two or three individuals. As long as no such tabulations are reported, the possibility of inadvertently revealing data on a single individual is virtually eliminated.

STRATEGIC CONSIDERATIONS

There are several strategic considerations that should be kept in mind when one is attempting to establish a comprehensive integrated student data base: the visibility of the project, the use of existing data, methods of data collection, item content, access to the data, and costs.

Visibility of the Project

The current conventional wisdom about assessment on the campus is that it should be a campus-wide affair and that all segments of the campus should be involved in the process (Ewell, 1984). While widespread involvement of the campus community in the utilization of the data is an important objective, I believe that the initial attempt to develop the data base should be undertaken with as little fanfare as possible. On several campuses I have seen attempts to establish a comprehensive data base fail, either because of the paranoia that the announcement generated or because certain officials felt that it was too costly or simply unfeasible.

Several issues are involved here. First, the value of the data base is very difficult to demonstrate in the abstract. (We can't expect all interested parties to read this book!) Since many members of the campus community are skeptical about any kind of assessment or data collection, they first need to be convinced that at least some value can be realized from such a project. Without some appreciation of the potential value of an integrated data base, many people may resist the idea because of the presumed costs or time involved.

Another problem is the suspicion and paranoia that such a project can generate. On a campus where there is no tradition of regular assessment of student or faculty performance, the announcement that there is a plan afoot to establish a comprehensive student data base can raise faculty concern that they are going to be evaluated. Again, until there is at least some minimal demonstration of the potential usefulness of the project and until the motives of those promoting the project are clearly understood, there is likely to be a significant degree of resistance.

What I am really suggesting here is that in establishing any kind of a comprehensive student data base, there is a substantial amount of learning that must occur among members of the campus community. Sufficient time needs to be allowed for the community to develop trust in those responsible for developing the project and to appreciate some of the potential value of the project. For this reason, it is important first to implement the preliminary stages of the project—the retention data base and the preliminary student surveys—before any attempts are made to "sell" the campus community on the idea of a more grandiose project.

Use of Existing Data

Another item of conventional wisdom in the assessment field today is that the first step in the development of a student data base should be the pulling together of all existing data on the campus (Ewell, 1984; Jacobi, Astin, and Ayala, 1987). While this is a laudable goal in theory, in practice it may generate as many problems as it solves. In my travels to different campuses I have observed that except for data from the admissions and registrar's offices, most campus data on students are either unusable, very difficult to retrieve, or both. Except for projects that attempt systematically to survey students in a complete cohort (the CIRP Freshman Survey, for example), most existing sources of data on students have either been obtained on accidental samples or are in a form that would make retrieval in machine-readable form very difficult.

A more productive approach would be to encourage other campus administrative units (the alumni office, for example) to collect their data in a form that would allow it to be added easily to the integrated student data base. This is a long-term proposition. Before other data collection units can be persuaded to modify their data collection or data storage techniques, it may first be necessary to demonstrate some of the potential of the project (the value of the retention data base, for example).

Special consideration needs to be given to the use of data from cognitive testing. Given the enormous expenditure of student time and the considerable cost of most standardized tests, it is worth investing a significant effort to convert the information obtained from these tests into a talent development context. The most obvious way to do this is to posttest the same students after an appropriate period of time. Most institutions already employ some kind of testing program for admissions, and many also use placement tests. From a talent development perspective, these admissions and placement tests can be viewed as a kind of input pretest. This is especially the case with placement tests, which are presumably used because they indicate something about the student's entry level of performance. If, for example, a student is placed in a remedial or developmental course or program because of poor performance on a placement test, why not repeat the test at the end of the course or program to see whether the entering deficit has been removed? A similar argument could be made for admissions tests and, in particular, for achievement tests that might be required as part of the admissions process, although the cost of posttesting with relatively expensive instruments such as the College Board's Achievement Tests may be somewhat more difficult to justify.

The same kind of reasoning can be made for standardized testing that is done at the upper-division or graduation level. Many institutions require upper-division competency tests for certification purposes. Why not pretest these same devices at the same earlier point in order to determine how much growth or improvement has occurred? Such longitudinal data would provide an excellent basis for evaluating various patterns of course taking in terms of their effectiveness in developing the particular skill being measured. A procedure much like this is currently being followed at Austin Peay State University (Rudolph, 1989).

A final possibility concerns nationally standardized tests used for professional certification (e.g., the National Teacher Examination) or for admission to graduate or professional school (e.g., LSAT, GMAT, MCAT, and GRE). Eckerd College, for example, pretests its new freshmen with the GRE (Paskow, 1988). Pretesting with these devices can provide a baseline for determining how effectively the institution is preparing the student for entry to a profession or for admission to graduate or professional school. Also, when such longitudinal cognitive testing results are incorporated into the larger comprehensive student data base, it becomes possible to determine the effects of various other student input and environmental characteristics on test performance. Some of the tests that are used for admission to graduate school are so much like the SAT and ACT that these latter instruments might well serve as pretests, thereby obviating the need for additional testing.

Methods of Data Collection

A prime consideration in developing strategies for collecting data from students is *timing*. By far the best time to collect data from students is at the point of initial contact with the institution: registration or orientation. A student who is in the process of matriculating for the first time is generally in an extremely cooperative frame of mind and is therefore an ideal subject for pretest or placement assessments. It is important to capitalize on this opportunity as completely as possible and to include as many assessments as might be needed for a full-fledged program. Follow-up assessments are always more difficult since students may never again congregate in a single place at the same time and in the same cooperative spirit. With cognitive testing, in particular, it may well be necessary to mandate follow-up posttest assessments. Our experience with the FIPSE value-added consortium showed that follow-up cognitive posttesting needs to be carried out with a lot of planning. Voluntary participation in follow-up testing may lead to a large amount of attrition because of noncooperation. Required participation, however, raises both logistical and ethical issues. It may be difficult and expensive to schedule posttesting sessions for all students in a cohort. Further, faculty and administrators may question the desirability of required testing if they have not as yet come to appreciate the potential benefits of the larger assessment program. It is important not to engage the institution in an extensive program of follow-up cognitive testing before all segments of the academic community have been educated to the need for such posttesting.

Regardless of whether the follow-up posttesting with cognitive assessments is voluntary or required, it is important to educate faculty and students alike about the possible benefits and the importance of their active participation and cooperation. Even so, certain incentives should probably be provided for both students and faculty in order to secure their cooperation. For students, participation in cognitive posttesting might be incorporated into the requirements for a course. Finding appropriate incentives for faculty might be somewhat more difficult. Perhaps the most obvious strategy is to identify faculty who are sympathetic to the assessment concept and to involve them in the project from the beginning. Here we come to an important point: while it may not be necessary or even desirable to involve faculty formally in the development of the preliminary retention data base (above), it is absolutely necessary that they be involved from the beginning in any attempt at cognitive data collection. The reason is simple: Most college courses deal with cognitive functioning of some sort, and faculty have a vested interest in any assessment activities that bear directly on cognitive functioning. Even though cognitive outcome assessment can provide teaching faculty with important informational feedback, it also represents a potential threat if faculty feel it will be used to evaluate their teaching performance.

Early involvement of faculty is also helpful in determining whether a particular cognitive assessment procedure is really relevant to course objectives. Often, faculty decide that externally developed standardized tests are inadequate for assessing cognitive learning. When this happens, faculty should be invited to design their own assessment techniques. This approach has been used, with considerable success, at Alverno College (Alverno College Faculty, 1985) and Kean College of New Jersey (Kean College, 1988) among others.

A final data collection issue concerns the use of follow-up questionnaires. The most convenient way to administer a follow-up questionnaire is to use upper-division classrooms in which students are a kind of captive audience. The main drawback to this technique is that it excludes all the dropouts, thereby limiting the outcome assessment to the "satisfied customers." This may not be a problem in institutions that have extremely high retention rates, but for the majority of institutions (where retention rates are less than 60 percent), following up only enrolled students can result in serious sampling biases.

The obvious alternative to classroom administration of follow-up questionnaires is the mail. Mailed surveys, of course, carry their own problems, the most serious being nonresponse bias. Indeed, research indicates that the dropouts are the ones least likely to respond to mail follow-ups (Astin and Molm, 1972). There is, however, a useful technique that can be applied to correct for much of the response bias that occurs with mailed questionnaires. This technique requires only that extensive personal data on the nonrespondents (e.g., the CIRP Freshman Survey) be available, so that the data from the respondents can be adjusted to give the greatest weight to those respondents who most resemble the nonrespondents in their personal characteristics. In this way, the weighted questionnaire data simulate what the results would have been if all students had responded (for technical details, see Hurtado et al., 1989; Astin and Molm, 1972). Obviously, the only requirement for being able to apply such statistical adjustments is to have extensive input data on the students to whom follow-up questionnaires are sent. An excellent discussion of issues in conducting questionnaire follow-ups of students has been presented by Stevenson, Walleri, and Japely (1985).

Item Content

In constructing questionnaires, the issue of item content is very tricky and needs a great deal of thought and planning. I have participated in the design of perhaps a hundred different student questionnaires over the years and these instruments have been administered to more than eight million students at more than 1,300 institutions. This experience has caused me to form a number of rather strong views about item content. With no validation other than my personal experience, I can summarize these views as follows:

- The best questionnaires and the best items are those that are developed in a cooperative group setting, in which people openly discuss and debate the content and wording of each item. The principal requirement for group membership is that each person have an interest in developing the best possible questionnaires.
- The worst system of all is one in which a questionnaire has been developed by one person or group and must then be reviewed and approved by a second committee or group such as the academic senate.
- *Any* question on *any* subject can be construed as intrusive or as an invasion of privacy.
- Complaints about questionnaire content are much more likely to come from faculty or parents than from students.
- Students are much more likely to be "turned off" by questions that are extremely difficult to answer or by questionnaires that are extremely time-consuming rather than by "offensive" item content.
- Questions about illegal activities or explicit sexual behavior should be avoided. Inquiring about student *attitudes* toward such matters seems to create few problems.
- Sensitive questions should never be flagged by the provision of alternatives such as "I prefer not to answer" or "I consider this information personal." The message in such flags is that there is something impertinent or improper about the question. If there is a concern that students are being coerced into providing personal information, such concerns are much better handled with a blanket caveat at the beginning of the questionnaire indicating that student participation is voluntary.

- Wherever possible, items should require a minimum of reading and a maximum of responding. Such items generate the greatest amount of information in the shortest possible time.

Access to the Data

My utopian ideal of a comprehensive integrated student data base also includes the notion that the data will be widely used by all members of the campus community. Provided that the confidentiality of individual data is protected (see above), there is no reason why any student, faculty member, or administrator cannot or should not have access to the data base.

Ideally, anyone who has an interest in student development should be encouraged to use the data base. Most people working in the area of student services or student activities, for example, should have an interest in analyzing the data. Such studies could help student affairs personnel determine, among other things, which of the various services that they provide are most effective and which are most in need of review or revision.

Individual faculty members and departments could use the data base in a variety of ways. Beyond its obvious uses for studying course or program effectiveness, the data base could also be used by the faculty as a teaching tool. They could use the data for class projects in courses in education or the social sciences, for example. Faculty could also use the data to help students understand principles of measurement, statistics, and probability in mathematics and statistics courses.

Professors and administrators with expertise in statistical analysis of data could access the data base through the college's mainframe computer or be provided with floppy disks containing appropriate subfiles of the data for use on their personal computers. Those who lack such expertise could be encouraged to utilize the data by enlisting help either from computer center staff or from students or colleagues who have such expertise.

The ultimate aim of maximizing access to the student data base is to encourage all members of the academic community to focus their attention on the most fundamental institutional function: the development of the students' talents and abilities. This focus would help not only to enlighten the academic community about the strengths and weaknesses of the educational program but would also generate a spirit of inquiry and self-study across the campus.

Costs

A very complex and politically sensitive issue is the cost of establishing and maintaining a data base. Several assessment specialists (e.g., Ewell and Jones, 1985; Lewis, 1988) have attempted to estimate the costs of certain assessment activities, but the estimates vary by a considerable margin, depending on the assumptions one builds into the estimating process. Lewis (1988) has suggested using cost-benefit analyses in which costs are broken down into direct, incidental, and opportunity costs and benefits into direct, incidental, and secondary benefits.

There are certain out-of-pocket costs, which can be calculated with relative ease, that are incurred whenever externally developed tests and assessment devices are used. The primary problem with computing other costs is how to account for faculty and staff time. In institutions such as Alverno College or Empire State College, where assessment of student performance is viewed as a regular part of each faculty member's ordinary responsibilities (Alverno College Faculty, 1985; Lehmann, 1988), it would make no more sense to compute the costs of assessment in faculty time than it would be to compute the costs of classroom teaching, advising, research, or committee work.

In other institutions, the involvement of faculty and staff in assessment might be seen as an additional cost because it is viewed as an add-on to their normal responsibilities. Under these conditions, it would be necessary either to hire additional personnel or to effect some kind of tradeoff between assessment activities and other regular responsibilities.

In the long run, if assessment is to become a meaningful and important function to be carried out by faculty and staff, it must eventually be incorporated as part of their regular responsibilities.

SOME TECHNICAL CONSIDERATIONS

There are several technical considerations that need to be taken into account in designing and operating an integrated student data base. These include hardware and software, sampling, missing data, and use of item data. Each of these is discussed in turn below.

Hardware and Software

The rapidly changing market for commercially available hardware and software makes it extremely difficult to formulate hard-and-fast recommendations. By the time this book has been published and reviewed the available products will probably have changed dramatically. Nevertheless, there are a few principles that persons responsible for developing a comprehensive student data base may wish to consider.

In all likelihood the most appropriate place to locate and operate the data base is in the institution's principal mainframe computer center (some of the largest research universities, of course, operate several mainframe computers). The personnel in these centralized computer centers are most likely to be familiar with the data bases maintained by the admissions office, the registrar, and other administrative units that have institutionwide responsibilities. Furthermore, the capabilities for developing, maintaining, and updating large data files are almost certainly going to be greater in the mainframe center. Remember that once several cohort files representing different entering classes have been developed, the size of the total data base is likely to be quite large, especially if the variety of input, environmental, and outcome data is extensive.

One potential drawback of using the institutionwide mainframe computer center is the possible loss of control. Technical people in these centers have very strong notions about how to design and maintain data files, and in my experience these viewpoints are often at odds with the needs of assessment specialists and others who would be using the integrated student data base. The main problem is that the data bases with which computer center personnel are most familiar are built on the information retrieval principle rather than the data analysis principle. This problem is analogous to the one discussed earlier in this chapter, where I made a distinction between data bases designed for administrative use (where it is necessary to look up information on an individual person) and data bases designed for longitudinal statistical studies of students. If the mainframe computer center serves as the focal point for the integrated student data base, it is extremely important for the assessment specialist to maintain control over the design of the data base. Most important is that the cohort design be implemented and that each cohort file be independently accessible with relative ease.

A related issue is how best to facilitate access to the data within the larger academic community. For the most part other users in the institution will wish to access the data base in two quite different ways: through terminals connected to the mainframe computer and through personal computers operating with their own software. If the personal computers are wired to the mainframe, software should be developed that permits the user to create a subfile from any designated cohort file containing any specified set of variables. These subfiles could reside either on the hard disk of the personal computer or, if the file is not too large, on a floppy disk that could be used on any personal computer using the same operating system. For users whose personal computers are not hard-wired to the mainframe, the computer center will have to develop the capacity to provide subfiles on a floppy disk.

In order to make the data files maximally accessible to users across the campus, two conditions have to be met. First, there has to be extensive documentation of each cohort file so that any outside user could know what the file contains with relative ease. Second, software must be available to facilitate the acquisition of appropriate subfiles by users.

With respect to statistical software for analyzing data from the cohort files, the packages of choice are SPSS and SAS. I happen to prefer SPSS because of the output formats it produces from its cross-tabulation and regression programs and also because it generates step-by-step results for all variables in its stepwise regression program. In recent years many users have been attracted to SAS because of the relative ease with which it permits the user to manipulate data files and individual variables. The most recent version of SPSS (1988), however, incorporates many of these same features. In my experience, SPSS also seems to operate much faster than SAS (1985).

Sampling

As already indicated, the basic retention file should serve as the nucleus around which the integrated student data base is constructed. Every attempt should be made to ensure that this basic file covers *all* students from a given cohort, including those who might drop out very shortly after matriculating. Even if important data (such as admissions test scores) are missing on certain students in the cohort, these students should be represented in the file along with students with complete data. The retention file, in other words, should define the population around which all other data are developed.

Because of the considerable expense of doing cognitive testing with commercially available standardized tests or conducting mailed questionnaire follow-ups, it may be necessary to sample students rather than to assess the whole cohort. This situation would be especially true in very large institutions where any given cohort might include several thousand students. Nevertheless, users should recognize that the smaller number of cases available through sampling may make it difficult to do some of the most interesting analyses, such as departmental comparisons. Also, sampling for one purpose (e.g., a questionnaire follow-up) limits the use of those data for analyses involving assessments that have been carried out using independent sampling (e.g., some kind of cognitive testing). Thus, if the questionnaire follow-up is done on a 25 percent sample and the cognitive testing is carried out on an independent 25 percent sample from the same cohort, we would expect to obtain both test and questionnaire data on only about 6 or 7 percent of the original cohort. For this reason it is important to keep track of all the different assessments being done on various cohorts so that any new assessment can be designed to maximize overlap with other data that have already been collected. In this manner, the institution can make the greatest use of its different assessment activities.

Missing Data

A technical problem that plagues all assessment activities and, indeed, social science research in general, is missing data. (Readers who will not be involved in actually developing a data base can skip this section.) From admissions to placement testing to questionnaire assessment, it is a sure bet that certain input, environment, and outcome variables will be missing on at least a few cases and that whole categories of data (questionnaire responses, for example) will be missing on certain students. The question is how to handle this problem most efficaciously with minimal damage to the assessment and analysis process.

One very practical question is how to represent missing data on the different student data files. My own preference has always been to utilize a common indicator for missing data on all variables. Over the years I have preferred to represent a missing value by a zero. The only problem with this particular approach, of course, is that some variables might legitimately have the value of zero. The traditional method of coding dummy variables, for example, is 0 and 1. To reserve 0 for missing data, I normally code the dummy variables as 1 and 2 (a procedure which, incidentally, has no effect on the multivariate relationships of the variable). Whatever alternative is chosen, it is strongly recommended that some kind of common code for missing data be developed and used consistently throughout the data file.

A more difficult issue concerns how to treat missing data in data analyses. While this highly technical issue might be better presented in the appendix, I will discuss it here instead because we are on the subject of missing data. The main problems with missing data are (a) the loss of cases that occurs when the analytical procedures used require that all subjects have values on all variables; (b) the possible bias that occurs when people with missing data are excluded.

Over the years I have developed some rules of thumb that seem to work well in handling the missing data problem. First, I generally avoid multivariate analyses utilizing correlations that have been computed on a pair-wise basis. Sometimes the results based on such correlations are bizarre, especially when there are extensive numbers of missing cases on certain variables. Second, I *never* replace missing data on the dependent or outcome variable. Such a practice contributes nothing to your knowledge of how environments affect outcomes and introduces unnecessary error (and possibly unknown biases) into the multivariate results. For similar reasons, I seldom replace missing data on environmental variables. Finally, I generally replace missing data on all other independent variables, with the important exception of the pretest on the outcome measure (if one is available).

How, then, to replace missing data? What values do we use? Generally, I prefer to use the mean value based on all students for whom the data on the variable in question are available, in part because software packages such as SPSS and SAS permit one to do this with relative ease. However, there may be certain occasions when the mean is not the most appropriate value. A more complicated but possibly more valid procedure is to replace missing data by regression analysis. The way this works is by means of regression questions that make it possible to estimate each input variable using all other input variables. Thus, if information on a particular input variable is missing for a particular subject, one can use the regression equation for that variable to estimate the missing value by plugging in information on the other variables that are available on that particular subject. This is an extremely costly and tedious procedure, but it offers perhaps the best solution to the question of how to replace missing data. Whether it really improves results to the extent that would justify the trouble and cost is really not known.

We now come to the question of whether the cohort data files should contain replacements for missing data. It can be extremely time consuming to replace missing data on the input variables every time we use a cohort file, especially if there are many input variables. Thus, it would represent a considerable convenience to the users of the file if missing data on the input variables were replaced in the master file. Since different users may have different needs with respect to missing data, it is perhaps not advisable to replace missing data routinely, but to offer it as an option for those users who desire it.

Use of Item Data

Considering the substantial costs of standardized tests and the heavy reliance of most colleges and universities on such tests, it is unfortunate that so little of the information contained in these tests is actually used for educational purposes.. A particularly important source of information is contained in the individual test item. If it were possible to know how students perform on individual items—which ones they find most difficult and which ones they find relatively easy—such information could be invaluable in examining the effectiveness of particular courses and in planning and evaluating the curriculum.

The purveyors of standardized tests have resisted providing information on how students perform on individual test items on the grounds that such information is unreliable. As pointed out in chapters 4 and 6, the "unreliability" argument may be valid in the case of individual students, but it is not relevant to information provided in *aggregate* form. That is, it would be extremely valuable for faculty members to know how a *group* of students performs on each test item. While most testing companies do not provide such information on a routine basis, I believe that they could be persuaded to do so if institutions insisted on it as a condition of using their tests. By identifying items with which students are having particular difficulties and by knowing which incorrect alternatives students are selecting, faculty will be in a much better position to know how to reshape the curriculum and to modify their pedagogical techniques.

The same arguments in support of using individual test questions could be made for locally developed instruments. If such test item information is included in the student data base, the potential value of the information is increased substantially, since it will be possible to identify which students (in terms of gender, ethnicity, major, class, and so on) are having particular difficulties with which kinds of test questions.

SUMMARY

The lack of a comprehensive data base greatly limits the potential value of any new outcome assessment activities that an institution might undertake. Among other things, such a data base makes it possible to determine how student performance is related to various environmental experiences (courses taken, place of residence, etc.) while controlling for student characteristics at the point of entry (inputs). But even if an institution has no interest in conducting studies of environmental impact, there are good administrative reasons for having an integrated student data base that simultaneously includes input, environmental, and outcome data.

A comprehensive student data base should be designed around a cohort principle, with each new group of entering students creating a new cohort. The actual development of the data base should be in stages. The first stage should consist of a retention file that combines information on each student's retention status with data from the admissions and registrar's offices. Much practical use can be made of such a file while the larger, more comprehensive file is being created.

Among the other practical matters that need to be taken into consideration are the security and confidentiality of the files, the visibility of the project within the campus community, ways to utilize existing campus data, methods of data collection, item content, hardware and software, missing data, and sampling.

9

ASSESSMENT AS DIRECT
FEEDBACK TO THE LEARNER

To this point we have been looking at assessment primarily as a means of informing or enlightening the educator: to aid the decision-making process by providing information on how various educational programs, practices, and policies affect talent development. In this chapter we shall examine the ways in which assessment can be used to influence talent development directly by serving both as feedback and as an incentive to the learner. We shall consider both students and faculty members as potential learners.

From the perspective of the input-environment-outcome (I-E-O) model, direct feedback constitutes one of the *environmental* variables that can be used to improve performance. The learner's performance which initially generates that feedback can be viewed as an *input* or pretest variable, while the learner's subsequent performance (following the feedback) can be viewed as an *outcome* or posttest variable.

Although measurement specialists have never developed formal theories to explain how or under what conditions assessment affects the learning process, there seem to be several implicit theories that underlie much of the discussion and debate about assessment. Since each theory implies a somewhat different approach to assessment, it is important to understand the reasoning behind each one. For simplicity I have identified two broad categories of theory: incentive theories and information theories.

ASSESSMENT AS INCENTIVE: THE CARROT AND THE STICK

Theories based on "carrot and stick" reasoning see assessment primarily as an external incentive to learn that operates both as a reward and a punishment. When it comes to facilitating learning, most of our traditional assessment in higher education can best be justified on the basis of its incentive value. Surely the most common example of assessment based on this particular theory is the grade. Grading in higher education is involved at several different levels: we grade course assignments, exams, and overall course performance (the final grade), and we aggregate course final grades into a cumulative grade-point average (GPA). I have already argued that grading in higher education is often justified on the basis of its usefulness in screening and certifying, but to the extent that it is regarded as being useful in the learning process, it is supposed to operate primarily as an incentive: students are expected to work harder because they know their performance will be graded. Grades, in turn, are important to the student not only because they can influence subsequent employment and educational opportunities but also because of their implications for the student's self-esteem. Getting good grades is presumably good for one's sense of self-worth, and getting poor grades is presumably detrimental to one's sense of self-worth. Thus grades can operate as both a carrot and a stick, depending on whether the student is oriented toward attaining success or avoiding failure.

While standardized tests and other types of student screening devices are viewed as aids to the talent development process even less often than grading is, to the extent that such tests in their present form might affect learning, they would operate once again under the carrot-and-stick principle. High school students are thus expected to study hard for the SAT or ACT because they want to gain admission to the best (i.e., most prestigious) college. Undergraduates will study hard for professional licensing exams or to prepare for the GRE, LSAT, MCAT, or GMAT because they want to be admitted to the best possible graduate or professional school. Finally, professional school students will study hard so they can pass the state bar or medical licensing exams. In all such situations these examinations can be regarded as external incentives or motivators.

Most assessments of college and university faculty follow the pattern for student assessments: to the extent that they are assumed to have any value in developing faculty talent, they are supposed to operate primarily as incentives. Professors' knowledge that their scholarly work will be assessed by their colleagues presumably serves to motivate them to do more and better writing and publishing, and their awareness that their students will evaluate their course is expected to motivate them to do a better job of teaching. Again, both the carrot and the stick are involved: college professors want to be respected by their colleagues and admired by their students, and they want to avoid losing their jobs because they fail to make tenure or, if they are already tenured, being regarded as "dead wood."

In a similar vein, the reasoning behind many of the state initiatives to mandate assessment activities in higher education (see chapter 11) is based on carrot-and-stick reasoning. To some state officials, student outcome assessment represents a kind of club that can be used to motivate faculty to be "more responsible" for their students' learning and to compel institutions to be more "accountable" in their teaching activities. Such officials thus believe that institutions and their professors can be forced to do a more effective job of teaching if the results of their pedagogical efforts are exposed to the public. (Assessment programs in Florida and Georgia appear to be based at least in part on such reasoning.) The not-so-subtle implication here, of course, is that current efforts at teaching are *not* very successful. Otherwise, why are the outcome assessments needed?

In other states, mandated assessment activities are viewed more like a carrot (Tennessee being one example). When assessment results show that an institution is doing a good job, it gets extra funding from the state. Of course, once such a program becomes established and most institutions are receiving incentive funding (the current situation in Tennessee), the distinction between carrot and stick becomes increasingly difficult to make. *Not* receiving full incentive funding is thus viewed as a punishment, i.e., a virtual loss of funding. (The pros and cons of state incentive funding programs are discussed in detail in chapter 11.)

ASSESSMENT AS INFORMATION: THE FEEDBACK PRINCIPLE

A very different way of looking at assessment is to regard it as a way of generating information that can facilitate the learning process. This approach is based on a well-established principle of learning called feedback or knowledge of results. Many hundreds of studies of human learning have shown that the learning process can be substantially enhanced if the learners have appropriate knowledge of results showing how much progress they have made and pointing out specific areas where additional work is needed. Without such feedback, learning can be very slow and difficult or, under some conditions, virtually impossible.

To illustrate how the feedback principle works in practice, let us consider a common learning situation in higher education, the freshman course in English composition, and contrast the feedback approach with the incentive approach to assessment. Assume that we have two students of equal writing ability but whose first essays are graded by different teaching assistants. Student A's essay comes back with just a grade, C−, and perhaps some "incentive" comments such as "You need to work harder in this course," "This is a very weak essay," "Not bad for a first try, but you need to improve." In contrast, Student B's essay comes back with no grade but with a series of specific comments: "This first paragraph should tell the reader briefly what the whole essay is about," "This is not a complete sentence. Rewrite it to make sure it has a subject and a verb," "Try writing shorter sentences," "This is a very interesting idea; try explaining it a bit more." Whereas the information given to student A might serve as an incentive to work harder, student

B has a much clearer idea of what he should do to improve his writing. There is no reason, of course, why both the incentive and the enlightenment principles cannot operate simultaneously; the point to keep in mind is that the two principles involve different mechanisms (reward and punishment versus knowledge of results) and imply different kinds of assessments (evaluative judgments versus feedback to steer the student's future efforts in particular directions).

Perhaps the best examples of the feedback principle as applied to the assessment of student learning are the specific narrative comments provided to students on exams, essays, term papers, and other student work. Some innovative institutions—Hampshire College and the University of California at Santa Cruz, for example—actually use narrative evaluations in place of the traditional course grades and GPA. Instead of a decimal number, students receive a written evaluation that attempts to touch not only on the overall quality of their work but also on specific strengths and weaknesses. Such comments usually cover cognitive skills (thinking, logic, writing, speaking, analysis) as well as work habits and motivation. Moreover, where appropriate, these evaluations also include specific suggestions for improvement.

Assessments of faculty performance are seldom done to provide "knowledge of results," with one notable exception: the pre-tenure review. In some institutions the work of assistant professors is reviewed in detail after their first three or four years of employment. One important purpose of such reviews is to identify any significant deficiencies in the assistant professor's performance far enough in advance to give the candidate an opportunity to remedy them. However, many academics seem to believe that if such reviews are even mildly negative (especially with respect to the candidate's scholarly work or research), the candidate's prospects for ever making tenure are bleak indeed. Negative reviews are thus taken to mean that the candidate should begin to seek employment elsewhere. Such beliefs, unfortunately, tend to undermine the potential educational value of this feedback.

One important form of assessment in higher education that is done *primarily* to provide feedback is the institutional accreditation process. Except for newly established institutions that are seeking accreditation for the first time, the accreditation process is seldom concerned with the question of whether the institution being assessed should be reaccredited. Consequently, a positive decision on reaccreditation is a foregone conclusion in the vast majority of cases. What is really involved in most such visits is a thorough review of the institution's curriculum, facilities, programs, policies, fiscal condition, and governance by an expert team of colleagues from peer institutions. The basic aim of most accrediting visits is thus to "enlighten" the institution concerning its major strengths and weaknesses. Most accreditation teams make a number of specific recommendations for how the institution can strengthen its programs and operations.

INCENTIVES OR FEEDBACK?

While there is no reason that a given assessment activity cannot simultaneously utilize both the incentive and feedback principles, it is important to realize that these two principles are based on quite different conceptions of the assessee. Thus, advocates of the incentive approach believe that external rewards and punishments are needed to motivate students and faculty to develop their talents. The feedback theory, on the other hand, implicitly assumes that students and faculty naturally want to learn and to develop their talents, and that what they need in order to do this is good information about their progress, their specific strengths and weaknesses, and the specific types of activities that are most likely to contribute to their future development.

So far we have been focusing on theories of how assessment can facilitate the talent development process directly. We have noted a few instances in which assessment in higher education is thought to operate on the feedback principle, but the educational rationale underlying most of our assessment activities, especially testing and grading of students and reviews of faculty performance, seem to be based more on the rewards and punishments of the incentive principle. I have already noted that incentive assessment can also have feedback value, but there are at least two instances in higher education in which the power of assessment to enlighten is seriously compromised by its use as an incentive.

The first of these is the course grade. The fact that professors must grade their students as well as teach them makes it difficult for students to develop the trust that is sometimes necessary for them to ask for the kind of feedback they really need. The incentive principle encourages students to impress their professors with their knowledge and competence so as to get a good grade. At the same time, it discourages them from exposing their ignorance, so to speak. If students are confused or uncertain about some aspect of the course, they may be reluctant to seek appropriate feedback because they are afraid that the professor will evaluate them negatively. For the past fifteen years I have taught a very technical and difficult graduate course in statistics and research methodology, and the biggest pedagogical problem I have is convincing students that they will not be punished or judged negatively if they are completely honest with me about what they do not fully understand. Unfortunately, our predilection for incentive-oriented assessment in education has conditioned many of our students to view the professor or teacher more as someone to impress or manipulate than as someone who can help them learn.

The other assessment activity in which the potential educational value of feedback is compromised by the incentive principle is student evaluations of teaching. Many of us who teach are in a position to benefit substantially (develop our teaching talents) from end-of-course evaluations by students. However, because the results of such evaluations are usually made available to others and used in personnel decisions, we often focus more on *getting* good ratings than on actually *learning* from the ratings (Gleason, 1986). (This situation is directly analogous to that in which students are motivated to study for the test rather than to learn the material.) One specific danger in such ratings is that we teachers will be tempted to "go easy" on our students for fear of getting poor ratings. Thus, we might give fewer assignments, easier exams, or fewer exams in order to get more favorable ratings. Or, we might be tempted to do more entertaining and less teaching in the class. The problem, in short, is that when such ratings are used as incentives, we are being encouraged to manipulate them rather than learn from them.

EFFECTIVE ASSESSMENT IN THE CLASSROOM: A PROTOTYPIC EXAMPLE

Since the classroom provides our greatest opportunity to influence student learning directly, let us now consider how classroom assessment and feedback can be used to enhance the learning process. Ironically, most principles of good assessment for learning can be illustrated by looking at some of our "softest" fields, especially the fine and performing arts. Let us take a prototypic example from the arts: the piano lesson. By examining in some detail just what happens during a typical piano lesson, we can discover virtually every principle by which assessment and feedback can be used to enhance the talent development process directly. As we discuss the lesson, I will spell out each principle in italics.

To begin with, both the teacher and the student are interested in improving the quality of the student's piano playing. In other words, *both the teacher and the student are committed to a common goal or set of goals*. These goals, at least in part, have to do with talent development: growth or improvement on the part of the student. Most students, however, are also interested in another type of goal: *that the learning process itself should be enjoyable, gratifying, meaningful, interesting, or in some other respect pleasurable or rewarding*. Piano teachers sometimes forget this, and when they do, learning the piano from the perspective of the student often becomes boring, unpleasant, or pure drudgery. When all the fun and enjoyment is taken out of the learning process, the only remaining incentive is the learning outcome itself (improvement in playing ability), and often this rather remote goal is simply not enough to sustain the student's interest in taking lessons and practicing. Again, such problems underscore the importance of having the teacher and the student committed to a *common* set of goals.

What about the learning process itself? Let's first look at what the teacher does. Once the teacher has defined the task ("practice this scale," "learn that piece," "try playing it like this"), the student is asked to perform, and the teacher *watches* and *listens*. Basically, what the teacher is doing here is *assessing the student's performance*. Clearly, the *performance assessments should be relevant to the shared goals of the learning process*. While it is possible to make a single overall judgment of the student's performance (excellent, good, fair, poor), performance assessments are inevitably based on several criteria rather than one. Thus, the student's playing can be judged in terms of accuracy (playing the right notes), tempo, dynamics (loudness and softness), touch, interpretation, and so on. Such *outcome* assessment might also be coupled with *process* assessments, whereby the teacher sees how the student sits or holds her hands, observes her emotional state, or inquires about how she practices between lessons. In short, *the teacher's assessments of student performance should be multidimensional and can involve observations of the learning process (environment) as well as of learning outcomes*.

The information obtained through the teacher's assessments is then used by the teacher to generate *feedback* to the student, usually in the form of spoken comments and suggestions. Sometimes this feedback consists simply of the raw assessment data ("you should have played an A-flat here instead of an A"), sometimes it consists of direct suggestions for improvement ("try counting out loud while you play"), and sometimes it is intended merely to serve as encouragement ("you played it much better that time"). Whatever the form, *assessment and feedback is intended to serve the goals of teaching and learning: to facilitate student learning and talent development and to make the learning process itself more rewarding*.

Once feedback has been provided, the student typically is asked to perform once again, and the assessment process continues. When feedback from the teacher does not serve its intended purposes (performance does not improve, the student becomes frustrated or discouraged), the teacher may simply repeat the feedback ("you still played an A instead of an A-flat; try it again"), or she may try using a different form of feedback ("try playing this passage more slowly"). In other words, *assessment and feedback should be an ongoing, iterative proceeding that is integral to the learning process rather than a one-time activity carried out only at the end of the learning process*. It would appear that, in the fine and performing arts at least, much of what we refer to as "teaching" activity consists of providing assessment and feedback to the student. Whether assessment and feedback should have the same priority in teaching other academic fields is perhaps debatable, but there seems to be little question that *assessment of student performance and providing feedback to students should constitute a significant part of any teacher's pedagogical activities*.

Let's now look at the piano lesson from the student's perspective. The nature of almost any performing art is that the performance itself generates direct feedback to the student. The student, in other words, can listen to what she plays (feedback) and make a judgment about it (assessment). It is thus possible for the student to learn to play the piano without the aid of a teacher (and, in fact, many people do), since a good deal of feedback is automatically built into the performance process. In short, *students can learn by generating their own feedback and assessment.* However, if the student is ever going to achieve a high level of proficiency in playing, a substantial amount of assessment and feedback from others (fellow musicians, friends, teachers) is almost always required. *Most "learners," in other words, eventually need "teachers" to provide assessment and feedback.*

It is difficult to overestimate the importance of assessment and feedback in the learning process. Consider what would happen if the feedback were eliminated. Imagine what it would be like for a deaf person to try to teach someone else how to play the piano. Or imagine how difficult it would be for a deaf person to teach herself how to play. Similar problems arise in other fields of the arts. How could a blind person learn how to paint or to teach anyone else to paint or draw? And how could you teach somebody to write if you could never read their writing?

It might be added here that the importance of assessment and feedback to the learning process is just as great when we reverse the roles and view the *teacher* as a learner. How do people learn to be good teachers? Again, we see the essential role of assessment and feedback. The piano teacher can make assessments of the student's performance, provide feedback, and then observe the student's performance once more. If the performance gets worse, fails to improve, or improves too slowly, the teacher can try something else. Gradually, the teacher learns what works and what doesn't work, and under what conditions. Note, however, that the student's performance in this instance serves as feedback to the *teacher*. The teacher still does the assessment, but without such feedback provided on a regular basis, it is difficult to see how anyone could learn to be an effective piano teacher.

In many respects the need for assessment and feedback in learning any performing art is self-evident. Indeed, if the performing arts constituted the whole of our curriculum in higher education, there would be little need for a book such as this one, since the role of assessment and feedback is fundamental to the implicit theories that govern the activities of all teachers of the performing arts. No performing arts teacher in her right mind would employ techniques that contradict or ignore these principles. However, the central role of assessment and feedback is often overlooked in the implicit theories used by teachers in most other fields. If professors in these other fields were to apply the principles of effective assessment and feedback more fully in their own teaching activities, the educational impact of our higher education programs would improve substantially.

I have chosen the performing arts to illustrate the importance of assessment and feedback in the learning process for two reasons. First, the essential role of assessment and feedback is patently obvious in the arts; it would be next to impossible for either teachers or students to learn without it. Second, in the performing arts it is easier to see the importance of timing in providing feedback. Imagine how difficult it would be for the beginning piano student to benefit from feedback that came two weeks after she performed. But problems in timing can also occur when there is too much feedback provided too soon. For example, if the teacher stops the student from playing when there is the slightest error in any aspect of the performance, the student can quickly become frustrated and discouraged. Or, if the teacher provides too much feedback at one time or asks the student to attend to too many different things while performing, the student can become confused and not really be able to benefit from the feedback.

FEEDBACK IN OTHER FIELDS

What is the nature of feedback in the humanities, social sciences, and natural sciences? Unfortunately for the learner, most teachers in these other fields have chosen to employ teaching methods that do not, in themselves, generate timely and appropriate assessment and feedback for either the student or the teacher. This is partly due to the nature of the fields themselves, and partly an economic matter—large lecture sessions do not readily lend themselves to individualized feedback.

What can professors do to simulate the kinds of feedback available to those who teach in the performing arts? A unique approach to assessment in the classroom is what Patricia Cross (1989) has called "classroom research." Cross's basic idea is for classroom teachers to develop a series of small-scale assessments that can be given regularly in a class to provide information about what and how students are actually learning. Cross and Angelo (1988) have developed a detailed handbook of such classroom assessment techniques for use by teaching faculty. Three different kinds of assessment techniques are presented and described: those for assessing intellectual development, those for assessing students' self-awareness as learners, and those for assessing student reactions to both the teacher and the course.

Part of the difficulty with academic fields outside the arts is that the "talents" that are being developed are not as salient as performance talent in music, art, or theater. One cannot directly observe the student's critical thinking ability, cultural understanding, esthetic appreciation, or knowledge of history or chemistry. For this reason, student assessment in these fields has traditionally come to rely on indirect measures called *tests*. What is especially significant about testing in higher education is that most of it is *not* done to provide students and faculty with feedback to enhance the talent development process. Rather, as we have already seen, testing is done primarily to produce course grades and to sort, select, classify, and certify students. As a consequence, both the nature of most tests and the timing of their administration are ill suited to the teaching-learning process and therefore of limited value in furthering the institution's talent development mission.

To illustrate these last points, let's look at how we test students in the light of the (italicized) principles set forth in the preceding paragraphs. For purposes of this discussion we will consider the kinds of assessment and feedback that the student is likely to encounter in a typical lower-division undergraduate course offered in a large public institution (where the majority of undergraduates are to be found). While the problem illustrated here may not occur as frequently in smaller institutions or in upper-division courses, there are few courses outside the performing arts where some improvement could not be achieved through more diligent application of the principles of effective assessment and feedback.

SHARED GOALS: TALENT DEVELOPMENT AND SATISFACTION. Are the teacher and student in the typical psychology or history course committed to a common set of goals? Not necessarily. The student may merely want to be entertained or to satisfy a course requirement while the professor may be more focused on helping students learn. Or, the professor may be more interested in impressing students with his knowledge whereas the students may be focused more on getting a good grade.

RELEVANCE OF ASSESSMENT AND FEEDBACK TO SHARED GOALS. Even if professor and student were committed to the common goal of talent development, the single most common assessment procedure, the course final examination, would be of limited value because it does not really say much about what has been learned (i.e., about talent development). This and the preceding principle are, of course, closely linked: without a common student-faculty commitment to talent development, it is highly unlikely that assessment and feedback will be used to further this purpose.

MULTIDIMENSIONALITY. Students in many college courses receive little feedback beyond a single score on a final examination (the number or percent of correct answers) or worse yet, a relativistic assessment in the form of a letter grade (A−, C+, etc.). Even when the student prepares a term paper rather than (or in addition to) an exam, the feedback often consists of little more than a final grade or a few written comments.

INCLUSION OF "PROCESS" DATA. This category includes information such as how the student behaves in class (interaction with others, note taking) as well as out-of-class behavior such as reading and study habits and use of the library. Only in very rare instances do faculty members even bother to gather such information, much less use it in providing feedback to students. It is true that many institutions now have programs or centers to enhance students' learning skills, but such activities are usually not directly linked to courses, and student participation is usually voluntary and therefore infrequent.

ENHANCEMENT OF LEARNING. Perhaps the best assessment for learning that goes on outside the performing arts occurs in laboratory work or with the homework assignments that are common in the natural sciences. Laboratory work is usually monitored closely, and homework (e.g., problem sets) is usually evaluated on an individual basis. Otherwise, about the only widely used assessment approach that might be useful in enhancing the learning process is the mid-term exam. Depending on the form of such exams and the type of feedback provided, such assessments have the potential for being of significant value in the learning process. The typical final exam, of course, comes far too late in the process.

ASSESSMENT AS AN ONGOING, ITERATIVE PROCESS. Except for mid-term exams and lab work and homework assignments in the natural sciences (above), most assessment and feedback is a one-shot activity conducted in connection with specific courses. Daily "pop" quizzes are perhaps the only exception, and they are seldom used. Furthermore, assessments from different courses are seldom compared and contrasted over time. Thus, for any student it is very difficult to determine how much or what type of talent development is actually occurring.

FACULTY TIME AND EFFORT DEVOTED TO ASSESSMENT AND FEEDBACK. Outside the arts, the greatest degree of faculty involvement in assessment and feedback probably occurs in courses in English composition. Among professors who teach most large undergraduate lecture courses, however, only a very small fraction of total teaching time is devoted to assessment and feedback. Indeed, in many large undergraduate courses, professors devote no time to assessment and feedback, relying entirely on teaching assistants to administer examinations and grade papers. When professors do conduct their own assessment activities, they often utilize multiple-choice tests that can be scored and graded by machines.

STUDENT-GENERATED FEEDBACK. The most common form of student-generated feedback occurs with term papers and other written assignments: students can read what they have written and adjust their writing accordingly. Students can also generate feedback from each other by sharing and critiquing written assignments. Some institutions (e.g., Evergreen State College in Washington) actually structure their general education courses in this fashion. But formal opportunities for students to generate assessment and feedback from professors are relatively rare, especially in large undergraduate lecture courses. Nevertheless, an enterprising student in almost any type of institution can generate a considerable amount of feedback by staying after class to talk to professors and by meeting with professors during office hours. Unfortunately, few students take advantage of such opportunities, nor do most institutions encourage students to do so.

OPTIMAL TIMING OF FEEDBACK. Most feedback occurs at the worst possible time: at the end of the course. Once the student finishes the final paper or final exam, interest in any meaningful feedback (beyond the final grade) diminishes considerably, as the student goes on vacation, prepares for the next term, or graduates. As already mentioned, mid-term exams are well timed, but what may be the best time for assessment—at the beginning of a course—is seldom used.

In summary, this overview indicates that the best principles of assessment and feedback are seldom followed or applied in the typical lower-division undergraduate course. And if we include standardized tests in our review, the picture is even more discouraging. The most widely used tests, of course, are the national undergraduate admission tests (the SAT and ACT) and the graduate and professional school admissions tests (GRE, MCAT, GMAT, LSAT). The feedback from these tests consists primarily of norm-referenced scores that tell the student how well he is performing only in relation to other students. The feedback is multidimensional (in that most tests generate more than one score), but the student is generally at a loss to explain how or why he performed as he did on the various subtests. This is especially true for "aptitude" tests like the SAT and GRE. Finally, the normative feedback tells the student almost nothing about what or how much has been learned over time (no two tests produce scores that can be compared to derive change measures), and even less about what the student might do in the future to improve his performance.

Feedback from lower-division assessment activities is of equally limited value to the *professor*. Standardized, norm-referenced test results tell the professors virtually nothing about the effectiveness of their pedagogical efforts, and course grades are not much better. Final examination results offer somewhat better information, especially if they are aggregated across students in some fashion to provide a picture of the class's specific strengths and weaknesses (a practice that is, unfortunately, greatly underutilized). Final exam results would, of course, be much more informative if they could be compared with pretest results given at the beginning of the class. Perhaps the best single source of feedback for the professor is the student course evaluations that are now widely used in many institutions.

DEVELOPING FACULTY TALENTS

Throughout this book I have tried to emphasize that the philosophical and practical arguments underlying effective student assessment can be applied with equal validity to the assessment of faculty. Unfortunately, most of our traditional procedures for assessing faculty are carried out in much the same spirit as traditional assessments of students: they are intended to evaluate faculty for purposes of hiring, promoting, and tenuring rather than to provide feedback for purposes of enhancing talent development among faculty.

When it comes to developing the faculty member's *research* talents, existing feedback systems probably work reasonably well. The faculty review process—which tends to assign a high priority to research and scholarship—certainly provides plenty of incentive for faculty to develop their research and writing talents. In addition, the peer review procedures that operate within most academic disciplines to determine who gets research grants and whose work gets published or displayed provides not only plenty of incentives but also excellent feedback for developing research talents. An article submitted for publication in a scholarly journal ordinarily receives one or more detailed written critiques that spell out its particular strengths and weaknesses and that often include suggestions for improvement. Useful feedback is also obtained from colleagues during the conduct of collaborative work and from peers who might be asked to review creative work prior to its showing, performance, or submission for publication. In short, the peer review system seems to be well designed to provide the kind of feedback that faculty members need to develop their research, writing, and performing skills.

The feedback that comes with reviews of scholarly work done in connection with the personnel review process are probably of less value for developing the faculty's research and creative talents. Details of these reviews are not always made available to the candidate. In the case of most hiring decisions, candidates have no idea what has been said about their work either by outside reviewers or by members of the search committee. Reviews of scholarly work are sometimes shared with candidates who have come up for promotion or tenure, but often these reviews are so generalized and so judgmental that it is difficult for the candidate to realize any useful feedback from them. The one exception to this generalization, as already noted, is the pre-tenure review that some colleges and universities now conduct with their assistant professors several years before the tenure decision must be made.

Concerning the enhancement of the faculty's pedagogical talents, by far the most common feedback comes from student ratings of classroom instruction. These ratings have become so widespread during the past several decades that most institutions and faculty members now take them for granted. Although many professors continue to argue that student ratings have no validity and are little more than popularity contests, there is a growing body of evidence (Centra, 1973; Cohen, 1980; Murray, 1985) showing that the feedback from student ratings can indeed improve teaching.

Other than student ratings, the most common way of assessing teaching performance is peer review. In the typical review, the professor's syllabi are examined by faculty colleagues. Unfortunately, this method of evaluation falls prey to all the problems of the *environment only* approach to assessment (see chapter 2). Moreover, it looks at only a narrow piece of the total environment (course content).

There are several steps that can be taken to improve the quality of feedback that faculty members receive from their pedagogical efforts. For one, student ratings of instruction should cease to be an option. Given their great potential value as feedback, they should be mandated on an institution wide basis, with the proviso that the results be for the instructor's eyes only. There are several ways in which these ratings might be designed to avoid some of the problems usually associated with the typical rating scale. In particular, it is important to design the rating procedure so each faculty member receives feedback about specific changes that might improve the course.

Despite their widespread use, student ratings are frequently used in ways that run contrary to the principles of good feedback for learners. When ratings are made public (for instance, in student-published guides) or are used as a basis for making personnel decisions, the instructor is motivated to manipulate the ratings rather than to view them as a way to improve teaching. Thus, the potential learning value of the feedback is compromised by the incentive system that is set up. Moreover, when poor ratings are made public, the professor is tempted to rationalize the results away rather than to learn from them. If institutions feel that students' evaluations must be made public or that they are necessary for personnel actions, it is probably best to employ two sets of ratings, one for the record and one for the private edification of the professor.

Because student ratings of classroom instruction are so common, institutions might well invest a good deal of effort in evaluating and improving the procedures used. Under some conditions, for example, student ratings are subject to biases that have little if anything to do with the quality of instruction. Bassin (1974), for example, has shown that courses with quantitative content tend to get lower ratings than nonquantitative courses.

Another potentially useful form of feedback can be provided by teaching consultants (Katz, 1985). Ideally, teaching consultants would make periodic visits to the classrooms of all instructors to provide feedback in the form of consultation and constructive criticism. If it comes from a trusted colleague or outside teaching consultant, such consultation can help faculty members "examine and enrich their current assumptions and skills in a supportive but challenging climate" (Carrier, Dalgaard, and Simpson, 1983, p. 196). Few faculty members are able to view their own classroom performance with complete objectivity; therefore, a consultant who observes a class directly can help faculty members see the implicit theories on which they operate (Argyris and Schön, 1974; Hunt, 1976). If a faculty colleague rather than an outside teaching consultant serves in this capacity, the colleague should be exempted from participating in any personnel actions involving the instructor being evaluated.

One of the most thorough analyses of different methods for appraising faculty performance has recently been presented by Blackburn and Pitney (1988). They make the very important point that in order to be of maximal use in facilitating faculty development, any form of feedback should be individualized . For this reason they are skeptical about the value of the typical rating forms used to evaluate classroom instruction since these tend to force faculty members into a common yardstick for purposes of evaluation. They point out, for example, that most such forms explicitly value being "well organized" in the class. Under such circumstances, certain kinds of more open-ended pedagogical techniques will certainly be discouraged, and faculty may be deterred from experimenting with new instructional techniques. Blackburn and Pitney also make the important point that feedback about the service aspect of the faculty member's performance (advising, committee work, etc.) usually contains little information on the *quality* of that service. Thus, while the review might indicate how many and what kinds of committees the faculty member participated in, it ordinarily says very little about whether that participation was helpful or obstructive to the committee's activities. Blackburn and Pitney conclude that the most useful form of feedback might be a personal portfolio that contains detailed documentation about the candidate's performance as well as personal commentary from the candidate about that performance and any future plans for change or improvement.

SUMMARY

In several ways, assessment can be used to enhance talent development directly through its immediate effects on the student or faculty member being assessed. There are at least two different theories about how assessment can benefit the assessee: the carrot-and-stick theory by which assessment serves as an incentive, and the feedback theory by which assessment provides information that can be useful to the assessee in the learning process. Because a given assessment activity can serve both as an incentive and as feedback, the potential value of the feedback can be compromised when the assessment is also used to evaluate the assessee's performance for purposes of grading, awarding credits, hiring, or promotion.

To illustrate some of the principles underlying effective feedback, a hypothetical scenario was borrowed from the field of the performing arts: the piano lesson. By observing how a skilled piano teacher can use assessment and feedback to enhance the student's ability to play, one can deduce several principles of good practice to use in designing feedback systems in the classroom.

The chapter concludes with a discussion of current procedures for assessing faculty performance and presents several suggestions for how these assessments can be improved to assist faculty in developing their scholarly and pedagogical talents.

10

ASSESSMENT AND EQUITY

Among proponents of equal access and expanding opportunities in higher education, there are few issues that generate as much heat as testing and assessment. The basis for much of their resistance to the use of assessment in higher education is easy to understand, given the following facts: (1) blacks, Hispanics, and poor students are substantially underrepresented in American higher education, especially in the more select or elite institutions; (2) American higher education institutions rely heavily on two measures—the high school grade point average and scores on standardized college admission tests—to select their students; and (3) blacks, Hispanics and poor students tend to receive lower high school GPAs and lower test scores than do other groups. Obviously, the continuing reliance on such measures by college and university admission offices will make it very difficult for any educationally disadvantaged group to attain equal or proportionate access to higher education opportunities.

The use of grades and test scores for admission to higher education has serious equity implications beyond the competitive disadvantage that it creates for certain groups in the college admissions process. Because the lower schools tend to imitate higher education in their choice and use of assessment technology, there is a heavy reliance on school grades and standardized tests all the way down to the primary schools. Given the normative nature of such measures (students are basically being compared with each other; see chapter 3), students who perform below "the norm" are receiving important negative messages about their performance and capabilities. At best, they are being told that they are not working hard enough; at worst, they are being told that they lack the capacity to succeed in academic work. A young person who regularly receives such messages year after year is not likely to view academic work in a positive way and is certainly not likely to aspire to higher education. Why continue the punishment? In other words, it seems reasonable to assume that the use of normative measures such as school grades and standardized test scores causes many students to opt out of education altogether long before they reach an age at which they might consider applying to college.

Even among students who will finish high school and apply to college, the institution's reliance on grades and standardized test scores has a major impact on *where* any student chooses to send applications (Astin, Christian, and Henson, 1975). A great deal of college and university selectivity is, in fact, *self*-selection by application. Very few students with mediocre grades or test scores apply to highly selective institutions. While some high-scoring students do apply to nonselective institutions, most of them apply instead to the more selective institutions. As a matter of fact, the self-selection by student applicants is so extreme that most of the highly selective institutions could admit students at random from their applicant pools and have an entering class that differs only very slightly, in terms of high school grades and test scores, from those admitted through the usual applicant screening process (Astin, 1971).

In short, the colleges' and universities' continuing reliance on high school grades and test scores in the admissions process poses a serious obstacle to the attainment of greater educational equity for disadvantaged groups, not only because of the handicap that it poses in the admissions process but also because of the profound effects that it has on students' decision making at the precollegiate level.

As pointed out in chapter 1, the principal driving force behind the use of grades and test scores in the admissions process is adherence to the resources and reputational views of excellence: high-scoring students are seen as a valuable resource (and, by implication, lower scoring students as a liability) and having a select (high-scoring) student body enhances an institution's reputation because it is regarded as a sign of "excellence." The educational folklore that has evolved out of this process consists primarily of a hierarchy or pecking order of institutions with the most selective ("highest quality") institutions at the top and the least selective ("lowest quality") ones at the bottom. That students, parents, teachers and counselors are well aware of this folklore is reflected in the considerable amount of self-selection that takes place among high school students before they ever apply to college.

Some observers have likened the American institutional hierarchy to a kind of de facto tracking system. Defenders of public systems of higher education such as California's, where institutions are segregated on the basis of selectivity as a matter of public policy, would have us believe that there is some kind of educational (e.g., talent development) rationale involved: a special type of college for each student based on the level of that student's preparation. But the fact is that California's and every other state's educational hierarchy differs in important respects from a true tracking system. Institutions at every level of the hierarchy seek the best-prepared students they can find and many institutions use their own scholarship resources to lure such students. In a true tracking system, the best-prepared students would be admitted only to the top track, the middle students only to the middle track, and the weakest students only to the bottom track. However, as pointed out in chapter 6, the best-prepared students are allowed to enter *any* public institution, while the middle-scoring students are allowed to enter all except the most selective universities. Only the poorest prepared student is limited to a single choice of institutional type.

Despite its hierarchical nature and its strong inclination to favor the best-prepared students, American higher education has made substantial efforts to mitigate the handicaps posed by selective admissions and reliance on norm-referenced tests and grades. First we have "special" admissions or "affirmative action" admissions wherein an institution accepts black or Hispanic applicants whose grades and test scores fall below the minimum levels required to admit other students. Practically all selective institutions practice some form of special admissions, and many invest substantial resources in actively recruiting minority students. Beyond this, most institutions have some form of remedial or developmental educational programs for specially admitted students; these provide special tutoring and counseling to help students raise their performance levels to those of regularly admitted students. Nevertheless, judging from the continuing underrepresentation of blacks and Hispanics at both the admissions and graduation levels (Astin, 1982), these special admissions and educational programs have not been able to achieve a level approaching proportional representation of Hispanics and blacks among college students and college graduates.

OPPORTUNITY FOR WHAT?

One of the problems with the rhetoric that one frequently encounters in discussions of equal access and equal opportunity is a great deal of fuzziness about the meaning of the term *opportunity*. Opportunity for what? Opportunity to do what?

Perhaps the best way to approach this issue is from the student's perspective. What sorts of benefits can students derive by attending a postsecondary institution? I see three major types of benefits (Astin, 1985): *educational* benefits, *fringe* benefits, and *existential* benefits. Educational benefits have to do with the changes in the student—in intellectual capacities and skills, values, attitudes, interests, mental health, and so forth—that can be attributed to the college experience. Educational benefits relate directly to the talent development model: to what extent are students able to develop their talents as a result of being exposed to particular educational programs?

From the student's perspective, the fringe benefits of college include those post-college outcomes that are related to the institutional credential that the student receives rather than to the student's personal attributes. This has been called the sheepskin effect by some educators. Having a degree from a particular institution can confer certain social and occupational advantages that have little to do with the graduate's personal characteristics or qualifications. Since many graduate schools and employers regard the candidate's undergraduate institution as one of the most important considerations in admissions or hiring, a degree from one institution may constitute a much better entree to later educational or vocational opportunities than the same degree from another institution.

The last category of benefit, existential benefits, refers to the quality of the undergraduate experience itself, independent of any talent development (educational benefits) or sheepskin effect (fringe benefits). Existential benefits have to do with the student's subjective satisfaction derived from the learning process, peer contacts, interactions with faculty, extracurricular and academic experiences, and recreational activities. Such experiences may, of course, lead to educational benefits, but the existential aspects of attending college are important in and of themselves.

Viewed from the perspective of these different kinds of benefits, the question of equal opportunity or equal access becomes much more complex. To measure educational benefits we have to do before-and-after assessments of changes in students' competencies and affective characteristics. To assess fringe benefits we have to look at the kinds of postgraduate educational and occupational opportunities available to the student upon leaving. Finally, existential benefits must ultimately be assessed by getting inside the heads of the students to understand how they perceive their college experience.

Highlighting the complexity of the benefits question is not intended to obfuscate this discussion of educational equity. Indeed, there are several relatively simple measures that can give us at least some rough estimates of benefits to gauge how opportunities are distributed. Economists, for example, might encourage us to determine how much is invested in the education of a given student. How much an institution spends does bear some positive relationship to the fringe benefits of attending particular colleges (Henson, 1980), but expenditures bear only a tenuous relationship to educational or existential benefits (Astin, 1975). Better indicators of educational benefits are the type of college attended (public institutions and community colleges, in particular, reduce the student's chances of completing a degree program) and the availability of residential facilities (living in a campus residence hall confers a number of educational and existential benefits; see Astin, 1977).

DEFINING EQUITY

Some policy makers prefer to define educational equity in terms of the access concept. These observers would be content to believe that educational equity will be attained when overall enrollments in postsecondary education reach proportionate or near-proportionate representation for ethnic minorities, poor students and other underrepresented groups. Measured by this standard, the United States, of all the countries in the world, has achieved the greatest degree of equity. If "opportunities" in American higher education were indeed equal, such a gross measure of equity might be acceptable. However, given the great disparities in educational resources and reputations that are associated with the institutional hierarchy, any definition of equity or equality of access must also take into consideration the quality of the opportunity offered. Guaranteeing that opportunities are available for all does not ensure equity unless the opportunities themselves are comparable.

To provide some rough indication of the great discrepancies among institutions in the United States, let us consider two extreme groups of institutions: the most selective (those whose entering freshmen average 1300 or above on the SAT) and the least selective (those whose entering freshmen average below 775 on the SAT). Computed on a per-student basis, for every dollar invested in educational and general expenditures in the least selective institution, the most selective institutions invest *three* dollars. The most selective institutions pay their faculty 60 percent more than do the least selective institutions (Astin, 1985a). And more than 90 percent of the freshmen entering the most selective institutions live in residential facilities, compared to fewer than half the students entering the least selective institutions. Furthermore, there is considerable evidence (e.g., Henson, 1980) that graduates of selective institutions enjoy a great many fringe benefits not available to students at the least selective institutions. Among these would be access to the best job opportunities and to the top graduate and professional schools, and increased lifetime earnings (Solmon, 1975). Finally, longitudinal research suggests that a student starting out at a selective institution has a much better chance of completing a degree program than a comparable student who starts at a nonselective institution (Dey and Astin, 1989).

After thinking, researching, and writing about these issues for twenty years, I came to realize that the issue of equity versus excellence is really more a matter of how we define excellence. If we accept the reputational or resource approach to excellence, there is clearly a conflict with the goal of equity: there are only so many resources to go around and there are only so many institutions with great reputations. If we allocate more resources to the educationally unprepared or admit more of these students to the prestigious institutions, we spend less on the best-prepared students and admit fewer of them to prestigious institutions. In other words, under the reputational and resource approaches, we are playing a zero-sum game when it comes to excellence: there is only so much of it to go around and if we want to distribute more of it in the direction of the underprepared students we must dilute the "excellence" of education provided to the best-prepared students. In short, when it comes to affirmative action and the expansion of educational opportunities to disadvantaged students, it is the reputational and resource views, more than anything else, that pose the greatest obstacles.

The conflict has still other dimensions. From the perspective of an individual institution, admitting more underprepared students forces us to admit fewer of the best-prepared students, thereby diluting the "quality" of our institution (quality in this context being defined in terms of the level of preparation of the students who attend). Conversely, if we decide to become more "excellent" by raising our admission standards, we must necessarily deprive more of the less-prepared students of a place in our institution. Under this definition of excellence there is an inherent conflict between excellence and equity.

This zero-sum game also serves to foster a great deal of wasteful competition among institutions. If my institution succeeds in becoming more "excellent" by recruiting away some of your faculty stars or National Merit scholars, then your excellence is proportionally reduced. And the resources invested in this competition are lost from the system with no gain in overall excellence.

A talent development approach to excellence creates a very different scenario. From this perspective, our excellence depends less on who we admit and more on what we do for the students once they are admitted. Thus our excellence is measured in terms of how effectively we *develop* the educational talents of our students rather than in terms of the mere level of developed talent they exhibit when they enter. While it is possible to create a competitive pecking order of institutions using the talent development approach (e.g., which institutions' students show the greatest change, learning, and development?), there is nothing inherently competitive or normative about talent development. If my institution manages to be highly successful in developing the talents of our students, this in no way constrains or limits what any other institution can do. Under a talent development approach institutions can learn from each others' successes and failures in the talent development enterprise, thereby enhancing the talent development (human capital development) that occurs in the system as a whole. In my more optimistic moments I imagine how assessment can play a central role in such a cooperative process: by documenting the talent development that occurs at each institution and by understanding which particular enviromental interventions are most successful in enhancing the talent development process, it becomes possible for all institutions to exchange information resulting from these assessments and to adopt those practices and approaches that are most likely to yield maximal talent development.

My advocacy of the talent development perspective toward excellence is by no means intended to suggest that there are not powerful forces supporting the resource and reputational approaches. College administrators are heavily rewarded for acquiring resources and enhancing their institutions' reputations. Regardless of where institutions stand in the pecking order, most of them want to move up, so administrators put a very high premium on enhancement of reputation and resources. At the same time, virtually every constituency of the institution—students, faculty, administrators, trustees, alumni, members of the local community—support the institution's drive for greater resources and reputation. Being associated with a prestigious institution makes each of us feel more important; it gratifies our egos. For those who are interested in embracing a talent development conception of excellence and enhancing and expanding educational opportunities, it is an uphill struggle.

To me the most potent conceptual tool for expanding educational opportunities and achieving a greater degree of educational equity is the talent development approach. This is especially true in our public institutions since they are presumably committed to serving the public. The most appropriate public service that can be performed by such institutions is education. Since the explicit charter of the public institution is thus to serve society by educating its citizens, a public institution does not exist primarily to enhance its own resources and reputation or, to put it in the vernacular, merely to become as rich and as famous as it can.

What is particularly interesting about these issues is that many of the contemporary spokespersons for higher education have lately been arguing the human capital viewpoint as a basis for greater public support and funding. America's competitiveness, they argue, depends upon educating all of our citizens to the greatest extent possible, not only to maximize the number of high-achieving scientists, inventors, and leaders, but also to minimize the number of lower performing people who often represent a drain on the society's resources. The human capital argument, in other words, applies across the entire spectrum of ability and achievement. Such a view meshes very nicely, it seems to me, with the talent development approach.

ASSESSMENT AND ACADEMIC STANDARDS

While I believe there is considerable evidence supporting the idea that the primary justification for using high school grades and standardized test scores in college admissions is to support the reputational and resource conceptions of excellence, many college faculty will argue that the fundamental reason for selective admissions is to establish and maintain academic standards. Without further elaboration, such arguments resemble an endorsement of motherhood, God, the flag, and apple pie: Who can object to "maintaining standards"? But what, exactly, is meant by the term *academic standards?* I see at least two different meanings that can be extracted from this phrase. First, academic standards can be interpreted as referring to the level of performance the student must demonstrate in order to be awarded particular grades or to earn the bachelor's degree. When the term is used in this sense, the resistance to lowering admissions standards in order to accommodate more underprepared students is actually a concern that final (exit) performance standards will also be lowered. Those who make such an argument forget that changed admissions standards do not lead inevitably to changed performance standards, simply because performance standards can be maintained independently of admissions standards.

The lack of a necessary relationship between admissions standards and exit performance standards can perhaps best be understood with an analogy from the field of medicine. In much the same way that education seeks to develop the student's talent to a high level, the exit performance standard for all forms of medical treatment is a sound and healthy patient. If a patient is admitted to a hospital for a hernia repair, the exit standard is basically no different from what it would be for a patient who has to undergo a more difficult and complex procedure such as the removal of a tumor from the lung. In both cases, the goal is the same: a sound and healthy patient. It is understood, however, that more environmental resources will need to be invested in the patient with the tumor: much more complex surgery, more intensive postsurgical care, a longer stay in the hospital, and possibly postoperative treatment with radiation or chemotherapy. At the same time, it is recognized that the probability of success (reaching exit standards of soundness and health) is higher for the hernia patient, since the surgical risks are less and the prognosis better (e.g., much less chance of malignancy).

In short, if a hospital admits a patient who is more seriously ill than the typical patient at the hospital, the hospital does not automatically set lower performance standards for that patient: it is hoped that all patients will eventually recover from their illnesses and be healthy, productive citizens when they leave the hospital. Granted, the extremely ill patient may require a greater investment of resources to reach the hoped-for performance standards for discharge, and the probability of reaching those standards might be somewhat less than for an average patient, but the hospital does not automatically alter its performance standards simply because the patient has a poor prognosis at entry.

In terms of the I-E-O model, what I have just described is a situation in which (a) the expected outputs are somewhat different because the inputs are different, and (b) the environments (treatments) are designed in part to compensate for that difference. Since the inputs (diagnosis and prognosis) for the two patients are different, the environments (type, intensity, and length of treatment) must be different in order to achieve a comparable output (i.e., standards of health and well-being).

This medical analogy underscores one important reality about expanding educational opportunities: if an institution or a system of institutions wants to maintain exit performance standards *and* to enroll a greater proportion of underprepared students (students who, at college entry, have lower high school GPAs and lower standardized test scores than the average student), one or more of the following changes must occur: the underprepared students must be given more time to reach performance standards; a greater share of institutional resources must be deployed to deal effectively with the underprepared students; or the institution's drop out and failure rates must increase. In short, lowering admissions standards does not necessarily require any alteration in performance standards at the exit point.

In higher education our thinking about performance standards tends to be much more simplistic. Rather than attempting to achieve common performance standards by differential treatment, we try to maintain standards through selective admissions. This is basically no different in principle from trying to achieve performance standards in a medical setting by refusing to admit the sickest patients. In American higher education we have developed a set of elite institutions that are so selective in their inputs that high performance standards are almost guaranteed, even if the institution contributes little to the educational process. Moreover, these same institutions have the best facilities and the most resources of all. To replicate such institutions in the medical field would be almost absurd: we would have an elite group of hospitals or clinics that would have the finest and most advanced equipment and facilities and the best-qualified and highest paid staff but which would admit only people with common colds. All other prospective patients would be excluded in order to maintain the highest possible performance standards at exit.

A second meaning of the argument for maintaining academic standards expresses a concern for the talent development process itself. The argument goes as follows: If larger numbers of underprepared students are admitted to an institution, that institution's academic program will become less demanding and will therefore lose some of its potency in developing student talent. This argument implies that in attempting to gear its program to greater numbers of underprepared students, the institution will slight its better prepared students, giving them a watered-down education that will lead to less talent development among the better prepared students. It should be emphasized that this argument revolves around a problem that all institutions face, regardless of their admissions policies: how to deal effectively with students who come to college differing significantly in their levels of academic preparation. Even the most selective institutions face this difficulty, particularly when it comes to specific academic skills such as writing ability. Indeed, here is one place where good assessment can and has been used to enhance the talent development process: good diagnostic assessment and appropriate guidance and course placement are among the techniques most commonly used to deal with differences in academic preparation. When such diagnostic assessment and differential placement is done thoroughly and thoughtfully, there is no reason that students at all levels of performance cannot be exposed to rigorous courses that challenge them to develop their talents.

THE PREDICTION ARGUMENT

When challenged about their reliance on high school grades and test scores in making admissions decisions, many faculty will respond that these assessment devices predict grades in college. It has already been noted (chapter 1) that grades leave much to be desired when it comes to their use as a student outcome measure. But even if we accept college grades as a valid performance measure, the prediction argument does not really hold up under scrutiny. Basically, the prediction argument asserts that students with high grades and high test scores should be favored in the admissions process because they are likely to perform well later on in college. What this really means is that a high-scoring student is more likely than one with lower grades and test scores to do well on measures of academic performance (college grades, honors, retention, etc.). This is simply another way of saying that high school performance correlates with college performance. But does the argument really have anything to say about how much or how well the different students will actually *learn*? Does it say anything about how much talent development different students will eventually show? Unfortunately, it does not.

Consider the following scenario. Suppose we admit all applicants regardless of their grades and test scores, but instead of educating them we put them in a deep freeze or in a state of suspended animation for a period of four years. Then we revive them and give them a set of "final exams" in order to compute their college GPAs. As you might guess, those who had the best grades and the highest test scores at the point of entry will perform better on these final exams than those with lower grades and test scores, even though *no learning took place*! The point is a subtle but very important one: Just because past performance correlates with or predicts future performance does not mean that high performers in high school will learn more or develop their talents more in college than low performers. In other words, traditional selective admissions does not necessarily further the talent development mission of a college or university.

Supporters of selective admissions might respond that my argument is flawed because a student's college GPA is indeed a valid indicator of how much a student has learned in college. On a purely anecdotal level, most of us who have taught in college have had personal experiences that refute such an argument. For example, we have all had students who were so bright and so well-prepared at the beginning of a course that they could do well on the final examination without exerting much effort and without really learning very much. On the other hand, most of us know of students who showed great improvements (learned a lot) but whose final exam performance was mediocre because they came to us so ill prepared. But the evidence against the argument that grades reflect learning is not merely anecdotal. Harris (1970), for example, has shown that students who get mediocre grades in a course can be learning as much (as measured by score improvements in standardized tests given before and after the course) as students with the highest grades.

The evidence usually cited in defense of the prediction argument consists of moderate correlations of college grades with high school grades and admissions test scores. To see why prediction does not necessarily reflect learning, one needs only to understand what a correlation really shows. Suppose we have three people who have obtained scores of 4, 5, and 6, respectively, on a test given in the senior year of high school. Suppose they all gained two points during their four years of college so that, by the time they reached the senior year, they scored 6, 7, and 8, respectively. The prediction of college performance from high school performance would yield a very high correlation (+1.0 in fact), even though all three students learned the same amount in college. On the other hand, suppose that the students learned absolutely nothing in college, so that their scores remained the same over the four years. The correlation would *still* be +1.0, even though the students learned nothing! Even if the students got dumber during college, with each score declining two points to 2, 3, and 4, respectively, the correlation would *still* be +1.0! In other words, the only requirement for high school performance to correlate with college performance is that the students' positions relative to each other show some consistency over time. Nothing in the correlation tells us how much learning has occurred or even whether there has been any learning at all.

EDUCATIONAL OPPORTUNITY AND THE DEVELOPMENT OF HUMAN CAPITAL

The principal obstacle to expanding educational opportunities is posed not by the assessment devices themselves, but by the way they are used to promote the reputational and resources conceptions of excellence. While some critics have tried to argue that the talent development approach compromises and threatens academic standards, when we look at the educational system as a whole, *there is no better way to promote academic standards than to maximize talent development.* To see why this is so, imagine that we have ten people to educate and that they come to us at the point of admission with varying levels of developed talent. To simplify the argument, let us assume further that we can classify each person's level of developed talent on a scale from 1 to 10. Level 1 would represent illiteracy and level 10 would represent the intellectual talent level required for attaining a Ph.D. degree. Let us assume further that the minimum standards required for the bachelor's degree fall at 6 on the scale. If we were working in a large university, a typically diverse group of ten college freshmen might enter our college with the following levels of talent development: 2, 2, 3, 3, 3, 4, 4, 4, 4, 5. (This last student, who has a score of 5, is functioning at almost the minimal level required for graduation.) Our first job as an educational institution, then, is to help as many of these students as possible to reach level 6. In essence, a talent development approach seeks to *add* as much as possible to each student's entering level of performance. If we are indeed able to maximize talent development among these ten students, we accomplish at least three important goals:

1. We maximize the number of students who reach minimal performance standards (level 6).
2. We maximize the "margin of safety" by which students exceed this minimal level (that is, the number of 7s, 8s, 9s, and 10s).
3. We minimize the number of students with borderline skills (that is, levels 2 and 3).

This last accomplishment (3) is especially important since we will seldom be successful in bringing all entering students up to performance standards. So, even if some of our ten students fail to reach level 6 and drop out of college without a degree, we have still made some contribution to their intellectual functioning and have thus added to their chances of eventually becoming productive members of society. In other words, a talent development approach is the surest way not only to maintain academic standards but also to maximize the amount of human capital available to the society.

As suggested in chapters 1 and 2, the role of assessment changes dramatically under a talent development perspective. Rather than being used to promote institutional resources and reputation, assessment is used to place students in appropriate courses of study and to determine how much talent development is actually occurring by repeated assessments over time. These latter assessment activities would serve two functions: to document the amount and type of talent development that is occurring, and to provide, in combination with environmental information, a basis for learning more about which particular kinds of educational policies and practices are likely to facilitate talent development. If testing in higher education were revised along the lines suggested here, it seems likely that proponents of expanding access and opportunity in higher education would come to see assessment as an ally rather than as a threat.

TALENT DEVELOPMENT AND PROFESSIONAL COMPETENCY

While maximizing talent development is the most effective way for higher education institutions and systems of such institutions to serve their students and the larger society, there are certain circumstances under which selection and placement may have to be based on other considerations. Perhaps the most obvious situations are those in which we are trying to prepare students for entry into professions requiring very high levels of intellectual or technical competence: e.g., medicine, engineering, art, music, college teaching. Take engineering as an example. Since effective performance as a professional engineer almost always requires considerable competence in mathematics, engineering curricula place substantial emphasis on developing mathematical talent. Under these conditions, is it educationally wise to admit all comers to such programs? What about the person whose competence in mathematics is only at the eighth-grade level? Does it make educational or economic sense to admit such students to an engineering program?

The talent development philosophy suggests that any student, given sufficient motivation and sufficient time and resources, could, in theory, reach any desired level of competence. However, from the perspective of the profession there may be several negative consequences of admitting all applicants to certain types of programs. The student with eighth-grade mathematical skills who enters a bachelor's program in engineering may get discouraged and drop out, even if the program makes significant efforts at remediation. And even if such a student could manage eventually to finish the program, the resources needed to bring that student up to minimally acceptable performance standards might be more than the program could bear. Assuming that program resources are finite, programs that accepted all comers would end up producing fewer graduates. Finally, accepting all comers would almost certainly reduce the margin of safety by which the average program graduates exceed minimal performance standards. As a result, the overall quality of professional competence and performance in the field would decline.

This discussion suggests that there may be situations in which selective admissions should be based on considerations other than maximizing talent development. While such a view may well be reasonable and valid from the narrow perspective of a single program, institution, or profession, it seems less appropriate from the broader perspective of the entire educational system or the society at large. When we operate from the narrow perspective of one institution or a single profession, we are concerned only with what happens to those students we admit; the rejected candidates are not of interest to us. On the other hand, when we view such decision problems from a larger system perspective, we concern ourselves with the fate of *all* candidates, winners and rejects alike. This distinction is precisely analogous to the distinction between the use of assessment for selection versus assessment for placement (see chapters 1 and 2).

The real problem would seem to be *placement* of people in appropriate courses and programs within the total system. If a person with eighth-grade math skills wants to study engineering at the college level, there should be a means available to help develop that person's mathematical talent to the level at which it would not cause a disproportionate drain on the resources of the engineering program. Furthermore, the person should be assured that if the math remediation is successful, there could be a place available in the engineering program. This same set of principles—appropriate placement with assurances of future opportunity—should be applied to all persons at all talent levels and to all fields of academic and professional study. An educational system designed and operated according to such principles would not only provide educational opportunities for all but would also encourage each person to view education in its proper light: as a place to develop one's talents rather than as a place that merely screens and sorts or that limits opportunity. And, if students were permitted to avail themselves of educational opportunities as long as they continued to develop their talents, the public would also be getting the maximum "bang" for its educational "buck."

In short, when we view educational decisions—such as selection and placement—from a larger societal perspective, the goal of maximizing talent development makes more sense than any other educational philosophy. There is no better means by which we can maximize the human capital available in the society.

A SYSTEMS PERSPECTIVE

This discussion suggests that our conceptualization of the problem of equal access and equal opportunity would take on a very different character if educators were more willing to (a) look at the issues from a *systems* perspective rather than an institutional perspective and (b) see educational institutions as analogous to hospitals, clinics, or other organizations whose primary purpose is public service.

The systems perspective is an especially important viewpoint from which to examine issues of educational opportunity. Here again we can use assessment as a way to illustrate the issues. Imagine that we had some kind of a test that measured people's level of developed talent along a number of continua (e.g., verbal, quantitative, knowledge of various subject matter, citizenship, social responsibility). To simplify the illustration let us compress all these different talents onto a single continuum; keep in mind that the same argument can be made with multiple continua and indeed, if any of these ideas were to be put into practice, it would be necessary to develop such multidimensional assessment tools. Let us further demarcate three different points along this continuum: point C is at the low end, signifying relatively undeveloped talent. Point B is around the middle of the continuum, signifying a moderate level of talent development. Point A is at the upper end of the continuum, signifying a high level of talent development. If we were to look at this continuum from the traditional institutional perspective, we would be competing to recruit as many students as possible who perform at the A end of the continuum and rejecting most applicants who scored at the C end. We would, of course, make the usual arguments (discussed above) about why it is necessary to admit only those with the highest possible levels of developed talent. If all institutions were to adopt such a perspective, students scoring at the A end would have many choices among institutions and generous offers of scholarship support. The B students in the middle might be admissible to the institutions that were not highly sought after by the best-prepared students, whereas students at the C end would be limited to the open door institutions or, more likely, discouraged from attending higher education altogether.

While such a scenario might make sense from the perspective of the individual institutions involved, it might make no sense from a systems perspective. By systems perspective I mean the overall interests of the state and the nation as far as the education of its citizenry is concerned. The scenario just described (which, I think, portrays our current higher education system reasonably accurately) will have the effect of exaggerating existing differences in talent development within the population. The reason is quite simple: we are making a maximal educational investment in the A students, a modest investment in the B students, and little or no investment in the C students. In other words, the current system will tend to widen the gaps between B and A and especially between B and C.

The social significance of such policies depends on a number of factors, perhaps the most important being the absolute levels of competence or developed talent represented by points A, B, and C. If point C represents borderline literacy (which is probably the case with high school graduates who do not attend college and even with many community college students), the policy may have serious long-term social and economic repercussions. Because persons functioning at the C level may not be able to avail themselves of decent-paying work, they may end up on the welfare rolls or, worse, pursue a life of crime. Note that the failure of the system to develop these individuals' talents creates problems associated not only with limited vocational and job skills but also with those interpersonal and social skills that are very often learned in school and college and which become so important to effective community living and citizenship. In fact, the development of character and citizenship is one of the major goals of a liberal education (see chapter 3).

Thinking about educational objectives in these larger systems terms makes it possible for us to develop educational policies that are relevant to an entire population of citizens rather than to the more parochial interests of individual institutions. In earlier writings (Astin, 1973, 1985a) I suggested that there are at least three different social policies that can be symbolized by the continuum just discussed. A policy that primarily favors the A students might be termed *elitist* since it benefits greatest those whose talents are already well developed. A policy that distributes educational resources equally across all levels of the developed talent continuum might be termed *egalitarian*, whereas a policy that disproportionately invests resources in the least well educated citizens (the C students) might be termed *remedial* or *social welfare*. While American higher education tends toward the elitist model, it combines certain elements of both the egalitarian and the remedial model. An open admissions policy is certainly egalitarian, while having special services and programs for the educationally disadvantaged students might be characterized as remedial. The elitist character of the system is to be found primarily in the hierarchical arrangement of institution. This arrangement is supported by selective admissions and characterized by a pattern of allocation of resources and opportunities that is skewed toward the elite institutions within public and private systems.

Educators and policy makers who are concerned with educational issues at the state and federal levels need to address a number of critical questions that are suggested by a systems perspective. Following is just a sampling of such questions that need to be addressed through further assessment research and policy analysis:

- What are the relevant talents that need to be developed in the citizenry? How should these talents be assessed?
- What types of educational programs and interventions are most likely to produce the largest gains at various points on each continuum? Are certain policies more effective for some types of students than others (A students versus C students, for example)?
- What are the relative costs of these different interventions and programs?

- What are the various individual benefits (job, income, career, family) associated with increments at various points along the talent continuum?
- What societal benefits are associated with increments at various points on the continuum? Do investments at the low end have significant payoffs in terms of lower unemployment, less crime, and reduced reliance on welfare programs? Do investments at the high end of the continuum pay off in increased scientific and technical advances?
- Are there points of diminishing return with respect to investments at various places on the continuum? For example, are the generous investments currently being made at the high end of the continuum really necessary to produce the desired amount of talent development at that end?
- If students do not attend college, what increases or decreases in development of various talents can be expected?

Considering that each of these questions has significance for educational policy, it is unfortunate that they have received so little attention from policy makers, from researchers, and especially from those who fund policy research. One likely reason for the paucity of such research is the lack of good longitudinal information on talent development. Without systematic assessment data on how much people's talents change over time and on what environmental experiences they have been exposed to, it is very difficult to obtain reliable answers to these important policy questions. One would need to apply a model something like the I-E-O model (chapter 2) with extensive national data on all types of students and all types of institutions to obtain even preliminary answers to questions such as these. The closest approximation to such a data base is the National Assessment of Educational Progress, which periodically assesses the levels of development of several different talents at different grade levels. The capacity of this very ambitious assessment program to shed light on critical policy questions is extremely limited, however, because it is cross-sectional rather then longitudinal and incorporates virtually nothing about the educational environment. In other words, it periodically assesses outcomes but contains no assessment data on inputs and very little on environments.

WHAT ARE THE SOCIAL RESPONSIBILITIES OF PUBLIC SYSTEMS?

While the institutional hierarchy within the private sector of higher education developed more or less by historical accident, the hierarchies that exist within most of our state systems have been established as a matter of public policy. These systems, in turn, are sustained by a system of selective admissions that relies heavily on the students' high school grades and scores on standardized tests. In the typical state system, there is one (or more) "flagship" university that occupies the top rung in the hierarchy. The middle rungs of most public hierarchies are occupied by the state colleges and universities (many of them former teachers' colleges), and the community colleges occupy the bottom rungs. The prototype of this model is the system in the state of California, whose master plan formally recognizes these three levels. Most other states have emulated the California model with minor variations. As with the private hierarchies, the resources and opportunities are unequally distributed within the public hierarchies, with the greatest resources and opportunities concentrated in the flagship universities and the fewest resources and opportunities at the community college level (Hayden, 1986).

It is well known that poor students and members of educationally disadvantaged minority groups are severely underrepresented in higher education as a whole. It is often not recognized, however, that poor and minority students are not equally distributed across different types of institutions *within* most public systems. To achieve proportional representation, large numbers of minority and poor students would have to be moved from the community colleges to the state colleges and flagship universities, and some in the state colleges would probably also have to be moved into the flagship universities. Thus, to achieve proportional representation in the flagship universities, the number of blacks attending these institutions would have to be more than doubled, the number of Hispanics would have to be increased by more than 80 percent, and the number of American Indians would have to be increased by more than 60 percent (Astin, 1982). Note that "proportionate" in this context refers solely to the distribution of currently enrolled students within these public higher education systems. Given that all three of these groups are substantially underpresented in higher education as a whole relative to their proportions in the population, the problem of equal access to higher education is far more serious than these substantial figures suggest.

A similar result occurs when we look at how low-income students are distributed among the public institutions (Astin, 1985b). If we define low income as including each student whose family's income falls in the lowest 20 percent for college students nationally, the number attending flagship universities would have to be more than doubled to achieve proportional representation in these institutions.

In an earlier study of the sixty-five flagship universities across the country (Astin, 1982a), fifty-six had significant underenrollments of blacks, forty-eight had significant Hispanic underenrollments, and forty-six had significant underenrollments of American Indians. Moreover, the degree of underenrollment was greatest in those states with the largest minority populations. To attain proportionate representation of the underrepresented minorities in the flagship universities in New York, Texas, California, and most of the southern states, the numbers would have to be increased by between 200 percent and 600 percent!

The maldistribution of minorities and low-income students becomes even more pronounced if we look at only the twenty-four most selective flagship universities (those whose entering freshmen score above 1100 on the SAT composite test). While these institutions enroll 4.8 percent of all college students in the United States, they enroll only the following percentages of minorities: blacks, 2.1; Hispanics, 2.5; and American Indians, 2.3. Asians, who are slightly underrepresented in all public universities, are actually overrepresented by nearly 100 percent in the most selective public universities (these institutions enroll 9.3 percent of all Asians compared to only 4.8 percent of all students).

The flagship universities and their supporters are willing to defend this state of affairs primarily because, in one way or another, they all support the resources and reputational views of excellence. But what of the public university's broader mandate? To what extent is the pursuit of institutional self-interest through resource acquisition and reputation enhancement compatible with the public university's mission of serving the public interest? Does not the public interest include the education of *all* the citizens and expansion of opportunities for minority and low-income students?

While it might be argued that the flagship universities are not equipped to educate underprepared students, most universities have explicitly acknowledged their responsibilities in this area by introducing special admissions programs, remedial and support services for underprepared students, and other such assistance. Programs of this type are especially generous when it comes to academic assistance for specially admitted athletes. The real issue seems to be the *numbers* of such students that these universities are willing to take in. In this connection, it should be noted that several major research universities in the Midwest have a long-standing policy of open admissions. At the same time, virtually every state has acknowledged its commitment to expanding opportunities by providing all high school graduates with access to some type of public institution. This analysis indicates, however, that these opportunities tend to be confined to the community colleges and, to a lesser extent, the state colleges.

It seems clear that the flagship university's interest in expanding educational opportunities to disadvantaged groups directly conflicts with its quest for excellence in reputational and resource terms. Judging from the current distribution of low-income and minority students among our public institutions in most states, it appears that the quest for excellence has been given much higher priority than the issue of equal access. As a consequence, in most states low-income and minority students do not have equal access to the best educational opportunities.

Lest the reader be tempted to conclude that proportionate representation is a utopian ideal that would never receive much public support, the recent report from the Joint Legislative Committee that reviewed California's Master Plan for higher education has specifically established proportional representation of minorities and poor students as a specific goal for California for the year 2000 (California, 1989). This remarkable document challenges the University of California and the California State University not only to achieve proportional representation of disadvantaged minority groups by the year 2000, but also to reduce dropout rates for these groups to the level for white students. Whether the state of California will be able to achieve these objectives is debatable, but the fact that both houses of the state legislature are willing to commit the state to such a radical goal is remarkable in and of itself.

Let us return briefly to the role of assessment in promoting equal opportunity. Several years ago my colleagues and I obtained national college admissions test data from the College Entrance Examination Board and the American College Testing Program which allowed us to determine just how the representation of minority and low-income students would be affected by changing the way in which high school grades, test scores, and other assessment information is used in the college admissions process. Following are some of the major findings of that simulation study:

- Both blacks and Hispanics are put at a competitive disadvantage when high school grades and standardized admissions test scores are used in making admissions decisions. Test scores pose a greater handicap than high school grades, especially for blacks.
- The handicap resulting from the use of test scores and grades becomes greater as the selection ratio increases. A simple combination of test scores and grades produces an 80 percent underrepresentation of blacks when the selection ratio is one in four, but only a 65 percent underrepresentation when the selection ratio is one in two.
- Much of the handicap posed by the use of test scores and grades can be mitigated by the use of a disadvantagement index based on the income and educational level of the student's parents. This index gives special credit for students whose parents are poor and/or relatively uneducated.
- Minorities benefit differentially from the use of a disadvantagement index, but such an index must be given substantial weight to overcome the handicap imposed by test scores and grades.

- Given the considerable handicap posed by standardized test scores, the use of a disadvantagement index benefits minority students more if it is combined with grades alone rather than with grades and test scores.

This last finding is of particular relevance since a number of studies have shown that standardized test scores contribute little to the prediction of academic performance once the student's high school grades are taken into account.

Besides modifications in the use of different assessment devices for college admissions, there are other avenues available to public universities that may wish to enhance their enrollments of minority and low-income students. One such alternative relates to the structure of public higher education systems. The California model, with its three-tiered system, is not necessarily the only or even the best model. States such as Pennsylvania and Kentucky have developed public university systems that, in effect, combine the community college model with the research university model by means of two-year branch campuses that offer the first two undergraduate years. A student attending one of these branch campuses is admitted to the university for upper division work without having to go through the usual application and transfer paperwork. Another version of this alternative would be for universities to "adopt" existing community colleges and to standardize the lower-division transfer curricula. Although these alternative structures may degenerate into an implicit hierarchy (through comparisons of the branch campus with the main campus, for example), they appear to represent some advance over more rigidly stratified systems.

SUMMARY

The conflict between equity and excellence in American higher education is caused in part by our continuing reliance on the reputational and resource conceptions of excellence. Under these views, students with good grades and high test scores are highly sought after because they are seen as an important resource that enhances the institution's reputation; lower scoring students, on the other hand, are shunned as a liability that detracts from institutional excellence.

Under a talent development view, the performance level of entering students is of much less importance since the institution's excellence will depend primarily on how effectively the institution is able to *develop* its students' talents.

The traditional argument that lowering admissions standards necessarily erodes academic standards is challenged, as is the argument that test scores and high school grades should be used in admissions because they predict college grades.

Considering that public systems of higher education, in particular, are responsible for extending equal educational opportunities to all citizens of a state, the existence of hierarchical public systems supported by selective admissions based on test scores and grades is questionable. There is reason to believe that the flagship universities in most states could substantially increase their enrollments of underrepresented minorities without seriously compromising academic standards.

11

ASSESSMENT AND PUBLIC POLICY

One of the major driving forces behind the current assessment movement in American higher education is the executive and legislative branches of state governments. Why have so many states become so interested in assessment? One precipitating factor was the educational reform movement that began in the early 1980s with the publication of the much-heralded report, *A Nation At Risk*. While precollegiate education was the primary target of this very critical report, a virtual flood of reports critical of higher education has followed in its wake. One of the common themes running through these reports is that higher education needs to strengthen and improve its assessment practices. Moreover, all six regional associations that accredit colleges and universities in the United States now require some systematic assessment of outcomes as a condition of accreditation (Folger and Harris, 1989). Perhaps the most prescriptive of all regional associations is the Southern Association of Colleges and Schools (SACS), which recently stated that "the institution must define its expected educational results and describe how the achievement of these observable results will be ascertained" (Southern Association of Colleges and Schools, 1989, p. 14).

Another factor behind the assessment movement is the growing popularity of the concept of accountability in higher education. More and better assessment is presumably one way to make institutions more accountable for the success or failure of their educational programs. Given the strain on most state budgets caused by increasing deficits and decreasing domestic spending at the federal level during the 1980s, it is difficult to escape the conclusion that many state officials who push for greater accountability are really looking for ways to trim higher education expenditures. Thus, the argument that public institutions have not been sufficiently accountable carries with it the not-so-subtle implication that greater accountability will lead to increased savings in state monies.

But the institutions themselves have played a part, perhaps the biggest part, in laying the groundwork for state-sponsored assessment initiatives. Put yourself in the position of a typical legislator or state policy maker who is responsible for allocating resources for public colleges and universities. Suppose you are trying to persuade your colleagues in state government to support a request for increases in higher education expenditures. How would you go about answering questions such as the following: How effectively are the universities using the money we already give them? How much are students really learning? Are they learning what we expect them to learn? Are they developing the kinds of talents and skills that are needed by our state's economy? Are they developing the values and habits of citizenship that will make them responsible and caring parents, spouses, and members of the community? Are they developing the kind of leadership qualities that will help them to become productive and effective professionals, teachers, politicians, and government officials? What about the students who fail to complete their programs? What good has higher education done for all these dropouts? Are institutions doing all they can to reduce the dropout problem? Are we using the most up-to-date teaching techniques? How effective and efficient are our institutions in comparison to private institutions or to institutions in other states? How effective are our teacher training programs?

While these are all perfectly legitimate *educational* (talent development) questions, they are next-to-impossible to answer because few public institutions, if any, conduct studies directly bearing on these issues. The problem, of course, is that the assessment of student learning and development that has traditionally gone on in our public colleges and universities has been a completely private affair between the student and the professor or teaching assistant. Legislators and state policy makers know this very well, since most of them have themselves been students in these institutions. Under these circumstances, it is not surprising that many state officials are clamoring for better evidence of what is actually happening in the teaching-learning process.

State involvement in higher education assessment activities has been expanding at a dizzying rate. In their *Time for Results*, the report of the Task Force on College Quality of the National Governors' Association (National Governors' Association, 1986), the governors of the fifty states called on public institutions across the country to greatly expand and strengthen their assessment activities: "The public has a right to know what it is getting for its expenditures of tax resources; the public has a right to know and understand the quality of undergraduate education that young people receive from publicly funded colleges and universities" (p. 3). Indeed, assessment was about the only topic discussed in the report. Furthermore, a state-by-state synopsis of assessment activities that followed the report several years later (National Governors' Association, 1988) indicated that all but a handful of states (mostly with small populations) had already embarked on some major effort to expand assessment activities in public institutions. Because of the rapidly changing situation in the states and the availability of excellent summaries of current state activities (e.g., Boyer and Ewell, 1988), no attempt will be made here to enumerate or summarize state initiatives. Rather, I would like first to discuss what the legitimate state interests in assessment might be, then to critique four of the most unique state approaches that have already been tried, and to conclude with some specific recommendations for using this powerful tool to strengthen higher education in the states.

WHAT ARE THE REAL STATE INTERESTS?

What are the legitimate state interests when it comes to public higher education? Unfortunately, the rhetoric and controversy surrounding discussions of accountability and performance funding tend to obscure the most fundamental state interest: to develop the talents of the state's citizens as fully as possible. In other words, the *real* state interest in formulating higher education policy on assessment or on any other issue is to facilitate the institutions' task of developing the human capital in the state. The improvement of learning and student development, in other words, should be the bottom line. Research and community service are, to be sure, other important state and institutional interests, but just as teaching and learning represent the most fundamental and vital institutional functions of higher education, so does the development of human capital represent the most fundamental state interest.

If state legislators and policy makers are to embrace talent development or human capital development as the core function of their higher education systems, it would seem that any state policies with respect to assessment should be designed to enhance the talent development function. The true test of any state assessment policy is not whether it makes institutions more accountable but whether it serves to enhance the talent development function of its higher education institutions.

STATE POLICIES TO ENHANCE TALENT DEVELOPMENT: A LOOK AT FOUR OPTIONS

There seem to be almost as many state approaches to higher education assessment as there are states. Readers who are interested in learning about all the different approaches that are being tried should consult several of the excellent summaries and critical analyses that have already been published (Boyer and Ewell, 1988; Ewell and Boyer, 1988; National Governors' Association, 1988). Rather than attempting to review each state program, I will focus on four different approaches that have been tried and discuss their likely effects on the talent development process. For convenience these four approaches can be labeled, respectively, as value-added assessment for incentive funding, competency testing, mandated assessment with local control, and challenge grants.

Value-Added Assessment for Incentive Funding: The Tennessee Model

Probably the most radical type of state assessment initiative is one that mandates some form of testing and retesting of students and allocates money on the basis of how much improvement students show over time. Tennessee is the only state so far that has tried such a program, but the Tennessee incentive funding system merits special attention because it has achieved so much publicity and because it has been in operation for so long (more than ten years). In the Tennessee program value-added testing is only one of several bases for awarding state incentive funds (for a detailed description of the program, see Banta, 1986). My purpose here is not to offer an analysis of the Tennessee program as such, but to comment on this general approach. Readers who are interested in how the Tennessee program has affected one campus should consult Banta (1985).

The basic idea behind incentive funding based on value-added assessment is to motivate institutions to strengthen their educational programs in order that maximum growth or learning will occur among students after they enter the institution. The purpose of the pretesting and posttesting is to provide an empirical basis for judging whether the amount of growth shown by the institution's students is sufficient to merit incentive funding. Typically, students are pretested at the point of entry and posttested after completion of certain classes or programs of study. The change between the two testings is then used as an estimate of intellectual growth or *value added*. While this approach has the obvious advantage of affording institutions an opportunity to determine how much talent development is occurring among their students, mandating such assessments with a common instrument may, under certain conditions, be dysfunctional not only for the institution and its students but also for the state. By this time it should be clear to the reader that I remain a strong advocate of longitudinal or value-added assessment. However, I feel strongly that the conditions under which it is carried out can subvert the educational purposes of any longitudinal assessment activity.

First, let us consider the state perspective. Can incentive funding based on value-added testing really enhance the capability of public institutions to maximize talent development among their students? The usual justifications given for state-mandated value-added assessments are (1) to make institutions "more accountable to the public" and

(2) to ensure "excellence" or "quality control" in various educational programs. Let us consider the accountability argument. Proponents of greater accountability typically provide little or no indication as to what the state is supposed to *do* once the results are in. For example, if a value-added assessment program shows that an institution's students are not substantially improving their writing skills during college, what is the state supposed to do? Should it punish the institution's poor performance by withdrawing funds? Is such action likely to remedy the problem? What if the institution needs more funds in order to give professors released time so they can more frequently assign and individually critique written assignments and essay examinations? If funds are instead withdrawn, then the institution may be tempted to shortchange some other important area of learning (e.g., math) so it can focus more of its faculty resources on the teaching of writing. Such a tradeoff may or may not be desirable, and its overall consequences for talent development may not be detectable unless the institution has an assessment system that is sufficiently comprehensive and sophisticated to reflect the performance decrement (in some other skill area such as math) that accompanies the tradeoff.

A similar problem occurs with monetary rewards for "good" performance. If an institution succeeds in getting additional funds because its writing program is successful, it may be tempted to divert even more resources into that program to the detriment of other important institutional programs.

It might be argued that such tradeoffs can be avoided by a more comprehensive state assessment program that covers more areas of competence and knowledge in handing out the rewards. But this broader program introduces a new problem: how much weight to give each area. Further, tying the reward system exclusively to gains in cognitive performance might tempt some institutions to shortchange student affairs activities, thereby running the risk of exacerbating other problems such as dropout rates.

These difficulties with a simple system of rewards and punishments become even more serious when we consider competencies other than writing (which presumably can be assessed with some confidence through a writing sample). If monetary rewards are tied to improvements in test scores covering some area of substantive knowledge, you can bet that most institutions will first take a hard look at test content and then "teach to the test." Earlier (in chapters 3 and 6) I argued that teaching to the test is not necessarily a poor idea, provided the test comprises a representative sampling of the domain of knowledge to be learned. But that domain may vary from one institution to another. Perhaps the state mandates a test of American history to be administered on a value-added basis in all public institutions. Tying monetary incentives to student performance on such a test might well lead to a homogenization of history courses taught across the different public campuses. Thus, if one college's history department has a professor who is one of the world's experts on the Civil War, and if the mandated state history test gives only cursory treatment to the Civil War, students will be deprived of an opportunity to learn the best that this professor has to teach. Also if the test is a multiple-choice test (which it is highly likely to be), history departments will be tempted to overemphasize the student's acquisition of mere facts and give insufficient attention to developing the student's ability to synthesize, to write creatively, and to think critically about history.

In short, it would appear that a policy of simple rewards and punishments may not represent a productive approach to state-mandated value-added assessments in higher education.

Another possible state response to mandated assessments might be called the *remedial* approach. Instead of punishing poor performance, the remedial approach would provide more resources to the poorer performing institutions on the grounds that their programs are most in need of strengthening. The remedial approach is thus a kind of mirror image of the reward-and-punish approach since the poorest performing institutions are given more resources rather than less. The problem with this approach, however, is obvious: institutions will be tempted to encourage their students to "fake bad" in order to garner more resources. The remedial approach encourages institutions to look bad on the posttest while the reward-and-punish approach creates incentives for them to look bad on the pretest. Neither model, it seems, serves the state interest in getting more value added or more talent development out of its higher education system.

To examine this issue from an institutional perspective, suppose our institution does poorly on a value-added assessment, with the students showing little or no improvement from pretest to posttest. Assuming that we have subsequently been prodded into some sort of remedial action by a denial (or withdrawal) of incentive funding, what actions are we supposed to take? What is the source of the problem? What needs to be fixed? Is there something wrong with our institution, our curriculum, or what? Do we need to strengthen classroom teaching? Does the fault lie with our system of advising and counseling? Is there a problem with our residence halls or with our student activities program? Lacking any definite answers to such questions, perhaps we should take a shotgun approach and try to fix everything. But where are the resources for such widespread reforms to come from, especially considering that our funding has just been reduced? And if we decide to concentrate our finite resources on just one potential problem area, what other areas should we deprive of resources in order to do this? And how can we be sure that taking away such resources will not create new problems? In short, under a performance-based incentive funding program, there is no assurance that even the most well-intentioned institution will be able to remediate the problem identified through longitudinal value-added assessment.

A different set of problems confronts the high-performing institution under a state incentive funding program. Which effective activities should be preserved and strengthened? Which activities might be subject to improvement? Should the institution play it safe and continue doing business as usual? Should it avoid institutional reforms or innovations for fear of losing its competitive edge? Should experimentation be shunned?

This discussion suggests, once again, that value-added (input-outcome) information, by itself, is of limited value. As pointed out in chapter 2, to make the best use of such data, institutions also need to link it to other data about the student's educational experience (such as course-taking patterns, place of residence, and participation in special programs).

There is nothing inherently dysfunctional about value-added assessments (even those mandated by the state). Indeed, value-added assessments, coupled with other data, can be extremely useful to institutions as an aid to self-study, in student counseling, and for program evaluation. The problems arise when the state also ties a system of competitive rewards directly to gains in performance.

Competency Testing: The Florida Model

A variation of the value-added approach is the use of minimal competency exams required of students in order to gain certain credits, degrees, or other credentials. The much-discussed College Level Academic Skills Test (CLAST) program in Florida (Ciereszko, 1987; Losak, 1987) exemplifies this approach. In order to insure some minimal competencies at given transition points, the state sets scores below which students will not be licensed or certified or permitted to move to the next higher level. In Florida the CLAST program sets minimal scores below which students are not permitted to move from the sophomore to the junior year level. Assuming that the tests are valid indicators of appropriate competencies, there is nothing inherently objectionable about such a policy. What is not clear, however, is how the institutions are supposed to be affected by such tests and how states are supposed to use institutional results. As far as state policy is concerned, we have the same problems we had with value-added testing: whether to punish or reward particular institutions. But this decision problem is compounded by a new defect: the lack of a pretest. Without pretests, the institutions that enroll poorly prepared students are operating under a severe handicap when it comes to competency testing, and those that recruit the best-prepared students have an unfair advantage. Judging institutions on the basis of the overall performance of their students at some transition point (rather than on a value-added basis that measures improvement between pretest and posttest) creates institutional incentives that tend to work against the talent development process. Under such conditions, institutions will be reluctant (or perhaps even unwilling) to enroll underprepared students and will trip over each other in a rush to recruit the best-prepared students. Since underrepresented students from minority groups and poor students account for a disproportionate share of the underprepared students (see chapter 10), the net result of such a policy will be to limit severely the educational opportunities for these educationally disadvantaged students.

While the CLAST program may be unique to Florida, many other states are already using this basic approach in the area of professional certification. Most states, for example, require graduates of teacher training programs to pass a common certification exam (the most widely used being the NEA's National Teacher Examination) before being licensed to teach in the public schools. In most such states the test performance of each institution's teacher training graduates is closely monitored, and the quality of different programs is judged in terms of their students' pass rate. In the absence of any pretests to measure how much students have actually improved, such comparisons are not only spurious but are also likely to discourage institutions from recruiting more underrepresented minorities and poor students into the teaching profession.

This discussion suggests that if states mandate competency exams that must be passed at various educational transition points, they should also mandate pretests with the same or similar exams at an appropriate earlier entry point. These pretests can serve several useful purposes. First, they provide a baseline for measuring value added via the competency (posttest) exam. In this manner an institution's degree of success in raising its students' level of competence to acceptable levels can be judged against the point at which students started on admission. Under this approach an institution in which students were already functioning at a relatively high level at the point of entry would be expected to have a higher pass rate than one whose entering students were less well prepared. At a minimum, the less well prepared students should be given more time to reach acceptable levels of competency.

Another important use of competency pretests is in counseling and course placement of students. Students whose pretests indicate that they are considerably below the desired competency level can not only be placed in appropriate remedial or introductory level courses but should also be informed that more time and considerable effort will probably be required on their part to achieve these minimal levels of proficiency. At the same time, institutions will know which students are most likely to need special assistance in particular skill areas.

Still another important use of competency pretests is for program review and evaluation. From the point of view of the institution, this is potentially one of the most attractive features of value-added competency assessment. In the FIPSE-supported value-added project discussed in chapter 8, the members of the seven-institution consortium eventually came to the realization that the key to building an effective system of program evaluation is the existence of a comprehensive student data system. The system must include not only value-added data on cognitive growth but also data on retention and program completion, measures of student satisfaction with various aspects of the program, demographic and admissions data, course grades, and—most important—environmental information on the students' department or major, course-taking patterns, place of residence, participation in special programs, extracurricular participation, and so on. When data from these different sources are linked, it becomes possible to evaluate the impact of any course, department, program, or other environmental experience on outcomes such as cognitive growth, retention, and satisfaction.

The more I consider the prospects and problems of competitive state incentive systems based on students' test performance, the less attractive they become. During the late 1960s and early 1970s I was a strong advocate of performance funding, but I have since lost my enthusiasm for it. In reflecting on my earlier attraction to the idea, I think it appealed to me mainly because I felt that having such data on the campus would be of substantial value in program review and evaluation. The incentive or performance funding aspect of the program was simply a means—a gimmick or tactic—to the end of generating longitudinal data on the growth and development of a campus's undergraduates. Given the historical reluctance of institutions to assess systematically what is happening to their students educationally, the performance funding approach seemed to be a good way to get institutions to collect the necessary data. But like most Machiavellian approaches to problem solving, the ends seldom if ever justify the means. For the many reasons already mentioned, competitive incentive systems based on actual test performance do not really serve state interests because they create more problems than they solve. In the long run such systems may actually impede attempts to strengthen the talent development capabilities of public higher educational institutions.

This conclusion should not be taken to mean that I oppose assessment at the state level or that states should not use incentives to get institutions to do more and better assessment. At issue here is whether the incentives should be tied to student performance on specific tests or whether they should instead be designed to encourage institutions to conduct better assessments and to use the results in program review and evaluation.

Mandated Assessment with Local Control

Perhaps the most popular current state approach to higher education assessment is to mandate that all public institutions will utilize some form of assessment but that the decisions about which assessments will be used and how the results will be utilized will be left up to the individual institutions. This seems to be the approach currently being taken in Missouri, Virginia, Colorado, and other states. While it is possible to mandate the form of the assessment (for example, that it involve pretesting and posttesting), most states have so far specified only that some kind of outcome assessment be utilized.

The major benefits of this approach seem to be, first, that institutions are required to engage in some form of systematic assessment of student outcomes and, second, that control over the selection and use of the assessment tools is in the hands of the faculty. The obvious drawbacks are (a) the possibility that institutions will utilize the outcomes-only model or the input-outcome model with all their attendant limitations and problems (see chapter 2), and (b) that there will be no comparability among the data collected by different institutions. The lack of comparable data makes it very difficult for institutions to share or exchange findings from their respective assessment activities.

The state of Washington has recently been involved in preliminary attempts to implement mandated assessment systems with local control, and the generally unsatisfactory results obtained so far should be scrutinized carefully by other states that might be considering a similar approach. The project had an impressive beginning. In late 1987 Washington's Higher Education Coordinating Board (HECB) recommended that the public institutions in the state develop a "statewide performance evaluation program" that would strike a "balance between statewide assessment and strictly local evaluation conducted for institutional improvement." The board also stated that even though the performance evaluation system was to include student satisfaction questionnaires, alumni surveys, employee surveys, and locally developed cognitive tests, "one important aspect of an institution's evaluation system is the identification of a nationally normed test of computation, communication, and critical thinking skills . . . to compare the performance of Washington institutions with that of their peer institutions" (Higher Education Coordinating Board, 1987, pp. 26–27).

In the ensuing attempt to implement the board's recommendations, much of the interest was focused on the "nationally normed tests." Task forces from the two- and four-year systems examined various off-the-shelf instruments and decided to try three of them by testing 1,300 students statewide and by having more than 100 faculty take abbreviated versions of the tests to check for appropriateness of content and potential usefulness for curriculum improvement and student advising. No pretests were used.

The committee concluded that the tests added "little reliable new information," that the "test scores were not sensitive to specific aspects of the college experience," and that the test content failed to provide "an adequate match with curricular content" (Daley, 1989, p. iv). In short, the idea of using a common assessment instrument was rejected outright as far too costly and as providing too little of value. The report "reaffirmed the value of assessment activities" while at the same time concluding that "the development of meaningful assessment measures is both difficult and time consuming" (Daley, 1989, p. iv).

While it is still too early to know what will happen to this part of the state's assessment plan, there is little question that this preliminary experience represents a major setback. The published documents suggest that several crucial mistakes were made in the early conceptualization and implementation of the plan.

1. Undue emphasis was placed on finding nationally normed instruments that could permit institutional comparisons. Institutions will see such an approach as threatening, especially if they feel they might suffer in the comparisons.
2. Too little emphasis was placed on developing "home-grown" instruments, which would have offered much greater opportunities for faculty to assume some ownership over the results.
3. The initial commitment to using commercially available off-the-shelf instruments almost guaranteed that faculty would remain in the role of external critics rather than assume responsibility for finding or developing satisfactory instruments.
4. Conclusions about the appropriateness of test content could have been reached without having to test any students.
5. The failure to obtain longitudinal (pretest-posttest) data made it virtually impossible to determine, with any confidence, whether test scores were indeed "sensitive to particular aspects of the college experience." That the committees were able to reach definitive (and negative) conclusions about such matters suggests (the reports are unclear on this) that some environmental data, such as time spent studying and credits earned, were directly linked to test performance. However, with no controls for pretest performance levels at college entry, there is simply no way to interpret simple correlations between environmental data and test performance (see chapter 2).

Challenge Grants

Some of the most interesting and innovative assessment activities have been elicited through the mechanism of challenge grants. The purpose of challenge grants is to encourage institutions to bring their creative talents and energies to bear by proposing innovative assessment activities that will be funded by monies from the challenge grant. Perhaps the best example of the potential benefits associated with challenge grants is Kean College of New Jersey, which was awarded a 3.5 million dollar challenge grant by the state of New Jersey in 1986. Primarily as a result of the grant and the leadership of top administrators, Kean has initiated one of the most comprehensive and sophisticated systems of outcome assessment currently in operation. Judging from a preliminary evaluation of the grant's impact (Kean College, 1988; Ross and Weiss, 1989a), Kean's assessment program has had beneficial effects on the college's general education program and on practically every academic department.

THE IMPORTANCE OF TRUST

No state incentive program can be expected to work effectively unless the institutions and the state can develop a mutual sense of trust. State legislators and other officials need to realize that the defensiveness and suspicion institutions are inclined to display in response to externally mandated assessment programs are based, at least in part, on legitimate concerns. Faculty and administrators, for their part, need to realize that most state officials are genuinely concerned about enhancing the quality and effectiveness of educational programs. It is this talent development goal—to enhance and improve the educational experience—that can best serve as the common core around which states and institutions can work together to build a greater sense of trust in each other. There is really no reason that states cannot provide incentives to encourage institutions to develop the kind of data base described in chapter 8. A comprehensive longitudinal student data system can play a critical role in helping to bring about this mutual trust and understanding. Serious use of such a data base can help institutions to identify those programs that are most effective and those that are most in need of strengthening. It can also provide a basis for knowing whether attempts to strengthen and improve programs are ultimately effective.

To my mind, the best kind of performance-based funding scheme is the one that encourages and rewards good practice. Because we already know much about what constitutes good practice in higher education (Chickering and Gamson, 1989), any state incentive system should be designed to encourage institutions to adopt such practices: to develop a comprehensive data base,[1] to conduct more and better talent development assessments (and to use the results in program planning and review), to increase faculty-student contact, and to increase student involvement through the use of more active modes of learning.

1. Ewell, Parker, and Jones (1988) described an attempt to design a longitudinal student tracking system for a state community college system

COOPERATION: AN ATTRACTIVE ALTERNATIVE

One of the dilemmas posed by most performance-based funding systems is the competition it engenders among institutions. Since we are usually playing a zero-sum game when it comes to state resources, one institution's success, in effect, depletes the resources available to other institutions. Colleges are implicitly rooting for each other to fail.

What has not yet been considered by any state, as far as I know, is a *cooperative* system of performance-based funding, in which monetary incentives are based on the aggregate performance of an entire *system*. Under such a cooperative model, institutions would have maximum incentive to *facilitate* each other's performance, since the success of any one brings in resources that are shared by all the others. It is interesting to consider how relations among institutions in a state might change under such a cooperative system of incentives.

Cooperative incentive systems can be used to cope with a wide range of educational problems. In California, for example, we are plagued by a very low transfer rate from the community colleges to the four-year universities. What if the states were to establish a program that simultaneously rewarded both two-year and four-year institutions for increasing the proportions of community college students who transfer and successfully complete their baccalaureate work? The size of the reward could be pegged to the size of the increase. Under such a program, all public institutions in the state would have a strong incentive to strengthen the transfer process and to share information with each other about how best to get the job done. Because all institutions would share equally in the rewards, the poorer performing institutions would be under pressure from their institutional peers to improve their performance, and these same peers would have equally strong incentives to help them bring about such improvements.

A similar system could be established to enhance institutional retention rates. In many states, the state colleges and universities have very high dropout rates (Astin, Green, and Korn, 1987). In such systems, all colleges could participate in a cooperative program in which various financial rewards would be geared to specified increases in systemwide retention rates. Each institution would thus have a stake in bringing about increased retention rates across the system as a whole. Performance-based funding on a cooperative, systemwide basis could be designed to enhance a number of other outcomes, such as enrollment and retention of underrepresented minorities, or enrollment and program completion in critical career fields (e.g., school teaching, nursing, social work).

Cooperative arrangements can also be used to overcome some of the problems associated with incentive systems that are geared to test performance. Institutions might first determine whether they can agree on a common approach to assessment in a certain area, such as basic skills in writing or mathematics. The current performance level of all students in the system could then be used as a base for a state incentive funding program, with financial rewards tied to future improvements beyond that base.

Test-based funding schemes might also be tied to professional certification exams (e.g., school teaching, accounting, nursing) or to some of the widely used admissions tests for graduate or professional school (GRE, MCAT, LSAT, or GMAT). Given that all undergraduates who aspire to professional certification or to graduate or professional school have a stake in being able to perform well on such tests, both states and institutions might well be able to justify a program that rewards a system of institutions for managing to improve its students' performance on such tests. Pretesting new students with these exams would be an important first step in determining how best to maximize the growth between pretest and posttest. Again, a cooperative system would provide maximum incentive for different institutions to pool their expertise about ways to bring about such improvement. The underlying strategy, of course, is to encourage all institutions in the system to pool their skills, expertise, and resources in the interest of enhancing student development, learning, and achievement.

CONCLUSIONS

In this essay I have discussed the pros and cons of various state assessment initiatives from both a state and an institutional perspective. The analysis seems to warrant the following conclusions:

1. The basic state interest is not necessarily to make institutions more accountable, but rather to find ways to assist them in carrying out their talent development mission as effectively and as efficiently as possible.
2. Performance-based funding should not be designed simply to reward and punish good and bad performance. Rather, it should be designed to improve the educational effectiveness of entire public systems.
3. The most simplistic (and inequitable) system is one that rewards only competence as assessed at some exit point. Such systems are also the least likely to result in real improvements in educational effectiveness and the most likely to discriminate against educationally disadvantaged students.
4. Value-added (talent development) systems are far more equitable across institutions since they require entry (pretest) as well as competency (posttest) assessments.

5. The usefulness of value-added assessments in program improvement can be greatly enhanced if they are linked to such environmental information as course-taking patterns, participation in special programs, study habits, and extracurricular participation.

6. Focusing too heavily on nationally normed tests and institutional comparisons is likely to generate minimum faculty ownership and maximum faculty resistance.

7. A potentially powerful state tool is the challenge grant. Experience with challenge grants so far indicates that they can be used to encourage institutions to adopt a variety of reforms, including the use of comprehensive assessment programs.

8. Cooperative performance-based systems, in which institutions are given incentives to work together and to exchange knowledge and expertise, are far more likely to produce positive results than competitive systems that pit one institution against another. Under a cooperative arrangement, all institutions share equally in the rewards.

9. A promising way to initiate cooperative incentive systems would be to tie monetary rewards to systemwide improvements in such outcomes as transfer rates, retention rates, and performance on professional certification exams and on graduate and professional school admissions tests.

12

THE FUTURE OF ASSESSMENT

Like most authors, I thought I had a pretty clear idea of what I was going to say about assessment when I sat down to write this book. What has happened in the meantime, however, can be described only as a major transformation of some of my views about assessment. I have gradually come to three new realizations:

- Assessment issues are basic to just about everything we do in higher education: admissions, teaching, mentoring, grading, certifying, research and scholarship, hiring and promotion, evaluation, governance, administration, accreditation, and fund raising.
- Many of our most serious problems in higher education are, at root, problems with what we choose to assess (or not assess), how we choose to assess it, or what we decide to do with the resulting information.
- Assessment is a potentially powerful—but greatly misused, misunderstood and underused—tool for improving higher education policy and practice.

In this chapter I shall first summarize the major arguments set forward in the preceding chapters and then discuss some of the possible futures for the practice of assessment in American higher education.

A SYNOPSIS OF MAJOR ARGUMENTS

The book is based on two fundamental premises: that an institution's assessment practices are a reflection of its values (the "is" of assessment), and that assessment practices should further the basic aims and purposes of higher education institutions (the "ought" of assessment). While different types of institutions might emphasize somewhat different aims and purposes, all institutions share a common commitment to teaching and to enhancing student learning and development. I prefer to label this the institution's talent development mission.

The problems with our current assessment practices can best be understood in terms of the concept of excellence in higher education.

231

While most institutions claim to be committed to educational excellence (that is, to the talent development mission), what institutions actually *do* in the name of excellence seems to reflect two other very different conceptions: the reputational and the resource views of excellence. Under the reputational view, an institution's excellence is defined in terms of its ranking in the institutional hierarchy or pecking order. Under the resource view, excellence is equated, for example, with the level of academic preparation of the entering students, the faculty's scholarly visibility, the endowment, or the physical plant.

The assessment practices of most institutions are inadequate because they are used primarily to promote the resources and reputational views of excellence rather than the talent development view. Thus, admissions testing is required in order to enroll the most select or elite student body, classroom testing and grading is used primarily to "certify" students for purposes of awarding credits and degrees, and various forms of competency testing are done more for quality control than for educational purposes. About the only commonly used form of student assessment designed primarily to enhance talent development is placement testing.

If institutions wish to revise their assessment practices to focus more on their talent development mission, they must view assessment much more as a form of feedback that can be used to enlighten both teacher and student about the student's progress and the effectiveness of the teaching. Such a view of assessment frequently requires that repeated (longitudinal) assessment be used so that growth or change in the student can be assessed.

Traditional procedures for assessing faculty fall prey to the same limitations as student assessment practices. Thus, faculty are evaluated for purposes of hiring, tenuring, and promoting rather than to enhance the development of their research and teaching skills. The major exception to this generalization is the pre-tenure review that some institutions use several years prior to the actual tenure decision.

There are basically two ways in which assessment can be used to promote talent development: as direct feedback to the learner, and indirectly by informing the practitioner about the effectiveness of various educational practices. Most of the book has been devoted to a discussion of the latter use of assessment, with one chapter (chapter 9) devoted exclusively to a consideration of assessment as direct feedback.

The I-E-O Model

How can assessment be used to inform or enlighten the practitioner? Educators, like most other professionals, "do things" to and for the clientele they serve, presumably for the benefit of that clientele. These "things" include an incredible array of actions and procedures such as teaching, advising, testing, mentoring; establishing a curriculum; hiring and promoting faculty and staff; admitting, testing, and grading students; establishing rules and requirements; and shaping a physical environment. Each action involves choices among alternative courses of action: what to teach, how to teach it, whom to hire. My basic view of assessment is that it should be used primarily as an aid to educational decision making by providing information on the likely impact of alternative courses of action. My preferred approach to using assessment for this purpose is through the application of the input-environment-outcome (I-E-O) model. Outcome refers to the characteristics of the student that the institution either does influence or attempts to influence, input refers to the characteristics of the student at the time of initial entry to the institution, and environment refers to the various "things"—institutional programs, practices, and policies—that are designed to promote the desired outcomes. However, since outcomes are always influenced to some extent by inputs, it is important to control for the effects of inputs before attempting to assess the effects of environmental characteristics. The focus of the I-E-O model is on the possible effects of environments on outcomes. The environment is of particular importance because it includes those aspects of the student's experience that can be directly controlled. The ultimate purpose of the application of the model is to learn better how to structure educational environments so as to maximize talent development.

Most assessment activities and much of what passes for educational "evaluation" leave out one or more components of the I-E-O model. Basing educational decisions on the results of assessment and evaluation studies done with incomplete models forces the practitioner to make a number of assumptions that are usually very difficult to justify.

Assessing Outcomes

A critically important task in any assessment project is to define the relevant student *outcomes* and to choose methods for assessing them. As there is no way that outcomes can be empirically validated, the definition and measurement of educational outcomes is inevitably based on value judgments. Which outcomes are most appropriate will depend upon the values or perspective of the concerned parties (faculty, departments, disciplines, professions, employers, state agencies, parents, and students). Values affect not only *what* we choose to assess, but also *how* we choose to assess it. Given the diverse perspectives of the constituencies that have an interest in higher education and the multiple objectives of most educational programs, it is essential that any assessment program utilize multiple outcome measures reflecting at least some of these diverse values. Here again we encounter another major limitation of contemporary assessment practices: most institutions rely primarily on a very limited number of relatively narrowly defined outcomes (the grade-point average, for example).

Contemporary discussions of assessment frequently misuse the term *outcome* to imply that "what is being measured is what has been learned." Given the heavy influence of inputs on outcomes, there are few circumstances under which such an assumption can be justified. The I-E-O model, by contrast, uses the term "outcome" to refer simply to the level of developed talent as measured after exposure to the educational environment. The relative influence of input and environmental variables on these outcomes remains to be determined through application of the I-E-O model.

Considering the need for multiple outcome measures in most assessment projects, it is important to utilize some form of outcome taxonomy to develop an appropriate battery of measures. My preferred taxonomy is one that utilizes three dimensions: the type of outcome (cognitive versus affective), the type of measure used (psychological or behavioral) and the time interval involved between input and outcome assessment (see chapter 3).

Despite the ready availability of standardized multiple-choice tests and the ease with which they can be scored, the heavy or exclusive reliance of most assessment programs on such tests is questionable. As these tests are usually scored normatively, most students are encouraged to view themselves as mediocre at best and as failures at worst. Beyond this, normatively scored tests are usually inadequate for measuring talent development or growth since they tell us little about the absolute level of the student's learning or performance. Perhaps most important, the multiple choice methodology would appear to be inappropriate for assessing many of the important outcomes of higher education programs.

Assessing Inputs

Input measures are required by the I-E-O model primarily because they are related to both outcomes and environments. That is, outcomes are to some extent dependent on inputs, and different environments (programs, practices) attract different kinds of students. Under these conditions, any observed relationship between educational environments and educational outcomes might well be reflecting the effects of inputs rather than the true effects of environments on outcomes. Therefore, it is important first to control inputs before assessing the effects of environments on outcomes. Ideally, any set of input assessments would include pretests on the important outcomes to be investigated later. When pretests are unavailable or inappropriate, self-predictions about likely performance on the outcome measure are a good substitute. Besides their use in I-E-O analyses, input measures are of potential value for admissions and recruitment, curriculum and program evaluation, and public information.

Assessing Environments

The environment includes everything that happens to students during the course of an educational program that might conceivably influence the outcomes under consideration. Despite their obvious importance in educational assessment and evaluation, environmental measures are the most neglected area of assessment activity. Even if the investigator has available good input and outcome information, the findings will be of limited value without environmental information since there will be no basis for interpreting why certain students' outcome performances deviate from what would be expected from their input characteristics.

Environmental assessment presents a number of technical and methodological difficulties. One of these is the problem of defining the relevant unit of observation. Environmental assessment can thus measure something about the entire institution, a particular school or college within the institution, a particular department or major, or such individual elements as the student's living quarters, courses taken, extracurricular participation, and the personal attributes of those professors, advisers, counselors, administrators, and student peers with whom the student comes in contact. Commercially developed instruments for assessing educational environments are of limited use because they are designed primarily to assess the environment of the total institution rather than the environmental experiences of individual students within that institution.

The Data Base

Institutions wishing to perform assessment activities involving the I-E-O model need to develop a comprehensive longitudinal student data base that includes input, environmental, and outcome information on each student. The most efficacious approach is to design such data files on a cohort basis, with each cohort representing a new population of entering students. Few institutions, however, have such a data base—a further reflection that traditional assessment activities are not really designed to enhance the talent development process. The lack of an adequate comprehensive student data base is perhaps the single biggest obstacle confronting any institution that wishes to use assessment to enhance talent development.

While the ideal data base would include all relevant information currently collected by various administrative units on the campus (admissions, registrar, financial aid, student affairs, alumni) as well as any specially designed assessments, it is important to aim initially at a very modest data base that can be put into use immediately. Other data elements can be added over time. It is recommended that this initial data base be conceived of as a "retention" file that incorporates basic data from the admissions and registrar's offices, with the possible addition of a survey of incumbent students' views about their educational experience. This retention file can produce usable results in a relatively brief period of time. It can also serve as a nucleus around which the more comprehensive data file can be developed.

Analyzing Assessment Data

No matter how comprehensive and sophisticated the data base, it will be of little benefit to the talent development process if proper methods of analysis are not employed or if the results are used inappropriately. Indeed, most modern treatises on outcomes assessment say very little about actual methods of analysis.

Assessment data can be analyzed in two different ways. *Descriptive* analyses are designed simply to portray the current state of affairs with respect to some input, environmental, or outcome measure (or set of measures), while *causal* analyses are designed specifically to estimate the comparative effects of different environments on student outcomes. The two most commonly used techniques for analyzing assessment data are cross-tabulation and correlational analyses. Cross-tabulation is useful for descriptive analyses, although it can also be used, under certain conditions, for causal analyses. Correlational and regression analyses are especially well suited to causal analyses of assessment data because they permit the investigator to control simultaneously a large number of potentially biasing input variables.

Actual examples of the application of cross-tabulation and correlational analyses are provided in chapter 6. The appendix has been provided for those readers who will be responsible for analyzing assessment data or who want more in-depth exposure to the statistical and technical aspects of analyzing assessment data.

Using Assessment Results

An assessment program will be most effective if it is based on some kind of theory concerning how users are supposed to translate the assessment results into action. I have found it useful to employ a "performing arts" theory, wherein faculty and staff use assessment results as feedback to enhance their understanding of those educational practices that are most likely to enhance talent development. Just as artists, dancers, and musicians rely on sensory feedback to perfect their craft, so do teachers and administrators need feedback to develop their skills in teaching, mentoring, planning, and decision making. A major role of assessment is to enhance the quality and quantity of feedback available to faculty and staff in order to assist them in becoming more effective practitioners. More specifically, the feedback from assessment should be designed to illuminate the causal connections between different educational policies and practices and various student outcomes.

Assessment results will have their greatest impact when they are designed for the particular audience that will view the results (faculty, administrators, student affairs, etc.). Consideration should also be given to strategies for avoiding the "So what?" reaction and for dealing with the many academic games that faculty are inclined to play when they are confronted with data suggesting the need for change. Whenever possible, efforts should be made to encourage all interested parties to experiment with the assessment data as a means of exploring various alternative ideas and possibilities.

Assessment as Direct Feedback

Most of this book has been devoted to a discussion of ways in which assessment can be used to enhance the talent development process by enlightening the practitioner about the likely consequences of different courses of action. However, assessment can also be used to facilitate talent development more directly when it is used as direct feedback to the learner. There are at least two theories concerning the ways assessment can work as direct feedback: the carrot-and-stick theory whereby assessment serves as an incentive to the learner, and the feedback theory whereby assessment provides information that can be useful to the assessee in the learning process. While any assessment activity can serve both as an incentive and as a source of feedback, the potential value of the feedback can be compromised when the assessment is also used to evaluate the assessee's performance for purposes of grading, awarding credits, hiring, or promotion.

Several principles can be applied to ensure that the direct feedback from assessment can be maximally beneficial to the learner. First, the teacher and the learner should both be committed to the shared goal of enhancing talent development and student satisfaction, and the assessment and feedback procedures should be directly relevant to these goals. Feedback should also be multidimensional (reflecting the multidimensional nature of learning outcomes) and should include *process* data concerning how the learner approaches the task. Feedback should also be optimally timed, and the learners themselves should be encouraged to generate their own feedback. Finally, feedback should be considered the result of an ongoing, iterative process (rather than as a one-time activity done at a single point in time) and the institution should specifically recognize the importance of assessment activities in faculty job descriptions and in the personnel review process. Most of these principles can be applied with equal validity in using direct feedback to enhance talent development among faculty and administrators.

Assessment and Equity

The much-discussed conflict between equity and excellence in American higher education is caused in part by our continuing reliance on the reputational and resource conceptions of excellence. These traditional views encourage us to regard students with good grades from high school and high scores on standardized admissions tests as an important resource that enhances the institution's reputation; lower achieving students, on the other hand, are shunned as a liability that detracts from institutional excellence. Reliance on the traditional conceptions of excellence in terms of resources and reputation thus leads us to employ assessment practices that directly conflict with the goals of expanding educational opportunities and increasing educational equity. Further, regular use of such norm-referenced assessments at the precollegiate level serves to discourage many students from pursuing further education beyond high school. In other words, continuing reliance on high school grades and test scores in the admissions process poses a serious obstacle to the attainment of greater educational equity for underrepresented groups, not only because of the handicap that it poses in the admissions process but also because of its negative effect on students' aspirations during the precollegiate years.

Under a talent development view, the performance level of the *entering* student is of much less importance, since the institution's excellence is defined primarily in terms of how effectively that institution is able to *develop* the student's talents. At the same time, adherence to the talent development approach leads to assessment practices that focus much more on *changes* or *improvements* in performance than merely on students' relative performance at a single point in time.

There are two traditional arguments used by those who oppose more flexible admissions standards or who resist using assessment that focuses on talent development. The first argument asserts that lowering admissions standards necessarily erodes academic standards. The second justifies the use of test scores and high school grades in admissions on the grounds that these assessment devices predict college grades. A careful examination of these arguments (see chapter 10) reveals that they are both fundamentally flawed. Indeed, it would appear that reliance on a talent development model of excellence is the surest way not only to enhance educational opportunity and equity but also to maintain the highest possible academic standards.

Assessment and Public Policy

Many states have undertaken ambitious programs of assessment in higher education, presumably in order to encourage public institutions to be more accountable. Under a talent development perspective, accountability is a means to the end of more effective education rather than an end in itself. In other words, the basic state interest is not necessarily to make institutions more accountable, but rather to find ways to assist them in carrying out their talent development mission as effectively and as efficiently as possible.

Different states have tried a variety of approaches to higher education assessment, including performance-based funding, competency testing, and challenge grants. Most of the performance-based funding approaches have been deficient in important ways. A particularly promising but untried approach is one that ties the incentive funding to improvements in the performance of an entire system. Thus, incentive funding could be geared to overall improvement in systemwide measures, such as transfer and retention rates and increased enrollments of underrepresented groups, and incentive funds could be shared equally by all institutions in the system. Under such an arrangement, institutions would have maximum incentive to cooperate and collaborate with each other.

Competency testing represents an attempt at "quality control" that can be imposed at various transition points (say, from the sophomore to the junior undergraduate year). The educational values of such assessments could be substantially increased if the same competencies could be pretested at some earlier point in time, thereby providing a means for assessing how much improvement or change has taken place over time. Since no state has as yet attempted to use competency testing in this fashion, its educational value is uncertain.

Challenge grants represent what may be the most promising state approach to assessment. Recent experience in several states indicates that institutions can be encouraged to develop very sophisticated assessment programs and to undertake other significant institutional reforms in response to a program of challenge grants.

A LOOK BACK

Before discussing the issue of what is likely to happen (or what *should* happen) with assessment in the future, it is useful first to examine briefly some of the history of assessment in higher education. By getting a glimpse of where we have been, it becomes easier to chart a course for the future.

Throughout this book I have repeatedly suggested that our assessment practices in higher education will serve our talent development mission much more effectively if we do less meritocratic assessment (for purposes of ranking, screening, and certification) and more assessment designed to benefit the assessee (i.e., to provide feedback to the learner and to enlighten the practitioner). To make such a conversion in our way of thinking about assessment will be no easy task, given the long history of meritocratically based assessment.

The first such use of assessment was probably the Chinese civil service examinations, which date back to 2200 BC (Dubois, 1970). With no aristocratic tradition to determine successive generations of government officials, the Chinese needed a meritocratic procedure to identify the most competent people. The civil service examinations were thus used to select new officials and also to reassess the competence of incumbent officials every three years.

While the earliest uses of assessment in American higher education were also primarily meritocratic, it would appear that many so-called contemporary ideas about assessment are nearly as old as American higher education itself. In the early colonial colleges of the seventeenth and eighteenth centuries, assessment was used for such diverse functions as advanced standing, the award of honors, quality control, setting entrance requirements, developing the curriculum, awarding degrees, transfer between institutions, and public relations (Smallwood, 1935). Most of the early examining, however, was done through debate or oration, and it was not until the nineteenth century, when printing technology became more efficient, that written exams and printed examinations were introduced.

One of the pioneering institutions in the field of outcome assessment was Mount Holyoke College. In the early part of the nineteenth century Mount Holyoke declared that "a student should not progress according to the time spent . . . but should be judged by the results indicated in an examination" (Smallwood, 1935, p. 24). A number of educators however, also recognized the possible use of exams to enhance talent development. In 1841 President Quincy of Harvard noted that exams can be useful as "a stimulus to the student" (Smallwood, 1935, p. 26). Similarly, in 1817 the College of William and Mary identified four "classes" of graduates using terminology that sounds very much like talent development or value added: "The first in their respective classes . . . have made the most flattering improvement." "[The fourth] have learnt little or nothing and we believe on account of escapaide [sic] and idleness." These assessments of individual students at William and Mary also sound a bit like narrative evaluations: "[The student] has made some progress but has been by no means as attentive as he might have been."

At about the same time, however, a number of now-familiar objections to assessment appeared. Thus, in 1848 President Everett of Harvard argued, "It may be doubted whether the benefit of these examinations is in proportion to the inconvenience, labor, and expense with which they are attained" (Smallwood, 1935, p. 29). Smallwood also notes that faculty generally abhorred the practice of cramming, blaming it on written examinations. Similarly, in 1857 the President of Harvard objected to "the necessary absence of personal communication between the mind of the examiner and the mind of the one who is examined" (Smallwood, 1935, p. 39). Sound familiar?

The meritocratic view of higher education assessment during the twentieth century has been most dramatically influenced by the advent of intelligence testing and especially by the introduction of techniques of mass testing. It is important to realize that intelligence testing was originally introduced as a device for selecting and screening people. In the case of the individually administered tests developed by the Frenchman Alfred Binet, the purpose was to identify children who could not cope with the usual school curriculum and who would need special schooling and remediation. While the I.Q. score was not, strictly speaking, a normative measure, it prompted the use of normative jargon with strong meritocratic connotations: genius, superior, dull, normal, imbecile, and so forth. Since this form of assessment required an individual examiner for each examinee, it was too expensive to be used on a mass scale. Nevertheless, these individually administered intelligence tests served as a model for the group-administered tests used today.

Large-scale group testing was initially conducted by the military during World War I in order to screen out illiterate and "mentally defective" recruits and draftees and to identify candidates for officer training. Again, this application of group testing is basically meritocratic: it is designed to facilitate selection and screening by identifying the "best" and "worst" candidates. The meritocratic view of group testing continued to grow in popularity between the two world wars but received a substantial boost after the end of World War II when the crush of applicants forced many colleges to institute screening procedures that could be applied on a large scale at relatively low cost. Normative scores provided a simple and seemingly fair means to identify the "best" students. As already discussed in chapters 1 and 10, this meritocratic view of assessment has been reinforced by the competitiveness of the colleges themselves as they attempt to amass resources and enhance their reputations in part through the recruitment of "highly able" students.

In the 1950s and 1960s, this meritocratic orientation was reinforced by competitiveness at the international level: the launching of the first Soviet Sputnik led many Americans to believe that the United States had slipped behind because some of its brightest students were not going to college. One manifestation of this belief was the National Merit Scholarship Corporation, which annually tested close to one million students just to identify the 1500 or so with the highest scores, and which then awarded each of them scholarships to assure their college attendance. Colleges, of course, have become highly competitive in their quest for Merit Scholars, and the number of scholars in the student body is widely regarded as a sign of academic excellence. A similar competition has developed among the high schools to see which schools could produce the largest numbers of Merit Scholars.

The point of this brief historical excursion is to show that our predilection for meritocratically oriented assessment in higher education has a long history and is a natural outgrowth of our approach to intelligence testing. American higher education has, perhaps unwittingly, adopted this same meritocratic approach to assessment, whereby we test not to enhance the learning process but rather to identify the best, the average, and the worst students for purposes of selection, screening, and certification. While a meritocratic approach to assessment probably makes sense in the case of business or the military, when the intention is to weed out the least competent people and to identify the most competent for positions of leadership, it makes much less sense within an educational context, in which the goal is less to exploit talent than to develop it.

Many years ago it occurred to me that this distinction between talent exploitation and talent development can be illustrated with an analogy from the field of thoroughbred racing (Astin, 1969). If thoroughbred horses can be regarded as analogous to students, the typical institution operates very much like a handicapper: it tries to pick the best or most promising candidates to bet on. By "picking winners" we enhance our resources and reputation. Under a talent development perspective, on the other hand, the institution would see itself much more in the role of jockey or trainer: to help the horse run better and faster. With this perspective, assessment would be used more to enhance the horse's performance than merely to pick the one most likely to win the race.

MANAGING THE FUTURE

While it makes for an interesting intellectual exercise to sit back and try to forecast what is going to happen on the assessment front in the near future, I personally try to resist engaging in this form of crystal-ball gazing. I prefer to see us each as active participants in shaping our own futures, especially those of us who work in institutions of higher learning. The great autonomy that we all enjoy in many of the most important areas of our work-life means that we do indeed have the power to develop any kind of assessment program we please. The real question is whether we have the will and the know-how to do it.

It is my strong belief that the future course of assessment in American higher education will be primarily determined not by what the federal and state legislators and policy makers do, but rather by how we in the institutions respond to the challenge of the assessment movement. Despite our increasing dependence on governmental support and governmental policies, we still maintain direct control over most of the things that really matter: whom we admit and on what basis we admit them; how we place our students in different courses of study; what we teach and how we teach it; how we assess, grade and certify our students; whom we hire and on what basis we reward and promote them; and how we operate our institutions internally. And even if we find ourselves under a state mandate to do outcome assessment or value-added testing, most of us still retain the right to decide what we test and how we test it. In many respects the difficulties that we encounter in trying to reform our assessment practices stem in part from our resistance to changing anything about our educational policies and practices (Astin, 1985a). What is especially ironic about our reluctance to change our assessment practices is that the arguments that we typically use to resist any such reforms seem to be at variance with our own time-honored practices!

This contradiction was illustrated to me recently when I had an opportunity to debate the whole assessment movement with a very articulate and witty humanist who was also a high-ranking administrator at one of the campuses of the California State University. In the debate, I was cast, albeit somewhat reluctantly, as the "pro-assessment" person, while my protagonist assumed the role of the assessment skeptic. The humanist-administrator spoke first and recited the usual litany of objections to systematic assessment: one or even several test scores simply cannot accurately reflect the rich diversity of a liberal education; the multiple choice test is not an appropriate methodology for assessing many important student outcomes; the typical standardized test cannot tell us much about the learning process because it generally yields only normative information showing how students perform in relation to each other at a particular point in time; and, finally, the use of outcome assessments is a serious threat to the curriculum because it inevitably forces us to "teach to the test."

While each of these standard criticisms of outcome assessment has merit, during the debate it began to dawn on me that there was a considerable degree of irony in my opponent's position: namely, that these same criticisms could be leveled with equal if not greater justification against the very same assessment procedures that my opponent and his colleagues have been using all of their professional lives. These procedures, of course, are also the ones that most of the rest of us in academe have been using as well. Just look at our undergraduate and graduate and professional school admissions procedures: we rely heavily on nationally normed, standardized, multiple-choice tests that yield a single or perhaps three or four scores at most. Such a system not only encourages students to study for the test, but for the Advanced Placement Examinations and the Bar exam, the teachers are clearly teaching to the test. And what about our classroom assessment procedures? Since grades are usually awarded on the basis of final exam performance, we've created an incentive system that certainly encourages students to study for the test. And letter grading itself is a relativistic or comparative measure that reduces the richness and diversity of the learning process to a single score. The point here is really a very simple one: Our traditional assessment practices in higher education are vulnerable to exactly

The same arguments that we invoke to resist external pressures to be "more accountable" or to conduct better "outcome assessments."

Sooner or later, in one form or another, most institutions in the United States will have to come to terms with the assessment issue. Simply continuing to ignore it or hoping that it will go away is becoming increasingly unrealistic, in light of mounting pressures from regional accrediting bodies and state governments, not to mention the growing number of internal initiatives being brought by a rapidly expanding pool of individual administrators and faculty members who see assessment as a powerful tool for self-study and reform. The real question is just what form each institution's response will take.

Getting Started

Any state or individual institution that wishes to introduce a systematic student assessment program needs to start somewhere. I have already suggested some of the critical first steps: to develop a clear understanding of institutional mission and goals; to design a series of outcome measures that reflect these goals; to begin developing a comprehensive longitudinal student data base; to read this book!

Although I have made frequent references throughout the book to the work of other investigators in the assessment field and have mentioned a number of institutions that have pioneered in this area, the book makes no pretense of being a thorough review of the assessment literature or a comprehensive analysis of exemplary assessment programs. I would strongly recommend to anyone undertaking a major assessment effort to examine more of the assessment literature and to take a look at some of the more innovative and sophisticated assessment programs that have actually been implemented around the country. As far as the assessment literature itself is concerned, there are a many excellent collections of essays that can be consulted (e.g., Adelman, 1988b; Banta, 1988; Ewell, 1984, 1985a; Folger and Harris, 1989; Halpern, 1987). Furthermore, there are at least three pioneering institutions whose well-developed and well-documented assessment programs merit some careful scrutiny: Alverno College (Alverno College Faculty, 1985; Mentkowski and Doherty, 1984; Mentkowski and Strait, 1983), Northeast Missouri State University (McClain and Kreuger, 1985; Northeast Missouri State University, 1984), and the University of Tennessee at Knoxville (Banta, 1985, 1986). Programs that have gotten off the ground much more recently but which show tremendous innovativeness and promise include Kean College of New Jersey (Kean College, 1988; Ross and Weiss, 1989b), Northwest Missouri State University (1987), Virginia Commonwealth University (McGovern, Wergin, and Hogshead, 1988), Empire State College (1989), and a number of other programs summarized by Paskow (1988; see especially the programs of

James Madison University, Kings College, and SUNY College at Platts-burgh).

Other excellent resources can be found in some of the national associations, assessment centers, and institutional consortia. The one national organization that has probably exerted the most leadership in this field is the American Association for Higher Education (AAHE). The AAHE Assessment Forum, under the leadership of Pat Hutchings, has served as a national clearinghouse for information on assessment and has compiled what is probably the most extensive library of resources on the topic. AAHE also sponsors the annual National Conference on Assessment which has shown enormous growth in popularity during the four years it has been operating. Another excellent source is the Assessment Resource Center at the University of Tennessee at Knoxville. The director of the center, Trudy W. Banta, is not only one of the most sought-after consultants on assessment but has also recently become the editor of a new newsletter on assessment activities, *Assessment Update*. The National Center for Higher Education Management Systems in Boulder, Colorado, provides extensive consulting services to states, systems, and individual campuses on assessment matters. Its stable of consultants includes Peter Ewell and Dennis Jones, two of the country's leading assessment experts.

The Problem of Expertise

While the political problems of establishing a comprehensive student data base and getting faculty involvement in the assessment of student outcomes are formidable, perhaps the biggest obstacle to successful implementation of a comprehensive student assessment program is the paucity of people who are adequately trained to undertake such an effort. This problem was discussed at length in chapter 7, in which I attempted to outline some of the personal qualifications for an ideal director of assessment. The basic difficulty is that there are few people around these days who understand the basic philosophical, technical, statistical, and educational issues or who have the communication and other interpersonal skills needed to guide such a program through its development and to enlist faculty involvement and support.

Where do institutions find such people, given the fact that there are few, if any, graduate programs currently designed to produce them? Those doctoral programs that are most likely to produce people with at least some of these qualifications would include (a) graduate departments of psychology with strong programs in measurement or educational psychology, (b) graduate sociology departments with strong quantitative programs, or (c) graduate schools of education with strong programs either in research methods or in higher education with an emphasis in empirical research.

What prompted me in part to write this book was a recognition that these three types of programs—psychology, sociology, and higher education—typically offer little in their curricula that attempts to bring together the diverse topics of higher education theory and practice, measurement, evaluation, statistical analysis, test construction, and utilization of assessment data to improve educational practice. I believe that this book could serve as a text for a year-long graduate course that could supplement the usual curricula offered by graduate programs. It could also serve as a text for postdoctoral seminars or workshops for institutional researchers, student affairs researchers, or faculty members who have been assigned responsibility for developing assessment programs at their institutions. And even if those who are responsible for running these doctoral or postdoctoral programs take issue with some of what I have to say, I believe that the book's coverage of content is diverse and unique enough to warrant its use as a kind of straw man: "If not this, then what?"

Traditional Assessment Practices

If an institution undertakes an ambitious program of assessment and self-study designed to enhance its talent development mission, what is to become of our traditional course grades and of the GPA? What future is in store for these time-honored indicators? Most of the assessment experts and much of the conventional wisdom about assessment finesses the whole issue of what is to become of course grades and the GPA. Given that we have been exposed to these meritocratic practices beginning with the early school grades and continuing through graduate and professional education, we cannot realistically be expected to abandon them immediately or even in the near future. The grading habit is simply too deeply ingrained in our educational psyches.

Does grading serve any legitimate educational purpose? Perhaps the most cogent argument in defense of our continuing use of course grades is that the students need to know how they are doing, and that employers and graduate and professional schools need to know how well the student has done. We academics also need to realize, however, that the course grade and the GPA are by no means the only, and probably not the best, way to satisfy these needs. Those few institutions that have had the temerity to abandon traditional grading systems and to institute systems focused more on the talent development process have all had generally positive experiences with their alternative systems. To date, most of these institutions, such as Empire State College, Hampshire College, Alverno College, and the University of California at Santa Cruz, have employed some form of narrative evaluation. Unfortunately, there has so far been no systematic research on the efficacy of narrative evaluations vis-à-vis traditional course grades. On a purely anecdotal level, however, students seem to get much more out of narrative evaluations, and these evaluations do not seem to pose any particular handicap to students in employment or in applying to graduate or professional school.

The narrative evaluation system at the University of California's Santa Cruz campus received a good deal of criticism during the 1970s on the grounds that students were handicapped in applying to graduate or professional school. So far as I know, no systematic documentation of these claims has ever been produced. Again, anecdotally, colleagues at Empire State and Hampshire College have assured me that their students are able to gain admission to some of the best graduate and professional schools, and that the admissions offices at these schools often report that the narrative evaluations reveal much more useful information about the candidates than do simple course grades and GPAs. Given the obvious importance of this issue, it would seem essential that the higher education community embark upon some systematic research into the matter at the earliest possible date. If employers and graduate and professional schools prove to be receptive to alternative forms of evaluation, the way would seem to be clear to introduce alternatives to traditional course grades.

One imperative for seriously considering alternative approaches to classroom assessment is that American higher education (indeed, American education in general) must find a way of assessing that *allows all students to succeed*. Our traditional normative approaches to assessment—grading on the curve and especially norm-referenced standardized testing—guarantees a significant proportion of failures and a very large number of mediocre performers, no matter what the absolute level of student performance turns out to be. Few people want to be average and practically nobody wants to be a poor performer or a failure.

I have two suggestions for surmounting this problem. First, of course, is to replace our norm-referenced assessment procedures with criterion-referenced measures. This latter form of measurement has two principal advantages: it tells us something about the student's absolute level of performance, and it in no way limits the number or proportion of students who can achieve excellent performance. Excellence, under a criterion-referenced approach to assessment, is not artificially rationed.

My second suggestion is to diversify and broaden what we are attempting to assess. While a single measure such as the GPA or SAT score might be convenient for purposes of selecting the "best" candidates for jobs or for graduate or professional schools, the use of a single measure—norm-referenced or otherwise—does great violence to the diversity of human talents and distorts the diverse purposes of any liberal education program. Moreover, the convenience of a single measure for use in hiring or selection is a dubious benefit. There are few employers or admissions officers who really want to rely on a single index of a candidate's worth or potential. If we stop for a moment and consider what the employers of college graduates are looking for, it becomes clear that the GPA simply will not do the trick. Most employers have a considerable stake in selecting people who exemplify traits such as creativity, leadership, honesty, and social responsibility. Intellectual or academic ability, to be sure, is a valued trait in a prospective employee, but consider the diverse ways in which this generalized trait can be manifest: reasoning ability, critical thinking skills, knowledge of particular subject matter, writing ability, and speaking ability.

In other words, a system of student assessment that is both criterion-referenced and multidimensional not only provides maximum opportunity for all students to succeed but also reflects more accurately the goals of a liberal education and provides prospective employers and graduate schools with a much richer source of information about the individual's capabilities and potentials.

Assessment of Faculty

Although the primary focus of this book has been on issues related to assessing student performance, many of the principles and strategies can be applied with equal validity to the assessment of college faculty. In thinking about the future of faculty assessment, it is important to realize that many educators are still unclear about why we need to assess faculty performance and what aspects of that performance should be assessed.

As I was putting the finishing touches on the manuscript for this book, I happened to be browsing through the October 4, 1989, *Chronicle of Higher Education* and encountered an article that reminds me of how far we still have to go before actual assessment practices catch up with what we really know. Michael Moffatt, an anthropology professor at Rutgers, authored an excellent essay about the need for each academic discipline to develop a national system for evaluating the teaching performance of its members. If such systems could be developed, argues Moffatt, the hiring and review process might eventually put as much value on teaching as it does presently on research. Moffatt argues further that since peer review has succeeded so well in evaluating research, why not use peer review to evaluate teaching? Moffatt argues that peers could evaluate each other's teaching by means of class visitations. What Moffatt and others who support such an approach to the peer review approach fail to realize is that peer review of research is assessing a tangible *product* (written research articles, books, artistic performances and products) while peer reviews based on classroom visitations assess only the teaching *process* (teaching practices and styles). (In terms of the I-E-O model, peer review of research looks at the *outcome* while peer review of teaching looks at the *environment.*)

Moffatt's appeal for the academic disciplines to take more of an interest in this subject is to be applauded, but his proposed remedy reflects a widely held misconception about assessment. What if Moffatt's proposed approach to assessing teaching were actually used in evaluating research? We would ignore the professors' completed research articles and books and concentrate instead on how they act in the laboratory or the library, how they sit in front of their word processors, and so on. As long as they are honest and ethical, does it really matter what *processes* professors use to conduct their research provided that the products (articles, books, creative performances) are up to standards? Indeed, do we ever try to get information on the professor's style of doing research during the peer review process? We do not, since it is the product that is of primary interest.

If we were really to apply the peer review system used for research to the evaluation of teaching, the most important information should reflect the product: how students are being affected by the professor's teaching and advising. Much of this book has been devoted to a discussion of how we might go about doing such evaluations. While many of the examples have dealt with more aggregated sorts of environments (programs, institutions) rather than with individual classrooms, exactly the same principles can be applied to the assessment of classroom teaching. For example, the peer review process recommended by Moffatt could be used to focus less on technique (environment) and more on student outcomes if the classroom visitor would concentrate more on student reactions to the class. (See the description below and in chapter 9 on teaching consultants.) In short, the most promising future direction for improving our assessment of the professor's teaching and mentoring is to focus on the product of these activities: the educational and personal development of the student. This is not to say that student evaluations of teaching are necessarily the best way to get this kind of information; one would presumably prefer to have data that show how much students have actually changed, how much they have learned, or the kinds of creative products that they have produced as part of their academic work.

One of the basic dilemmas and challenges in assessing faculty performance is how to utilize teaching performance in the personnel process without compromising faculty development. As pointed out in chapter 9, the potential value of faculty assessments for improvement of performance can be compromised if the assessment information is also used in the personnel review process.

There are several ways in which faculty assessment can be designed to avoid these problems. First, the institution can mandate institution-wide student assessments of classroom teaching performance for the "eyes only" of the professor. If this kind of information is also required in the personnel review process, a separate set of ratings should be used and the students should be told which rating is to be used for which purpose. Second, the institution could employ teaching consultants to visit classrooms (without the professor being present) in order to conduct a teaching seminar in which the students discuss with the consultant the strengths and weaknesses of the course. The consultant can subsequently summarize for the faculty member what transpired during the seminar. Finally, the institution can implement procedures for evaluating nonclassroom contacts between the faculty member and the student. This would involve getting students to evaluate the effectiveness of the professor's advising and mentoring, and their informal interactions with the professor. As far as I know, few institutions currently attempt to collect such nonclassroom performance information in any systematic way. Given that national surveys show academic advising to be among the most heavily criticized services that students receive (Astin, Green, and Korn, 1987), it seems obvious that faculty members need much more systematic and consistent feedback about their performance of this very important task.

We have really been very unimaginative about our faculty review procedures. Faculty handbooks typically create the illusion that faculty members should be equally proficient in all the usual areas under review (teaching, research, professional activities, institutional service). This expectation is quite unrealistic, given that many faculty are much more capable in some areas than in others. One possible approach to this problem is to let the faculty negotiate how much weight will be given to their teaching and how their teaching will be evaluated. A faculty member who wishes that considerable weight be given to teaching could specify one or several methods that would be used to evaluate that teaching: traditional student rating forms, open-ended student evaluations, talent development as measured by tests given before and after a course, creative products emanating from students' course work, and teaching consultants' judgments based on seminars with class members. No matter what techniques are used for personnel review purposes, a faculty member should also be given a chance to react, either in writing or in person, to the performance information being collected. This kind of feedback from faculty would enhance our ability to evaluate the assessment information and would also encourage faculty members to use the feedback coming from personnel reviews to develop their own pedagogical and mentoring talents.

Another potent use of assessment for faculty development is to engage faculty directly in the development of instruments for assessing student development. Experience at a number of institutions that have engaged faculty in this fashion (Alverno College and Kean College of New Jersey are excellent examples) appears to have a number of salutary effects:

- Faculty begin to talk to each other about course goals and objectives.

- Given that such discussions must eventually lead to some form of assessment, the discussion must eventually move from the purely abstract to a more concrete consideration of what various goals and outcomes actually mean.
- When students are also involved in the process, the exercise of trying to develop outcome assessments tends to break down status barriers and encourage greater trust between faculty and student.
- Faculty engaged in developing outcome assessments often begin to rethink not only curriculum content but also pedagogical technique (a much neglected topic in most discussions of curriculum).
- Many faculty, for the first time, begin thinking critically about their examining and testing procedures.
- Attention is focused on individual differences among students and on the multidimensional nature of learning outcomes.
- Course expectations become much clearer from the student's perspective.
- When the task involves assessing the outcomes of general education, it generates cross-disciplinary communication. Traditional disciplinary competitiveness is reduced, and faculty from different disciplines begin to focus on areas of common interest and concern rather than on differences.

What Would an Assessment-Oriented Institution Look Like?

If an institution were to commit itself to its talent development mission and attempt to implement a comprehensive assessment program designed to further that mission, how would such an institution change? How would its climate for learning and teaching differ from the typical institution? Below are just a few of the many ways in which such an institution might be unique.

- The environment will be characterized by a widespread spirit of inquiry and self-study. The comprehensive student data base will provide a common tool for all members of the community — students, administrators, faculty, and staff — to engage in a continuous process of self-examination.
- A much higher priority will be given to teaching, advising, mentoring, and similar institutional functions that are designed to enhance talent development.
- There will be a much greater spirit of experimentation and innovation, not only to improve areas of institutional functioning that are found to be in need of change, but also because a built-in mechanism for assessing the effectiveness of innovations (the data base) will be available.
- More of the faculty's expertise in research and scholarship will be devoted to studies of teaching, learning, and student development.

- Discussions about pedagogy will become more commonplace.
- Rigid lines between departments and disciplines will begin to break down.
- Teacher training programs and schools and departments of education will be accorded higher status and will receive higher priority in institutional planning.
- Hiring of faculty and administrators will give greater weight to the candidate's interest in and capacity to enhance the talent development function.
- Administrators will be expected to be educational leaders rather than mere managers.
- More students will be encouraged to take up careers as school and college teachers.

SOME FINAL THOUGHTS

Some readers may view the kind of assessment program suggested in this book as a sort of utopian ideal that has little chance of implementation in the real world. Paradoxically, such a belief may well be the principal obstacle to implementing a truly comprehensive and effective assessment program as the formal charters of most higher education institutions already provide the conceptual justification for such a program. The principal business of higher education is, after all, education. Assessment turns out to be an excellent device for helping us understand how effectively we are carrying out this mission. Moreover, assessment is a potentially powerful tool for assisting us in building a more efficient and effective educational program. Assessment can enhance our educational mission directly—by strengthening the teaching-learning process—and indirectly—by informing or enlightening us about which of our programs, policies, and practices are most and least effective. If an institution succeeds in developing an assessment program that serves these two functions, the external critics of higher education who seek to make us more accountable will have little left to complain about.

Most of the great philosophical and religious traditions have promoted, in one form or another, the maxim "know thyself." Self-knowledge is regarded by most of these traditions as a prerequisite for all of the other virtues: honesty, love, compassion, empathy, maturity, and social responsibility. It seems to me that the individual benefits of self-understanding can be generalized with equal validity to the case of an organization or institution: an institution that really understands itself—its strengths and weaknesses, its limitations and its potential—is likely to be much more successful in carrying out its educational mission than an institution that lacks such self-understanding. In short, it would seem that any institution—large or small, public or private, community college, liberal arts college, or university—has plenty of justification— logical, moral, and even legal—to embark upon a comprehensive program of assessment that focuses on the teaching-learning process.

While the current assessment movement is a potentially promising development for American higher education, I am concerned about its almost exclusive emphasis on cognitive outcomes. In chapter 3 I tried to show that there is plenty of justification in the catalogues and mission statements of most colleges and universities for including such qualities as interpersonal competence, leadership, empathy, honesty, citizenship, and social responsibility in any battery of outcome measures. Even so, the current balance between cognitive and affective seems to be tipped much too far in the cognitive direction.

Modern society provides many examples of our outstanding cognitive achievements: atomic energy, genetic engineering, modern agriculture, modern medicine, and computers and other electronic marvels of every conceivable type. It is truly astounding. At the same time we can see the great affective and emotional and spiritual divisions that threaten our very existence: religious fanaticism and hatred, racial prejudice, fanatical nationalism, noninvolvement in the political process, rampant dishonesty in business and government, escalating criminal behavior in the land of opportunity, and widespread poverty and homelessness in the face of unprecedented affluence. It is time to redress the balance. It is time to begin shifting some of our educational interest and energy in the direction of our affective side—to begin concerning ourselves much more directly with the development of beliefs and values that are going to heal our divisions and that will help to create a society that is less materialistic and competitive and selfish and more generous and cooperative.

Let me add a final word about our different conceptions of excellence. In the long run, the kinds of assessments that we perform and how we use the results will depend heavily on our values, which means in part the conception of excellence we ultimately choose. During my days as a clinical psychologist I would have looked at the reputational and resource views as basically egocentric, in the sense that they emphasize what possessions we have and what others think of us. (Perhaps *narcissistic* would be even more accurate than *egocentric*.) Under a talent development view, we identify ourselves instead in terms of what we do, what we contribute to others and what they in turn contribute to their communities and to the society. In other words, by adopting a talent development perspective, we, in effect, transcend our institutional egos to some extent and begin to view our institutions more in terms of their impact on the larger society.

The basic point to be made is a rather simple one: When an institution exists primarily for its own sake, and when it identifies itself primarily in terms of its resources and reputation, its relationship with the society it is supposed to serve becomes exploitative and defensive, and its capacity to serve as an instrument for improving the society is compromised. In short, the biggest obstacle to higher education's serving as a major instrument for societal improvement is the institutional ego. Our colleges and universities need to learn how to transcend their institutional egos and to become more actively involved in what is going on in the society.

Many years ago when I was doing psychotherapy, I was continually aware that my ability to help a troubled patient was limited to the extent that I allowed my ego to become a prominent part of the therapeutic process. Egotistical therapists are less helpful to patients because their sense of worth comes primarily from the power they wield over the patient and from the patient's sense of helplessness and dependency. The most effective therapists, on the other hand, are those who are able to transcend their egos to the extent necessary to empathize fully with the patient and to create an accepting and supportive therapeutic clinical environment. The therapeutic focus should be on the patient rather than the therapist.

I believe that there is an analogy here between patients and therapists, on the one hand, and students and institutions, on the other: The capacity for higher education to be a positive change agent in American society will depend upon our ability to transcend our institutional egos, our narcissism, and our self-interest, and to concern ourselves more directly with the impact we are having on our students and communities.

I believe that the key to achieving this kind of institutional transcendence is in how we ultimately define our own excellence. Rather than continuing to see our excellence as limited to what we have (resources) or to our status and prestige (reputation), we need to see it more in terms of what we do and what we accomplish. And to do this we need to rely heavily on assessment. We need to know many things: How much and how well do our students learn? How are we affecting their values and attitudes? What kinds of citizens and what kinds of parents and spouses do they make? Are they becoming humane, more honest, and more concerned with the welfare of others? Are they becoming more active and better-informed participants in the democratic process? If we who are involved in the assessment game could succeed in persuading our faculty and administrative colleagues simply to *begin* seeking answers to such questions, we would be taking a major step toward institutional transcendence.

Appendix

STATISTICAL ANALYSIS OF LONGITUDINAL DATA

This appendix is designed to serve two purposes. First, for those readers who are not well-versed in statistics, the section entitled "Basic Statistics" reviews some fundamental statistical concepts. I have included a minimal amount of math that even the least mathematically inclined reader should be able to follow. Second, for those readers who are interested in applying the I-E-O model in practice, the remainder of the appendix covers what I consider to be the fundamental statistical and analytical concepts needed to apply the model to real data. My basic aim has been to convey the logic behind the I-E-O model as it can be expressed through statistical analyses. Again, no math beyond the simplest algebra is used. Statistical purists may be upset by what I have left out, but if the reader can master the material presented here, he or she should be able to use appropriate statistical tools responsibly and, more important, to understand what the results mean in practical terms.

What are we really doing when we use traditional statistical procedures to analyze assessment data? To begin with, it should be recognized that the most widely used statistical methods—correlation, regression, factor analysis—are fundamentally *relativistic* or *normative*. By this I mean that these procedures work by *comparing* the scores of the different persons being assessed.

A SAMPLE PROBLEM

Let's say we're trying to analyze the Graduate Record Examination (GRE) scores of our graduating seniors with the goal of trying to find out what we can do to help future generations of students get the best possible scores. With our problem formulated in this manner, the seniors' GRE scores would constitute an *outcome* measure (see Chapter 2). To simplify, we will limit our discussion to the GRE Verbal score. If we test 200 graduating seniors,[1] we get 200 GRE Verbal scores (one for each student).

BASIC STATISTICS

In this section we will discuss the definition and meaning of basic statistics—the mean, standard deviation, and correlation coefficient— together with other statistical concepts such as variable, constant, and standard (z) scores. Readers already familiar with such concepts can skip to the section entitled "Environmental Effects." However, even if you think you already understand these concepts, reading pages 256 to 263 might still give you some new perspectives.

Let's use the letter Y to stand for the GRE score of any student. Letters like X and Y are used to designate *variables*, in this case the GRE Verbal score of the students. The reason we call them variables is that the scores can *vary* from one student to another (i.e., not all students will get the same score). In statistics we conventionally use Y to represent an outcome or dependent variable, and X to represent an independent (i.e., input or environmental) variable. Since in our hypothetical problem the GRE Verbal score is an outcome or dependent variable, we are using Y to represent the GRE score. The reason we use a letter instead of an actual score is that we have 200 different scores to

---

1. In the jargon of educational research, we could also refer to the seniors as "subjects," "cases," or "units of observation." Basically, the units of observation in research are the entities from which we take our measures (such as GRE). Units of observation might be students, classrooms, schools, or even school systems, depending on the nature of the problem being studied.

deal with. The symbol Y can thus represent *any* student's score, or *all* of the scores considered together, depending on how we use it.

For example, if we wanted to add up all the 200 students' scores, we would use the Greek capital letter sigma ($\sum$) to indicate the summing operation, so that $\sum Y$ would mean the sum total of the 200 GRE Verbal scores. Any time you put a $\sum$ in front of a variable (in this case, Y), it means that you're adding up all of the scores on that variable for your entire sample. What if we wanted to find the average of the 200 scores? Clearly, we'd have to divide the sum ($\sum Y$) by the number of scores (200) to get the average. In this case we would use the letter N to indicate how many scores we have, so that the average becomes

$$\sum Y \div N \text{ or } \frac{\sum Y}{N} \text{ or } \frac{\sum Y}{200}$$

In statistics, of course, we refer to this value as the *mean*. Suppose the mean of 200 students' GRE Verbal scores turns out to be 500. Instead of the formula shown above, let's use the shorthand $\overline{Y}$ to stand for the mean. (Any time you draw a flat bar across the top of a variable, it means the mean of that variable.) From this point on, *all* of the commonly used statistics that we might use to analyze these GRE scores use this mean ($\overline{Y}$) as a *reference point*. So, in effect, any time we analyze an individual student's score we are basically comparing that score with the mean for all 200.

Let's look at why this is so. All statistical procedures are basically analyzing *variability*. (It is, incidentally, unfortunate that one of these procedures happens to be called "the analysis of variance," since *all* procedures—correlation, regression, etc.— analyze variance.) In our example, the practical reason underlying our interest in analyzing variability is our desire to answer the following questions: Why do different seniors get different GRE scores? Why don't they all get the same score? What do students do and what do *we* do in our institution that *influences* how well the students do on the GRE? Obviously, being able to answer such questions puts us in a good position to set up programs and implement policies that will help students get better scores.

Thus, the first task confronting us is how to define variability. We *could* compare a given student's score with the highest score or with the lowest score to see how far away it is. However, as already indicated, the statistical procedures discussed in this chapter all rely on the mean ($\overline{Y}$) as the common reference point. By "reference point" we mean simply that each student's GRE score (Y) is to be compared to the mean score for all students ($\overline{Y}$), and that the "variability" in our 200 GRE scores will be judged in terms of *how far they are from the mean*. So, if the mean GRE Verbal score for all 200 seniors is 500, a student with a score of 600 is 100 points above the mean, a student with a score of 450 is 50 points below the mean, and so on. This "distance from the mean" for any individual student's score is indicated by the following term:

$$Y - \overline{Y}$$

The letter Y stands for any student's GRE score, and $\overline{Y}$ stands for the mean of the 200 scores, which is 500. We can call this the student's GRE "deviation score." We can, of course, compute a deviation score for each of the 200 students. The reason we subtract the mean from any student's individual score rather than the other way around is so that students who score above the mean will get positive deviation scores and students who score below the mean will get negative deviation scores. If the student happens to get the mean score, the deviation score is, of course, zero.

We are now in a position to visualize what we have so far been discussing only with words and algebraic symbols. Let's look at all the possible GRE Verbal scores that our students might get, and represent these by a *continuum*:

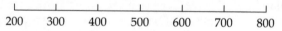

200	300	400	500	600	700	800

Any student's Y score can be represented by a *point* on this continuum and any student's deviation score $(Y - \overline{Y})$ can be represented by the *distance of the student's score* from the mean score of 500.

So far we've been talking about how far any individual student's score deviates from the mean score. How do we describe the deviations of all students considered together? The mean score $(\overline{Y})$ describes the average score for all students. What can we use to describe the average *deviation* score? One possibility, of course, would be simply to compute the average deviation. To do this we would sum up the 200 deviation scores $[\sum(Y - \overline{Y})]$, and divide by 200. Unfortunately, the average deviation, by definition, always turns out to be zero. Partly for this reason, most statistical techniques require a somewhat different measure of variability—one that is similar to an "average deviation"—but with an important difference: Instead of just taking the average of all 200 deviations, we first *square* each deviation, i.e., multiply it by itself:

$$(Y - \overline{Y}) \times (Y - \overline{Y}) \text{ or } (Y - \overline{Y})^2$$

This squaring procedure has two effects: It makes all deviations positive (a minus deviation multiplied by itself becomes a plus), and it *magnifies the larger deviations*. Note that if Mary is 100 points from the mean GRE, her squared deviation is 100×100 or 10,000, but if John is 200 points (twice as far) from the mean, his squared deviation is 200×200 or 40,000. Now, with the deviations squared, instead of being twice as far from the mean as Mary is, John is *four* times as far away (40,000 versus 10,000.)[2]

These squared deviations can be summed across all 200 seniors:

$$\sum(Y - \overline{Y})^2 \text{(called the } sum\ of\ squares)$$

and the sum can be averaged:

$$\frac{\sum(Y - \overline{Y})^2}{200}$$

This last quantity is called the *mean square* or, more commonly, the *variance*.

Our last step is to take the square root of the variance

$$\sqrt{\frac{\sum(Y - \overline{Y})^2}{200}}$$

which is called the *standard deviation* or "SD." The basic reason we take the square root is to compensate for the fact that we originally squared the deviations. The point to keep in mind is that the standard deviation is very much like the average deviation, except that we have given more weight to the larger deviation scores.

The most important thing to remember about the standard deviation is that it represents a *distance* along the continuum of GRE scores. In our particular problem the standard deviation would come out somewhat near to 100 GRE points. If the distribution of the 200 students' scores is bell shaped or "normal" (see below), about two-thirds of the students (133 of the 200) will have scores that fall between minus one and plus one standard deviations from the mean (that is, between 400 and 600), and about 95 percent of the students (190 of the 200) will have scores that fall between minus two and plus two standard deviations (that is, between 300 and 700).

In most statistical procedures we conventionally express each subject's deviation or distance from the mean in *standard deviation units*. That is, we first compute the deviation score:

$$Y - \overline{Y}$$

and then divide it by the standard deviation:

$$\frac{Y - \overline{Y}}{SD}$$

---

2. The mathematical justification for this is not really germane to our discussion. Logically, we might argue that, since large deviations are much rarer than small ones, they should get more weight.

This quantity is commonly called a "z score." What a person's z score tells us is how far from the mean, in standard deviation units, that person's score is. Or, how many standard deviations away from the mean (and in what direction, plus or minus) is the person's score. If the person's GRE score is 700, our formula looks like this:

$$z = \frac{700 - 500}{100} = 2.0$$

In other words, a verbal score of 700 is 2 standard deviations above the mean. A GRE score of 400 would produce a z score of −1.0 ([i.e., (400 − 500) ÷ 100]), meaning that the person who got that score is exactly one SD below the mean.

It should be noted that z scores have one main advantage: They equalize (or "standardize") the units of measurement. (A z score can also be called a *standard score*.)[3] Thus, a z score of 1.5 means that the person's score is one and one-half standard deviations above the mean, regardless of whether we are talking about GRE scores, SAT scores, GPAs, height, weight, or whatever. In other words, z scores provide a basis for *comparing* people's scores on two or more variables, even if the different variables are based on completely different units of measurement (GRE points, inches, pounds, and so on). This ability to compare people's scores on two or more variables is what makes it possible to compute *correlations* between different variables.

Correlation

What, indeed, is a correlation coefficient? To answer this question, let's return briefly to our practical problem: to learn how to raise students' GRE scores. Our basic approach to this problem is to search for environmental factors that influence the student's GRE score, that make her perform better or worse than she might otherwise do if she were not exposed to those factors. We can refer to these environmental factors as environmental *variables*, since the actual experience of students can vary, i.e., different students could be exposed to different aspects of the college environment. Correlation coefficients would help us determine if any of these environmental variables is associated (correlated) with the variable of GRE performance.

But exactly what do we mean by "associated with" or "correlated"? Let's take a concrete example. It is reasonable to expect that the stu-

---

3. A standard score expresses any raw score in terms of how many standard deviations it is from the mean. The z score is just one form of standard score in which the mean has been set to zero and the SD to 1. SATs and GREs were originally developed as standard scores with a mean of 500 and an SD of 100. ACT standard scores were designed with an SD of 5.

dents' performance on the GRE Verbal test might be affected by how much reading they've been required to do during their undergraduate years. Since performing well on a test like the GRE Verbal depends in part on one's ability to read and comprehend unfamiliar written prose under pressure of time, it stands to reason that the more practice a person gets in reading prose, the better he should do on the test. People who have had a lot of practice should do better on the GRE than people with little practice. What we are describing in this last sentence is a *positive correlation*, where people with high scores on one variable (practice in reading) tend to get high scores on the other variable (GRE Verbal score), and people with low scores on one tend to get low scores on the other. Note the hedge in my statement: "tend to get." By this I mean to suggest that there is merely a tendency for the two variables to be positively associated, but that not all students' pairs of scores on the two variables will follow the pattern of high-high and low-low. The extent to which students *do* follow that pattern will be indicated by the *size* of the correlation.

Let's say we compute for each student a score on an environmental variable called *practice in reading*, which we define as the total number of pages of assigned prose that any student actually reads during the undergraduate years. Let's assume further that our 200 students read between 500 and 5,000 pages each, with a mean of 2,000. Let's say further that the standard deviation for pages read turns out to be 500. Keep in mind that *each* of the 200 students now has a *pair* of scores: practice in reading and GRE Verbal.

How do we determine whether there is any correlation between these two variables, practice in reading and GRE Verbal? How large is the correlation? And what does it *mean*?

The first thing we would do is to compute z scores for all 200 seniors separately on each of the two variables. What we are doing here is converting their raw scores on the two variables, practice in reading and GRE Verbal, into two z scores. Thus, for each student we would determine how far above or below the mean, in standard deviation units, each of their two scores was and to substitute two z scores for their two original scores. Let's take a specific student, Mary, whose GRE Verbal score was 600 and whose practice in reading score was 3,000. In other words, she scored 100 points better than the average senior on the GRE and she read 1,000 more pages than the average . Mary's two z scores would look like this:

	Raw score	Computation	=	z score
GRE Verbal	600	$(600 - 500) \div 100$	=	+1.0
Reading practice	3,000	$(3,000 - 2,000) \div 500$	=	+2.0

Since both of Mary's scores are above the mean, both of her z scores are positive. Note that we have accomplished one important goal in converting Mary's data into z scores: We can now *compare* her two scores (GRE Verbal and reading practice), even though they were originally measured in entirely different ways. Basically, what we are doing is comparing these scores by determining how far (and in what direction) each one *deviates* from its respective mean. Mary's reading practice score is twice as far above its mean as her GRE Verbal score is above its mean. Let's take another student, John. He did 200 points worse than average on the GRE Verbal—a score of 300, and also read 750 pages less than average—only 1,250 pages. John's two z scores would be as follows:

	Raw score	Computation	=	z score
GRE Verbal	300	$(300 - 500) \div 100$	=	-2.0
Reading practice	1,250	$(1{,}250 - 2{,}000) \div 500$	=	-1.5

If we repeat the computations we did for Mary and John for all the other 198 seniors, we have 200 z scores for GRE Verbal and 200 z scores for practice in reading. Remember, however, that the z scores come in *pairs*: two for each student. To keep track, let's call the z score for practice in reading z_1, and the one for GRE Verbal z_2. The correlation (between practice in reading and GRE Verbal performance) turns out to be very simple to compute:

$$\text{Correlation } (r) = \frac{\sum(z_1 z_2)}{N}$$

In other words, to compute the correlation, we first take the product of each senior's two z scores,

$$z_1 z_2$$

sum the products across all 200 seniors,

$$\sum(z_1 z_2)$$

and then divide by the number of seniors:

$$r = \frac{\sum(z_1 z_2)}{N} \text{ or } \frac{\sum(z_1 z_2)}{200}$$

The lower-case letter (r) is traditionally used to designate the correlation coefficient involving two variables.

Now what have we really done here? We have determined, for the group of 200 seniors as a whole, the extent to which high or low scores on one variable "go together" with high or low scores on another variable. By "go together" we are referring to the fact that z_1 and z_2 scores come in pairs, that is, each student has one of each. For Mary and John at least, high and low scores *did* tend to go together. What the correlation coefficient tells us, then, is the extent to which this holds true for all 200 seniors. In trying to understand correlation coefficients, keep in mind the following:

1. When both z scores for any person are positive (i.e., when that person's scores on both variables are high or above the mean), the product (z_1, z_2) will be positive.
2. When both z scores are negative (i.e., when both scores are low or below their means), the product $(z_1 z_2)$ will *also* be positive.
3. If positive z's tend to occur together and negative z's tend to occur together, the sum of all the products $\sum(z_1 z_2)$ will *also* be positive, and the correlation $\sum(z_1 z_2)/N$ will be positive.
4. When positive z's on one variable tend to be paired with negative z's on the other variable, the products $(z_1 z_2)$ will tend to be negative, and so will the correlation coefficient.
5. The largest possible size of the correlation coefficient (r) is either +1.0 or −1.0.
6. When there is no overall tendency for high or low z's on one variable to be paired with high or low z's on the other, there will be just about as many positive products (two positive z's or two negative z's) as there are negative products (a negative z paired with a positive z). Under these conditions, the positive and negative products will tend to cancel each other out when you add them together, so that the $\sum(z_1 z_2)$ (and thus the correlation coefficient) will be near zero.

The logic behind the zero or near-zero correlation coefficient is that high scores on one variable are no more likely to be paired with low scores than with high scores on the other variable. There is, in other words, no consistent *association* between scores on one variable and scores on the other. In the case of our practical example, a zero correlation would mean that seniors who read a lot during their undergraduate years performed no better or no worse on the GRE than did students who had read very little.

Environmental Effects?

But let's assume that we *did* find a positive correlation between the environmental variable of practice in reading and the outcome variable of GRE Verbal performance. Let's assume further that the correlation coefficient turned out to be .40, which would be only a modest positive correlation, but highly significant statistically.[4] In effect, such a correlation means that those seniors who read a lot tended to do well on the GRE Verbal test, while those who read little tended to do relatively poorly. (Note that you can describe a positive correlation in two ways: in terms of either the high-high students or the low-low students.) What we have here, then, is a significant positive association between an environmental variable (practice in reading) and an outcome variable (GRE Verbal score).

While this particular correlation coefficient confirms our expectation about the effects of practice in reading on the student's GRE Verbal score, how confident can we be that this positive correlation reflects a *causal* relationship between the two variables? By "causal" we mean that the students who read a lot tended to score better on the GRE *because* they read a lot. Obviously, the degree of confidence that we have in the existence of a causal relationship will determine in part our future policies: Should we consider increasing the amount of outside reading required in our courses? Are we justified in expecting that this will help future generations of students do better on the GRE Verbal test?

As indicated in chapter 2, we are always free to interpret any environment-outcome correlation in causal terms; the real issue is how *confident* we can be in such a conclusion. This degree of confidence, in turn, will help to determine whether, and to what extent, we will base future policies and practices on such a causal interpretation.

In chapter 2 we also suggested that the greatest risk in making causal interpretations of environment-outcome correlations is the possibility that the correlation may have come about instead as a consequence of *input* variables. In our current example, is it reasonable to ask whether the correlation of .40 reflects the effect of some student input characteristics on the GRE, rather than the effect of practice in reading? Even a cursory examination of this problem suggests that it does.

One such input characteristic would be the verbal ability of the students when they first entered the college as freshmen. We are safe in assuming that not all of the students began college with the same degree

---

4. By "significant" we mean simply that a coefficient of that size or larger would be very unlikely to occur by chance. If we decide that a correlation is significant (meaning that it is not zero), we make such a decision with a certain "level of confidence." If we make the decision at, say, the .01 level of confidence, this means that the odds of getting a coefficient of that size or larger by chance are fewer than 1 in 100. The .05 level means that the odds are fewer than 5 in 100 (or 1 in 20). With correlation coefficients, statistical significance at a given level of confidence depends on two factors: the size of the coefficient and the size of the sample on which it is based. A coefficient of .40, for example, would not be considered significant, even at the .05 level of confidence, if it were based, say, on a sample of only ten students. The concept of statistical significance, which is treated at length in almost all books on statistics, is not covered further here.

of skill in taking a test like the GRE. Their verbal skills, in other words, *varied* from student to student. We know this because their scores on a very similar test—the Scholastic Aptitude Test (SAT) Verbal subtest—were by no means all the same. Let's assume that these SAT Verbal scores—like their GRE scores four years later—yielded an SD of 100 when they started college as freshmen. It stands to reason that these freshman SAT scores would have at least some effect on their senior GRE scores; that is, that *variation* in the SAT would be related to *variation* in the GRE. Or, to put it in nontechnical terms, that the students who got the highest scores on the SAT would also *tend* to get the best GRE scores, and that those with the lowest SAT scores would tend to do relatively poorly on the GRE. In other words, we would expect to find a *positive correlation* between input and outcome or between SAT and GRE. (As suggested in chapter 2, such an expectation is based on the observation that differences among people tend to persist over time.)

Research has shown that SAT Verbal scores *do* correlate positively with GRE Verbal scores obtained from the same students several years later (Astin, 1968; Nichols, 1964; see also chapter 6 and below). It would not be unusual, for example, for the correlation coefficient to be as high as .80. What we have, then, is a substantial correlation between input (SAT) and outcome (GRE).

Is it reasonable to suggest that the positive correlation between SAT and GRE may account for the positive correlation between GRE and practice in reading? Returning once more to the principles outlined in chapter 2, we need to determine whether the observed correlation of .40 between environment and outcome can be attributed to the effects of input. For this to occur, input (SAT) also must correlate with environment (practice in reading). Is this a plausible possibility? Is it reasonable to expect that input (SAT) is related to outcome (GRE) *and* to environment (practice in reading)? The answer to this question would seem to be yes, given that students who enter college with highly developed verbal abilities (high SAT Verbal scores) would be expected to read more while in college (high practice in reading scores), whereas those with less well developed verbal skills would be expected to read less. This correlation could come about for a number of reasons: students with highly developed reading skills might enjoy reading more, they might take more courses that require a lot of reading, and so on.

Regression Analysis: Controlling for Input

How, then, do we go about determining whether the observed correlation between GRE and practice in reading can be attributed to SAT scores? The basic strategy for answering this question is first to "control" the student input variable (SAT) and then to determine whether the environment (practice in reading) is still related to outcome (GRE). In effect, what we do when we *control* the input variable is to eliminate its effect on the outcome variable. In other words, what we strive to do is to eliminate the correlation between input and outcome.

My favorite statistical procedure for eliminating the effect of input variables on the outcome variable is called *regression* analysis, and it requires some explanation.

Let's say that an independent (input) variable such as SAT is correlated with a dependent (outcome) variable such as GRE, and that instead of just determining the strength of the correlation between the two, we want to use the input variable to predict or *estimate* the outcome variable. Prediction or estimation of one variable from another is the major purpose of regression analysis, and it has a lot of practical advantages. Many colleges use regression to get an estimate of what the student's college GPA is likely to be, given their high school grades and admission test scores.

To see how regression works, let's return to our z scores. If we're trying to estimate the student's GRE z from her SAT z, the formula is really very simple:

$$\hat{z}_{GRE} = r \times z_{SAT}$$

In other words, you simply multiply the student's SAT z score by the correlation coefficient, and this gives you an estimate of her GRE z. Note that we put the little "hat" (^) above the z_{GRE} to show that this is a *prediction* or *estimate* based on SAT rather than the actual z.

Look at the logic behind this last formula. If Mary's SAT is above the mean, and if SAT and GRE are positively correlated, we would also expect her GRE to be above the mean. If John's SAT is below the mean, we'd expect his GRE also to be below the mean. Thus, if the person's X variable (SAT) is above the mean, and if there is a positive correlation between X and Y (SAT and GRE), $\hat{z}_{GRE}$ will be a positive value. So, for example, if the student's SAT score is above the mean, then the z score based on that SAT score, $(X - \overline{X}) \div SD$, will also be positive. Thus, multiplying z_{SAT} by r will yield a positive estimate of z_{GRE}:

$$\hat{z}_{GRE} = r \times \left(\frac{X - \overline{X}}{SD_x} \right)$$

A simpler way of saying this is that whenever we have a positive correlation, we can be sure of two things in regression: (a) if a person's score on X is above the mean of X, the $\hat{Y}$ based on that X will be above the mean of Y; and (b) if the person's X score is below the mean of X, the $\hat{Y}$ based on that X will also be below the mean of Y.

It is also important to realize that, except when the correlation is perfect (either +1.0 or –1.0), the estimated $\hat{z}$ for GRE will always be *smaller* than the z for SAT. This is true simply because any time you multiply a value by less than 1.0, the result is always a smaller value.

Note, however, that in that rare case when r is 1.0, $\hat{z}_{GRE}$ will be the *same* as $\hat{z}_{SAT}$. On the other hand, if the correlation (r) is zero, we also estimate the $\hat{z}$ for Y to be at zero (which is, of course, the mean of the z scores for Y). Another way of saying this is that when X is of no help in predicting or estimating Y, your best bet is to estimate $\hat{Y}$ to be the same as $\overline{Y}$, or $\hat{Y} = \overline{Y}$.

Since z scores can be awkward to use in practice, the regression formula shown above ($\hat{z}_Y = r z_x$) can, with a little algebraic manipulation, be rewritten without resorting to z scores, as follows:

$$\hat{Y} = a + bX$$

This is the usual regression formula, and it is also the geometric formula for a straight line. Two of the terms are familiar:

X = input or independent or predictor variable

$\hat{Y}$ = an estimate of the outcome or dependent variable Y

These are the two *variables* in the regression equation, meaning that they can vary from one person to the next within a sample. The terms a and b are *constants*, meaning that, in any given problem situation (say, predicting GRE from SAT among our 200 seniors), they will have the same value from student to student. The constant b is called the *regression coefficient*, and it functions very much as r does in the z score formula; that is, you multiply it by X. As a matter of fact, there is a simple formula for translating r into b:

$$b = \frac{r \times SD_Y}{SD_x}$$

In other words, the only difference between r and b is caused by the standard deviations. When the SDs for X and Y are the same, r and b are the same. The constant a is usually called the *intercept*, for reasons to be discussed shortly.

Basically, then, if you want to use X to get the best estimate of Y, you simply multiply X by b and add the result to a.

There is a peculiarity about regression that may already be apparent: Since you need to know the actual correlation (r) between X and Y in order to use regression, what good is it? Since you need to know everyone's SAT (X) *and* GRE (Y) before you can compute the correlation between X and Y, why bother to "predict" or "estimate" something that you already know?

The answer to this question has to do with the value of knowing the *strength* of the relationship between X and Y. Let's take our example of the 200 seniors with their GRE (Y or outcome) and SAT (X or input) scores: To what extent has the variation in the seniors' GRE scores been affected by variation in their SAT scores obtained four years earlier? If we know the magnitude of that effect (i.e., if we know the correlation between SAT and GRE), we can use regression analysis to *eliminate* or remove that effect statistically. In other words, by using regression we can eliminate the correlation between any two variables (in this case, between SAT and GRE). Let's see how this works.

Recall first the formula for simple regression:

$$\hat{Y} = a + bX$$

This represents the best estimate of the outcome or Y (GRE) that we can make from input or X (SAT). (We'll discuss shortly what is meant by "best"). Imagine for a moment that we computed $\hat{Y}$ separately for each of the 200 seniors. Since the constants a and b will be the same for all 200 equations, the only variable is X. In other words, for each of the seniors, $\hat{Y}$ *is an expression of* X. Or, to put it more concretely, the regression formula allows us to convert the student's SAT score into an "expected GRE score" ($\hat{Y}$). Or, to use the more generalized terminology from chapter 2, $\hat{Y}$ *is an expected outcome score based on input*. Regression, in other words, allows us to express the student's input score in terms of an expected outcome score called $\hat{Y}$. Each student's $\hat{Y}$ value, then, represents the GRE score that we would expect that student to get, given her freshman SAT score.

$\hat{Y}$ has some other interesting properties:

1. The correlation between $\hat{Y}$ and Y is exactly the same as the correlation between Y and X (this is not surprising, given that $\hat{Y}$ is derived from X).
2. The $\hat{Y}$ *mean* for all cases is exactly the same as the mean Y.
3. The variation (SD) in $\hat{Y}$ is always less than the variation in Y, except when the correlation is +1.0 or −1.0 (in which case the variations are equal).

RESIDUALS. The really important application of regression begins when we start *comparing* each student's $\hat{Y}$ (the expected outcome score) with his or her Y (the actual outcome score). The simplest way to do this is to subtract one from the other:

$$Y - \hat{Y}$$

This value is called the *residual* (for reasons to be explained shortly). It can also be called the *error*, meaning that, if our predicted outcome ($\hat{Y}$) for a student doesn't match the actual outcome (Y) for that student, then there is some error in our prediction for that student.

But what is the residual in reality? In the terminology of chapter 2, the *residual* is that part of the student's outcome score that we cannot *predict* (or account for) from the student's input score. Look at the expression: $Y - \hat{Y}$. What we are doing is taking away (subtracting) from the student's actual outcome score (Y) that part of the score that is caused by input ($\hat{Y}$). Or, to go back to our example, the residual represents that part of the student's GRE performance that cannot be explained by (or predicted from) her SAT score.

Let's say we calculate a residual GRE for each of our 200 seniors. These 200 residual scores, like $\hat{Y}$, have some interesting properties:

1. The stronger the correlation between X and Y, the smaller the residuals.
2. The mean residual (computed across all students) will be zero.
3. The correlation between the residual GRE score and the original SAT score will be *zero*. Or, in the terminology of chapter 2, the correlation between input and residual outcome is always zero.

This last property is probably the most important consequence of regression analysis. It allows us to compute a new outcome measure (the residual outcome or $Y - \hat{Y}$) which is *independent of input*. In other words, we can eliminate (or control, as the statisticians prefer to say) the effects of input on outcome by replacing Y with $Y - \hat{Y}$ (that is, by substituting a residual outcome measure, $Y - \hat{Y}$, for the original outcome measure (Y). Regression analysis, of course, is the statistical tool that allows us to do this.

VISUALIZING REGRESSION. Perhaps the best way to understand regression is to visualize it. Thus, let's once again look at our continuum of GRE scores. But this time let's also show what scores our 200 students actually got. For this purpose we shall use some real data taken from UCLA students who took the SAT in high school and who took the GRE four years later when they were seniors. There are 97 students in all (see figure A.1). Each of the 97 dots in figure A.1 represents a different senior, and the dots are positioned along the continuum according to what scores each student got. Note that when more than one student gets the same score, we have to pile one on top of the other. Thus, the height of any column of dots above a given score indicates how many students got that score. In other words, the height of each column indicates the "frequency of occurrence" of the score corresponding to that column. We could also draw a line connecting the tops of the columns of dots, creating a curve that would be roughly "normal" in shape. Figure A.1 is called a *frequency distribution*, since it shows graphically how frequently different values of a variable occur within a sample. More specifically, we would call figure A.1 a *univariate* frequency distribution, since it shows how frequently the different values of a single (*uni*) variable occur.

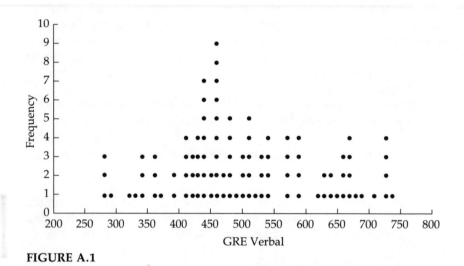

FIGURE A.1

Since regression involves at least two variables, in order to show regression graphically we have to create a different kind of distribution called a *bi*variate frequency distribution (*bi* referring to two variables) (figure A.2). What we have done in figure A.2 is to set up *two* continua, one for the GRE (the vertical one) and one for the SAT (the horizontal one). The horizontal continuum is also called the "X axis," since this is where we put the input or independent (X) variable, and the vertical continuum can be called the "Y axis" to signify the outcome

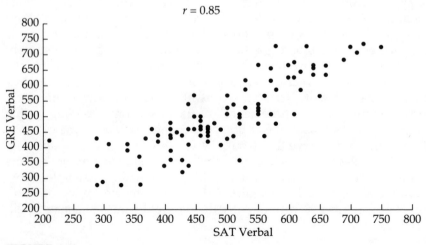

FIGURE A.2

or dependent variable. Again, each dot represents a different senior. The important thing to keep in mind about a bivariate frequency distribution is that each dot (student) represents a pair of scores (i.e., each student has *both* an SAT and GRE score), and the *position* of the dot in the two dimensional space of the chart is determined by the student's scores on the two variables. The SAT locates the student in the right-left (X) dimension, and the GRE locates the student in the up-down (Y) dimension. A bivariate frequency distribution, in other words, shows graphically how often different pairs or *combinations* of scores on two variables occur. If two people happen to have exactly the same combinations of scores, the proper way to show this would be to pile up the students on top of one another in a third dimension (i.e., up off the page). To avoid having to make three-dimensional figures, we usually "cheat" a bit by cramming students with identical pairs of scores as closely together as possible. Thus, in a bivariate frequency distribution, we can "eyeball" the degree of association or correlation between the two variables by seeing where the dots (people) are most heavily clustered.

Now in trying to predict or estimate GRE (Y) from SAT (X), it seems obvious that, except in the limiting case where the correlation is perfect ($+1.0$ or -1.0), there will necessarily be a certain amount of *error* $(Y - \hat{Y})$ in our estimates. The regression formula is a means of estimating Y from X that will *minimize the amount of error* in these estimates. Regression analysis uses a method called the *principle of least squares* to minimize the error in prediction. Let's see how it works.

Figure A.3 shows the same data from the previous figure, except that we have added an additional item: a straight line that has been

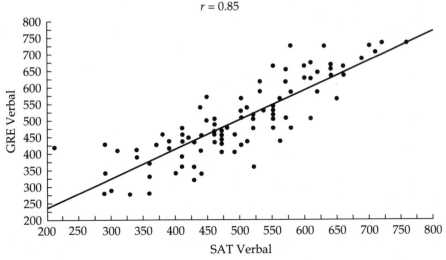

FIGURE A.3

drawn through the dots called the *regression line*. What the regression line represents is the $\hat{Y}$ corresponding to *every possible value of X*. Let's say we're trying to estimate Mary's GRE from her SAT. The procedures for using this line are as follows:

1. Find the point on the X axis corresponding to Mary's SAT score;
2. Draw a vertical line up from that point until it meets the regression line;
3. At the point where the vertical line touches the regression line, draw a horizontal line over to the Y axis (GRE score).
4. The point where the horizontal line crosses the Y axis is Mary's $\hat{Y}$ (her estimated GRE based on her SAT).

The graphic procedure for estimating Y just described gives exactly the same result that you would get using the algebraic formula, $\hat{Y} = a + bX$ to calculate Mary's estimated Y. In other words, the b and a coefficients in the formula serve the same purpose as the regression line in the bivariate frequency distribution. These two coefficients, in fact, determine the position of the line on the chart (see below). If you were to calculate all the possible values of $\hat{Y}$ (i.e., corresponding to all the possible values of X), and plot the points and connect them together, you would reproduce the regression line as shown in figure A.4.

Note from figure A.3 that Mary's actual GRE score (represented by the vertical height of her particular dot) might not match her $\hat{Y}$ or *estimated* GRE (as represented by the height of the regression line at the point on the X axis corresponding to her SAT score). Unless Mary's dot happens to fall right on the regression line, her $\hat{Y}$ and Y will not match. In other words, her residual $(Y - \hat{Y})$ may not be zero. We have shown

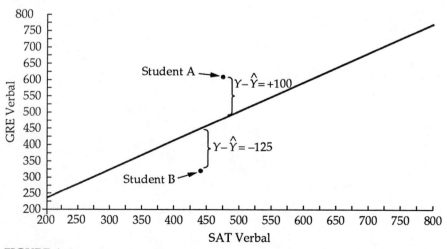

FIGURE A.4

two residuals in figure A.4: Student A, whose actual GRE falls above the line, has a positive residual of +100 points; student B, whose GRE falls below the line, has a negative residual of −125 points. In other words, student A's GRE score is better than we would have expected from her SAT, and student B's is worse than expected. An important thing about the regression line is that it is located so that the sum of all the squared residuals $[\sum(Y - \hat{Y})^2]$ is set to a *minimum*. (This is the so-called principle of least squares.) For any given bivariate frequency distribution, there is one and only one line that satisfies this principle.

The *a* coefficient or "intercept" is the point at which the regression line intersects the Y axis. The regression coefficient *b* is also called the slope of the regression line. By "slope" we mean the steepness or flatness of the line. Strong correlations make steep slopes, whereas weak correlations make flat slopes. When the correlation is zero, the line is completely flat, running exactly parallel to the X axis. When this happens, the regression line intersects the Y axis at the mean of $Y(\overline{Y})$ (see figure A.5).

Note that when this happens, $\hat{Y}$ (your estimate of Y based on X) is always $\overline{Y}$(the mean of Y), regardless of X. Algebraically, it works out like this:

$$\hat{Y} = a + bX, \text{ and since } b \text{ is zero,}$$

$$\hat{Y} = a + (0.0) \times X$$

or

$$\hat{Y} = a$$

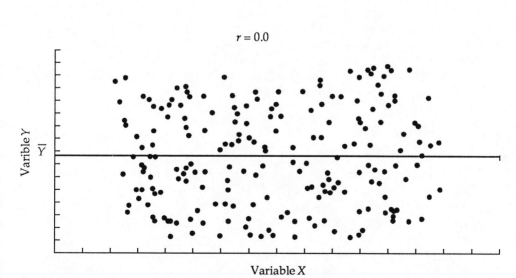

$r = 0.0$

Variable Y

$\overline{Y}$

Variable X

FIGURE A.5

Since a is the point where the regression line intersects the Y axis,

$$a = \hat{Y}, \text{ and } \hat{Y} = \overline{Y}.$$

In practical terms, then, when X has no correlation with Y, it is of no help in estimating Y, so the best (safest thing) you can do is to estimate $\hat{Y}$ to be at the mean of Y, or $\overline{Y}$. Since $\overline{Y}$ is a constant, for each person your best estimate of $\hat{Y}$ is always $\overline{Y}$.

On the other hand, when there is *some* correlation between X and Y, then b will not be zero, and the regression line will have *some* slope. The larger the correlation, the steeper the slope.

What, precisely, do we mean by b or by "slope"? Perhaps the best way to understand this is to think in terms of *changes* in X. If you start with any given value of X, it will have a corresponding $\hat{Y}$:

$$\hat{Y} = a + bX$$

Now if you *increase* X by *one point*, b tells you how much $\hat{Y}$ (your estimate of Y) will change. In other words, b shows how much $\hat{Y}$ changes for every *unit increase in* X. Put another way, we could say that b indicates the rate of change in $\hat{Y}$ per unit increase in X.

You can get a pretty good idea of how strongly X and Y are correlated just by "eyeballing" the bivariate frequency distribution. The way to do this is to see how far the dots (people) are from the regression line. The residual $(Y - \hat{Y})$ for any person is indicated by the vertical distance between that person's dot and the regression line. The closer the dots are to the regression line, the *smaller* the residuals, and the *larger* the correlation. If the correlation is perfect ($+1.0$ or -1.0), then residuals will all be zero $(Y - \hat{Y} = 0$, or $\hat{Y} = Y)$, and all the dots will fall on the regression line. When the correlation is large (but not perfect), the dots will be close to the line, forming an ellipse that slopes either up (figure A.3) or down (a negative correlation). When the correlation is zero or very weak, the dots will tend to form more of a circle (figure A.5) or an ellipse that does not slope.

Multiple Regression

In chapter 2 we noted that the outcome or dependent variable (Y) is usually affected by more than one input variable. Thus, if we really want to control inputs as thoroughly as possible, we need to be able to control more than one input variable simultaneously. The statistical technique for accomplishing this is *multiple* regression. (We call regression with just one X variable, i.e., $\hat{Y} = a + bX$, "simple" regression.)

The form of a multiple regression equation is very similar to the equation for simple regression, except we allow for two or more X

(input) variables rather than one. Thus, if we have two independent or input variables, our formula would be:

$$\hat{Y} = a + b_1 X_1 + b_2 X_2$$

Each X variable thus has its own b (regression coefficient). Notice that we have numbered the X variables and their corresponding b's in order to keep track of them. When we have more than two X variables we just write a separate $+bX$ term for each additional X variable. To save space, the general form of such an equation can be written as follows:

$$\hat{Y} = a + b_1 X_1 + b_2 X_2 + b_3 X_3 \ldots + b_n X_n$$

The ellipsis (...) stands for any omitted terms, and the $b_N X_N$ term stands for the last ("Nth") X variable.

Going back to our 200 students with SAT and GRE scores, let's say we wanted to use multiple regression to control two input variables: SAT and sex. We would first assign each student a "score" for sex. Since the variable of sex can only have two values, we could arbitrarily assign the men a score of 1 and the women a score of 2. (Such variables—those that can assume only two possible values—are called *dummy* variables; many researchers use 0 and 1 instead of 1 and 2, but such choices are arbitrary and really have no effect on the results.) Each student now has three scores: GRE, SAT, and sex. The procedures for estimating GRE from *both* SAT and sex involve first computing the sample means and standard deviations for all the variables, and then computing the simple correlations among all three variables (GRE-SAT, GRE-sex, and SAT-sex). We then set up a series of simultaneous equations in order to solve for our constants: a, b_1, and b_2. Since the mathematics of multiple regression are much more complicated than those of simple regression, they will not be shown here. Interested readers should consult Cohen and Cohen (1975), Pedhazur (1982), or the various Sage monographs (Achen, 1982; Berry and Feldman, 1985; Lewis-Beck, 1987; and Schroeder et al., 1988). Any modern computerized statistical package will produce these coefficients quite easily, even with large numbers of X variables. The important point to remember is that these algebraic operations will produce what you need to estimate the student's GRE: the constant a (the intercept), a regression coefficient for the student's SAT score (b_1), and a regression coefficient for the student's sex score (b_2). The formula will thus be:

$$\hat{Y} = a + b_1 X_1 + b_2 X_2$$

To get an estimate of Mary's GRE, you multiply her SAT score (X_1) by b_1, multiply her sex score (X_2) by b_2, add these two products together, and add that sum to a. The $\hat{Y}$ based on multiple regression has exactly the same properties as $\hat{Y}$ based on simple regression:

1. The mean of $\hat{Y}$ is equal to the mean of $Y(\overline{Y})$.
2. $\hat{Y}$ can be subtracted from Y to obtain a residual $(Y - \hat{Y})$.

The most important quality of such a residual is that it is uncorrelated with *both* X_1 and X_2. In other words, a residual outcome measure is uncorrelated with (independent of) *all* of the input variables that have been used in the multiple regression. In theory, one can use multiple regression to control as many input variables as one desires. The only practical limits are the capacity of the computer program used and the number of subjects available (in multiple regression one ordinarily should not use more variables than there are subjects; ideally one would want to have considerably more subjects than variables—perhaps four or five times as many).

In summary, if we were to apply any computerized multiple regression program to the raw GRE, SAT, and sex scores of our 200 students, the program would give us back the three coefficients we need: a, b_1, and b_2. We could then calculate an expected GRE $(\hat{Y})$ for each student, and then calculate a *residual* GRE $(Y - \hat{Y})$ for each student. These 200 residual GRE scores would have zero correlations with *both* the original SAT scores and the original sex scores.

Multiple Correlation

Like multiple regression, multiple correlation involves much more complicated algebra than simple regression and simple correlation. However, there is a very simple and direct way to calculate the multiple correlation between a dependent variable and several independent variables: it is the simple correlation between Y and $\hat{Y}$. In other words, no matter how many input variables you want to control, once you have determined the constant (a) and the regression coefficients (b's) for each input variable, all you have to do is to compute $\hat{Y}$ for each subject, and then compute the simple correlation between Y and $\hat{Y}$. The resulting multiple correlation (designated by the capital R rather than r) can be interpreted in exactly the same fashion as any simple correlation.

Since simple regression requires a three-dimensional chart (X by Y by frequency), it is not practical to show multiple regression graphically (it would require four or more dimensions). However, it is possible to show multiple regression in a bivariate distribution by plotting Y against $\hat{Y}$. In this connection, it is useful to keep in mind that $\hat{Y}$ is really *an expression of input*. That is, it is a way of expressing the student's input characteristics in the form of an *expected outcome*. Going back to our 200 students, $\hat{Y}$ provides us with a way of answering the question: Given this student's freshman SAT and *sex*, what score would we expect her to get on the GRE? Or, in more general I-E-O terms, given these input characteristics, how would we expect the student to perform on the outcome measure?

Once we have computed $\hat{Y}$, we are then in a position to compute the residual $(Y - \hat{Y})$, which provides an answer to the following questions: How well did the student's actual performance and her expected performance agree? Did she perform about as expected from her input characteristics? Did she perform better than expected, worse than expected? *How much* better or worse?

It might be easier to understand the function of the weights (*b*'s used in multiple regression) by taking an analogy from the art of cooking. Combining several input variables (*X*'s) in a multiple regression equation is much like combining different ingredients in a recipe. In the case of regression, the object is to get the best possible estimate ($\hat{Y}$) of the outcome variable; in the case of cooking, the different ingredients are combined to create the best-tasting dish. In cooking we must take care not only to use the right ingredients but also to use the correct *amounts* of each ingredient: a half-teaspoon of baking powder, a cup of milk, and so on. These measures or amounts of each ingredient used in cooking are very much like the weights (*b*'s) that we apply to each input variable in multiple regression: we weight each variable in such a way as to get the best possible estimate of the outcome variable. This end product—the estimate—is, of course, $\hat{Y}$. And just as we don't use ingredients that will not enhance our dish, so we give a zero weight to input variables that do not aid prediction. Giving a zero weight to a variable in regression produces the same result as excluding the variable altogether.

ASSESSING ENVIRONMENTAL EFFECTS

We are now ready to return to our practical problem: the effects of practice in reading on GRE Verbal scores. Now, there are basically two ways that we can approach this problem: (1) by analyzing residual GRE scores at different levels of the environmental variable, and (2) by adding the environmental variable to the regression equation. Let us consider each of these approaches separately.

Comparison of Residuals in Different Environments

The residual GRE score, it will be recalled, represents that part of the student's GRE performance that could not be accounted for (or predicted by) the student's SAT score and sex. In other words, it represents the extent to which the student's GRE performance exceeded or failed to reach the level that would be expected from SAT and sex. The practical question we need to ask is whether any of these deviations from expectation can be explained by how much practice in reading the students had.

If practice in reading has a positive effect on GRE performance, then we would expect to find more positive residuals among students who had a lot of practice in reading and more negative residuals among students with little practice in reading. In other words, we would expect to find a positive correlation between practice in reading and residual GRE Verbal performance.

The simplest way to test this expectation is first to divide the students into two groups: those who were above average in practice in reading and those who were below average. We could then compute the mean residual GRE score separately for the students who were above average and below average in reading practice. If these mean residuals turned out to be significantly different, we would then have a basis for concluding that practice in reading affects GRE Verbal performance.

There are many variations on the simple scheme just described. For example, it might be useful to compare only the residuals of persons at the extremes, say, those in the top 10 percent and bottom 10 percent on practice in reading. Or, we might want to divide our students into four or five different levels of practice in reading, in order to determine whether there is an equivalent benefit at each higher level of reading practice. Perhaps the benefit does not show up until the top two or three intervals, or perhaps there is a point of diminishing returns beyond which additional reading does not improve GRE performance. Such questions could be answered by determining whether the size of the increase in mean residuals is the same from one practice in reading interval to the next. Mean residuals could be plotted against the practice in reading intervals. If the plotted points (one for each mean residual) formed a straight line, we would be justified in concluding that there is an equivalent benefit at each successive higher level of reading practice. Another approach would be simply to plot the individual student's residuals against their individual practice in reading scores. If the points tended to form an ellipse from the lower-left to the upper-right section of the plot (like that in figure A.2), we would have visual evidence suggesting that the more reading practice the student has, the higher will be the student's subsequent residual performance on the verbal scale of the GRE.

An interesting application of residual analysis has been suggested by Drew (1983). This method is useful when some environmental *change* has been introduced (e.g., a new program, policy, teaching technique, etc.), the effects of which might be expected to emerge over time. Residual outcome measures are computed at several different time points, and the mean residual scores are plotted over time to determine whether they change in the expected direction.

ADDING ENVIRONMENTAL VARIABLES TO THE REGRESSION

The second procedure for assessing environmental effects involves adding the environmental variable to the original regression equation formed by the input variables. In our hypothetical example, this would amount to determining whether practice in reading *adds* anything to the prediction of GRE performance over and above what has been contributed by SAT and sex. In other words, what we would do in this instance would be to move from a two-variable regression involving two input variables (SAT and sex) to a multiple regression involving the two input and one or more environmental variables. The test of "the environmental effect" thus involves determining whether practice in reading adds significantly to the prediction of GRE performance over and above what can be predicted by SAT and sex. The procedure for exploring such a possibility is traditionally called stepwise regression. Stepwise regression is really a form of multiple regression in which the independent variables (input or environmental) are added to the regression equation one at a time. Thus, the first step really involves simple regression (one independent variable). At the second step a second independent variable is added to the regression, forming an entirely new multiple regression equation. If there are more than two X variables, we keep adding additional X variables until none of the remaining ones is capable of adding significantly to the prediction of the dependent variable. Each step in a stepwise regression, in other words, involves computing an entirely new regression equation in which a new independent variable is added to the variable(s) used in the equation from the previous step. Of course, in our hypothetical example, there are only three independent variables, so there would be a maximum of only three steps in the stepwise regression.

What is actually happening at each step in a stepwise regression? Let us try to answer this question by once again using our hypothetical example. The first step in such a regression, as already indicated, involves a single independent or input variable: SAT Verbal score. Once this step has been completed, we compute a residual GRE score (now independent of SAT) and determine whether this residual score is significantly correlated with the next input variable, sex. If sex turns out not to be related to residual GRE, it should not be added to the regression. Assuming that there were no additional input variables to consider, we would then proceed to determine whether residual GRE was related to practice in reading. If the correlation is nonsignificant, then we conclude that practice in reading had no effect on GRE performance, and we do not proceed to the second step of the regression. On the other hand, if the correlation between residual GRE performance and practice in reading proves to be statistically significant, we then proceed to step two where *both* SAT and practice in reading are used as independent variables in a *multiple* regression equation. If there were additional environmental variables that we wished to consider for possible effects on GRE performance, we could continue this stepwise procedure—adding variables one at a time to the regression equation—until none of the remaining variables could add anything to the prediction of GRE performance. Each added variable constitutes another step in the regression.

Let's pause for a moment and review what we have been doing. Recall first that any statistical procedure is designed to *analyze variation*. In our hypothetical example we were primarily interested in understanding variation in GRE scores: Why do students differ from each other in their GRE performance? Is it merely because they differed initially in their SAT scores and sex when they first entered college? Or do they vary in part because of how much reading they do in college? Note that these would be meaningless questions if everyone was of the same sex and started college with the same SAT score and if everyone did the same amount of reading in college, since SAT, sex, and practice in reading would be constants (i.e., each student would get the same SAT and sex scores and the same practice in reading score). A constant, in other words, cannot correlate with GRE scores or with anything else. In short, as long as people *vary* in their SATs and sex and in the amount of reading they do in college, there is the possibility that we can explain or account for differences in their GRE scores on the basis of these other three variables. The multiple correlation coefficient (R) tells us *how much* of the variation among the students' GRE scores can be accounted for by SAT, sex, and practice in reading, and the three individual standardized regression coefficients (B's or betas) tell us how much GRE variation can be explained or accounted for by each of the other three variables.

Partial and Part Correlations

The correlation between practice in reading and the residual GRE score (independent of SAT) is typically called a *semipartial* or *part* correlation. Such a correlation is obtained by computing a simple correlation between a residual variable (GRE) and a nonresidual variable (practice in reading). Most modern computerized regression programs, however, do not utilize part correlations but instead rely on partial correlations.

Partial correlations require a bit of explaining. What they are, in effect, are simple correlations between *two* residual variables. For example, the partial correlation between practice in reading and GRE Verbal (controlling for SAT) would be the simple correlation between residual GRE and *residual practice in reading*. The residual score on practice in reading is computed in precisely the same manner as the residual score on GRE Verbal, except that practice in reading is used as the dependent variable instead of the GRE Verbal. SAT Verbal is used as the independent variable in both situations. In other words, to compute a residual score on practice in reading, we temporarily treat the raw score on practice in reading as a dependent variable and use the SAT Verbal as the independent variable in a simple regression analysis. If we use the subscript *pir* to indicate the practice in reading score, the equation would be as follows:

$$\hat{Y}_{pir} = a + bX_{SAT}$$

$$Residual = Y_{pir} - \hat{Y}_{pir}$$

The correlation between this residual practice in reading score and the residual GRE score would be a *partial* correlation, since both residual scores have been obtained from the same independent variable (SAT). If we used more than one independent (input) variable (e.g., SAT and sex), we would perform two separate multiple regression analyses on GRE and practice in reading, compute residual scores on these two variables, and then correlate the residuals with each other. As long as the same independent variable or set of independent variables is used in computing the two residuals, the resulting correlation is a partial correlation.

How does one interpret a residual score on practice in reading? One way of looking at this question is to consider the I-E-O design. As we have already stated on numerous occasions, the I-E-O design is necessary because inputs are usually correlated with environments as well as with outputs. In our hypothetical example the positive correlation between SAT Verbal and practice in reading suggests that people differ in the amount of reading they do in college in part because they enter college with differential *inclinations* to read a lot. The SAT, then, can be viewed as a rough indicator of people's predisposition to read a lot in college. By computing a residual score on practice in reading (that is, by controlling for the effects of SAT on practice in reading), we are able to obtain a measure of how much reading the student does *independently* of the student's verbal ability at the time of entering college. In other words, part of the variation in how much reading the students do in college cannot be attributable to their verbal ability at the time of college entry, but rather to environmental factors such as the courses they take, the co-curricular activities they engage in, their friends and associates, and so on. It is this independent part of the students' practice in reading score (that is, the part that cannot be predicted from SAT Verbal) that might have an effect on their eventual GRE performance.

Since it is possible to compute a residual score on practice in reading just as we can do for GRE Verbal, it is also possible to compute a *part* correlation between residual practice in reading and the student's nonresidual (raw) score on GRE Verbal. Thus, for every partial correlation there are two corresponding part correlations. The requirements of the I-E-O design (that is, to control inputs) can be satisfied with either part or partial correlations. That is, as long as the effects of input on *either* environment or outcome are controlled, the resulting part or partial correlation between environment or outcome cannot be attributed to input. Although there are certain interpretive advantages to part correlations (see Astin, 1970a, 1970b), the fact that all of the major computerized regression programs utilize partial correlations requires that we will henceforth deal only with partial correlations in discussing statistical methodology. It might also be noted that partial correlations maximize one's chances of detecting significant environmental effects on outcome variables, since they remove the effects of input variables from *both* environmental and outcome variables.

Let us now return to our discussion of stepwise regression analysis. In our hypothetical example, we would apply a computerized regression routine to the data from our 200 student cases. For each student we would supply four scores: SAT Verbal, sex, GRE Verbal, and practice in reading. We would instruct the computer routine to conduct a stepwise regression in which GRE Verbal was the dependent variable (Y) and SAT Verbal, sex, and practice in reading were the three independent (X) variables. The computer would then take the raw data from the 200 seniors, compute the means and standard deviations for each variable, compute the intercorrelations among the four variables, and then begin the stepwise regression. However, we would instruct the computer routine to begin the first step of the regression routine by looking only at the two input variables (SAT Verbal and sex) and picking the one (in this case, SAT Verbal) with the highest correlation with GRE. Once having done this, the computer would then compute a *partial* correlation between GRE Verbal and sex (holding constant or controlling for SAT Verbal). If this partial correlation turned out not to be significant, sex would not be added to the equation, since it would not improve the prediction of GRE. At this point, the computer would then go on to compute a partial correlation between GRE and practice in reading (still holding constant SAT). If this second partial correlation turned out to be statistically significant, the computer routine would then go on to the second step in the regression where it would compute a *multiple* regression equation using both independent variables (SAT Verbal and practice in reading). The purpose of computing the partial correlation is to determine whether practice in reading adds anything significantly to the prediction of GRE Verbal. If the partial correlation turns out to be nonsignificant statistically, there is no point in proceeding to the second step in the regression because the addition of that environmental variable to the regression equation would not significantly enhance the prediction of GRE Verbal. In practical terms, this would force us to conclude that the amount of reading that students do in college does not have any effect on their eventual GRE performance.

A REAL EXAMPLE

Chapter 6 contains an actual example of a stepwise regression using a sample of UCLA students for whom both SAT and GRE scores are available. That particular example was designed primarily for the non-technical reader. In this appendix we shall present a different example, together with a great deal more technical detail, which is being provided for investigators who plan to do the actual analysis of such data. Those examples use a standard statistical package, SPSS-X (1988), which has the unique advantage of providing a great deal of information about what is happening to each variable in the analysis at each step in the regression. This particular software routine is available for most large-scale mainframe computer systems, and is also increasingly available on many personal computers as well.

The problem to be shown in this illustrative analysis involves one of the more important outcomes of postsecondary education: student retention. Rather than using data from a single institution, we have utilized here data from the Cooperative Institutional Research Program (CIRP). The subjects include 4,078 students who entered college as full-time freshmen in the fall of 1981 and were followed up four years later in 1985. The sample includes students attending some 300 four-year colleges and universities who completed the CIRP freshman questionnaire in 1981 and whose institutions provided SAT and retention data four years later in 1985. Earlier analyses (Astin, 1982) indicate that such students are a representative sample of all freshmen entering such institutions.

The outcome variable for these analyses consisted of a dichotomous or dummy variable: the student completed a degree (score 1) or failed to complete a degree (score 0) within four years after entering college.[5] This represents a rather stringent definition of retention since quite a number of students eventually complete degrees, but not in four years (Astin, 1982). It would, of course, be possible to generate a more liberal definition of retention which would include, say, students who were

---

5. Some methodologists believe that there are certain circumstances under which conventional stepwise regression is not as effective as other statistical techniques. One such condition occurs when we use dichotomous or "dummy" dependent variables such as degree attainment (versus dropping out). Some methodologists recommend instead that either "discriminant analysis" or "logit analysis" be used with dichotomous dependent variables. My preference for regression over these other techniques is based primarily on two lines of evidence: (a) The regression weights obtained in discriminant analysis are exactly proportional to the weights obtained in regression; and (b) logit analysis does not seem to produce any better "fit" between the dependent and independent variables than does regression (Dey and Astin, 1990). About the only circumstance that might justify the use of logit analysis is when the split between 1's and 0's on the dependant variable is very extreme (say, greater than 90 or less than 10%).

still enrolled in pursuit of the degree as persisters rather than dropouts. Other analyses done at the Higher Education Research Institute, however, suggest that students who take longer than four years to complete the degree may more closely resemble the eventual dropouts than the four-year degree completers (Astin, 1975; Dey and Astin, 1989).

Input variables include nine student characteristics that have been shown in previous research to be among the strongest predictors of retention: average grade in high school as reported on the freshman questionnaire (A or A+ = 8, A− = 7, B+ = 6, B = 5, B− = 4, C+ = 3, C = 2, and less than C = 1), the student's composite score (verbal plus mathematical) on the Scholastic Aptitude Test (SAT) (ACT composite scores were converted to SAT equivalents following Astin, Christian, and Henson, 1978), sex (female = 2, male = 1), and seven dummy variables measuring different racial-ethnic group membership: white, black, Chicano, Puerto Rican, Asian, American Indian, and other (each scored as a separate dummy variable).

Environmental variables included four dummy variable measures of the type of institution the student entered as a freshman: public university, public four-year college, private university, private four-year college. Although it would make no sense to use such environmental variables in a single-institution study (they would all be constants), this type of analysis could be repeated at a single institution if these four between-college measures were replaced by measures of *within*-institutional variation in environmental experiences such as place of residence, major field of study, and extracurricular participation (see chapter 5). In other words, the kinds of environmental effects analyses performed in this example could be performed just as readily with retention data from a single institution, although the actual measures of environmental variation would obviously have to be different since only one institution would be involved.

In setting up this particular regression, the retention outcome measure was designated as the dependent variable, and the nine input and four environmental measures as independent variables. These independent variables were separated into two "blocks": input (block 1) and environment (block 2). Under these conditions, SPSS-X will enter the variables from the first block into the regression one at a time until no additional variable in that block is capable of adding significantly to the prediction of retention (in statistical jargon, we would say "until no additional variable is capable of producing a significant reduction in the residual sum of squares"). The user can specify different criteria for deciding whether variables within a block should be entered. In this particular example we established a confidence level of .05 ($F > 3.85$) for entering variables within a block. Once all of the predictive power of the variables in the first block has been exhausted, the program then moves to consider the variables in the second (environmental) block. These variables are in turn entered in a stepwise fashion until all of their predictive power is exhausted, at which point the program terminates.

Before moving to the actual results of this example, let us reiterate the logic behind this kind of analysis. The basic purpose of this illustrative study concerns the possible effects of environments on the outcome: to determine whether different types of institutions have differential effects on the student's chances of completing a bachelor's degree within four years after entering college. However, a large body of research on college student retention has shown that the student's chances of completing college are significantly affected by factors such as academic ability, admissions test scores, sex, and ethnicity (Astin, 1975). At the same time, it is known that different types of institutions attract student bodies that differ in grades and test scores, in the proportions of men and women, and in the proportions of students from different ethnic groups. In other words, we expect our nine input variables to correlate with both the outcome measure and the four environmental measures. Under these conditions, the retention rates of diferent types of institutions would be expected to differ simply as a result of the different types of students that they enroll. As a consequence, any observed correlation between institutional-type characteristics and student retention (degree completion) may well come about as a result of student input characteristics. If we wish to obtain a less biased estimate of the effects of institutional type on student retention, it is necessary first to control for these differential student inputs. The first stage (block of variables) in the regression is thus included to control for student input characteristics while the second block will tell us if college-type characteristics contribute anything to the prediction of student retention beyond what can be predicted from student input characterisctics.

Interpreting Regression Results

The results of this stepwise regression are shown in table A.1. The first column in the table shows the step number in the regression. In this instance, the regression included eight steps: the first six steps involved input variables and the last two, environmental variables. The column head "Variable Entering" identifies the variable that entered at each step. The column under R shows the multiple correlation coefficient at each step in the regression. In effect, R shows the simple correlation between the outcome variable (Y) and the estimate of that outcome ($\hat{Y}$) derived from the regression equation at that step in the analysis. The next column, r, shows the simple correlation between the entering variable and the outcome measure (degree completion). The last eight columns show the beta coefficients (standardized regression coefficients) for the variables at each step in the analysis. Since the use of these last columns will probably be unfamiliar even to readers who are

TABLE A.1 Predicting Degree Completion within Four Years after College Entry (N = 4,078 Freshman Entering in 1981)

STEP	VARIABLE	R	SIMPLE r	BETA[a] AFTER STEP							
				1	2	3	4	5	6	7	8
Input	Entering:										
1	High school GPA	30	30	30	20	18	18	18	18	18	17
2	SAT composite	34	29	19	19	21	19	19	19	20	18
3	Sex: female	34	05	02	07	07	07	07	07	06	06
4	Race: black	35	−13	−09	−06	−06	−06	−05	−05	−05	−06
5	Race: American Indian	35	−05	−04	−04	−04	−04	−04	−04	−04	−04
6	Race: Asian	35	04	03	03	03	03	03	03	03	02
Environment	Entering:										
7	Private 4-year	37	10	11	12	12	12	12	12	12	16
8	Private university	38	11	06	04	04	04	04	04	11	11
	Not entering:										
	Race: white	—	12	07	03	03	−02	−02	01	00	02
	Public university	—	−13	−14	−12	−12	−12	−12	−12	−08	−03

Source: UCLA Higher Education Research Institute, Cooperative Institutional Research Program. Follow-up of 1981 freshman conducted in summer 1985. Degree completion data were provided by the institutions.

Note: Decimals before numbers have been omitted.

[a] The coefficient for any variable not yet in the equation shows the beta that variable would receive if it were entered into the equation at the *next* step.

already acquainted with stepwise regression, some discussion of what these coefficients actually mean seems in order.

To begin with, a "beta" coefficient is simply a regression coefficient (b) which has been "standardized" (betas are also called *standardized regression coefficients*). Recall the standard multiple regression formula, $\hat{Y} = a + b_1X_1 + b_2X_2$. Earlier we noted that b can be interpreted like a correlation coefficient, but only if the variances in X and Y are the same. If the variances of X and Y are different, b must compensate for the difference so that the prediction of Y from X yields the correct variance in Y. Thus, if the variance in X_1 is larger than the variance in Y, b_1 will be proportionately reduced in size. Similarly, if the variance in X_2 is smaller than the variance in Y, b_2 will be increased in size. Once the variances are equated, b is the same as beta. To convert b to its equivalent beta, we use the following formula:

$$\text{Beta} = b\left(\frac{SD_X}{SD_Y}\right)$$

Unlike the b coefficients, which cannot be directly compared if the variances in the different X's are different, different betas can be compared to assess the relative predictive power of each X variable.

A unique feature of the SPSS-X regression routine is that after each step it provides, for each independent variable that has not yet been entered in the regression equation, something called "beta in." In effect, what the computer is doing here is looking one step ahead. For each variable that has not yet entered the regression, it determines what that variable's beta would be if the variable were to be entered into the regression at the next step. For example, the "beta in" for SAT composite after the first step in the analysis is .19. Since the variable at the first step was high school GPA, this "beta in" of .19 represents the beta that the SAT composite score would receive if a two-variable equation consisting of high school GPA and SAT composite were to be formed. Note that the beta for SAT composite after step 2 is indeed .19, since this variable was added to the equation at step 2. After each step, SPSS-X also provides partial correlations for variables not yet entered into the equation. These are partial correlations between each independent variable and the outcome (dependent) variable, holding constant the effects of variables already in the equation at that step. It might be preferable to show the partial correlations rather than the "beta in" for each variable not in the equation. However, we have shown the "beta ins" in order to have comparable coefficients across each row of the table (SPSS-X does not provide partial correlations for variables already in the equation).

The reader will note that the betas for all variables tend to get smaller at each successive stage in the stepwise regression analysis. The reason for this is that independent variables tend to be correlated with each other (a condition called *multicolinearity*). As more variables are added to the equation, they must share increasing amounts of predictive power with each other. Since the predictive power of the independent variables gets spread across larger numbers of variables, the predictive power associated with any individual variable gets smaller. There are, however, important situations in which a coefficient will actually get larger rather than smaller. This phenomenon, known as a "suppressor effect," will be discussed shortly.

First, let us consider the findings in table A.1 that bear directly on the primary purpose of the analysis: to assess the possible effects of college type on student retention. Note that two measures of college type *did* enter the regression equation in the second stage, even after student input characteristics were controlled. This result would suggest that the type of college attended does indeed affect the student's chances of completing a degree within four years. Such a conclusion must be tempered, of course, with a recognition that there may be some important student input characteristics that we have not controlled in this particular analysis. Indeed, a more definitive test of the effects of college type would involve controlling for more student input characteristics, such as initial degree aspirations and socioeconomic status. We have omitted such variables from this particular analysis, however, to keep the illustration relatively simple.

Let us now consider what we can learn from the beta coefficients shown in table A.1, beginning with the first step in the regression, where high school GPA enters. High school GPA was entered as the first variable because, of all the input variables in block one, it had the largest simple correlation (.30) with the dependent or outcome variable (degree completion). The beta for high school GPA after step 1 is also .30 because the simple correlation between two variables is the same as the standardized regression coefficient that would be obtained if one were to form a regression equation to predict one variable from the other. However, the beta for high school GPA drops substantially (from .30 to .20) when SAT enters at the second step. This tells us that there is a positive correlation between these two input variables, and they must therefore share some of the predictive power in the equation for predicting degree completion. Note for SAT Composite that there is a corresponding drop between its simple correlation and its beta after step 1 (from .29 to .19) when high school GPA enters the regression equation.

The beta for high school GPA also drops slightly (.20 to .18) when sex: female enters the regression at step 3. This tells us that there is a positive correlation between being female and high school grades (women get higher grades than men do), and that these two variables must therefore share some of their respective predictive power when they are both in the regression equation. (The same positive correlation between being female and high school grades is reflected in the drop—from .05 to .02—between the simple correlation and the beta after step 1 for sex: female.)

After step 3, the betas for high school GPA change very little, suggesting that the input and environmental variables that enter the regression between steps 4 and 8 do not share much in common with high school GPA. The only possible exception here would be at step 8, where the beta for high school GPA drops very slightly, from .18 to .17, when private universities enter the regression. The drop indicates that GPA and private universities are positively correlated (students enrolling at private universities tend to have higher GPAs than students enrolling at other types of institutions).

Suppressor Effects

Let us now consider another input variable, sex: female, in terms of how its beta coefficients change at each step in the analysis. As already indicated, the positive correlation between being female and high school grades is reflected in the drop (from .05 to .02) between its simple correlation and its beta after step 1. However, an interesting thing happens when SAT composite enters at step 2: the coefficient for sex: female *increases* from .02 to .07. This is an excellent example of a *suppressor* effect. The reason the coefficient for sex: female gets larger between steps 1 and 2 is that being female is negatively associated with SAT composite (that is, women tend to get lower SAT scores than men do). Thus, if two independent variables are positively associated with the dependent variable but negatively associated with each other, controlling for one of the variables will actually *increase* the correlation between the other independent variable and the dependent variable. I use the term "suppressor" to indicate that one variable is "suppressing" the observed relationship between two other variables. When that "suppressor" variable is controlled, the relationship between the other two gets stronger. In the current example, SAT composite is the suppressor variable because it is "suppressing" the relationship between sex: female and degree completion. Suppressor variables can be identified only after the fact: we know that one variable is suppressing the relationship between two other variables only when we control it and see the relationship between the other two get stronger . The suppressor effect is always symmetrical in the sense that controlling *either* independent variable will strengthen the correlation between the other and the dependent variable. Note that when sex: female enters the regression at step 3, the beta for SAT composite also increases, from .19 to .21. Which one of the two independent variables we choose to label as the "suppressor" variable depends upon the order in which we control them.

Basically, there are two different situations in which we can observe suppressor effects: (1) when the two independent variables have the *same* relationship (both positive or both negative) with the dependent variable and a negative relationship with each other; and (2) when the two independent variables have opposite relationships (one positive and the other negative) with the dependent variable and a *positive* relationship with each other.

We can learn a great deal about any one of the independent variables simply by following the history of its betas throughout the stepwise regression. Take race: black as an example. The simple correlation of −.13 between being black and degree completion tells us that blacks, in comparison to nonblacks, are less likely than other students to complete a bachelor's degree within four years after entering college. However, since the final beta (−.06) is smaller than −.13, we can learn something about *why* black students have lower retention rates by identifying those steps in the regression where the beta coefficient for race: black drops substantially. There are two steps in which substantial drops in the coefficient for race: black occur. The first is at step 1 when high school GPA enters (the coefficient drops from −.13 to −.09), and the second is at step 2 when SAT composite enters (the coefficient drops from −.09 to −.06). After step 2, the coefficient for race: black changes very little. This analysis tells us that black students have lower retention rates than nonblacks primarily because they have lower high school GPAs and lower admission test scores. If we wanted to express these findings in educational terms, we could say that the main reason black students drop out more often than other students is their poorer academic preparation at the secondary school level.

The coefficients for the environmental variable, private university, also show an interesting pattern. While the simple correlation between private university and degree completion is .11, the coefficient shrinks rapidly to only .04 after high school GPA and SAT composite are controlled. This tells us that private universities have higher retention rates in part because they attract relatively well-prepared students. However, note that the coefficient for private university jumps from a borderline .04 back to .11 at step 7, when private four-year college enters the regression equation. This is, of course, another example of a suppressor effect. The explanation for this effect is as follows: a dummy variable such as private university is scored as private university = 1, all others = 0. Since "all others" includes the private four-year colleges, which have a positive effect on degree completion, it tends to mask the positive effect of private universities on degree completion. Once the effect of the private four-year institution is controlled (step 7), the positive effect of private universities becomes stronger.

Another use of table A.1 is to help us understand why certain variables do *not* enter the regression equation at all. For example, race: white had a significant simple correlation with degree completion, but did not enter the regression equation. The betas for this variable show clearly that the reason it did not enter is that its coefficient was reduced to nonsignificance after the entry of the first two input variables (high school GPA and SAT composite). To put it more simply, white students are more likely to complete degrees than nonwhite students because they have better academic preparation at the time they enter college. Once their level of academic preparation is controlled, their retention rates do not differ significantly from those of nonwhites.

Investigators should exercise some care in interpreting the results when sets of mutually exclusive dummy variables are used. For example, the fact that two environmental variables, public university and public four-year college, did not enter the regression equation should *not* be taken to mean that attending such institutions does not affect one's chances of completing a degree. The simple reason they did not enter the regression is that their opposites—private four-year college and private university—entered first. The best way to understand how environmental variables operate is to examine the results of the regression equation after all input variables have been controlled but before any environmental variables enter. In this example, such an examination should occur after step 6. Note that the coefficients for *all* college-type variables are statistically significant after step 6: the coefficients for the two private dummy variables are positive and those for the two public dummy variables are negative. In fact, the coefficients for private four-year colleges and public four-year colleges are not significantly different but are in fact equal to the second significant digit (+.12 and −.12 respectively). Since the coefficient for private four-year colleges was slightly larger in the third digit than that for public four-year colleges, it entered the regression equation first. Given such trivial differences in coefficients, the proper conclusion is that attending a private institution has a positive effect on one's chances of completing a bachelor's degree in four years, and that attending a public institution has an equivalent negative effect.

Several other fascinating examples of suppressor effects are contained in the regression analysis reported in chapter 6, where GRE scores were predicted from SAT scores, gender, and the student's major (science versus nonscience). Table A.2 summarizes the stepwise regression results. Perhaps the most impressive effect occurs with the dummy variable, female (versus male). The simple correlation of this variable with GRE Verbal is .06, which is statistically nonsignificant in a sample of this size ($N = 97$). Since the beta at step one, after the SAT Verbal (the pretest) is controlled, remains nonsignificant at .07, we might well be inclined to conclude that the student's gender has no bearing on how well he or she does on the GRE Verbal test. However, after the SAT Math score enters at step 2, the beta for female jumps to a highly significant .18, suggesting that a woman is likely to do better on the GRE Verbal than is a man with comparable SAT Verbal and Math scores. The

TABLE A.2 **Prediction of GRE Verbal Scores Using SAT Scores, Gender, and Undergraduate Major** ($N = 97$)

Step	Multiple R	Freshman Predictor Entering	Simple r	Beta After Step			
				1	2	3	4
1	.850	SAT Verbal	.85	.85	.82	.80	.76
2	.857	SAT Math	.30	.11	.11	.21	.33
3	.870	Female (vs. male)	.06	.07	.18	.18	.17
4	.883	Science (vs. nonscience) major	−.11	−.06	−.21	−.19	−.19

Source: Data on UCLA undergraduates who applied to graduate school in 1985. (Also see table 6.5 in chapter 6.)

key phrase here is "with comparable SAT scores," since controlling for SAT Verbal and Math serves to "match" students statistically in terms of their SAT scores.

But why does this effect occur? How can we understand it in practical (rather than purely statistical) terms? The reason we don't see the effect of gender until we control for SAT Math is that men have higher SAT Math scores than women do. Since GRE Verbal performance is dependent not only on SAT Verbal but also to a certain extent on SAT Math scores, the women do slightly worse on the GRE Verbal because of their lower GRE Math scores. This decrement serves to compensate for and therefore mask the positive effect on the GRE Verbal of being a woman. Once the SAT Math score is controlled, this positive effect appears.

Another interesting suppressor effect occurs with the environmental variable, majoring in science. The simple correlation of this variable with GRE Verbal is −.11, which means simply that science majors do worse on this test than nonscience majors do. This correlation shrinks to a nonsignificant −.06 when the SAT Verbal is controlled at step 1. Consequently, if we were to content ourselves with controlling only this pretest measure, we would be forced to conclude that majoring in science has no effect on a student's GRE Verbal performance. But when we control for SAT Math at step 2, the beta for majoring in science increases to a highly significant −.21, and remains significant at −.19 after gender is controlled at step 3. Thus, by controlling the additional variable at step 2 (SAT Math), we find that majoring in science actually does have a significant (negative) effect on GRE Verbal. The explanation for this effect is similar to the explanation given for the suppressor effect involving SAT Math and gender. That science majors have higher SAT Math scores than nonscience majors do increases their GRE Verbal scores in such a way as to mask the negative effect of majoring in science on SAT Verbal performance. Once we control for the effects of SAT Verbal at step 2, the true negative effect of majoring in science appears.

Recalling that any suppressor effect operates in both directions, we also note that the beta for SAT Math also increases with the addition to the regression equation of being female (from .11 to .21) and majoring in science (from .21 to .33). Why does the beta for SAT Math increase from a very modest .11 to a much more substantial .30 when gender and major are controlled? The reason is that persons with high SAT Math scores are more likely to be men and to major in science than are persons with low math scores. The normally positive effect on GRE Verbal of having a high SAT Math score is thus masked to a degree by the fact that the people with high math scores include a disproportionate number of men and science majors. (We could also say that the normally negative effect of having a low SAT Math score on GRE Verbal is weakened by the fact that low scorers on the SAT Math include many women and nonscience majors.) Once we control for gender and major, the stronger positive effect of SAT Math appears.

Estimating the Magnitude of Input and Environmental Effects

One very practical application of regression analysis is in estimating the actual magnitude of effects associated with different independent variables. To see how this is done, let us first recall the standard formula for regression. The simple regression formula for a single independent variable is

$$\hat{Y} = a + bX$$

and the formula for multiple regression involving more than one independent variable is:

$$\hat{Y} = a + b_1X_1 + b_2X_2 \ldots b_nX_n$$

Keep in mind that stepwise regression yields a different regression formula at each step, with each successive formula involving one additional independent variable (X).

Table A.3 shows the actual regression formulas from the first three steps in the regression summarized in table A.2. However, in this case we have used the nonstandardized regression coefficients (b) rather than the standardized beta coefficients (B). These nonstandardized coefficients are always required when we are trying to estimate the actual value of Y for individual students. Table A.3 also provides the a coefficient (intercept) for each of the three regression equations. In

TABLE A.3 Estimating Chances of Degree Completion Using Different Formulae from Stepwise Regression (Data from Table A.1)

STEP	VARIABLE ENTERING AT STEP	b COEFFICIENTS FOR FORMULA		
		(1)	(2)	(3)
1	High school grades (X_1)	.0922	.0620	.0560
2	SAT composite (X_2)		.000474	.000526
3	Sex: female (X_3)			.0652
	Constant (a)	−.0716	−.3608	−.4137
	$\hat{Y}$ for a female student ($X_3 = 1$) with B average ($X_1 = 5$) and SAT Composite of 1,000 ($X_2 = 1,000$).	.389	.423	.458

order to obtain $\hat{Y}$ for any student using these formulas, we need only to replace each X in the formula with the student's actual scores on the corresponding input variable. The last row of data in table A.3 shows the computed $\hat{Y}$ values for a female student with a B average and an SAT composite score of 1000. What do these $\hat{Y}$ values actually mean? Since our dependent variable is a dummy variable with possible scores ranging from 0 (no degree) to 1 (bachelor's degree), the Y values obtained from these equations can best be interpreted as *probabilities* of obtaining a bachelor's degree within four years. Thus, if we use formula 1 (which utilizes only one input variable, high school grades), we obtain a $\hat{Y}$ value of .389, which can be regarded roughly as that student's probability of getting a bachelor's degree within four years. The probability can, of course, be converted to a percentage simply by moving the decimal point two places to the right. Thus, we can say that roughly 38.9 percent of all students with B averages in high school obtain bachelor's degrees within four years of entering college. Similarly, from formula 2 we can conclude that about 42.3 percent of the students who have B averages in high school *and* SAT composite scores of 1000 complete a bachelor's degree within four years. Finally, about 45.8 percent of women students with B averages and SAT composites of 1000 complete a bachelor's degree within four years.

How do these probabilities change when we change the value of the input variables? Let's suppose we have an outstanding female student with an A average in high school and an SAT composite score of 1300. Her probabilities of completing a bachelor's degree in four years using the three different formulas would be .666, .751, and .783, respectively.

By contrast, a male student with only a C average from high school and an SAT composite of 700 would have much lower probabilities: .113, .095, and .067, respectively. Thus, even though the multiple correlations (R^2) based on these input variables are quite low (see table A.1), students with excellent academic preparation from high school enjoy substantially greater probabilities of completing the bachelor's degree than do students with poor academic preparation from high school.

What about estimating the size of the effects of individual input and environmental variables? To illustrate how to do this, we can use the regression formula from the final step (step 8) in the regression shown in table A.1 and display the coefficients as the first column of numbers in table A.4. The first variable (X) shown in table A.4, high school GPA (X_1), has a b coefficient of .0542. The next two values in the same row show the range of possible student scores on high school GPA from the lowest (1) to the highest (8). The next two values show the products of the regression coefficient (b) and X_1 using the lowest and highest possible values of X (that is, of GPA). The final value shows the maximum difference that high school GPA can make, which is simply the arithmetic difference between the preceding two values. Basically, what this last value shows is the maximum possible difference that this particular variable can make in the final value of $\hat{Y}$. Clearly, the last

TABLE A.4 **Estimating the Magnitude of Input and Environmental Effects on Student Retention (Data from Table A.1)**

Variable	Final b	Range of X Low	Range of X High	Range of BX Low	Range of BX High	Maximum Difference[a]
Input:						
High school GPA	.0542	1	8	.0542	.4336	.379
SAT composite	.000453	550[b]	1600	.249	.725	.476
Sex: female	.060	0	1	.000	.060	.060
Race: black	−.109	0	1	.000	−.109	−.109
Race: American-Indian	−.208	0	1	.000	−.208	−.208
Race: Asian	.084	0	1	.000	.084	.084
Environment:						
Private 4-year	.161	0	1	.000	.161	.161
Private university	.160	0	1	.000	.160	.160

Source: Higher Education Research Institute, Cooperative Institutional Research Program.
[a]Shows how much difference each variable can make in the probability of a student's completing a bachelor's degree within four years after entering college.
[b]Lowest score in the sample. Theoretically a student can score as low as 400.

column of figures in table A.4 shows that most of the independent variables—but especially high school GPA and SAT composite scores—can make a substantial difference in a person's chances of completing a bachelor's degree within four years after entering college.

Of particular interest, of course, is the magnitude of possible differences associated with the type of college attended. Here we find almost identical results for attendance at a private four-year college and a private university. In both instances, attendance at a private institution improves the student's chances of completing a bachelor's degree within four years by about 16 percent. The reader will note an interesting fact about the dummy variables shown in table A.4: in each case the maximum difference that the variable can make is identical to the b coefficient. Thus, when both the independent and dependent variables are dummy variables, the final regression coefficient (b) associated with any independent variable can be directly interpreted as indicating how much of an effect that variable has on the individual's chance of being in one or the other category on the dependent variable.[6]

The literature on regression analysis usually advocates the use of the squared multiple correlation coefficient (R^2) as an indicator of the "percent of variance" in the dependent variable accounted for by the independent variables. Researchers are thus encouraged to use R^2 as an indicator of the predictive power of the independent variables in accounting for variance in the dependent variable. This literature further recommends that the importance of any given independent variable should be assessed by determining how much R^2 increases when that variable is added to the multiple regression equation. These interpretive guidelines often lead many researchers to conclude that any variable that makes only a small change in R^2 is not very important.

My two and a half decades of work with stepwise regression convinces me that R^2 or change in R^2 is *not* a good guide to assessing the importance of independent variables. Let's use the current regression example to illustrate the point. First, let's consider the absolute value of R^2. Table A.1 shows that R at the third step in the regression (when high school GPA, SAT composite and sex: female have entered the regression equation) is .34. The corresponding R^2 would thus be (.34 × .34) or .116. Using the "percentage of variance" approach, investigators might be tempted to conclude that these three input variables are not very important predictors of degree completion since they account for less than 12 percent of the variance. However, the analyses shown in Table A.3 suggest quite the contrary. We have already seen that a

6. This generalization will not hold if the equation contains dummy variables that are artificially correlated, e.g., if more than one racial category enters the regression or if one dummy variable represents a subset of a category on another dummy variable—for example, if the equation included a dummy for university (versus nonuniversity) and another for private university (versus all public universities and nonuniversities).

female student with an A average and an SAT composite of 1300 has about 78 chances in 100 of completing a bachelor's degree within four years, in contrast to a male with a C average and an SAT composite of 700, who has less than seven chances in 100 of completing the degree within four years. Clearly, such differences have great practical significance, even though the "percentage of variance accounted for" is very modest. This shows that, even when the multiple correlation is quite modest and the percent of variance accounted for quite low, differences represented by the extremes of the independent variables can be of great practical significance.

What about the "importance" of individual variables as judged from their regression coefficients? Let's take the case of the environmental variable, private university. When this variable entered the regression equation at step 8, the multiple R increased from .367 to only .380. The corresponding increase in R^2 associated with the entry of this environmental variable was thus only .0097, or less than 1 percent. Following the "percentage of variance" approach to interpretation, we might be tempted to conclude that this particular environmental variable is not of any practical importance, since it accounted for less than 1 percent of the variance in the dependent variable. However, we have already seen that this particular environmental variable was associated with an absolute increase of 16 percent in the student's chances of finishing the bachelor's degree. When we consider the large number of students who attend private universities, 16 percent is certainly not trivial, since it translates into literally tens of thousands of additional students receiving bachelor's degrees each year. Even for an individual student, an absolute change of 16 percent in that student's chance of completing a bachelor's degree can hardly be considered trivial. In short, this discussion suggests that the increase in R^2 can provide a misleading estimate of the importance of a given input or environmental variable, and that the regression coefficient provides a much better guide for judging that variable's potency or importance.[7]

At this point another note of caution should be interjected about interpreting the size of beta coefficients. Since there is a considerable degree of correlation among the independent variables (multicollinearity) in most data sets, any individual variable is forced to "share" increasing amounts of predictive power with other correlated variables as the number of variables in the equation increases. Under these conditions,

---

7. Elsewhere (Astin, 1970a) I have argued that the importance of a particular independent variable or class of independent variables (e.g., environmental variables) can be better evaluated through the use of part or semi-partial correlation coefficients than through traditional use of increases in R^2. One problem with R^2 is that it misclassifies suppressor effects as direct effects; part correlations, on the other hand, provide a better estimate of the *total* amount of variance in the dependent variable that is *uniquely* attributable to a particular independent variable or class of variables.

researchers should be cautioned against concluding that a particular variable is not important simply because its final beta is small. Such judgments should instead be tempered by attending to three factors: the variable's simple correlation with the dependent variable, the size of the beta at the point the variable enters the regression, and the other entering variables that cause the biggest drops in that variable's beta. For example, if several independent variables that enter the regression are highly correlated with each other, to conclude that any one of these is not important simply on the basis of its final beta may not be justified. Rather, it is important to look at the effect the variables have on one another as each of them enters the regression equation, and to determine how much the entire group as a whole adds to R^2 when it enters. Perhaps the simplest way to do this is to record the increase in R^2 that occurs when each variable enters and then to sum these amounts across all variables in the set. At the same time, the "maximum difference" in the outcome (see table A.4) attributable to the set could be estimated using the entire set rather than one variable at a time.

Interaction Effects

The meaning of interaction effects has already been discussed in chapter 6. Assessing interaction effects in the context of regression analysis presents a number of methodological problems, primarily because the number of possible interactions that can be investigated is very large. There can be as many simple (i.e., two-variable) interaction effects among a set of independent variables as there are correlations among these variables. If N represents the number of variables, the total number of possible interaction effects is $(N^2 - N) \div 2$. Thus, if we have twenty input and environmental variables in our analysis, there are $(400 - 20) \div 2$ or 180 possible simple interaction effects among these variables that could be investigated.

Many investigators examine only those interaction effects suggested by a particular theory. However, the paucity of comprehensive theory in the field of higher education greatly limits the variety of interaction effects that can be explored on the basis of theory alone.

Another approach is to select a limited number of student input variables on the basis of their intrinsic importance (sex, race, socioeconomic status, or ability, for example) and to determine whether any of these variables interact with environmental variables to affect the outcomes under investigation.

There are several possible methods for assessing interaction effects between environmental and student input variables. Perhaps the simplest approach is to establish various subgroups of students on the basis of input characteristics that might interact with environmental variables (women, men, whites, minorities, and so on) and to perform separate analyses on each subgroup. If, for example, we were to perform analyses for men and women separately, we could search for interaction effects by determining whether particular environmental variables had one effect for one sex and a different effect for the other sex. The main drawback to this approach, of course, is that it can become extremely burdensome, from a computational perspective, since it requires a completely separate analysis for every category on every input variable.

A more efficient approach is to search for interaction effects within a single analysis by generating new variables from *combinations* of the variables that might interact. These new "interaction variables" can be generated simply by taking the product of the input and environmental variables in question. Let's suppose that our outcome measure is student retention (completed a degree versus failed to complete a degree), and we are interested in determining whether there is any interaction between the student's academic ability (input measure) and the course load that the student takes (environmental variable). We want to know (a) whether the effect of ability on retention depends upon what course load the student takes, or (b) whether the effects of course load vary by ability level. To explore these questions, we might simply generate a new interaction variable which would be the product of the student's SAT score and the number of credit hours taken during the first term.

Interaction effects involving categorical or dummy variables can be explored in a somewhat different fashion. For example, in a study in which retention is the outcome measure, we might be interested in a possible interaction between the student's sex and participation in honors programs. Thus, we would want to determine whether the beneficial effect of honors participation on retention is the same for men as it is for women. In this case we would create one or more new dummy variables defined by *combinations* of the potentially interacting variables. For example, we could generate a new dummy variable: male honors program participation (score 1) versus all others (score 0). We could also create another dummy: female honors program participants (score 1) versus all others (score 0). There are also two other possible combinations here (male nonparticipants versus others and female nonparticipants versus others), but in this particular instance they would be redundant because they would be implied by the two participant combinations.

One peculiarity of studying interaction effects is that we cannot be sure we have identified significant interaction effects until we have first controlled for the *main effects* of the variables that make up the interaction term. (The problem here is identical to the one encountered in analysis of variance designs in which the main effects of the independent variables must first be removed before the interaction effects can be studied.) This requirement means that the specially constructed variables representing interactions between input and environmental variables must be withheld from the stepwise analysis until the simple effects of the input and environmental variables have been controlled.

In practical terms, we must form a separate block of interaction variables to be entered into the regression *after* the blocks involving input and environmental variables have been entered. The basic test of the existence of significant interaction effects is thus to determine whether any of the variables in the interaction block contribute to the prediction of the outcome measure over and above what is contributed by the simple effects of input and environmental variables that entered in earlier blocks.

If the stepwise regression shows that there are significant interaction effects, it is not always an easy matter to interpret what these effects *mean*. This is particularly true when interaction terms have been formed by multiplying the two variables. Even though such an interaction term may add significantly to the regression equation, the particular combination of the two variables that accounts for the significant interaction may not be apparent. Thus, if we were to create an interaction term by multiplying student ability and course load, and if that term contributed significantly to the prediction, we would still be unsure *which* particular combination(s) of the two variables accounts for the significant interaction. Is it the best prepared students who especially benefit from a heavy course load, are the less well prepared students handicapped by a heavy load, or what? To answer such questions, it may be necessary to treat the continuous variables like categorical or dummy variables. That is, it might be desirable to perform another analysis in which dummy variables representing combinations of various *levels* on the two continuous variables are generated. The analysis would then be rerun to determine which particular combinations of scores on the input and environmental variables in question account for the interaction effect.

Creating Dummy Variables

A final technical note about the creation of dummy variables for use in regression: Investigators who are unfamiliar with this practice sometimes find it difficult to understand that each subject must receive a score on *each* dummy variable, and that the set of scores for any given subject usually involves only one 1 with the rest being 0. For example, if we wanted to examine the effects of specific combinations of SAT scores and course load, we might divide both variables into three levels: high, medium, and low. We could then generate 3 × 3 or nine possible dummy variables, each representing a different combination of the two variables (high-high, high-low, low-medium, etc.). For each of these new dummy variables the higher score (1) would be assigned to those subjects whose pair of scores fit the combination (e.g., low-low) while the lower score (0) would be given to *all other* subjects. Each subject would then get nine such scores (one for each combination), and eight of the nine scores would be

0. The only score of 1 would be for that dummy variable that corresponded to that person's particular combination of scores on the two variables.

One final cautionary note: If the investigator creates a set of dummy variables representing all possible categories on a qualitative variable (e.g., such as race) or all possible interaction effects based on combinations of two variables, it is essential to insure that all combinations do not actually enter the regression.[8] Stepwise regression will usually prevent this from happening.

CAUSAL MODELING

The I-E-O design represents what some investigators might consider to be a simple "causal model." In causal modeling we are interested a determining the causal chain of events involving various independent variables that might ultimately affect the dependent or outcome variable. The chain of events implied by the I-E-O design is a very simple one: input precedes everything else, input leads the person into certain environmental experiences, these in turn combine with input to produce certain kinds of outcomes. A major conceptual distinction, however, between the I-E-O model and most other causal models is that the I-E-O is specifically designed to enhance our understanding of how *outcomes are affected by environmental variables*. By contrast, in causal modeling the investigator is more often interested in testing a particular theory concerning the causal chain of events among a set of variables. While the I-E-O approach is not by nature a theoretical model, it tends to treat input variables as a kind of necessary evil that have to be controlled in order to minimize bias in our examination of the effects of environments on outcomes. In causal modeling, these same input variables might indeed be the central variables in the theory being tested.

The method of choice for most persons interested in causal modeling is the technique of path analysis, which is a form of regression and partial correlational analysis specifically adapted for causal modeling. I

8. The problem here has to do with the degrees of freedom and the linear dependency that exist among such variables. The maximum degrees of freedom are always equal to the number of categories minus one. If you know a person's score on all but one of the dummy variables in the set, the person's score on the remaining one is not free to vary but is already determined. If all variables in such a set are used as independent variables in the same regression equation, the regression weights cannot be computed and the computer routine will abort the run. Stepwise regression usually avoids this problem by terminating the stepwise procedure before all combinations enter the regression. However, in such a situation the regression routine is sometimes unable to compute the "beta in" for those dummy variables that have not yet entered. One way to avoid such problems altogether is to omit one or more of the dummy variables completely from the regression.

shall present here only a few basic ideas about path analysis; readers interested in more details should consult other sources (e.g., Duncan, 1966; Land, 1969; Wolfel, 1985).

In path analysis one normally has a theory about the variables under investigation. Using the theory as a guide, the investigator organizes the variables in terms of their known or assumed order of occurrence (in principle this is very similar to the I-E-O model, which puts inputs first, environments second, and outputs last). Path analysis allows the investigator to visualize the theory by means of a series of boxes connected by arrows. Each box represents a different variable, and the arrows connecting any box with any other symbolize a direct causal path between the two, with the arrow pointing from the independent to the dependent variable. The investigator carries out a series of multiple regression analyses, one for each box that has arrows pointing at it. The independent variables in each of these analyses include all boxes from which the arrows pointing at the dependent variable box originate. These analyses permit the investigator to compute paths from each independent variable to its corresponding dependent variable. These direct paths are actually the standardized multiple regression coefficients (betas).

One practical difference between conventional stepwise regression and path analysis is that the latter technique permits the investigator to treat any variables falling between the earliest and latest variables in the chain as dependent variables. This can be accomplished in a single path analysis, whereas to do this with conventional regression would require a separate run for each of these dependent variables. On the other hand, most computerized path analytic routines do not provide the step-by-step betas that SPSS-X regression provides.

Path analysis does not require the investigator to examine all *possible* paths between the independent (antecedent) variables and the last (dependent) variable in the causal chain. The investigator specifies the paths dictated by his or her theory and can ignore all others, even though they might, in fact, produce significant beta coefficients. Stepwise regression, on the other hand, computes all direct paths to the dependent variable, and by blocking the independent variables and by following the step-by-step changes in betas, the investigator can, in fact, examine all indirect paths as well.

The particular extensions of the I-E-O model discussed below could very well be worked out using path analysis instead of stepwise regression. However, path analysis becomes unwieldy when large numbers of independent variables (especially input variables) are used since it basically requires the investigator to *model* all of these variables in some fashion. The I-E-O approach, on the other hand, does not necessitate such complicated modeling and instead focuses the investigator's attention on the major evaluative issue: the effects of environmental variables on outcome variables.

Modeling Environmental Variables

Many studies using the I-E-O model have utilized several hundred colleges and universities, with each institution representing a different environmental treatment (Astin & Panos, 1969; Astin, 1977, 1982). In such studies it is possible to conceive of at least two types of environmental variables: *between-institution* variables that are constant for all students in a given institution but which may vary from one institution to the next; and *within-institution* variables that may vary among students at a given institution. As discussed in chapter 5, between-institution variables include the institution's size, selectivity, type, and control, and within-institution variables include such things as the student's place of residence, work status, financial aid, and participation in extracurricular activities. Within-institution environmental variables are sometimes partially confounded with between-institution environmental variables. Many private colleges, for example, require new freshmen to live in campus residence halls. Many public colleges, on the other hand, have no residential facilities. Under these conditions, any observed difference in the comparative effects of private and public colleges might be attributable to the effects of the residential experience rather than to the effect of college type per se. Since the confounding of such variables is usually only partial (many public and private colleges have *both* resident and commuter students), it is possible to assess the effect of one variable while holding the other constant. This problem can be addressed by modeling the within- and between-institution environmental variables in separate blocks. My own preference is to include all the within-institution environmental variables, such as place of residence, in the first environmental block and then to include the between-institution variables in a subsequent block. The rationale for this recommendation is that such things as the student's major and place of residence are the more "proximate" environmental measures (see chapter 5) and therefore more likely to have a direct impact on any outcome measure. To put it more concretely, one would expect the student to be more directly influenced by her place of residence (a dormitory, sorority house, a private apartment on campus, or her parents' home) than by such things as the type or size or selectivity of the institution. By controlling first for these within-institution environmental experiences, we can then determine whether the type of college contributes anything else to the student's outcome performance.

For researchers working within a single institution, there are direct analogies to the modeling of between- and within-institution environmental variables just discussed. In a large university, the student's school (liberal arts, engineering, education) might be regarded as the equivalent of an institution in multi-institutional studies. In smaller colleges, different departments might likewise be regarded as analogous to different institutions. The modeling under these conditions would be similar to that just discussed: *within* variables such as place of residence, financial aid, and co-curricular participation could constitute the first block of environmental variables, and the characteristics of the department or college (institution) could be incorporated into a subsequent block.

In short, it is recommended that the most *proximate* environmental variables be controlled first and the most *distal* ones controlled last. (See chapter 5 for a fuller discussion of the various types of environmental variables that might be incorporated into such an analysis.)

Intermediate Outcomes

In its simplest form, the I-E-O model makes clear temporal distinctions between input, environmental, and outcome variables. That is, the student's input characteristics are assessed prior to any significant exposure of the student to the college environment, and the student is subsequently exposed to a known set of environmental characteristics (place of residence, type of institution, curriculum, etc.) before his or her outcome performance is assessed. In other words, inputs are known to precede exposure to the environment and exposure to the environment is known to precede the assessment of outcome performance. There is another class of environmental variables, however, that cannot be known at the time of initial exposure to the educational program (that is, when the input data are initially collected) but which can, nevertheless, have important effects on the student's development. The list is very long: participation in honors programs, membership in student organizations, interactions with particular professors or counselors or fellow students, exposure to particular courses, and so on. In chapter 5 such experiences were called *self-produced* environmental experiences because the student generally exerts some control over their occurrence. Viewed from a different perspective, such experiences might also be considered as outcomes. If, for example, a student joins a social sorority during her sophomore year, her subsequent experience with the sorority could be regarded as an environmental variable that could influence subsequent outcomes. However, that same event (joining the sorority) could also be viewed as a kind of *intermediate outcome* that occurs somewhere between initial entry to the college and assessment of outcome performance. Indeed, one could set up a complete I-E-O design in which joining a particular student organization is used as an outcome measure rather than an environmental measure. The same goes for any other intermediate outcome that occurs only after the person has been in the environment for some period of time.

But how do we deal with such intermediate outcomes when our ultimate concern is with later outcomes such as degree completion, entry to graduate school, changes in values and aspirations, and so on? My own preference in such situations is to treat these intermediate outcomes as environmental measures, but to model them only in the final blocks of independent variables to be entered into the regression analysis. In other words, we could examine their possible effects, but only after controlling for input and earlier environmental variables.[9]

The use of intermediate outcomes necessarily creates a certain degree of ambiguity in the final results. Let us look at a specific example. Some people who have studied student retention in higher education have used the student's college GPA as a kind of environmental variable. The (often unstated) assumption in such studies is that the student's GPA is causally antecedent to the act of dropping out, therefore justifying its use as an independent variable in studies in which retention is the dependent variable. Such a decision seems reasonable enough, given the fact that the class work that leads to particular grades is done *prior* to the actual act of dropping out or degree completion. On closer examination, however, it would appear that the direction of causation between GPA and retention could in fact work in reverse.

Suppose that a student was unhappy with his undergraduate experience and made a tentative decision to drop out at the end of the current term. This decision could well lead that student to neglect his studies during his last term, thereby lowering his overall GPA. Similarly, a student might drop out before the end of a term, receiving "incomplete" grades in that term's courses, and if that student fails to return, the incomplete grades could lapse into failing grades. In both of these hypothetical cases, the act of dropping out, or at least the decision to do so, is the intermediate outcome and the GPA is, in reality, the dependent variable.

Such interpretive ambiguities are almost impossible to avoid altogether if the investigator elects to include intermediate outcome measures as independent variables. The basic problem is that we are not able to assess input characteristics at the time of initial exposure to the

---

9. Another analytical method that is sometimes recommended over regression, especially in cases where intermediate outcomes are being utilized as independent variables, is called LISREL (Jöreskog and Sorböm, 1988) (A similar technique called EQS has been developed by Bentler, 1989.) While this is not the place to debate such arcane issues, my preference for stepwise regression is, once again, based on several factors. First, the computerized routines available for LISREL do not produce step-by-step changes in beta coefficients. Second, the combining of variables into factors is largely taken out of the hands of the investigator (I personally prefer to do separate factor analyses and to control the manner of scoring the factors directly). Finally, unpublished analyses conducted at the Higher Education Research Institute suggest that results obtained with LISREL may not be appreciably different from, and probably more difficult to interpret than, results obtained with stepwise regression.

intermediate outcome. Take another example: suppose we want to test the theory that fraternity membership strengthens conservative political beliefs. If a student decides to join a social fraternity during his sophomore year (intermediate outcome), the input measures obtained from that student at the beginning of the freshman year may no longer be appropriate, since some of these input measures might have changed during the interim, and these very changes might have affected the student's decision to join a fraternity or sorority.

How would such changes bias the results? After controlling for a pretest measure of political belief, other entering freshman input variables, and other environmental characteristics, we might still find that fraternity membership is positively associated with conservative political beliefs. Such a finding might tempt us to conclude that membership in such organizations fosters the development of conservative values and beliefs. The direction of causation, however, might actually work in reverse, since conservative values might lead students to *join* such organizations in the first place. If students decide to join fraternities during the first few weeks of the freshman year, the initial input assessments of political views obtained at the time of matriculation would probably suffice as an appropriate control for these self-selection biases, since the data would have been collected very close to the time the actual decision to join was made. However, when such decisions occur much later (say, in the sophomore year), that decision also may be affected by *changes* in political views that have occurred since initial freshman entry. Under these conditions, those students whose values have changed in a conservative direction since entering college may be more likely ultimately to join social fraternities than would students whose values changed in a different way. Thus, if two students enter college with identical political beliefs at "input," and one becomes more conservative during the freshman year while the other does not, the one who becomes more conservative may be more likely to join a fraternity. Unless some follow-up input assessment were to be made just prior to the decision to join, there would be no way to know for sure whether the greater (residual) conservatism of the fraternity members reflects changes that occurred prior to joining, changes that occurred after joining, or both.

Although such ambiguities can never be fully resolved, even with the most sophisticated analysis, the blocked stepwise regression procedure discussed in this appendix does provide some clues for resolving these ambiguities. Take the hypothetical example of conservatism and fraternity membership. If conservatism as assessed at the initial freshman input point is found to be strongly associated with a later decision to join a fraternity, then a weak correlation of fraternity membership with residual conservatism (after controlling for freshman conservatism, other input variables, and environmental variables) must be regarded with some skepticism, since it may well be that the residual correlation reflects changes in conservatism that occurred between freshman matriculation and the decision to join. On the other hand, if the effect of fraternity membership turns out to be stronger than the initial correlation of input conservatism with joining, then we have a stronger basis for inferring that membership itself strengthens conservatism.

Decisions about how to interpret results using intermediate outcomes should be based in part upon how the beta coefficients change as variables are added to the equation, and in part on the timing and inherent logic underlying the variables being investigated. If the student joins a fraternity in the sophomore year and we measure that student's posttest conservatism at the end of the senior year, we can at least be sure that exposure to this environment (Greek membership) occurred prior to the assessment of the outcome performance. Results of the analyses are still somewhat ambiguous (did the fraternity members' greater conservatism happen before or after they joined?), but at least we can be sure that the environmental event preceded the assessment of the outcome.

Researchers should be extremely skeptical of any causal analysis that treats intermediate outcomes as environmental variables when there is no reason to suppose that the environmental variable in question preceded the outcome variable in time. What if we decided to use an attitudinal question as our intermediate outcome? Suppose we devised a causal model to explore the possibility that student satisfaction with college is an important factor in student retention. We might ask the student at the time of the follow-up outcome assessment to indicate how satisfied he or she was with the college experience. In our follow-up we have thus assessed simultaneously the student's degree of satisfaction with college and whether that student finished college or dropped out. Our model would treat retention (degree completion versus dropping out) as the outcome variable and satisfaction as an environmental (intermediate outcome) variable to be entered into the regression after input and other environmental variables are controlled. The problem here is that there is simply no basis for assuming that satisfaction, as reported retrospectively by the student, *preceded* the decision to complete college or to drop out. Since satisfaction is being reported after the fact of completion or dropping out, it could well be argued that the direction of causation is reversed, that is, that the decision itself had an impact on satisfaction. Those students who know that they have completed their programs successfully are probably more inclined to be satisfied than are students who realize they were unable to complete the program and had to drop out. Since there is no way of knowing, in such cases, which variable preceded the other in time, any causal interpretations would seem to be hopelessly ambiguous.

In short, the recommended procedure for modeling environmental variables is to include in the first block all within (institution, school, or department) variables that can be known at the time that the input assessment is carried out, followed by *between*-program characteristics that are known at the time of input assessment, followed by intermediate outcomes. The intermediate outcomes can themselves be modeled according to their known or expected temporal sequencing, with the most ambiguous variables, such as student satisfaction with the college, consigned to the last block. On many occasions when I have modeled intermediate outcomes in such a manner, my suspicions about the temporal sequencing of the final block or blocks of environmental variables has prompted me to confine most of my interpretive reporting of results to the results obtained at the regression step immediately prior to the entry of these last blocks of intermediate outcomes. It often happens that entry of some of these intermediate outcomes into the regression radically changes the regression coefficients for the input and environmental variables that entered earlier. Such marked changes should be a red flag to any investigator, since they suggest that the intermediate outcomes may not really be appropriate independent variables for the outcome under investigation.

Modeling Input Variables

Since the I-E-O design does not require any modeling of input variables, the investigator can simply combine all input variables in a single group to be entered in the regression as the first block. For certain theoretical purposes, however, it might be of interest to model the input variables in terms of their known or expected sequence of occurrence. For example, since variables that can be known at the time of birth (sex, age, race, family socioeconomic status) can be assumed to precede any other input variables, they can be incorporated into a separate initial block. A second input block might include variables relating to the student's prior education (e.g., type of high school attended, courses taken, grades received). The final block of input variables might include any attitudinal and value questions that might be subject to change up to the very moment of matriculation to the institution. Generally, the order in which the input variables are entered will not substantially affect the final results of the analysis, although it sometimes happens that a variable that enters with a significant weight in an early input block ends up with a nonsignificant regression weight after input variables in subsequent blocks enter. Such a finding, in path analytic terms, suggests that the effect of the variable in question on the dependent variable is indirect, in the sense that its early relationship with the outcome can be explained entirely by the mediating effects of variables that entered the regression in later blocks.

Summary

Most modern computerized statistical packages (especially SPSS) allow the investigator to model the independent (input and environmental) variables in any number of blocks according to their known or expected temporal sequencing. In setting up such an analysis, it is important to remember that interaction effects can also be examined. A recommended procedure for ordering the different blocks of independent variables is shown below. Many problems may not use all the blocks, but these blocks that are used should be controlled in the order given:

1. Simple (main) effects of student input variables (may be several blocks; see above)
2. Interactions among input variables
3. *Within* environmental variables that can be determined at the time of entry to the environment
4. *Between* environmental variables that can be determined at the time of entry to the environment
5. Interactions among environmental variables (item 3 or item 4 above)
6. Interactions between input (item 1) and environmental (item 3 or item 4) variables
7. Environmental variables that occur subsequent to matriculation to the institution (intermediate outcomes) (may be several blocks; see above)
8. Interactions between intermediate outcomes and any antecedent variables (item 1 to item 7)

SOME FINAL INTERPRETIVE SUGGESTIONS

No matter how elegant the research design or how comprehensive the data base, the investigator can never be absolutely certain that true environmental effects have been identified. As already indicated in chapter 2, the main purpose of using the I-E-O model is not to prove causation but rather to minimize the risks involved in making causal inferences concerning the effects of environmental variables on outcomes. Nevertheless, there are certain situations in which the investigator can have more than the usual confidence that the data are indeed revealing true environmental influences.

Comparing Different Coefficients

One situation that justifies a high degree of confidence in one's causal inferences is that in which the environmental variable is uncorrelated with the input variables. In multi-institutional studies, for example, the size of the institution has been shown to have no relationship, or only a very weak one, with most student input characteristics (Astin, 1965). In other words, students who go to large institutions differ very little at the time of entry from students who go to small institutions. Under these conditions, any observed effect of institutional size on some student outcome measure is unlikely to be an artifact of the researcher's failure to control input differences.

A related situation arises when the correlation between the environment and outcome is substantially higher than the correlation between environment and input. Ideally, to have maximum confidence in the existence of true causal relationships, one would like to see the correlation between environment and outcome *increase* as differential inputs are controlled. The more usual situation, of course, is that the environment-outcome relationship shrinks consistently as input variables are controlled successively. Thus, if the environment-outcome correlation increases or at least holds its own as input variables are controlled, the investigator can be reasonably confident that the observed environmental effect is a true one. However, when the correlation between environment and outcome diminishes consistently as input variables are controlled so that only a weak relationship remains after all input variables have been controlled, there is the very real possibility that the environmental effect would have disappeared altogether if a few other input variables had been included in the analyses. Significant environmental effects found under these conditions cannot generate a great deal of confidence.

Sign Reversals

Perhaps the strongest evidence of true causation is when the sign (+ or −) of the regression coefficient for a given environmental variable in the final equation is the *opposite* of the simple correlation between that environmental variable and the outcome measure. Although rare, this reversal in sign has been observed in several studies. A good illustration is the effect of college selectivity on college grade-point average (GPA). On a number of different occasions (Astin, 1971, 1977), it has been shown that the simple correlation between college selectivity and the student's college GPA is positive. To put it more simply, the more selective colleges award higher grades than the less selective colleges. On the face of it, this finding suggests that the more selective colleges have easier grading standards than do the less selective colleges. However, when input characteristics such as the student's high school grades and admission test scores are controlled, the positive relationship between selectivity and college GPA not only disappears but actually becomes *negative*. This would suggest that the actual *effect* of college selectivity on college GPA is a negative one, even though the simple correlation between college selectivity and college GPA is positive. This causal conclusion is consistent with the belief that the grading standards of the more selective colleges are more stringent than those of the less selective ones, therefore making it more difficult for a student of a given level of ability to get good grades in the more selective college.

Another multi-institutional study showed a similar reversal between the simple correlation and the final beta following the control of input (Astin and Panos, 1969). In this study, *cohesiveness*, a measure of the college environment reflecting primarily the proportion of students who report having many close friends among their fellow students, was shown to have a positive effect on the student's chance of completing college. However, the simple correlation between cohesiveness and the college's retention rate was *negative*. When differential student input variables were controlled, the negative simple correlation switched to a positive partial correlation. This radical switch can be explained as follows. Students who go to highly cohesive institutions are, in terms of their input characteristics, more prone to drop out than are students who go to the less cohesive institutions (this accounts for the negative simple correlation between cohesiveness and retention). Only when we take into account the differential dropout-proneness of the entering students (i.e., input characteristics), does the true positive effect of cohesiveness on retention show up.

Interaction Effects

Any study in which significant *interaction* effects are found constitutes another situation in which causal inferences can be made from I-E-O analyses with more than the usual degree of confidence. Suppose we are interested in determining whether the student's peer group has any significant effect on an outcome measure, and that we develop several measures of the student's peer group by averaging the answers of all the entering students on certain items measuring such characteristics as values, attitudes, and academic preparation. Let us further assume that we have found a significant effect of one of these peer group measures on some student outcome. If this is a true effect rather than an artifact, we would expect to find a stronger effect among students who have had a good deal of exposure to their peers than among students who have had less exposure. We might hypothesize that the effect should be stronger among students living in residence halls than among commuters, given that the commuters would tend to have less direct and sustained contact with peers. To explore this possibility, we might conduct I-E-O analyses of the effects of the peer group variables separately for commuters and residents. If the effects turned out to be stronger among the resident students, we would have a stronger basis for inferring that the peer group effect is indeed a causal one. Since one would expect to find almost any aspect of the institutional environment to have a stronger effect on residents than on commuter students, it might be advisable routinely to check for the existence of interactions involving residency as a means of verifying almost any environmental effect.

Additional checks on the validity of causal inferences can be made by examining other types of interaction effects. For example, extroverts or gregarious students are presumably more susceptible to the effects of peer factors than are introverted or shy students. It might also be informative to check for interactions with length of attendance: the strength or magnitude of most environmental effects should increase the longer the student is at the college. The point here is that for many of the significant residual correlations between environments and outcomes that may be observed in I-E-O studies, it is possible to hypothesize the existence of certain interaction effects which, if subsequently confirmed by additional analyses, would lend support to the assumption that the observed relationship is, indeed, a causal one.

Types of Inferential Errors

The possibility that the simple correlation of an environmental variable with an outcome variable can actually be of *opposite* sign from the true effect of that environmental variable (see above under Suppressor Effects) raises an interesting question concerning our conventional notions about statistical inference. Normally we are taught that there are two kinds of inferential error in statistical studies. *Type I* errors (rejection of a null hypothesis when it is true) occur when there is no environmental effect, but the investigator concludes that there is an effect. *Type II* errors (acceptance of the null hypothesis when it is false) occur when there is a true environmental effect, but the investigator concludes that there is no effect. The aforementioned examples of sign reversals, however, indicate that there is yet a third type of inferential error which I call *Type III* errors (Astin, 1970a). Type III errors occur when there is a significant environmental effect, but the investigator concludes that the environmental variable in question has the *opposite* effect. In a sense, a Type III error combines both Type I and Type II errors, since it involves simultaneously the rejection of the null hypothesis which is true and (implicitly) the acceptance of a null hypothesis which is false. (A convenient mnemonic device for defining Type III errors is that $1 + 2 = 3$.) One advantage of the I-E-O model is that it minimizes the risk of committing Type III errors through the control of input variables.

Measurement Error

It is well known among measurement specialists that error in the measurement of any variable tends to shrink (attenuate) the observed correlation between that variable and any other. Thus, if we are using the student's GRE score as a dependent or outcome variable and the

SAT score as the input or control variable, error in the measurement of SAT will cause us to *underestimate* the true correlation between SAT and GRE. This attenuated correlation, in turn, will cause us to *under-correct* for the effects of SAT on GRE when we compute a residual GRE score. Under such conditions, this residual GRE score will still correlate significantly with the student's "true" SAT score. This underadjustment for the effects of SAT on GRE can actually produce spurious environmental effects, especially when the environmental variable in question is also positively correlated with input and outcome (that is, with SAT and GRE). (For a mathematical proof of this bias, see Astin, 1970a.) The seriousness of the bias is a function of two factors: the amount of measurement error in the input or control variable and the size of the correlations among input, environment, and outcome. Investigators should be especially alert to the possibility of such a spurious environmental effect under the following conditions: when the environmental measure correlates more with the input than with the outcome and when the environment outcome correlation shrinks but does not disappear completely when the input is controlled.

A solution to this problem when there is only one input variable is to inflate the regression coefficient associated with an input variable by adjusting for the degree of unreliability in the variable (Tucker, Damarin, and Messick, 1966). This procedure can be generalized to the multivariate case (that is, when there is more than one input or control variable) by adjusting the $\hat{Y}$ for unreliability. One problem with both of these procedures is that they require a knowledge of the reliability of each input measure, information that is too often not available in survey research. Since most test publishers report test reliabilities in their user manuals, the investigator can make such corrections relatively easily when the input variables are standardized test scores.

If there is a large number of both quantitative and qualitative variables in the regression composite ($\hat{Y}$), then it is possible to make a rough adjustment for the entire composite by dividing that composite by a factor of slightly less than 1.0. In one major study (Astin, 1977), such corrections were made when there was any suspicion about a spurious environmental effect, but the corrections turned out not to have any great impact on the final conclusions.

REFERENCES

ACHEN, C. H. 1982. *Interpreting and Using Regression*. Beverly Hills, Calif.: Sage.

ADELMAN, C., ed. 1985. *Assessment in American Higher Education: Issues and Contexts*. Washington, D.C.: U.S. Department of Education Office of Educational Research and Improvement.

_____. 1988a. Difficulty Levels and the Selection of "General Education" Subject Examinations. In *Performance and Judgement: Essays on Principles and Practice in the Assessment of Student Learning*, ed. C. Adelman. Washington, D.C.: U.S. Department of Education Office of Educational Research and Improvement.

_____, ed. 1988b. *Performance and Judgement: Essays on Principles and Practices in the Assessment of College Student Learning*. Washington, D.C.: Department of Education Office of Educational Research and Improvement.

ALLPORT, G. W., P. E. VERNON, and G. LINDZEY. 1960. *Study of Values*. 3rd ed. Boston: Houghton Mifflin.

ALVERNO COLLEGE FACULTY. 1985. *Assessment at Alverno College*. Liberal Learning at Alverno Series. Milwaukee, Wis.: Alverno Productions.

ARGYRIS, C., and D. A. SCHÖN. 1974. *Theory in Practice: Increasing Professional Effectiveness*. San Francisco: Jossey-Bass.

ANASTASI, A. 1988. *Psychological Testing*. 6th ed. New York: Macmillan.

APPELBAUM, M. 1988a. Assessment of Basic Skills in Mathematics. In *Performance and Judgement: Essays on Principles and Practice in the Assessment of College Student Learning*, ed. C. Adelman. Washington, D.C.: U.S. Department of Education Office of Educational Research and Improvement.

_____. 1988b. Assessment through the Major. In *Performance and Judgement: Essays on Principles and Practice in the Assessment of College Student Learning*, ed. C. Adelman. Washington, D. C.: U.S. Department of Education Office of Educational Research and Improvement.

ASSOCIATION OF AMERICAN COLLEGES. 1985. *Integrity in the College Curriculum: A Report to the Academic Community*. Washington, D.C.: Association of American Colleges.

Astin, A. W. 1962. "Productivity" of Undergraduate Institutions. *Science* 136:129–135.

———. 1963. Differential College Effects on the Motivation of Talented Students to Obtain the Ph.D. Degree. *Journal of Educational Psychology* 54:63–71.

———. 1964. Personal and Environmental Factors Associated with College Drop-Outs Among High Aptitude Students. *Journal of Educational Psychology* 55:219–227.

———. 1968a. *The College Environment.* Washington, D.C.: American Council on Education.

———. 1968b. Undergraduate Achievement and Institutional Excellence. *Science* 161:661–668.

———. 1969. Folklore of Selectivity. *Saturday Review,* December, 57–58, 69.

———. 1970a. Measuring Student Outputs in Higher Education. In *The Outputs of Higher Education: Their Identification, Measurement, and Evaluation,* 75–83. Denver, Colo.: Western Interstate Commission for Higher Education.

———. 1970b. The Methodology of Research on College Impact, Part I. *Sociology of Education* 43:223–254.

———. 1970c. The Methodology of Research on College Impact, Part II. *Sociology of Education* 43:437–450.

———. 1971. Two Approaches to Measuring Students' Perceptions of Their College Environment. *Journal of College Student Personnel* 12 (2):169–172.

———. 1973. Measurement and Determinants of the Outcomes of Higher Education. In L. C. Solmon and P. J. Taubman, eds. *Does College Matter? Some Evidence of the Impacts of Higher Education.* New York: Academic Press.

———. 1975. *Preventing Students From Dropping Out.* San Francisco: Jossey-Bass.

———. 1976. *Academic Gamesmanship: Student-Oriented Change in Higher Education.* New York: Prager.

———. 1977. *Four Critical Years.* San Francisco: Jossey-Bass.

———. 1982. *Minorities in American Higher Education: Recent Trends, Current Prospects, and Recommendations.* San Francisco: Jossey-Bass.

———. 1984. Criterion Centered Research. *Education and Psychological Measurement* 24:807–822.

———. 1985a. *Achieving Educational Excellence.* San Francisco: Jossey-Bass.

———. 1985b. Selectivity and Equity in the Public Research University. In *The Future of State Universities: Issues in Teaching, Research, and Service,* ed. L. W. Koepplin and D. Wilson. New Brunswick, N.J.: Rutgers Univ. Press.

———. 1988. Appendix C: Preliminary Assessment of Factors Influencing General Education Outcomes. In *Assessing Outcomes of General Education Program.* A proposal prepared for the Exxon Education Foundation. Los Angeles: Higher Education Research Institute.

Astin, A. W., H. S. Astin, A. E. Bayer, and A. S. Bisconti. 1975. *The Power of Protest.* San Francisco: Jossey-Bass.

———, and F. Ayala, Jr. 1987. Institutional Strategies: A Consortial Approach to Assessment. *Educational Record* 68 (Summer):47–51.

———, and R. F. Boruch. 1970. A "Link" System for Assuring Confidentiality of Research Data in Longitudinal Studies. *American Educational Research Journal* 7 (4):615–624.

———, C. E. Christian, and J. W. Henson. 1975. *The Impact of Student Financial Aid Programs on Student Choice.* Los Angeles: Higher Education Research Institute.

_____, K. C. GREEN, and W. S. KORN. 1987a. *The American Freshman: Twenty Year Trends.* Los Angeles: Higher Education Research Institute.

_____, K. C. GREEN, and W. S. KORN. 1987b. *Undergraduates Two and Four Years After Entry.* Los Angeles: Higher Education Research Institute.

_____, K. C. GREEN, W. S. KORN, M. SCHALIT, and E. BERZ, 1989. *The American Freshman: National Norms for Fall 1988.* Los Angeles: Higher Education Research Institute.

_____, and J. L. HOLLAND. 1961. The Environmental Assessment Technique: A New Way to Measure College Environments. *Journal of Educational Psychology* 52:308–316.

_____, C. J. INOUYE, and W. S. KORN. 1986. *Evaluation of the CAEL Student Potential Program.* Los Angeles: Higher Education Research Institute.

_____, and L. D. MOLM, 1972. Correcting for Nonresponse Bias in Followup Surveys. Manuscript.

_____, and R. J. PANOS. 1969. *The Educational and Vocational Development of College Students.* Washington, D.C.: American Council on Education.

_____, and L. C. SOLMON. 1981. Are Reputational Ratings Needed to Measure Quality? *Change* 2 (5):14–19.

BAIRD, L. 1988. Diverse and Subtle Arts: Assessing the Generic Academic Outcomes of Higher Education. In *Performance and Judgement: Essays on Principles and Practice in the Assessment of College Student Learning,* ed. C. Adelman. Washington, D. C.: U.S. Department of Education Office of Educational Research and Improvement.

BANTA, T. W. 1985. Use of Outcomes Information at the University of Tennessee, Knoxville. In *Assessing Educational Outcomes,* ed. P. T. Ewell. New Directions for Institutional Research, No. 47. San Francisco: Jossey-Bass.

_____, ed. 1986. *Performance Funding in Higher Education: A Critical Analysis of the Tennessee Experience.* Boulder, Colo.: National Center for Higher Education Management Systems.

_____, ed. 1988. *Implementing Outcomes Assessment: Promises and Perils.* New Directions for Institutional Research, No. 59. San Francisco: Jossey-Bass.

BANTA, T. W., and H. S. FISHER. 1987. Measuring How Much Students Have Learned Entails Much More than Simply Testing Them. *Chronicle of Higher Education,* 4 March, 45.

_____, and J. A. SCHNEIDER. 1988. Using Faculty-Developed Exit Examinations to Evaluate Academic Programs. *Journal of Higher Education* 59 (1):69–83.

BASSIN, W. M. 1974. A Note on the Biases in Students' Evaluations of Instructors. *Journal of Experimental Education* 43:16–17.

BENTLER, P. M. 1989. *EQS: Structural Equators Program Manual.* Los Angeles: BMDP Software.

BERNE, E. 1964. *Games People Play.* New York: Random House.

BERRY, W. D., and S. FELDMAN. 1985. *Multiple Regression in Practice.* Beverly Hills: Sage.

BLACKBURN, R. T., and J. PITNEY. 1988. *Performance Appraisal for Faculty: Implications for Higher Education.* Ann Arbor: National Center to Improve Postsecondary Teaching and Learning.

BOGUE, E. G., and W. BROWN. 1982. *Performance Incentives for State Colleges: How Tennessee is Trying to Improve Its Higher Education Investment.* Nashville, Tenn.: Higher Education Commission.

BOWEN, H. R. 1977. *Investment in Learning.* San Francisco: Jossey-Bass.
———. 1980. *The Costs of Higher Education.* San Francisco: Jossey-Bass.
———. 1981. Cost Differences: The Amazing Disparity among Institutions of Higher Education in Educational Costs per Student. *Change* 2:21–27.
BOYER, C. M., and A. AHLGREN. 1987. Assessing Undergraduates' Patterns of Credit Distribution. *Journal of Higher Education* 58 (4):430–442.
BOYER, C. M., and P. T. EWELL. 1988. *State-Based Approaches to Assessment in Higher Education: A Glossary and Selected References.* Denver, Colo.: Education Commission of the States.
BUROS, O. K., ed. 1978. *The Eighth Mental Measurements Yearbook.* University of Nebraska–Lincoln, Buros Institute of Mental Measurement.
CALIFORNIA TASK FORCE TO PROMOTE SELF-ESTEEM AND PERSONAL AND SOCIAL RESPONSIBILITY. 1990. *Toward a State of Self-Esteem: The Final Report of the California Task Force to Promote Self-Esteem and Personal and Social Responsibility.* Sacramento, Calif.: California State Department of Education.
CARRIER, C. A., K. DALGAARD, and D. SIMPSON. 1983. Theories of Teaching: Foci for Instructional Improvement through Consultation. *Review of Higher Education* 6(Spring):195–206.
CARTTER, A. M. 1966. *Graduate Education: A Study of the Assessment of Quality.* Washington, D. C.: American Council on Education.
CENTRA, J. A. 1973. Effectiveness of Student Feedback in Modifying College Instruction. *Journal of Educational Psychology* 65 (3):395–401.
———. 1988. Assessing General Education. In *Performance and Judgement: Essays on Principles and Practice in the Assessment of College Student Learning,* ed. C. Adelman. Washington, D. C.: U.S. Department of Education Office of Educational Research and Improvement.
CHICKERING, A. W. 1974. *Commuting Versus Resident Students: Overcoming Educational Inequities of Living Off Campus.* San Francisco: Jossey-Bass.
CHICKERING, A. W., and Z. F. GAMSON. 1989. Inventories of Good Practice in Undergraduate Education Available Soon. *Wingspread Journal,* July.
CIERESZKO, A. 1987. Mandated Testing in Florida: A Faculty Perspective. In *Student Outcomes Assessment: What Institutions Stand to Gain,* ed. D. F. Halpern. New Directions for Higher Education, No. 59. San Francisco: Jossey-Bass.
COHEN, P. A. 1980. Effectiveness of Student-Rating Feedback for Improving College Instruction: A Meta-Analysis of Findings. *Research in Higher Education* 13 (4):321–342.
CRONBACH, L. J. 1984. *The Essentials of Psychological Testing.* New York: Harper & Row.
CROSS, K. P. 1989. Feedback in the Classroom: Making Assessment Matter. In *Proceedings of the Second Annual AAHE Assessment Forum.* Washington, D.C.: American Association for Higher Education.
———, and T. A. ANGELO. 1988. *Classroom Assessment Techniques: A Handbook for Faculty.* Ann Arbor, Mich.: National Center for Research on the Improvement of Postsecondary Teaching and Learning.
CURRY, W., and E. HAGER. 1987. Assessing General Education: Trent State College. In *Student Outcomes Assessment: What Institutions Stand to Gain,* ed. D. F. Halpern. New Directions for Higher Education, No. 59. San Francisco: Jossey-Bass.

DALEY, A. 1989. *Institutional Report on Assessment: Executive Summary.* Olympia, Wash.: Higher Education Coordinating Board, 5 May 1989.

DeLORIA, D., and G. K. BROOKINS. 1984. The Evaluation Report: A Weak Link in Policy. In *Evaluation Studies Review Annual,* ed. R. Conner. Beverly Hills: Sage.

DEY, E., and A. W. ASTIN. 1989. *Predicting College Student Retention: Comparative National Data from the 1982 Freshman Class.* Los Angeles: Higher Education Research Institute.

————, and A. W. ASTIN. 1990. *A Comparison of Results Using Logit and Regression Analysis.* Los Angeles: Higher Education Research Institute.

DREW, D. E., and R. KARPF. 1981. Ranking Academic Departments: Empirical Findings and a Theoretical Perspective. *Research in Higher Education* 14 (4):305–320.

DUBOIS, P. H. 1970. *A History of Psychological Testing.* Boston: Allyn and Bacon.

DUNBAR, S. 1988. Issues in Evaluating Measures of Basic Language Skills for Higher Education. In *Performance and Judgement: Essays on Principles and Practice in the Assessment of College Student Learning,* ed. C. Adelman. Washington, D. C.: U.S. Department of Education Office of Educational Research and Improvement.

DUNCAN, O. D. 1966. Path Analysis: Sociological Examples. *American Journal of Sociology* 72:1–16.

EMPIRE STATE COLLEGE. 1989. *Assessment at Empire State College: A Strategic Plan and Position Statement for the Future.* Saratoga Springs, N.Y.: Empire State College Office of Research and Evaluation.

ENDO, J., and T. BITTNER. 1985. Developing and Using a Longitudinal Student Outcomes Data File: The University of Colorado Experience. In *Assessing Educational Outcomes,* ed. P. T. Ewell. New Directions for Institutional Research, No. 47. San Francisco: Jossey-Bass.

EWELL, P. T. 1984. *The Self Regarding Institution: Information for Excellence.* Boulder, Colo.: National Center for Higher Education Management Systems.

————. ed. 1985a. *Assessing Educational Outcomes.* New Directions for Institutional Research, No. 47. San Francisco: Jossey-Bass.

————. 1985b. Some Implications for Practice. In *Assessing Educational Outcomes,* ed. P. T. Ewell. New Directions for Institutional Research, No. 47. San Francisco: Jossey-Bass.

————. 1987. Establishing a Campus-Based Assessment Program. In *Student Outcomes Assessment: What Institutions Stand to Gain,* ed. D. F. Halpern. New Directions for Higher Education, No. 59. San Francisco: Jossey-Bass.

————. 1988. Implementing Assessment: Some Organizational Issues. In *Implementing Outcomes Assessment: Promises and Perils,* ed. T. W. Banta. New Directions for Institutional Research, No. 59. San Francisco: Jossey-Bass.

EWELL, P. T., and C. M. BOYER. 1988. Acting Out State-Mandated Assessment. *Change* 9:41–47.

————, and D. P. JONES. 1985. *The Costs of Assessment.* Boulder, Colo.: National Center for Higher Education Management Systems.

————, R. PARKER, and D. P. JONES. 1988. *Establishing a Longitudinal Student Tracking System: An Implementation Handbook.* Boulder, Colo.: National Center for Higher Education Management Systems.

FELDMAN, K. A., and T. M. NEWCOMB. 1969. *The Impact of College on Students.* San Francisco: Jossey-Bass.

FOLGER, J., and J. HARRIS. 1989. *Assessment in Accreditation.* Washington, D.C.: Fund for the Improvement of Post-Secondary Education.

FORREST, A., and J. STEELE. 1982. *Defining and Measuring General Education, Knowledge, and Skills (Report 1976–81).* Iowa City: American College Testing Program.

GLEASON, M. 1986. Getting a Perspective on Student Evaluation. *AAHE Bulletin* 39 (February):10–13.

GRAHAM, S. 1988. Indicators of Motivation in College Students. In *Performance and Judgement: Essays on Principles and Practice in the Assessment of College Student Learning,* ed. C. Adelman. Washington, D.C.: U.S. Department of Education Office of Educational Research and Improvement.

GRANDY, J. 1988. Assessing Changes in Student Values. In *Performance and Judgement: Essays on Principles and Practice in the Assessment of College Student Learning,* ed. C. Adelman. Washington, D.C.: U.S. Department of Education Office of Educational Research and Improvement.

HALPERN, D. F., ed. 1987. *Student Outcomes Assessment: What Institutions Stand to Gain.* New Directions for Higher Education., No. 59. San Francisco: Jossey-Bass.

HARRIS, J. 1970. Gain Scores on the CLEP General Examination and an Overview of Research. Paper presented at the Annual Meeting of the American Educational Research Association, Minneapolis, Minn.

HAYDEN, T. 1986. *Beyond the Master Plan.* Sacramento: Joint Publications.

HEFFERLIN, J. L. 1969. *Dynamics of Academic Reform.* San Francisco: Jossey-Bass.

HEFFERMAN, J. M., P. HUTCHINGS, and T. J. MARCHESE. 1988. *Standardized Tests and the Purposes of Assessment.* Washington, D.C.: American Association for Higher Education.

HELMSTADTER, G. C. 1985. Review of Watson-Glaser Critical Thinking Appraisal. In *The Ninth Mental Measurements Yearbook,* ed. J. V. Mitchell, Jr. Lincoln, Nebr.: University of Nebraska–Lincoln, Buros Institute of Mental Measurements.

HENSON, J. W. 1980. Institutional Excellence and Student Achievement: A Study of College Quality and Its Impact on Education and Career Achievement. Ph.D. diss., University of California at Los Angeles.

HIGHER EDUCATION COORDINATING BOARD (HECB). 1987. *Building a System . . . to Be among the Best . . . The Washington State Master Plan for Higher Education.* Olympia, Wash.: Higher Education Coordinating Board.

HUNT, D. E. 1976. Teachers are Psychologists, Too: On the Application of Psychology to Education. *Canadian Psychological Review* 17:210–218.

HURTADO, S., A. W. ASTIN, W. S. KORN, and E. L. DEY. 1989. *The American College Student, 1987.* Los Angeles: Higher Education Research Institute.

JACOBI, M., A. ASTIN, and F. AYALA, Jr. 1987. *College Student Outcomes Assessment* (ASHE-ERIC Higher Education Report No. 7). Washington, D.C.: Association for the Study of Higher Education.

JOINT COMMITTEE FOR REVIEW OF THE MASTER PLAN FOR HIGHER Education. 1989. *California Faces . . . California's Future: Education for Citizenship in a Multicultural Democracy.* Sacramento: Joint Committee for Review of the Master Plan for Higher Education.

JONES, L. V., G. LINDZEY, and P. H. COGGESHALL, eds. 1982. *An Assessment of Research-Doctorate Programs in the United States.* Washington, D.C.: National Academy Press.

JÖRESKOG, K. G., and D. SÖRBOM, 1988. *LISREL 7, A Guide to the Program and Applications.* Chicago: SPSS.

KARABEL, J., and A. W. ASTIN. 1975. Social Class, Academic Ability, and College "Quality." *Social Forces* 53 (3):381–398.

KATZ, J. 1985. *Teaching Based on Knowledge of Students.* New Directions for Teaching and Learning, No. 21. San Francisco: Jossey-Bass.

KEAN COLLEGE OF NEW JERSEY PRESIDENTIAL TASK FORCE ON STUDENT LEARNING AND DEVELOPMENT. 1986. *A Proposal for Program Assessment at Kean College of New Jersey: Final Report of the Presidential Task Force on Student Learning and Development.* Union, N.J.: Kean College of New Jersy.

KEAN COLLEGE. 1988. *Kean College of New Jersey Challenge Grant: Interim Performance Report, January 1, 1988–June 30, 1988.* Union, N.J.: Kean College of New Jersey.

KINNICK, M. K. 1985. Increasing the Use of Student Outcomes Information. In *Assessing Educational Outcomes,* ed. P. T. Ewell. New Directions for Institutional Research, No. 47. San Francisco: Jossey-Bass.

KNAPP, R. H., and H. B. GOODRICH. 1952. *Origins of American Scientists.* New York: Russell and Russell.

KNAPP, R. H., and J. J. GREENBAUM. 1953. *The Younger American Scholar: His Collegiate Origins.* Chicago: Univ. of Chicago Press.

KRUEGER, D. W., and M. L. HEISSERER. 1987. Assessment and Involvement: Investments to Enhance Learning. In *Student Outcomes Assessment: What Institutions Stand to Gain,* ed. D. F. Halpern. New Directions for Higher Education, No. 59. San Francisco: Jossey-Bass.

LAND, K. C. 1969. Principles of Path Analysis. In *Sociological Methodology,* ed. E. F. Borgata. San Francisco: Jossey-Bass.

LEHMANN, T. 1988. Fulfilling Democracy's Promise through Education: The Empire State College Experiment. *Golden Hill Issue,* Vol. 4. Saratoga Springs, N.Y.: Empire State College.

LENNING, O. T., Y. S. LEE, S. S. MICEK, and A. L. SERVICE. 1977. *A Structure for the Outcomes of Postsecondary Education.* Boulder, Colo.: National Center for Higher Education Management Systems.

LEWIS, D. R. 1988. Costs and Benefits of Assessment: A Paradigm. In *Implementing Outcomes Assessment: Promises and Perils,* ed. T. W. Banta. New Directions for Institutional Research, No. 59. San Francisco: Jossey-Bass.

LEWIS-BECK, M. S. 1980. *Applied Regression: An Introduction.* Beverly Hills: Sage.

LOSAK, J. 1987. Assessment and Improvement in Education. In *Issues in Student Assessment,* ed. D. Bray and M. J. Belcher. New Directions for Community Colleges, No. 59, San Francisco: Jossey-Bass.

McCLAIN, C. J., and D. W. KRUEGER. 1985. Using Outcomes Assessment: A Case Study in Institutional Change. In *Assessing Educational Outcomes,* ed. P. T. Ewell. New Directions for Institutional Research, No. 47. San Francisco: Jossey-Bass.

McGOVERN, T. V., J. F. WERGIN, and D. L. HOGSHEAD. 1988. *Virginia Commonwealth University: The Varieties of Undergraduate Experience.* Final Report.

MENTKOWSKI, M. 1988. Paths to Integrity: Educating for Personal Growth and Professional Performance. In *Executive Integrity: The Search for High Human Values in Organizational Life,* ed. S. Srivastra and Associates, 89–121. San Francisco: Jossey-Bass.

———, and A. DOHERTY. 1983. *Careering after College: Establishing the Validity of Abilities Learned in College for Later Careering and Professional Performance.* Final report to the National Institute of Education.

———. 1984. Abilities that Last a Lifetime: Outcomes of the Alverno Experience. *AAHE Bulletin* 37 (February): 5–14.

MENTKOWSI, M. and G. LOACKER. 1985. Assessing and Validating the Outcomes of College. In *Assessing Educational Outcomes,* Institutional Research, No. 47. San Francisco: Jossey-Bass.

MENTKOWSKI, M. and M. STRAIT, 1983. *A Longitudinal Study of Student Change in Cognitive Development and Generic Abilities in an Outcome-Centered Liberal Arts Curriculum.* Milwaukee, Wis.: Alverno Productions.

MILLER, R. I. 1988. Using Change Strategies to Implement Assessment Programs. In *Implementing Outcomes Assessment: Promise and Perils,* ed. T. W. Banta. New Directions for Institutional Research, No. 59. San Francisco: Jossey-Bass.

MILLMAN, J. 1988. Designing College Assessment. In *Performance and Judgement: Essays on Principles and Practice in the Assessment of College Student Learning,* ed. C. Adelman. Washington, D.C.: U.S. Department of Education Office of Educational Research and Improvement.

MITCHELL, J. V., Jr. 1985. *The Ninth Mental Measurements Yearbook.* 10th ed. Lincoln: University of Nebraska–Lincoln, Buros Institute of Mental Measurements.

MOLM, L. D., and A. W. ASTIN. 1972. Some Personal Characteristics and Attitude Changes of Student Protesters. *Journal of College Student Personnel* 13 (2):32–39.

MUJERS, C. 1986. *Teaching Children to Think Critically.* San Francisco: Jossey-Bass.

MURRAY, H. G. 1985. *Classroom Teaching Behaviors Related to College Teaching Effectiveness.* New Directions for Teaching and Learning, No. 23. San Francisco: Jossey-Bass.

NATIONAL COMMISSION ON EXCELLENCE IN EDUCATION. 1983. *A Nation at Risk: The Imperative for Educational Reform.* Washington, D.C.: National Commission on Excellence in Education.

NATIONAL GOVERNORS' ASSOCIATION. 1988. *Results in Education: State-Level College Assessment Initiatives, 1987–1988.* Washington, D.C.: National Governors' Association.

NICHOLS, R. 1964. Effects of Various College Characteristics on Student Aptitude Test Scores. *Journal of Educational Psychology* 55:45–54.

NORTHEAST MISSOURI STATE UNIVERSITY. 1984. *In Pursuit of Degrees of Integrity: A Value-Added Approach to Undergraduate Assessment.* Washington, D.C.: American Association of State Colleges and Universities.

NORTHWEST MISSOURI STATE UNIVERSITY. 1987. *Strengthening the Foundations: An Agenda for Improving Undergraduate Education at Northwest Missouri State University.* Maryville: Northwest Missouri State University.

OSTERLIND, J. 1989. *College Base: Guide to Test Content.* Chicago: Riverside Publishing Company.

PACE, C. R. 1960. Five College Environments. *College Board Review* 41:24–28.

———. 1963. *College and University Environmental Scales.* Princeton, N.J.: Educational Testing Service.

———. 1985. Perspectives and Problems in Student Outcomes Research. In *Assessing Educational Outcomes*, ed. P. T. Ewell. New Directions for Institutional Research, No. 47. San Francisco: Jossey-Bass.

———, and G. G. STERN. 1958. Approach to the Measurement of Psychological Characteristics of College Environments. *Journal of Educational Psychology* 49:269–277.

PASCARELLA, E. T. 1985. The Influence of On-Campus Living Versus Commuting to College on Intellectual and Interpersonal Self-Concept. *Journal of College Student Personnel* 25 (4):292–299.

PASKOW, J., ed. 1988. *Assessment Programs and Projects: A Directory.* Washington, D.C.: American Association for Higher Education.

PEDHAZUR, E. J. 1982. *Multiple Regression in Behavioral Research* (2nd ed.). New York: Holt, Rinehart, and Winston.

PETERSON, R. E., J. CENTRA, R. T. HARTNETT, and R. L. LINN. 1970. *Institutional Functioning Inventory: Preliminary Technical Manual.* Princeton, N.J.: Educational Testing Service.

———, and N. P. UHL. 1972. *Formulating College and University Goals: A Guide for Using the Institutional Goals Inventory.* Princeton, N.J.: Educational Testing Service.

POPHAM, W. J. 1978. *Criterion-Referenced Measurement.* New York: Prentice-Hall.

RATCLIFF, J. L. 1988. Development of a Cluster-Analytic Model for Identifying Course Work Patterns Associated with General Learned Abilities of College Students. Paper presented at the American Educational Research Association, New Orleans, La.

ROOSE, K. D., and C. J. ANDERSEN. 1970. *A Rating of Graduate Programs.* Washington, D.C.: American Council on Education.

ROSS, H., and N. WEISS. 1989a. *Achieving Institutional Reform through Shared Governance.* Union, N.J.: Kean College of New Jersey.

———, and N. WEISS. 1989b. Sharing the Challenge of Institutional Reform. *AGB Reports*, November-December, 15–19.

RUDOLPH, L. B. 1989. Assessment at Austin Peay Stimulates Improvement. *Assessment Update* 1 (3):50.

SAS INSTITUTE INCORPORATED. 1985. *SAS User's Guide: Basics, Version 5 Edition.* Cary, N.C.: SAS Institute Incorporated.

SCHROEDER, L. D., D. L. SJOQUIST, and P. E. STEPHAN. 1988. *Understanding Regression Analysis: An Introductory Guide.* Beverly Hills: Sage.

SMALLWOOD, M. L. 1935. *An Historical Study of Examinations and Grading Systems in Early American Universities.* Cambridge: Harvard Univ. Press.

SOLMON, L. C. 1975. The Definition of College Quality and Its Impact on Earning. *Explorations in Economic Research*, Fall, 537–587.

SOLMON, L. C., and A. W. ASTIN. 1981. Departments without Distinguished Graduate Programs. *Change* 2 (4):23–28.

SOUTHERN ASSOCIATION OF COLLEGES AND SCHOOLS. 1989. *Criteria for Accreditation.* Atlanta: Southern Association of Colleges and Schools.

SPSS-X User's Guide. 1988. Chicago: SPSS.

STEVENSON, M., R. D. WALLERI, and S. M. JAPELY. 1985. Designing Follow-up Studies of Graduates and Former Students. In *Assessing Educational Outcomes*, ed. P. T. Ewell. New Directions for Institutional Research, No. 47. San Francisco: Jossey-Bass.

STUDY GROUP ON THE CONDITIONS OF EXCELLENCE IN AMERICAN HIGHER EDUCATION. 1984. *Involvement in Learning: Realizing the Potential of American Higher Education. Final Report of the Study Group on the Conditions of Excellence in American Higher Education.* Washington, D.C.: National Institute of Education.

TUCKER, L. R., F. DAMARIN, and S. MESSICK. 1966. A Base-Free Measure of Change. *Psychometrika* 31:457–473.

TURNBULL, W. 1985. *Student Change: Why the SAT Scores Kept Falling.* College Board Report 85–2. New York: College Entrance Examination Board.

WEBB, N. J. 1984. Using Student Data for Academic Improvement: One College Experience. *Educational Record.* 65 (Summer):58–60.

WIRTZ, WILLARD, chair. 1977. *On Further Education: Report of the Advisory Panel on the Scholastic Aptitude Test Score Decline.* New York: College Entrance Examination Board.

WOLFEL, L. M. 1985. Applications for Causal Models in Higher Education. In *Higher Education: Handbook of Theory and Research*, ed. J. C. Smart. Vol. 1., New York: Agathon.

ZEMSKY, R. 1989. *Structure and Coherence: Measuring the Undergraduate Curriculum.* Washington, D.C.: Association of American Colleges.

INDEX

A

A Nation at Risk, 30–32, 216
AAHE Assessment Forum, 245
Academic games, 133–37, 138, 150
Academic Profile II, 49
Accountability, *vii*, 2, 30, 216
Accreditation, 36–37, 155, 231
Accrediting teams, 1, 181, 244
Achen, C. H., 275, 315
Achievement tests, 132
ACT Proficiency Examination Program, 8, 30, 49–51, 71, 96, 132, 152, 161, 168, 179, 189, 213
Adelman, C., 50, 244, 314, 317, 318, 319, 320, 323
Administrators, *vii*, 1, 14, 92, 129–30, 143–44, 200, 227, 236, 251
Admissions, 8–10, 68, 152, 157, 177, 231, 235–36, 238, 243
  examinations, 97, 160
  offices, 154, 162, 167
Advanced Placement (AP) Examinations, 12, 71, 73, 132, 243
Advising, 118, 144, 232, 250, 251
Affective-behavioral outcomes, 59–60
Affirmative action, 196, 199
Ahlgren, A., 92, 318

Allport, Vernon, Lindzey, *Study of Values*, 58, 315
Alumni, 61, 200, 235
  offices, 152, 154, 157, 167
  surveys, 225
Alverno College, *viii*, 40, 42, 50, 55, 60, 132, 142, 148, 169, 172, 244, 246, 250
Alverno College Faculty, 50, 169, 172, 244, 315
American Association for Higher Education (AAHE), 245
American College Testing (ACT) Program, 48
American history, 132, 220
American Indians, 68, 211, 212
Anatasi, A., 51, 315
Andersen, C. J., 36, 323
Angelo, T. A., 186, 318
Appelbaum, M., 47, 50, 315
Argyris, C., 192
Armacost, P., *x*, 151
Asian students, 68, 212
Assessment
  definition of, 2
  uses of, *vii*
Assessment Resource Center, 245
Assessment Update, 245
Assessment movement, 1
Assessment of faculty. *See* Faculty: assessment of

Association of American Colleges (AAC), 2, 315
    Project on Redefining the Meaning and Purpose of Baccalaureate Degrees, 42
Astin, A. W., 6, 7, 12, 17, 23, 33, 43, 47–50, 55, 57–59, 65, 67, 69, 72, 87, 89, 115, 117, 120, 134, 135, 148, 152, 161, 164, 165, 166, 169, 170, 195, 196–98, 211, 228, 242, 250, 283– 85, 303, 310, 311, 313, 316–17, 319, 320, 322, 323
Astin, H. S., xi, 316
Austin Peay State University, 167
Average deviation, 258
Ayala, F., Jr., xi, 43, 47–50, 148, 152, 166, 315, 320

B

Baird, L., 50, 316
Banta, T. W., xi, 39, 61, 143, 148, 219, 244, 245, 317, 322, 323
Bar exam, 39–40, 50, 243
Basic skills, 47
Bassin, W. M., 191, 317
Bayler, A. E., 316
Behavioral Event Interview (BEI), 48–49
Belcher, M. J., 322
Bentler, P. M., 317
Berkeley, 6
Berne, E., 134, 317
Berry, W. D., 275, 317
Beta coefficient. *See* Standardized regression coefficient
Between-institution measures, 86–90, 303
Binet, A., 241
Bisconti, A. S., 316
Bittner, T., 158, 319
Bivariate distribution, 270–74
Black students, 68, 78, 194, 196, 211–13
Blackburn, R. T., 192, 317
Bogue, E. G., *vii*, 317
Bok, D., 57
Boruch, R. F., 165, 316
Bowen, H. R., 8, 42, 318

Boyer, C. M., 2, 92, 218, 316, 319
Bray, D., 322
Bridge measures, 74
Brookins, G. K., 139, 319
Brown, W., *vii*, 317
Buros, O. K., 58, 318

C

California, 57, 195, 211, 213, 228
California Master Plan for Higher Education, 125–26, 213
California State Legislature, 57, 72, 213
California State University, 13, 30, 40, 57, 213, 243
Campus Compact, 57
Canada, 164
Career placement, 143
Carnegie-Mellon University, xi, 152
Carrier, C. A., 192, 318
Cartter, A. M., 36, 318
Causal analyses, 97, 102, 103, 108, 236
Causal inference, *ix*, 29
Causal modeling, 301–9
Causation, 88
Centra, J. A., 49, 191, 318
Certification, 8, 12, 167, 223
Challenge grants, 219, 226–27, 230, 239
Chief executive officers, 14
Chickering, A. W., 23, 227, 318
Chilton, L., *xi*
Chinese civil service examinations, 240
Christian, C. E., 195, 316
Chronicle of Higher Education, 248
Church, M., *xi*
Ciereszko, A., 40, 222, 318
Civil War, 221
Classroom
    experiments, 35
    research, 186
    testing, 186–87
CLAST. *See* College Level Academic Skills Test
CLEP. *See* College Level Examination Program

Coggeshall, P. H., 36, 321
Cognitive-psychological assessment, 48
Cohen, P. A., 191, 318
Cohort files, 156–58, 159, 173, 176
College and University Environmental Scales (CUES), 86–87, 90, 91
College Base, 49
College Characteristics Index (CCI), 87
College Entrance Examination Board (CEEB), 12, 161, 213
College impact, 34
College Level Academic Skills Test (CLAST), 24, 30, 222
College Level Examination Program (CLEP), 50, 71
College of William and Mary, 240
College Student Experiences (CSE), 87, 91
Collegial model, 139–40
Community college, 4, 82, 125–26, 160, 211, 214
Comparative evaluation, 23–24
Competition
  among colleges, 9–10
  in assessment, 52-53, 54
COMP test, 48
Competency testing, 4, 23, 50, 224, 239
  Florida model, 222–23
Comprehensive examinations, 41
Conceptual outcome, 38
Confidence, statistical, 264
Confidentiality of data, 162–65
Confounding, 88, 91, 303
Congress, U.S., 57, 164
Conner, R., 320
Consequents, 18
Conservatism, 72, 79, 80
Constant, 280, 284. *See also* Regression
  definition of, 267
Continuum, 82, 146, 208, 258
Control group, 23, 25–28, 29
Cooperative Institutional Research Program (CIRP), 57, 59, 63, 64,

68, 69, 71–73, 75, 98, 99, 116, 144, 152, 161, 167, 169, 283. *See also* Freshman survey
Correlation, 29, 66, 74–80, 97, 105, 204, 236
  and causation, 19, 29
  meaning of, 101–2, 260
  multiple, 116–17
    formula for, 276–77
  negative, 101, 102
  part, 280–82
  partial, 280–82
  positive, 101, 261
  pretest-posttest, 74–77
  semipartial, 280–82
  simple, 276, 280
  zero, 101, 263
Cost-benefit analyses, 172
Council for Adult and Experimental Learning (CAEL), 48
Course examinations, 2, 10
Credentialing, 8, 12
Criterion variables, 18
Criterion-referenced testing, 53,247
Cronbach, L. J., 51, 317
Cross, K. P., 186, 317
Cross-tabulation, 97, 98–101, 103–4, 236
Curriculum, 26, 32, 34, 176, 181, 233, 235, 240, 251
Curry, W., 48, 318

D

Daley, A., 226, 319
Dalgaard, K., 192, 318
Damarin, R. F., 313, 324
Data analysis, 94–127, 173 (*see also* the Appendix, 255–313)
Data base, 151–77, 235–36
De Loria, D., 139, 319
Demographic characteristics, 64, 70, 82, 161
Departmental perspective, 39
Department of Education, U.S., 86
Dependent variables, 18. *See also* Outcome
Descriptive analyses, 95–97, 102
Deviation score, 258–59

Devine, J., *xi*
Dey, E. L., *x*, 115, 198, 320
Disadvantaged groups, 195
Disadvantagement index, 213–14
Disciplinary perspective, 39
Discriminant analysis, 283
Displacement and projection, 136, 138
Diversion, 138
Doherty, A., 40, 42, 132, 142, 244, 322
Drew, D. E., *xi*, 36, 278, 319
dropping out, 35, 65, 159, 202, 220, 307
Dubois, P. H., 240, 319
Dummy variables, 96, 102, 283, 275, 300–1
Dunbar, S., 47, 319
Duncan, O. D., 319

E

Eckerd College, *x*, 51, 151
Education Commission of the States (ECS), 57
Educational benefits, 125, 196–97
Educational Opportunity Program (EOP), 116
Educational policy, 23, 130, 209, 243
Educational psychology, 245
Educational Testing Service (ETS), 49, 50
Empire State College, *xi*, 55, 152, 172, 244, 246, 247, 319
Empirical research, 245
Employee surveys, 225
Employer perspective, 40
Endo, J., 158, 319
Endogenous variables, 18
Enteman, W., *xi*, 151
Environment-only assessments, 30, 36–37, 89–90, 191
Environment-outcome assessments, 30, 32–34
Environmental Assessment Technique (EAT), 87–88
Environmental effects:
  assessment of, 81–93, 277–308, 235
  estimating size of, 293–98
Environmental experiences, 83, 233

Environmental variable, 18–19, 35, 85, 125, 154, 157–59, 160, 175
  and regression, 279–280
EQS, 305
Equity, 194–215
  and assessment, 238
  definition of, 198–99
  systems perspective of, 207–10
Error. *See,* Residual, definition of
Escalante, J., 132
Estimating outcome from input, 266
Ethnicity, 22, 67, 68, 70, 100, 117, 161, 284
Evaluation, 146
  curriculum, 37, 68–69
  definition of, 2–3
  narrative, 56, 181, 240, 246, 247
  normative, 56
  program, 23, 68–69, 224, 235
Everett, 240
Evergreen State College, 189
Ewell, P. T., *xi*, 50, 137, 140, 141, 145, 148, 158, 166, 171, 218, 244, 245, 318, 319, 322, 324
Excellence, 4–8
  and assessment, 4–8
  reputational view of, 5, 6, 9, 13–14, 53, 147, 199, 201, 205, 212, 214, 232, 238, 242, 253
  resources view of, 5–6, 9, 13–14, 53, 147, 199, 201, 205, 212, 214, 232, 238, 242, 253
  talent development view of, 6–7, 8, 14, 199–200, 233, 238
Existential benefits, 196–97
Expected outcome, 276
Experimental group, 25–28
Expertise in assessment, 139–41, 245–46
Extracurricular activities, 71, 92, 154, 155, 161, 224, 230

F

Faculty, 1, 5, 41, 129–30, 132–33, 200, 233, 236, 245
  assessment of, 1, 4, 14, 181, 190, 248–51

and assessment results, 142–43, 148–50, 236
morale, 90
performance, 8, 13, 190
salaries, 7
FBI, 164
Feedback, 12, 129, 146, 150, 178, 183–85, 186–91, 193, 232, 236, 250
Feedback principle, 129–30, 180–82
Feldman, K. A., 23, 34, 44, 275, 316, 320
Financial aid, 85, 92, 143, 152, 154, 155, 157, 161, 162, 235
Fisher, H. S., 143, 317
Florida, 13, 24, 30, 40, 51, 151, 180, 222–23
Folger, J., 244, 320
Follow-up surveys, 59, 61, 72, 98, 99, 103, 120, 152, 160–162, 163, 169–70
Forrest, A., 48, 320
Fraternities, 71, 144
Frequency distribution, 96, 269–71
Freshman survey (CIRP), 59, 61, 68, 69, 72, 73, 75, 98, 99, 152, 161, 167, 169
Fringe benefits, 196–97
Fund for the Improvement of Post-Secondary Education (FIPSE), *x*, 151–52
value-added consortium, 131, 148, 168

G

Games People Play, 134
Gamson, Z. F., 227, 318
Garfield high school, 132
Gender, 67, 70, 98, 100, 107, 121, 293
General education requirements, 62, 142
Gleason, M., 183, 320
GMAT. *See* Graduate Management Admissions Test
Goodrich, H. B., 17, 321
Governance, 140, 181
Governmental support, 242
GPA. *See* Grade point average

Grade point average (GPA), 7, 8–9, 10, 11, 22, 41, 46, 48, 70, 97, 98, 99, 124–25, 155, 179, 181, 194, 202, 203–4, 246, 247, 248
Grading, 11–12, 178–79, 182, 231, 237, 246
on the curve, 52
Graduate Management Admissions Test (GMAT), 10, 49, 97, 168, 179, 189, 229
Graduate Record Examination (GRE), 10, 22, 39, 44, 49, 50, 52, 53, 75, 82, 97, 100, 102, 105–9, 122, 148, 168, 179, 189, 220 (*see also* the Appendix, 255–313)
Graduation, 34
Graham, S., 57, 320
Grandy, J., 44, 57, 320
GRE. *See* Graduate Record Examination
Green, K. C., 57, 69, 228, 250, 317
Greenbaum, J. J., 17, 321

H

Hager, E., 48, 318
Halpern, D. F., 148, 244, 318, 319, 322
Hampshire College, 55, 181, 246, 247
Hardware, 172–74, 177
Harris, J., 11, 204, 244, 320
Harvard, 6, 57, 240
Harvard Board of Overseers, 57
Hayden, T., 211, 320
Health services, 143
Hefferlin, J. L., 89, 320
Hefferman, J. M., 51, 320
Heisserer, M. L., 39
Helmstadter, G. C., 47, 320
Henson, J. W., 195, 197, 198, 316, 320
Hetrick, B., *xi*
Hierarchy, institutional, 195, 198, 210
Higher education, purposes of, 3–4, 252
Higher Education Coordinating Board (HECB), 225, 320
Higher Education Research Institute (HERI), 115, 284

Hispanics, 68, 194, 196, 211–13
Hogshead, D. L., 244, 321
Holland, J. L., 17, 88, 317
Honors program, 80, 92, 124, 144
Hood College, *xi*, 152
Human capital viewpoint, 199–200, 204–6
Hunt, D. E., 192, 320
Hurtado, S., *x*, 116, 161, 169, 320
Hutchings, P., 52, 245, 320

I

I-E-O model, *ix*, 15, 37, 56, 84, 98, 108, 116, 119, 147, 162, 178, 201, 210, 248
  application of (*see* the Appendix, 255–313)
  and cross tabulation, 103
  as a causal model, 301–4
  definition of, 16–19
  and multiple regression analysis, 105
  purposes of, 19–20, 232–35
  student data base for, 153, 156
  student input data for, 64, 65–67, 70, 80
Incentive funding, 180. *See also* Value-added assessments
  Tennessee model, *vii*, 219–20
Incentives, 11, 168, 182–83, 193, 224, 227
Independent assessor model, 139
Independent variable, 18. *See also* Environmental variable; Input variable
Inferential errors, 312
Information retrieval, 173
Inouye, C. J., 48, 317
Input variable, 153–55, 157–59, 160, 175–76, 308–9
  assessment of, 234–35
  controlling for, 265–67
Input-environment-outcomes model. *See* I-E-O model
Input-outcome assessments, 30, 34–36
Institutional Functioning Inventory (IFI), 89, 91

Institutional Goals Inventory (IGI), 89
Institutional research office, 157–58
Interaction effects, 67, 120–27, 311–12
  estimating the size of, 298–300
  higher order, defined, 122
  simple, defined, 122–23
Intercept, definition of, 267, 273. *See also* Regression
Intermediate outcomes, 84, 304–8
Intervention, 37
Inventory of College Activities (ICA), 87, 91

J

Jacobi, M., *xi*, 43, 47, 49, 50, 320
James Madison University, 245
Japely, S. M., 170, 323
Joint Committee for Review of the Master Plan for Higher Education, 319. *See also* California Master Plan for Higher Education
Jones, D. P., 158, 172, 245, 319
Jones, L. V., 36, 321
Joreskog, K. G., 321

K

Karabel, J., 23, 321
Karpf, R., 36, 319
Katz, J., 135, 192, 321
Kean College, 50, 132, 143, 148, 169, 227, 244, 250, 321
Kiesler, C., *xi*
Kings College, 245
Kinnick, M. K., 142, 321
Knapp, R. H., 17, 321
Koepplin, L. W., 317
Korn, W. S., 48, 57, 69, 228, 250, 317, 320
Kreuger, D. W., 39, 321
Kurtosis, 97

L

Land, K. C., 321
Law School Admissions Test (LSAT), 49, 97, 168, 179, 189, 229

Learning, 124, 129, 183–85, 218
Least squares, principle of, 271–74
Lee, Y. S., 42
Lehmann, T., *xi*, 172, 321
Lenning, O. T., 42, 321
Lewis, D. R., 321
Lewis-Beck, M. S., 172, 275, 321
Liberal arts college, 156
Liberalism, 72, 79, 80
Lindzey, G., 36, 314, 321
Link file, 164
LISREL, 305
Loacker, G., 60, 322
Logit analysis, 283
Longitudinal assessment, 31
    designs, 34
Longitudinal multivariate studies, 67
Longitudinal research, 151–77
Losak, J., 222, 321
LSAT. *See* Law School Admissions
    Test

M

Macmillan, *xi*
Main effects, 123, 299
Marchese, T. J., 51, 320
Marital status, 155
Matching, 25
Matriculation, 158
MCAT. *See* Medical College
    Admissions Test
McClain, C. J., *xi*, 39, 321
McGovern, T. V., 244, 321
Mean square, 259
Mean, 96, 257
Measurement error, 77, 312–13. *See
    also* Reliability
Median, 96
Medical College Admissions Test
    (MCAT), 10, 49, 97, 168, 179,
    189, 229
Mental Measurements Yearbook, 47, 48
Mentkowski, M., 40, 42, 60, 132, 142,
    244, 322
Mentoring, 231, 233, 249, 251
Merit Scholars, 17, 199, 241
Meritocratic orientation, 241–42
Meritocratic procedure, 240

Messick, S., 313, 324
Micek, S. S., 42
Miller, R. I., 322
Millman, J., 47, 322
Minorities, 115, 144, 165, 211, 213,
    228
Mitchell, J. V., Jr., 47, 320, 322
Mode, 96
Moffatt, M., 248
Molm, L. D., 169, 170, 316, 322
Mount Holyoke College, 240
Mujers, C., 322
Multicollinearity, 288, 297
Multiple choice methodology, 234
Multiple choice testing, 49, 51–52,
    148, 234, 243
    critique of, 51–55
Multiple regression. *See* Regression
Multivariate statistical analyses. *See*
    Regression
Murray, H. G., 191, 322

N

Narrative feedback, 56
National Assessment of Educational
    Progress (NAEP), 30, 210
National Board exam, 40
National Center for Higher
    Education Management Systems
    (NCHEMS), *xi*, 245
National Commission on Excellence
    in Education, 30, 322
National Conference on Assessment,
    245
National Education Association
    (NEA), 223
National Governor's Association,
    217–18, 322
    Task Force on College Quality, 217
National Merit Scholarship Program,
    9, 16, 199
National Science Foundation (NSF),
    17
National Teacher's Exam (NTE), 39,
    167, 223
Natural experiment, 28–29
New Left, 136
Newcomb, T. M., 23, 34, 44, 320

Nichols, R., 265, 322
Norm-referenced tests, 189, 238, 247
  critique of, 52–54
Normative assessment, 52, 56
Normative measures. *See*
  Correlation; Regression
Northeast Missouri State University,
  viii, 39, 51, 244, 322
Northwest Missouri State University,
  244, 322

O

Obfuscation, 135, 138
Omnibus Personality Inventory
  (OPI), 58
Open admissions, 212
Orientation, 168
Orwell, G., 135
Osterlind, J., 49, 322
Outcome, 38–63, 184, 233, 234
  affective, 44, 56–57, 58, 61, 152
  affective-behavioral, 59–60
  cognitive, 43–44, 46–47, 55–58, 144,
    152
  existential, 46
  expected, 268
  intermediate, 304–6
Outcome-only assessments, 30–32
Outputs. *See* Outcome

P

Pace, C. R., 51, 60, 86–87, 323
Panos, R. J., 88, 303, 311, 317
Parker, R., 319
Pascarella, E. T., 23, 323
Paskow, J., 168, 244, 323
Passing the buck, 135, 138
Path analysis, 301–2
Pedagogical technique, 81, 128, 142,
  176, 189, 191–92, 251, 252
Pedhazur, 275, 324
Peer group, 23, 91, 92, 99, 311
Penna, T., *xi*
Percentile score, 52
Performance-based funding, 228, 239
Peterson, R. E., 89, 322
Ph.D. productivity, 17, 19, 33
Pitney, J., 192, 316

Placement, 67, 124, 126, 167, 168,
  206–7
Popham, W. J., 53, 322
Posttests, 34, 77, 167, 223, 225, 229.
  See also Outcome
Predictive validity, 54
Predominantly black colleges, 79
Preliminary Scholastic Aptitude Test
  (PSAT), 8–9, 22
Pre-tenure review, 13, 181, 190, 232
Pretest, 24, 26, 35, 51, 64, 65, 72, 80,
  103, 168, 223, 225, 229, 234
Pretest-posttest, 34, 120, 219, 226
Probabilities, 294–95
Professional certification programs,
  229
Professional schools, 3, 10, 11, 13, 39,
  40, 49, 144, 179, 229, 243, 247
Professional perspective, 40
Professors. *See* Faculty
Proprietary schools, 39, 40
Protestant colleges, 78
PSAT. *See* Preliminary Scholastic
  Aptitude Test
Psychological data, 44, 61–62
Public policy, assessment and,
  238–39
Public service, 3, 4, 57, 69, 200

Q

Qualitative assessment, 21
Quality of Effort scales, 91
Quality control, 24, 239, 240
Quantitative data, 21
Quincy, President, of Harvard, 240

R

Random selection, 25
Ratcliff, J. L., 92, 323
Rationalization, 134, 138
Recitation, 136
Recruitment, 68
Reference point, 257
Regents' External Degree Program,
  12
Regional accrediting bodies, 216
Registrar, 3, 152, 154, 157, 162, 177,
  235–36

Regression, 105–13, 176, 236
  blocking variables in, 284–309
  coefficient, 267
  formula, 267, 268
  interpreting results of, 285–313
  meaning of, 265–66
  multiple, 102, 105, 108, 146, 274–76
  multivariate statistical analyses, 28
  simple, 266-68
  stepwise, 279, 282
  visualizing, 269–74
Regression line, 272
Reliability, 77. *See also* Measurement
  error
Reliability-validity game, 137
Remedial, 68, 71, 92
Remedial approach, 221
Reputational polls, 7
Residual, definition of, 268–69. *See
  also* Regression
Retention, 22, 65, 71, 90, 96, 98, 109,
  121, 144, 283
Retention data base, 159–60, 166, 174,
  177
Retention rates, 96, 99, 100, 112–13
Rhetorical question game, 135
Rhode Island College, *xi*, 151
Roose, K. D., 36, 322
Ross, H., 227, 244, 322
Rudolph, L. B., 167, 323
Rutgers, 248

S

Sampling, 172, 174, 177
SAS, 141, 174, 175, 322
SAT. *See* Scholastic Aptitude Test
Satisfaction measures, 65
Schneider, J. A., 39
Scholarly productivity, 36
Scholarship, 231, 252
Scholastic Aptitude Test (SAT), 8,
  22–23, 30, 44, 49, 51, 53, 71, 75,
  82, 96, 97, 98, 101, 105–10, 112,
  123, 132, 148, 168, 179, 189, 198,
  212, 247 (*see also* the Appendix,
  255–313)
Schön, D. A., 192, 315
Schroeder, L. D., 275, 322
Screening. *See* Selection

Selection, 11, 67, 124, 127, 247
Selective admissions, 9, 125, 201–2,
  203, 209, 211
Selectivity, 69, 82, 85, 195, 198
Self-concept, 21, 161
Self-esteem, California Task Force to
  Promote Self-Esteem and
  Personal and Social
  Responsibility, 72, 318
Self-predictions, 64, 66, 67, 71
Service, A. L., 42
SES. *See* Socioeconomic status
Simpson, D., 192, 318
Skewness, 96
Slope of regression line, 273–74
Smallwood, M. L., 240, 322
"So what?" reaction, 91, 103, 130–31,
  150
Socioeconomic status, 22, 33, 117,
  155, 288
Software, 172–74, 177
Solmon, L. S., 6, 198, 317, 323
Sörbom, D., 321
Sororities, 71, 144
Southern Association of Colleges and
  Schools (SACS), 36, 216, 323
Special admissions, 196, 212
Special education programs, 68. *See
  also* Remedial
Spelman College, *xi*, 152
SPSS, 141, 174, 175, 284, 287, 323
Sputnik, 241
Srivasta, S., 323
Stand and Deliver, 132
Standard deviation (SD), 96, 267
Standard score, 52, 260. *See also* z
  score
Standardized regression coefficient,
  285–93, 302
Standardized tests, 12–13, 44, 69, 70,
  132, 167, 174, 194, 204, 211, 238,
  243
Standards, 23, 201–2, 205, 214–15
Stanford, 6
State University of New York
  (SUNY), 12
State agencies, 13, 233
State appropriations, 7
State governments, 216, 244
State legislators, 213, 217–18, 227, 242

State-mandated assessment, 180, 221, 223, 225–26, 243
State perspective, 40, 219
Statewide assessment, 2
Statistical significance, defined, 264
Statistics, 94–95, 182, 94–127, Appendix, 255–313. *See also* Correlation; Regression
Steele, J., 48, 320
Stepwise regression analysis, 279–80, 282. *See also* Regression
Stern, G. G., 87
Stevenson, M., 170, 323
Stewart, D., *xi*
Strait, M., 244, 322
Student affairs, 152, 154, 162, 235
Student affairs personnel, 143, 171
Student attitudes, 61
Student development, 45
Student housing, 155, 162
Student perspective, 40, 184, 251
Student-faculty relations, 54–56, 227
Student-generated feedback, 188–89
Study Group on the Conditions of Excellence in Higher Education, 2, 55
Subject-matter competency, 50
Sum of squares, 259, 284
SUNY College at Plattsburgh, 245
Suppressor effect, 288–89, 293

T

Talent development, 12, 18, 34, 118, 124, 146, 152, 158, 161, 167, 182, 210, 217, 218, 229, 231. *See also* Excellence: talent development view of
  and assessment, 240, 242, 246, 252
  and faculty, 190, 192
  and feedback, 187, 188
  and equity, 199–200, 202, 203
  and professional competency, 206, 207
Task Force on College Quality, 217
Taubmann, P. J., 317
Taxonomy, 42, 44, 46, 234

Teaching consultants, 192, 250
Teaching-learning process, 4, 10, 252
Teaching to the test, 39, 220, 243
Tenure, 13–14, 181, 190, 232
Time for Results, 217
Time diary, 60, 73, 161
Trade schools. *See* Proprietary schools
Transfer curricula, 214
Transfer rates, 35, 156, 160
Treatment group, 25
Trevino, J., *x*
True experiment, 25–28, 33
Tucker, L. R., 313, 324
Turnbull, W., 32, 324

U

Uhl, N. P., 89
Units of observation, 81–82, 84, 235, 256
Univariate distribution, 269–70
University of California, 125, 213
University of California, Los Angeles, *vii*, 86, 152
University of California, Santa Cruz, 55, 181, 246, 247
University of Chicago, 17
University of Colorado—Boulder, 158
University of Tennessee at Knoxville, 61, 244, 245
Upper-division competency tests, 167
Utilization of data, 128–150, 166

V

Validity, 38
Value-Added Consortium, *x–xi*, 131, 148, 168. *See also* Fund for the Improvement of Post-Secondary Education (FIPSE)
Value-added assessments, 34, 118, 151–52, 223–24, 230, 240. *See also* Talent development
  for incentive funding, 219–22
  Tennessee model, *vii*, 219–20
Values, 3, 8, 38–41, 43, 53, 161, 233
Variable, definition of, 18, 256
Variability, analysis of, 257

Vernon, P. E., 315
Virginia Commonwealth University, 244

W

Walleri, R. D., 170, 323
Wang, Y., x
Watson-Glaser Critical Thinking
    Appraisal, 47
Webb, N. J., 324
Weiss, N., 227, 244, 323
Wergin, J. F., 244, 321
Wesleyan University, 17

Wilson, D., 317
Wirtz, W., 32, 324
Within-institution measures,
    91–92, 99, 115–16, 303
Wolfel, L. M., 324

X, Y, Z

X axis, 270, 272, 273
Yale, 6
Y axis, 270, 272, 273
z score, 260
Zemsky, R., 92, 324
Zero-sum game, 199, 228